Sales and Revenue Generation in Sport Business

David J. Shonk, PhD

James Madison University

James F. Weiner, PhD

University of Tampa

HUMAN KINETICS

Library of Congress Cataloging-in-Publication Data

Names: Shonk, David J., 1969- author. | Weiner, James F., 1988- author.
Title: Sales and revenue generation in sport business / David J. Shonk,
  James Madison University, James F. Weiner, University of Tampa.
Description: Champaign, IL : Human Kinetics, Inc., [2022] | Includes
  bibliographical references and index.
Identifiers: LCCN 2021031404 (print) | LCCN 2021031405 (ebook) | ISBN
  9781492594222 (paperback) | ISBN 9781492594239 (epub) | ISBN
  9781492594246 (pdf)
Subjects: LCSH: Sports administration. | Sports--Marketing. | Revenue
  management. | Sports--Economic aspects.
Classification: LCC GV716 .S478 2022 (print) | LCC GV716 (ebook) | DDC
  796.06/9--dc23
LC record available at https://lccn.loc.gov/2021031404
LC ebook record available at https://lccn.loc.gov/2021031405

ISBN: 978-1-4925-9422-2 (print)

Acquisitions Editor: Andrew L. Tyler; **Senior Developmental Editor:** Christine M. Drews; **Managing Editor:** Melissa J. Zavala; **Copyeditor:** Bob Replinger; **Proofreader:** Rodelinde Albrecht; **Indexer:** Nan Badgett; **Permissions Manager:** Dalene Reeder; **Graphic Designer:** Dawn Sills; **Cover Designer:** Keri Evans; **Cover Design Specialist:** Susan Rothermel Allen; **Photograph (cover):** Ira L. Black/Corbis via Getty Images; **Photo Asset Manager:** Laura Fitch; **Photo Production Manager:** Jason Allen; **Senior Art Manager:** Kelly Hendren; **Illustrations:** © Human Kinetics, unless otherwise noted; **Printer:** Sheridan Books

Printed in the United States of America   10 9 8 7 6 5 4 3 2 1

The paper in this book is certified under a sustainable forestry program.

Human Kinetics
1607 N. Market Street
Champaign, IL 61820
USA

United States and International
Website: **US.HumanKinetics.com**
Email: info@hkusa.com
Phone: 1-800-747-4457

Canada
Website: **Canada.HumanKinetics.com**
Email: info@hkcanada.com

E7961

Tell us what you think!
Human Kinetics would love to hear what we can do to improve the customer experience. Use this QR code to take our brief survey.

I dedicate this book to Jen, the love of my life; to my wonderful children, Ashley and Ryan, who make me proud every day; and to all my current and former students.

David Shonk

I dedicate this book to my beautiful wife, Stephanie, who is all the evidence I need that I must have become a good salesman. She is the best thing that has ever happened to me, and I am thankful every day that she agreed to share our lives together.

James Weiner

CONTENTS

If you can sell, you can stay, and be very successful in the sport industry. Generating revenues is a skill set that launches careers within the sport industry and is a key to longevity. The sustainability of every organization, especially sport organizations, is absolutely dependent on the generation of new revenues. In some sport organizations everyone is expected to be involved in generating revenues. Ask almost anyone working within the sport industry what they believe is the most important skill and you will likely hear that it is the ability to sell. Sales is unique in that it integrates communication, persuasion, marketing, motivation, and social, leadership, and psychology skills. But it also demands perseverance, resolve, dedication, and passion to thrive. Users of this textbook should be able to demonstrate an understanding of the skills necessary to be successful in sales and generating revenues. In addition, they should be able to use the steps outlined in what we call the PRO method, described in the text.

Sales and Revenue Generation in Sport Business is written both for students seeking to enter the world of sport and for those currently working in the industry. Sales is one of the easiest ways to break into the sport industry for students graduating from college. But you do not have to pursue a career in sales to appreciate and use the information in the text. The sales process and the persuasion used to sell are germane to every aspect of life. For example, on a job interview you are selling yourself. Persuading your friends and family to go to a certain restaurant for dinner involves a form of selling, and making a presentation in the classroom involves sales.

Scope of the Book

Sales and Revenue Generation in Sport Business takes a diverse and broad approach to sales and revenue generation. Textbooks have traditionally focused on sales as it relates to tickets, sponsorships, and advertising. Although this text covers those areas, it branches out to provide the reader with a context for fundraising, grant writing, multimedia, and hospitality and tourism. The reader is not pigeonholed into one type of sales but instead gains a better understanding about how to generate revenues in many ways through creative processes. This textbook is a resource for anyone serious about working in the sport industry, and it sheds light on how to tackle the economic challenges that organizations face in this third decade of the 21st century.

Organization

Each chapter provides the reader with various sidebars focusing on business-to-business (B2B) and business-to-consumer (B2C) sales. In addition, each chapter helps the reader apply the PRO method of sales as it applies to the content within. This approach helps the reader understand the importance of the process involved in sales. Finally, each chapter ends with learning activities and a short case study. Various figures, tables, checklists, charts, and examples provide a real-world context that helps the reader garner the skills necessary to be successful within the industry. Students and practitioners alike will appreciate the glossary at the end of the book that defines the boldfaced sales terms that appear in the text.

Sales and Revenue Generation in Sport Business provides a comprehensive overview of the many ways in which sport organizations generate revenues, from inside sales to sponsorship to fundraising to corporate and foundation grants to concessions and merchandising to broadcasting and multimedia to social media revenues. A five-step process for generating revenues is presented in the textbook. The ability to generate sources of revenue continues to be the most important skill for people who currently work or wish to work in the sport industry. Students who understand the concepts applied in this text are more likely to gain rewarding employment in the sport industry, and practitioners who apply these concepts are likely to have more meaningful and longer-lasting careers in the industry. Finally, the text does not focus on one segment of the industry (e.g., professional sport); the concepts can be applied in many segments of the industry, from elite sport organizations to those more recreational in nature.

Benefits of the Book

Sales and Revenue Generation in Sport Business is intended for anyone who wants to generate revenues: both students entering the sport industry and current practitioners in the industry. It provides the reader with a strong conceptual, theoretical, and, most important, practical basis for understanding the sales process. By providing a sales process called the PRO method, the book provides the reader with a strong conceptual framework for sales. We have also drawn on current and past research to provide the reader with a strong theoretical framework for understanding sales and revenue generation. By their nature, the current examples we have added throughout the text may change over time, but the principles they illuminate will endure. Finally, through practical application and the experiences of the authors, the reader is prepared from day one to understand key terms, skills, methods, strategies, and processes for entering the industry and becoming a key contributor.

Students

This text can be used by upper-level undergraduate and graduate students interested in working in professional, Olympic, intercollegiate, interscholastic, or youth sport. The text is broad enough that students in multiple disciplines would benefit from learning the PRO method described within the text along with the many concepts explained. The book may be useful for students interested in careers in sport marketing, sales, communication, public relations, broadcast journalism, or social media content creation.

Sales and revenue management is an important course within the curriculum of any sport management program. Some programs have stand-alone sales courses, and others combine their marketing course with sales. Learning about sales and revenue generation is crucial because most of the entry-level jobs within the industry are sales related. Students may not have a title related to inside sales, sponsorship sales, corporate sales, or sales account executive. Instead, they may start their career in marketing, events, or other functional areas and gradually drift toward sales. We believe that this book can be useful not only for the graduating student but also for the industry practitioner as a resource that will be used many times over the course of a career.

The online resource will provide the student with useful tools for selling. We provide a video explanation of the sales process using the PRO method and introductory videos for each major segment of the sport sales industry (ticketing, sponsorships, fundraising, etc.) to explain how the topic of sales applies within that area. For each of these areas, which correspond to chapters 3 through 7, we provide students with interactive scenarios and downloadable and editable script templates to assist with the sales process. Visit HK*Propel* to access the online activities.

Professors

The textbook will help faculty members in multiple disciplines teach the sales process. Important conceptual and theoretical frameworks are described within the text. Faculty are guided through the process of sales using the PRO method as a helpful tool for providing students with key conceptual skills when selling. In addition, key sales terms are bolded in the text to help faculty provide students with a broad vocabulary for selling. Techniques such as sales role-playing, scripting, and trackable interactive scenarios are helpful to faculty. As faculty members ourselves, we have taught students using many of these techniques. More important, we have worked in both sales and development capacities within the sport industry and understand these concepts from a practical perspective. Finally, although most textbooks have focused on ticketing and sponsorship sales, this text helps faculty prepare students not only for these types of jobs but also for fundraising, grant writing, retail, hospitality and tourism, and multimedia and broadcasting.

Several ancillaries are provided online through HK*Propel*. The comprehensive package of resources includes an instructor guide with chapter summaries, chapter objectives, key terms, learning activities, and case study applications. A presentation package that includes slides for each chapter can be used for teaching a class or for sales managers who want to train their sales force. The test package, which is particularly helpful for faculty, includes 30 multiple-choice and true-false questions per chapter. The files may be downloaded for integration with a learning management system or printed as paper-based tests. Instructors may also create their own customized quizzes or tests from the test back questions to assign to students directly through HK*Propel*. Ready-made chapter quizzes are also provided online in HK*Propel*. Each quiz contains 10 questions, drawn from the larger test bank, that assess student comprehension of the most important concepts in each chapter. Each quiz may be downloaded or assigned to students within HK*Propel*. Test package and chapter quiz questions are automatically graded, and student scores can be easily reviewed by instructors in the platform.

The chapters within the text are organized by key areas that can be monetized such as ticketing, broadcasting and multimedia, sponsorships, corporate and foundation revenues, fundraising and development, grant writing, hospitality, concessions, and merchandising. Each chapter provides chapter objectives, key terms bolded and listed in the glossary, B2B and B2C sidebars, applied learning activities, and a case study with discussion questions.

Current Industry Professionals

The text serves as an important resource for sales professionals who are looking to train salespeople or simply want a refresher course. Examples from various organizations will help industry professionals stay current about how other organizations are approaching sales and revenue generation. The text can also be useful for those who would like to do independent study, consulting, training, and development. Although technology will change, industry professionals will find the key terms and definitions useful as they progress through their career. Understanding these terms is often easier after you have gained experience working.

Need for the Book

Although many textbooks focus on ticketing or sales, we take a macro perspective that includes both but also provides a comprehensive approach that can be applied in professional sport, intercollegiate and interscholastic athletics, other amateur sport, and organizations in recreational settings. It is the only textbook that covers the many varied ways in which a sport organization can generate revenues. It also includes sidebars that can be applied to customer service, B2B, and B2C perspectives. The textbook includes a variety of case studies, videos, online student resources, and a complete complement of instructor resources. We have found great reward in our careers in sport business and in teaching others, and we wish you the very best as you pursue this dynamic field.

ACKNOWLEDGMENTS

Knowing where to start with acknowledgments is difficult because many people have contributed in various ways to the success of this book. The ideas in this book are drawn from numerous people who have taught and inspired me over many years. First, thanks to Drew Tyler and Chris Drews of Human Kinetics. Every week, I am approached by students asking for advice about entering the sport industry, and my response has never changed over the years: "Learn to sell and generate revenue." When Drew approached me with the idea for this book, I simply could not pass up the opportunity to put into writing what I have learned by working in sales and development and by teaching sales within the classroom. Thanks to James Weiner for working with me. I deeply appreciate your expertise, and it has been awesome to watch you grow and to follow your accomplishments since you left James Madison University as an undergraduate. I could not have completed this book without the help of my student Spencer Haiges. Thanks, Spencer, for all your hard work and help! Thanks to Sam Lazzaro, who provided me with my early training in sport sales and baseball. Special thanks to Dennis Robarge, a mentor and great friend who has done so much for me over the years. I am forever indebted to Larry Lorenzi, Ellis Sulser, Ed Davis, Shirlee Kyle, Tim Coffee, and Cindy Allen at DECA for their training in sales and development. Ed was our executive director at National DECA, and he always jokingly asked me how much money I had made him today. Thanks to all my colleagues in the Hart School at James Madison University (JMU), the University of Louisville (U of L), and to both current and former students. Many JMU alumni provided me with ideas and inspiration for the book, in fact too many to mention without forgetting someone. Thanks to Michael Brown and Scott Gray of Tremont Global for helping me meet salespeople with numerous sport organizations who have guided this text. Of course, I would be remiss if I did not thank Chella, my mentor in the field of sport management and research. Thanks to Dad, Jim, and Arlie, my earliest sales instructors. Thanks to Jen, Ashley, Ryan, Mom Shonk, Mom Brady, Dad Brady, Bill and Margie, and Mike and Robyn. Last, but certainly not least, thank you Jesus for this opportunity and for guiding me along the way.

David Shonk

First, I give a sincere thank you to my coauthor, Dave, who invited me to participate on this book and walked me through every step of the process. Also, I want to express my appreciation for my friends at Human Kinetics, who probably gave me more slack on deadlines than they should have. This book (and topic) is important to me, and I enjoyed working on it thoroughly. I was very fortunate during my time working in sales; I learned from some of the best, and this book draws on many of their lessons: Thank you to Marc Tuttle, who gave me a chance, and to Chris Kautza, who showed me what a great boss looked like early in my career. Thank you to all my friends at IMGLTS (now LIMGTS) who provided support and guidance as well as to Mike Sobb and Jon Jackson at Duke. Your lessons on leadership were invaluable to me. Lastly, thank you to all the friends and family who supported me throughout the creation of this book. Your encouragement made all the difference.

James Weiner

Getty Images/Cecilie_Arcurs

CHAPTER 1

Introduction to Sales and Revenue Generation in Sport Business

CHAPTER OBJECTIVES

After completing the chapter, you should be able to do the following:

- Understand the importance of generating revenues within the context of sport
- Demonstrate the broad and diverse nature of the sport industry
- Explain the inventory available to sell in the sport industry
- Describe the characteristics of effective salespeople, or revenue generators
- Report what we know about whether salespeople are born or made
- Understand the importance of influence and persuasion skills

It seems that everyone wants to work in the sport industry. Thousands are currently working in the industry, and many more want to enter this exciting industry. Some of these people are former or current athletes or long-time fans. Others may not have any interest in sport but have specific skills that make them marketable within the field. What has led you to pick up this book? Yes, it might be required in your university's curriculum, but what led you to seek out this area of study? Have you played sports or been a fan for many years? Do you have sales and business skills that make sport business appealing to you? Or do you possess a combination of sport and business aptitudes and skills? Regardless of your background, the sport industry has something for everyone, including robust opportunities that involve revenue generation.

More than 500 academic programs in sport management are currently offered at colleges and universities across the United States and Canada. In addition, Europe has over 30 programs, Australia and New Zealand have almost 20 programs, and more than 20 programs are offered throughout Asia, Africa, and the Middle East (NASSM, 2020). Although sport management programs produce many employees, others within the sport industry come from wide-ranging academic backgrounds including business, communication, history, biology, psychology, sociology, and others.

The sport industry is large and includes a broad array of functional areas (e.g., marketing, sales, operations, and communication) and segments (e.g., professional sport, college sport, and recreation). As in many industries (e.g., automotive, retail, and technology), organizations within the sport industry have realized the need to break through one-way communications and use memorable experiences to engage their customers. Sport organizations are in show business. These companies must be entertaining and engaging when customers

INDUSTRY PROFILE

Pete Stuart

Senior Director, Marketing Communications at NASCAR

© Pete Stuart

Question: Describe your role as Senior Director, Marketing Communications at NASCAR.

Answer: From a communications standpoint, I operate on the commercial side of NASCAR's business and have day-to-day oversight of communications activities that support marketing, content, digital platforms, and diversity and inclusion. It is a strategic role with a robust emphasis on storytelling around key functional areas, amplifying the great work being done, and championing the overall business narrative around NASCAR. Additionally, I oversee executive communications and develop and execute strategies designed to elevate the profiles of our senior leaders. I also lead internal communications with a focus on keeping our NASCAR employees both informed and engaged through various channels.

Question: Describe the importance of partnerships and revenue generation for NASCAR.

Answer: Partnerships are critical to NASCAR and represent the lifeblood of our sport in general. A massive portion of our revenue is through the current, long-term deals with a pair of best-in-class broadcast partners in FOX and NBC. On the sponsorship side, NASCAR partners are among the most recognized in all of sports, and they trust us to deliver a return on their investments. There are other revenue streams, of course, including ticket revenue, which is now even more significant after NASCAR acquired International Speedway Corporation and its several racetracks in 2019. But partnerships have been and will continue to be incredibly important to the overall health and viability of our business.

Question: What sets NASCAR apart from other sports leagues (e.g., NFL, MLB, and NHL) when it comes to sponsorships?

Answer: When you look across the broader NASCAR industry, the sheer volume of partnerships is substantial. Nearly half of Fortune 100 companies and roughly one in four Fortune 500 companies are invested in the sport. Within the sanctioning body, iconic brands in Busch Beer, Coca-Cola, GEICO, and Xfinity have strengthened their investments as Premier Partners, part of a new sponsorship model introduced in 2020. One of the reasons corporate investment is so significant is because NASCAR has the most sponsor-loyal fans in sports, a claim proven over and over and recently by MarketCast in a study published in *Sports Business Journal.* It is much easier for companies to invest their dollars when they feel confident knowing our fans are more likely to support their business.

Question: You previously worked for Taylor, a PR and communications firm. With Taylor, you had a lot of different responsibilities. There, you managed strategic marketing communications planning and execution around Allstate Insurance's College Football, NCAA, Soccer, and Olympics properties. You developed brand and sponsorship marketing strategies. You also planned PR activation around various high-profile events including the Allstate BCS National Championship, Allstate Sugar Bowl, NCAA Men's Basketball Championship, MLS All-Star Game, and the MLS Cup. How did this job prepare you for your current job at NASCAR?

Answer: The agency role with Taylor specialized in public relations, but it also gave me insight into the sponsorship landscape and how brands put their dollars to work through unique and targeted activations. I had the opportunity to work with several brands on partnership promotion and activation, and among those Allstate Insurance, Alltel Wireless, and Crown Royal had deals with NASCAR teams or tracks. The experience helped me learn how to navigate the NASCAR landscape, particularly through the lens of the sponsor. After transitioning to the property side at NASCAR, it was helpful to have that experience and understand both perspectives.

Question: How important is it for a student studying sport management to understand sales and revenue generation? Do you have any specific advice for students wishing to work in the sport industry?

Answer: Understanding how your company or institution makes money can be of paramount importance, particularly if your role supports the broader business objectives. As a communications professional, I'm not personally signing the contracts, but my role through strategic public relations is to help elevate the value of the opportunity for brands. So, when our sales lead is pitching new prospects, his or her job is that much easier. The same goes for current NASCAR partners—if I can add value to the partnership, the brand is more likely to renew. In terms of advice, it'd be along those same lines. Students should have a solid, foundational understanding of how the machine works and, even more importantly, how it runs smoothly and successfully.

---

demand an experience that goes beyond the expected and delivers real value (Schmitt et al., 2003).

Do you want to be part of the show or are you already in show business? This text was designed for those who want to enter the sport industry, and it can serve as a refresher for those who are already working in the industry. People who are passionate about this industry and the business of sport know that it takes significant time and energy to succeed in this arena. Many have set aside the ball cap of their favorite team and put on their business hat instead. Often, the long hours that are required in the sport industry do not translate to the higher salaries we see in occupations like medicine, law, or engineering. Many skills are required to break into and to be successful in the sport industry. As noted in the title, and as you will see throughout the text, the ability to generate revenue is at the top of the list.

"You Sell, You Stay": The Importance of Generating Revenue

"If you can sell and produce revenue, you can stay!" In other words, anyone who can sell will have a long career in the sport industry. This phrase, uttered by many within the field of sport management, especially sales managers, underscores the importance of revenue generation. Anyone can spend money, but generating revenues is difficult. Almost every professional sport league, amateur sport entity and governing body, and major sport event is dependent on various revenue streams provided from ticket and sponsorship sales or media rights (Popp et al., 2019). For many sport organizations, ticket sales are the lifeblood that sustains the production of revenues (Popp et al., 2017). Most entry-level job openings in sport, particularly professional sport, are in ticket sales. Therefore, much of the content related to sales within sport management education has focused on ticketing and sponsorship sales.

Although sport is a multibillion-dollar industry, if enough funds are not generated to earn a profit or keep an organization functioning, the team or organization will fail to thrive or even fail altogether. For example, the Kansas City T-Bones, an independent professional baseball team based in Kansas City, was not generating enough revenues to pay their lease and utility bills. The team received a notice in September 2019 stating that they would be required to vacate the stadium unless they paid the county $358,439 for delinquent utility payments and $75,545 in late lease payments (Lieberman, 2019). The T-Bones subsequently struck a deal with the local government to keep the team playing. The NCAA reported that only 25 Division I athletics departments generated more revenues than expenses in 2018-2019, and all of these were in Power Five conferences (NCAA, 2020). For most intercollegiate athletics programs across the country, expenses exceed revenues. These examples demonstrate the vital importance of sales and revenue generation.

Although much of the focus on selling throughout the years has focused on professional sport, students in the 21st century must have a more holistic understanding of revenue generation and have the ability to monetize multiple inventories. The financial health and stability of a sport organization depend not only on ticketing and sponsorships but also on a much wider variety of sources for generating revenues. The next generation of sport managers and marketers must be able and willing to facilitate a sales process that helps their organization sustain their market position within a highly competitive industry. An intercollegiate athletics director must understand the principles of **fundraising** related to major gifts, annual funds, planned giving, capital campaigns, and special events. Interscholastic athletics directors may charge athletes to participate or require them to generate funds for sponsorships, sell tickets, or interact with boosters to solicit funds. Likewise, sport executives in the nonprofit sector write and secure grants from corporations and foundations, and recreational executives sell memberships, tickets, concessions, and merchandise as well as other inventory.

The modern sport industry continues to grow, and revenue generation is the number one source for sustaining this growth. Recent estimates of the sport industry in the United States suggest that it is valued at $498.4 billion (Plunkett Research, 2018), comprising sectors such as sporting goods, advertising and marketing, professional sport, fitness and recreation, golf courses, racetracks, amusement and recreation, other spectator sport leagues, and NCAA sports (Miller and Washington, 2018). The coronavirus pandemic has created some uncertainty moving forward. Before the pandemic, however, thousands of jobs across the United States were being created in youth sport by the creation of new sport facilities; the youth pay-to-play sport tournament sector is estimated by the National Association of Sports Commissions to be worth $11.8 billion per year (Greenwell et al., 2019). In 2017 the market for primary and secondary online ticketing services (including ticketing for concerts, sporting events, live theater, fairs, and festivals) was estimated to be worth $9 billion (IBIS World, 2017).

The dynamic growth within the sport industry is being driven by further specialization of sport managers and an appeal to servicing the more sophisticated and luxurious wants and needs of today's consumer. In 1990 the sport consumer bought their ticket at the gate, walked to the concession stand for traditional fare such as a hot dog or hamburger, and returned to their seat in the stands. In 2020 the consumer often bought a ticket online and may never have moved out of their seat for food. Instead, using a simple mobile application, the consumer may be sitting at club level or in a luxury box where the order is delivered in the comfort of an air-conditioned room furnished with sofas and a flat-screen television. Sport executives with titles such as suites sales manager, account manager of luxury and suite sales, or suite attendant spend significant portions of time selling multiyear suite leases and attending to the needs of the consumers in the suites.

Students studying sport management today must understand not only this more specialized and sophisticated appeal but also the broad and diverse nature of our industry. The idea of a broad and diverse industry suggests an industry in which one end of the continuum consists of elite sport competition (e.g., professional sport) and at the other end is sport for all (e.g., recreation and amateur sport). Sport management students are finding jobs at both ends of the continuum and everywhere in between. Furthermore, a sport management student may start their career as an account manager in minor league baseball, move to fundraising

in intercollegiate athletics, and end their career as the executive director at a nonprofit sport governing body. This type of dynamic change and fluidity suggests that the average sport executive needs to be prepared for generating revenues within a wide range of settings.

We believe that the ability to generate revenue is the most important skill for any student wishing to work in the sport industry or any practitioner currently working in the industry. Although many textbooks focus on ticketing or sales, this text takes a more comprehensive approach to generating revenue. Sport managers and marketers may generate revenue through ticketing, sponsorships, grants, concessions, merchandise, and fundraising. But the text does not limit sport executives in terms of revenue generation because they can use their creativity in many ways to monetize inventory. The incredible growth of the industry highlights the many employment opportunities available where revenue generation is important. Granted, some sectors and jobs place more focus on generating revenues than others. Chelladurai (2014) provides a partial list of the different types of organizations that make up the broader sport industry ranging from international sport governing bodies to recreation departments. We have used his list of organizations to classify them in figure 1.1 based on jobs available and importance of revenue generation as well as level of sport (i.e., participant or recreational to professional or elite).

The text provides a five-step process for generating revenues that connects theory and practice. Students and practitioners who can grasp the conceptual nature of this process and apply it within the industry will have a competitive advantage over their counterparts. Let's be honest: Sales is a highly competitive occupation. Achieving success is not easy, and many have failed. But regardless of your personality, age, or background, you can learn to sell. More important, those who can apply the revenue-generating ideas, concepts, and processes discussed in this text are on their way to mastering a skill that could lead to a robust career in the broad sport industry.

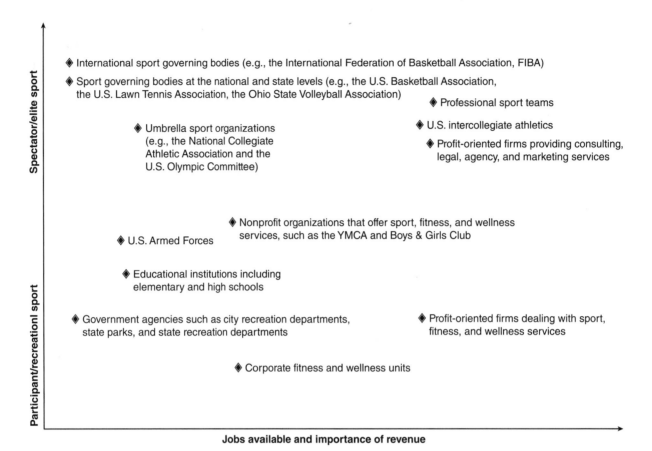

FIGURE 1.1 Broad array of job sectors in the sport industry. Classified based on jobs available and importance of revenue generation as well as level of sport (e.g., participant or recreational to professional or elite).

Revenue-Generating Jobs in Sport

A wide variety of jobs related to sales and revenue generation exist within the sport industry. There is no magic formula for generating revenues, but there is a general process, which we call the PRO method. We outline this method in chapter 2. The jobs in sales within the sport industry vary in two key ways. First, sales jobs vary in terms of functional area or department. In other words, you may find a sales job in the marketing department, food and beverages (concessions), retail sales (merchandising and licensing), sponsorship sales, ticketing, or fundraising. Second, these jobs vary based on the segment of the industry. For example, in professional sport, ticket sales and sponsorships sales are vitally important, and most of the jobs are in those areas. If you work

for a nonprofit sport organization, however, fundraising, a type of sales, is crucial.

If you are working within intercollegiate athletics, both sales and fundraising are important. Someone working in intercollegiate athletics may be employed by the athletics department, by a separate fundraising arm or nonprofit foundation (e.g., Buckeye Club), or by a separate outsourced marketing organization (e.g., Learfield Sports). Job titles include associate director for ticketing, ticket sales associate, director of athletics marketing and promotion, and associate athletics director for external relations. Many of the jobs within the athletics department relate to sales in ticketing and sponsorship, although sponsorship is often outsourced to companies like Learfield Sport, IMG College, and other companies that have strong connections with corporate sponsors, especially when it comes to selling naming

INTERCOLLEGIATE ATHLETICS

Job Duties for Associate Director of Corporate and Foundation Relations Position

The following are some of duties and responsibilities carried out by an assistant or associate athletics director, for revenue generation and sales within an athletics department.

- Manage a portfolio of major gift prospects
- Collaborate with team to identify, cultivate, and solicit corporate philanthropic support
- Assist in the development and implementation of strategies for corporate and foundation prospects
- Achieve core fundraising metrics including identification of new prospects and face-to-face visits
- Develop effective grant materials and communications (e.g., proposals, presentations, letters of inquiry, budgets, and stewardship reports)
- Conduct prospect research to identify potential individual, corporate, and foundation donors
- Create annual reporting or stewardship plans for each foundation grant and corporate gift

rights for facilities. Fundraisers (e.g., associate director of corporate and foundation relations) may work inside the athletics department or for athletics or university advancement.

Jobs in sport are mostly focused on sales. The easiest way to break into professional sport is to work in ticketing, which involves selling season tickets, partial plans, and group and event sales. Beyond ticketing, the emphasis in professional sport is on sponsorship sales, which requires contacting local, regional, and national corporations. Retail sales jobs available within the sport venue entail merchandise sales at retail shops located both within and outside the sport venue. Concessions, which are food and beverage sales, occur within the sport venue and consist of full upscale restaurants, food vendors and kiosks, and traditional concession stands. Both merchandising and concession sales are often outsourced to companies that

PROFESSIONAL BASEBALL

Job Description for Account Executive Position in Professional Baseball

The following is an example of job duties and responsibilities you may find for the position of account executive. Responsibilities may include areas such as group ticket packages, hospitality, and full and partial season ticket plans.

- Represent the organization with the utmost professionalism in the community
- Prospect and sell group, hospitality, and season ticket packages
- Be responsible for renewing all group, hospitality, and season ticket clients
- Develop and grow a database comprised of businesses and individual prospects
- Work closely with sales and marketing departments to develop sales programs
- Maintain a database of contacts and sales progression using CRM (customer relationship management)
- Meet or exceed personal sales goals while providing superior customer service

Job Duties for a Fundraising Position in the Private Sector

Revenue-generating positions in nonprofit organizations may entail some of the following duties and responsibilities:

- Secure sport events and tournaments
- Book event room blocks at local hotels
- Work with event promoters and directors to enhance attendance, engage fans, and attract business sponsors
- Serve as liaison between the organization and local sporting arenas, collegiate teams, and professional sport teams
- Work with consulting agencies in an advisory capacity to assist organizations and event directors

have expertise in the areas of merchandising and licensing, and food and beverage sales. Job titles may include senior director of licensing; manager, corporate partnerships; director of ticketing sales; inside sales representative; director of food and beverage; concessions stand lead; and others.

You may consider a job within the nonprofit sector if you are less concerned with the bottom line and more focused on serving a particular mission. Many of the jobs are focused on fundraising. For example, you may find positions like the director of major gifts or annual fund director for a nonprofit like Special Olympics. But sales jobs are also available in the nonprofit sector. A good example would be the director of sport sales for a convention and visitors bureau or sports commission.

Preparing for a Sales Job in the Sport Industry

Job descriptions for sales jobs normally include a description of the job along with the duties and responsibilities and the requirements for the job. Students must read the job description carefully because employers are looking for candidates that best fit their needs. Therefore, students need to develop the necessary skills and seek to gain experience in sales before graduating and applying for jobs in this competitive industry. Here are some practical tips

for ways that a student can gain sales experience and build a resume.

Intern

Complete a practicum or internship in sales with a sport organization of your choice. Although sales skills are transferable from one segment of the industry to another, the best approach is to do it within your preferred segment of the industry. In other words, if you want to work in Major League Baseball (MLB) then you should seek out jobs in MLB or minor league baseball. Although working for the local parks and recreation department or in your college or university athletics department might be more convenient, you will develop many more contacts if you work in baseball. The old saying "Birds of a feather flock together" applies here. Those who work in MLB can network with others who work in MLB or minor league baseball, whereas parks and recreation professionals know others working in their segment of the industry.

Volunteer

Volunteer with a sport organization or local nonprofit to help sell or to assist with customer service. One suggestion is to talk to people at your university to find out if you can volunteer to make phone calls to alumni or help the athletics department with calling season ticket holders. This type of volunteer work will help you develop relationship-building skills, and you will better appreciate the difficulty of making telemarketing calls and dealing with the rejection that goes with sales. Another option is to contact a local nonprofit that may need help with making phone calls, running an event, registering participants, or performing other duties that will help you gain experience.

Take Courses

Enroll in a course in communications, public speaking, sport media, graphic design, or something similar. Both oral and written communication are important to sales, and these types of courses are helpful in developing these skills. The program in which you are majoring at your institution may allow you to take such courses as an elective or may require them. You may also consider taking one of these courses at a local community college.

Network

Network, network, network. Students in sport or recreation management will probably get tired of hearing their faculty talk about the importance of networking. But it is not only about whom you know but also about who knows you. Here are some ideas about the many ways to network in sport:

- Attend one of the sport conferences for students (e.g., Sport Industry Networking Conference).
- If you are in sport or recreation management, alumni of your program are always looking for ways to help. Find out which alumni are working in jobs that you would be interested in and email or call them.
- Enroll in a study abroad course focused on sport where you can meet sport executives.
- If your courses include guest speakers from the sport industry, take a few minutes after class to shake the speaker's hand and introduce yourself. Request

a business card and ask if you can add them on LinkedIn. After class is over, make sure to follow up by adding them on LinkedIn and emailing them. Do not forget to stay in touch with this person regularly during your time in college. Remember that sales is all about relationships, and relationships become deeper and stronger based on factors such as the length of the relationship, frequent positive communication, and trust developed over time. If you have been in regular communication with this person over two to four years of your college career, they can serve as a helpful contact when you graduate and are looking for a job.

Role-Playing

Students may laugh at the notion of role-playing or may not take it seriously in a classroom setting. Role-playing, however, is widely used in sales training because it can significantly help a person develop confidence. **Role-playing** has been defined as a method that "encourages thinking and creativity, lets students develop and practice new language and behavioral skills in a relatively nonthreatening setting, and can create the motivation and involvement necessary for learning to occur" (Tompkins, 1998, p. 143). In the same way that a sport team would not go onto the field against their opponent without practice, a salesperson needs to practice and prepare what they are going to say, be able to respond to questions and objections, and interact confidently with a prospective customer. Role-playing offers numerous advantages (Craig & Amemic, 1994):

- Demonstrates differences between thinking and doing
- Permits practice in carrying out actions
- Provides rapid feedback for students
- Permits training in the control of feelings and emotions
- Accomplishes attitude changes by placing people in specified roles

- Trains people to be sensitive to the feelings of others
- Enables people to discover their personal faults
- Helps people better appreciate how feelings determine behavior in social situations

B2B Versus B2C Sales

Sales executives within the sport industry sell to both businesses and consumers. **B2B sales**, short for business-to-business sales, refers to an activity in which a business is selling its products or services to another business. **B2C sales**, short for business-to-consumer sales, refers to sales to individuals rather than businesses. Cohn (2015) describes the following differences between B2B and B2C selling:

- *B2B involves a longer decision-making process*: When selling B2B, the salesperson must be prepared to invest time in cultivating a relationship that may involve multiple telephone calls to more than one person within the company.
- *B2B involves a greater number of stakeholders*: As discussed earlier, the salesperson will likely have to speak to multiple decision-makers when pursuing a B2B partnership. If even one person at any step in this process declines the sale, the salesperson must begin again with someone else in the company or with another business.
- *B2B relationships are generally lengthier than B2C*: In comparison with selling to an individual person, companies typically seek longer relationships. For example, it would be tremendously challenging and costly for the James Madison University to change their athletics concessions contract with Aramark every year.
- ***Prospecting*** *for companies in B2B involves a smaller lead pool than B2C*: A prospect is a potential customer who has been qualified as fitting the following three criteria: (1) fits the target market, (2) has the money to buy, and (3) is authorized to make a buying decision. In contrast, a **lead** is an unqualified contact. Any potential client or customer the salesperson meets who has not been qualified as a prospect is a lead. Thus, prospecting is the act of finding leads and turning them into prospects. It makes sense that B2B involves a smaller pool of prospects than B2C because most communities have a greater number of residents (consumers) than they do businesses.
- *B2B requires a different type of product knowledge*: Typically, B2B requires a deeper technical knowledge. Consider the scenario of a business organization such as PepsiCo, which is considering buying a 30-second television advertisement for the Super Bowl costing $3.5 million versus a consumer who is thinking about purchasing a $15 ticket for a baseball game. The business executive with PepsiCo must understand what they are receiving in exchange for the money being spent. In other words, they must consider the return on investment. The consumer purchasing a $15 ticket faces much less risk.

Why is it important to understand the differences between B2B and B2C sales? Because sales within the sport industry involves both. For example, a sales executive may start their career as an account executive selling tickets in which most of the sales are to individual ticket holders. Later the executive may change jobs from selling season tickets to selling premium seating. Although premium seating may involve selling to individual seat holders, many of the sales will be to corporations. Selling corporate partnerships is another example of B2B selling, and sales executives must have a keen understanding of the benefits of their inventory and how the corporation will achieve a return on their investment. You will find that B2B and B2C selling will be a theme throughout the text. Many of the sidebars within the text will be relevant to these two concepts. In the next section, we describe various types of inventory. Although some inventory is sold primarily to businesses and other inventory is sold primarily to consumers, much of the inventory can be sold to both. A sales executive will need to understand the needs and wants as well as the objectives of both businesses and consumers when they are purchasing inventory.

Inventory in Sport: You Can Monetize Almost Anything

Regardless of the segment of the industry in which you work, you must understand the inventory that can be monetized for sale. Table 1.1 displays a variety of inventory that can be sold within the industry. Keep in mind that

we have defined the sport industry broadly, ranging from professional and elite sport to recreational sport. If you are working for a team in Major League Baseball, you are not likely to be selling moorings fees, whereas this activity may be common for those working for a community recreation organization. In the following section, we discuss some common sources of revenue for a variety of segments in the industry.

Community Programs

Many sport organizations have a community relations office that interacts with and builds relationships with people to improve the quality of life in the community. "Community relations provides a unique opportunity for sport organizations to enhance their dealings with outside groups and individuals while

TABLE 1.1 Sources of Revenue in the Sport Industry

Sources of revenue	Examples
Community programs	Camps, clinics, education programs, school assemblies, awards, banquets, luncheons, dinners, golf tournaments
Contractual or outsourced activities	Concessionaire or snack bar, golf course or tennis professional, operation of facilities, marketing and media rights, ticketing
Dues, fees, and permits	Greens fees, membership dues, initiation fees, camp fees, tennis permits, program fees, rented equipment, rental fees, permits for facilities, moorings fees
Electronic inventory	Television, radio, web page, social media, electronic newsletter, blogs
Fundraising	Major gifts, annual giving, planned giving, capital campaigns, scholarships, endowments, entitlements, and trusts
Grant writing	Corporations, private and community foundations, governmental grants
Naming rights	Arena, stadium, jerseys, team, practice facility, ball fields, playgrounds, staging areas, amphitheaters, swimming pools, community gardens, community rooms, trails
Print inventory	Game program, recruiting guide, media guide, scorecard, rosters, ticket back, credentials
Promotions	Premium items (e.g., bobbleheads), on-field or on-floor promotions, scoreboard, contests, raffles, music and other entertainment pregame and postgame, LED, Jumbotron
Signage	Billboards, dasher boards, scoreboards, matrix, message boards, ball fields, swimming pools, playgrounds, marquees, medallions, concourse areas, picnic areas, blimps, turnstiles, LED signage, community rooms, trails, community gardens
Taxes	Federal, state, and local revenues from taxes
Tickets and hospitality	General admission seats, reserved seats, box seats, club seats, suites, personal seat licenses (PSLs), group tickets, parties, special events, parking, hospitality tents

contributing to society in a meaningful way" (Misener, 2011, p. 246). Examples of community programs include sport camps, clinics, education programs, school assemblies, awards, banquets, luncheons, dinners, and golf tournaments. Although programs like camps, luncheons, dinners, and golf tournaments are easier to monetize, note that every touchpoint with the community is an opportunity to build relationships that can lead to sales. Almost every professional team is involved in various forms of community relations, and many have foundations. Many current and former professional athletes also seek to give back with various types of foundations. Athletics departments at most colleges and universities also ask their athletes to be involved in these types of programs as a way to give back to the community.

Of course, community recreation (e.g., local parks and recreation departments) and nonprofit nongovernmental organizations (e.g., YMCA, YWCA) are vitally involved in offering numerous types of programs that benefit the community at large. Youth sport is the foundation for developing athletes. In the United States, sport development occurs at the youth level in which young athletes participate in youth programs like Little League and high school athletics. In Europe, sport development occurs through a club system, but community involvement still offers many benefits. Regular involvement in sport can benefit individuals and communities and contribute to a range of positive outcomes (Sport England, 2019). Such outcomes include more volunteer participation; greater voice in decision-making; more cohesive, sustainable, and inclusive communities; and a reduction in crime.

Contracting or Outsourcing

To achieve their objectives, many sport organizations outsource their operations to other organizations. **Outsourcing** is defined as "turning over all or part of an organizational activity to an outside vendor" (Barthelemy, 2003, p. 87). It is normally part of a strategic business decision when an organization transfers one of its operations, which used to be handled in-house, to an external third party (Busi, 2008). For example, companies like Aramark, Centerplate, and Levy's Restaurants operate concessions in many sport venues throughout the United States (Greenwell et al., 2019). Stadiums hosting professional teams throughout North America are hiring executive chefs, pastry artisans, and bartenders and are serving more inventive and locally inspired cuisine, which is often associated with upscale restaurants. If you attend a game at Safeco Field in Seattle, you can get burgers and fries from Great State Burger, a Seattle-area favorite (Smith, 2018). At Camden Yards in Baltimore, legendary Oriole Boog Powell is often around to serve at Boog's Barbeque in center field. Alternatively, you can dine at Dempsey's Brew Pub & Restaurant at Camden Yards.

A sport organization's decision on whether to outsource is important strategically because it has an effect on revenues. Outsourcing involves the evaluation by the organization of possible cost savings compared with the consequences of loss of control over the product or service (Dinu, 2015). Outsourcing allows a company to specialize on its main objective, ensure the highest profit, lower costs, gain access to skilled resources, and offer faster and better services. Disadvantages include the loss of managerial control, less innovation and creative capacity, social and transaction costs, and threats to security and confidentiality (Dinu, 2015).

A sport organization may choose to outsource their sales to another company for several reasons. Burden and Li (2009) point to the following reasons as to why companies generally outsource their operations (quoted in Greenwell et al., 2019, pp. 165-166):

1. Outsourcing helps companies operate in a more efficient manner by focusing in-house resources on core competencies while outsourcing peripheral functions.

2. Outsourcing provides the company with economies of scale because the unit cost charged by the service providers is generally reduced when they are dealing with multiple organizations at one time.

3. Companies that outsource eliminate personnel costs such as recruitment,

retention, and employee relations. The company gains access to highly skilled and knowledgeable personnel who may not be available in-house.

4. Companies outsource because they do not have the technical expertise in-house, the resources to invest in new technology, or the ability to train staff.

Colleges and universities throughout North America outsource items such as merchandise, tickets, advertising, and radio and broadcast rights. The largest marketing and multimedia rights deal currently belongs to the University of Texas ($12.7 million annually). A recent trend is for professional sport organizations to provide services for an intercollegiate program. As an example, the University of South Florida (USF) has a 10-year agreement with Tampa Bay Entertainment Properties LLC (TBEP), who has full control of USF's marketing rights for athletics (Sutton, 2017). According to Sutton, when Fenway Sports Group agreed to represent Boston College and assume control of the marketing rights related to athletics in 2001, this contract became the first notable instance of a professional sport organization providing sponsorship sales and consulting services to a college athletics program.

Outsourcing occurs in many other segments of the sport industry beyond professional and intercollegiate athletics. Community recreation programs operated by local jurisdictions are constantly dealing with the effects of government budgets. For example, because of budget cuts in Florida, the leisure services department for the city of Altamonte Springs outsources the operation of its sport programs to private companies year-round to provide sports instruction and league and tournament play in 12 different sports. The city earns 15 percent of program registration fees and event tickets sales, and depending on the program provider's level of marketing sophistication, it may also earn a percentage of merchandise sales (Bynum, 2007). In another case, a town council in Palm Beach, Florida, struggling with financial shortfalls, asked the Recreation Department to study the feasibility of privatizing the par 3 golf course and tennis operations

that were costing the town about $1 million more to operate than they took in each year (Kelly, 2012). Under this type of privatization scenario, a private company pays a municipality a fee for the privilege of managing a recreation program and its facilities for the purpose of making a profit. A typical contract might last five years. Finally, swim lessons and lifeguarding are often outsourced within recreation. For example, several recreation facilities in New York and Connecticut use the services of WML Aquatics (www.wmlaquatics.com), which focuses on lifeguard and water safety instruction, swimming lessons, and CPR, AED, and first aid instruction.

Dues, Fees, and Permits

Many sport organizations generate revenues through charging dues for membership. In the United States, 60.8 million adults have membership to one of the country's 38,000 gyms, fitness, and health clubs and pay an annual, monthly, or daily fee to work out (Crockett, 2019). The industry average for membership fees in the United States is $58 per month, or $696 per year. Most private country clubs charge both an initiation fee and monthly membership dues. In 2018 the average membership dues for country clubs in the United States was $5,998 per year (Reilly, 2019). Public golf courses charge greens fees, a charge to play a round on the course. Governmental recreation departments at the local, state, and national level may charge fees for camping, program fees, rented equipment fees, permit fees to use facilities (e.g., picnic area or pavilion), and moorings fees (a time-based fee applied to a vessel for the use of buoys).

Electronic Inventory

Electronic inventory (what some call digital marketing) refers to the many modern advertising techniques used online, particularly social media, blogging platforms, pay-per-click (PPC) advertising, content and video, and mobile applications. Electronic inventory also refers to television, radio, and web page advertisements along with electronic newsletters.

Social Media

Sport organizations throughout the world use numerous types of social media platforms to reach their audiences. Sport teams in particular have jumped into this digital space. The most used social media platforms are Twitter, Facebook, Instagram, and Snapchat.

Twitter Twitter is often used to promote a team or organization, increase consumer engagement, build relationships, and drive revenue (e.g., game attendance, merchandise) (Williams et al. 2014). The value of Twitter to various sport organizations stems from advertising vehicles such as promoted tweets, promoted trends, and promoted accounts. Advertisers can purchase the promoted tweets to expand their marketing reach. The promoted tweets can also appear on a search result page, user timeline, and enhanced profile page or through official Twitter clients and third-party clients (e.g., Hootsuite).

Facebook With a slightly older demographic than Twitter, Facebook is a social networking site where a user can post comments, share photographs, and post links to news or other interesting content on the web, chat live, and watch short-form video (Nations, 2019). Recent statistics suggest that Real Madrid leads all sport teams with over 107 million Facebook followers. The Columbus Blue Jackets in the National Hockey League have used Facebook to boost the sales of their playoff and season tickets using lead ads and custom audiences. Lead ads are Facebook ads that a potential customer taps on, whereby a prepopulated form pops up with Facebook contact information that is sent to the organization. Custom audiences take data from the organization's customer relationship management (CRM) system or customer contact lists (e.g., phone numbers or email addresses) to help with connecting to customers and contacts on Facebook (Facebook Business, 2019).

Drew Hallowell/Getty Images

Social media can be used to cultivate an audience and identify customers.

Instagram   Instagram is a social networking app used for sharing photos and videos from a smartphone. With 8.8 million followers, the Los Angeles Lakers in the National Basketball Association use Instagram to engage fans with exciting plays and with content about former and current players. Instagram provides the opportunity for businesses to advertise through photo, video, or carousel ads. In addition, sport organizations can add professional-looking photos, develop stories, stream live videos, interact with other users, and sell products on Instagram (Driver, 2020).

Snapchat   Snapchat is a multimedia messaging app that allows users to take pictures or videos and send messages that are available only for a short time before they become inaccessible to their recipients. Unlike Facebook, Instagram, and Twitter, Snapchat does not open to a news feed, nor does it allow you to search for individual users without knowing their exact details. It is a messaging service for close friends and is particularly popular with the teenage population. Advertisers can buy the right to create their own bespoke animations and adornments. Snapchat has also offered rights holders the chance to have these products built for them in a value-in-kind arrangement to capture engagement around major events. Examples in sport include the UEFA Champions League final, the FIFA World Cup, and the PyeongChang 2018 Winter Olympics (Connolly, 2019).

Blogging Platforms

A blog refers to "frequently modified web pages in which dated entries are listed in reverse chronological sequence" (Herring et al., 2004, p. 1). Although websites and blogs are similar, the primary differences between the two is that blogs are updated more frequently than websites and allow reader engagement (Duermyer, 2019). Examples of some of the most popular sport blogs include SB Nation, Deadspin, Bleacher Report, Yahoo Sports, MLB, ESPN, Fans Edge, and Fanatics. Although bloggers can make money in several ways, the most common is through readers clicking on advertisements on the blog.

Pay-per-Click Advertising

A digital marketing strategy, pay-per-click (PPC) advertising allows businesses to advertise products and services on the site's page. Each time a visitor on the publisher's web page clicks on that advertisement, the business pays a certain amount to the publisher of the page (Farris et al., 2010). Sport organizations may use PPC to improve listings in search engines to enhance ticket and merchandise sales or services for game and sporting events (Simmons, 2018).

Content Marketing and Video Production

The production of valuable online content and relevant videos is vitally important to most sport organizations in the 21st century. Content marketing is defined as "a strategic marketing approach focused on creating and distributing valuable, relevant, and consistent content to attract and retain a clearly defined audience—and, ultimately, to drive profitable customer action" (Content Marketing Institute, 2019). For example, a youth sport organization might publish unique online content on sport parenting, safety issues for young athletes, and sports skills to engage their audience and promote their organization. Many sport organizations also use video-sharing services such as YouTube to share content with their customers. For example, Bundesliga, a German soccer league, shares highlights and funny videos on their YouTube Channel. ESPN also hosts a YouTube Channel with up-to-the-minute news, scores, highlights, and commentary for several sport leagues (NFL, NBA, etc.).

Mobile Applications

Mobile applications ("apps") represent a unique feature of smartphones: They are developed specifically for mobile devices and are available for a small fee or even for free to help users perform specific tasks (Kang et al., 2015). Apps are used in a variety of contexts from fitness and recreation to youth sports, within professional sport, and in a variety of other contexts. Kang and colleagues suggest the following uses for apps within sport:

Sport-related apps such as MLB At Bat and ESPN ScoreCenter allow users to quickly gain information about teams and view game highlights. Other sport-related apps cater to consumers interested in fitness. Workout trainer apps such as Daily Workout Apps feature videos and images of professional trainers to help users improve their fitness. As the apps support a wide range of sport spectrums, they have become an integral part of people's lives—especially for those who have embraced various aspects of sports. (p. 272)

Television Advertising

One of the most powerful ways for businesses to reach their target audience is to work with a local or national broadcast company, cable company, or sport league by placing a television ad. The power of television advertising is evident when considering that businesses spent $3 billion on television ads for just playoff games in the National Basketball Association (NBA), National Football League (NFL), Major League Baseball (MLB), and National Hockey League (NHL) in 2018 (Blustein, 2019). The National Football League earns $6 billion per year from their television contract with NBC, Fox, and ESPN, which runs from 2014 to 2022 (Statista, 2016). Consumers are still attracted to watching live events, particularly sports, mainly because of the uncertain outcome and emotional suspense that comes with them. Today, many people watch the Super Bowl just for the commercials. Super Bowl XLIX in 2015, between the New England Patriots and Seattle Seahawks, saw a record 114.4 million viewers tune in to the game, and businesses are willing to pay the price to reach those audiences. The advantage of television advertising is the large number of people that can be reached with the company's brand, although the cost is high and consumers are prone to changing the channel during breaks in the game (Irwin et al., 2008).

The broadcasting of college football games is another area where brands do a lot of advertising. Various brands spent almost $1.7 billion in television advertising in 2019 on college bowl games. AT&T alone spent more than $70 million on bowl advertising. College football was responsible for 10 percent of all television ad impressions on Fox and 9.5 percent for ESPN. The national championship game on January 13, 2020, between Louisiana State University and Clemson was broadcast on ESPN and accounted for an estimated $91 million in advertising. The postponement of much of the college football season because of the coronavirus pandemic, however, could account for more than $1 billion in lost revenues from advertisers in 2020 (Hsu, 2020).

Web Page Advertising

Sport organizations can sell ads on their websites. Several factors are important in relation to this type of digital advertising. First, the content on the website must be relevant, original, and useful, and it must be updated often to drive unique visitors to the site. The measure of unique visitors refers to the number of distinct individuals requesting pages from the website during a given period. The second factor is the amount of traffic that is driven to the site. Of course, new and original content will drive more traffic to the site. Finally, the site should be designed in such a way that users can easily navigate it. The header for a sport organization's website will likely prominently feature the sponsorship name. The website should be easy to navigate and could include advertisements along with social media, featured videos, upcoming events, podcasts, and photo galleries.

Fundraising

Many types of sport organizations engage in fundraising. Sectors of the industry such as intercollegiate athletics, nonprofits (e.g., Special Olympics), and youth sport organizations depend on receiving gifts. Fundraising is closely tied to philanthropy, a Greek word that means "love of mankind" (Ciconte & Jacob, 2011, p. 2). Fundraising has been defined as "the creation and ongoing development of relationships between a not-for-profit organization and its various donors for the purpose of increasing gift revenue to the organization"

(Lindahl, 2010, p. 4). The various sources of fundraising include individual donors, companies, foundations, and public support (Gallagher et al., 2012). Endowments, entitlements, and trusts are also a source of fundraising revenue. Fundraising methods such as major gift solicitation, annual giving, planned giving, capital campaigns, and event fundraising are discussed later in the text.

Grant Writing

A **grant** is a specific quantity of money that is awarded by a government, foundation, organization, or person for a specific purpose. A nonprofit may apply for a grant for several reasons, such as to run a program (e.g., a softball clinic), fund a new building, or pay for equipment or uniforms. For example, nonprofit youth sport organizations in the United States are apt to apply for grants. Many colleges and universities apply for various types of federal funding

to cover expenses for programs. In European countries, community sport clubs commonly apply for governmental funding. The process for applying for grants is discussed in more detail later in the book.

Naming Rights

Sport organizations may sell the rights to naming an arena or stadium, practice facility, jersey, or team. The first naming-rights deal for a stadium occurred in 1973 when the Buffalo Bills of the National Football League sold the right to name their new stadium to Rich Foods (Leeds et al., 2007). Although they are more common in professional sport, naming-rights arrangements are not unheard of in recreation. For example, the County of San Diego Parks and Recreation Department offers naming-rights opportunities for existing park amenities including ball fields, playgrounds, staging areas, sport arenas, amphitheaters,

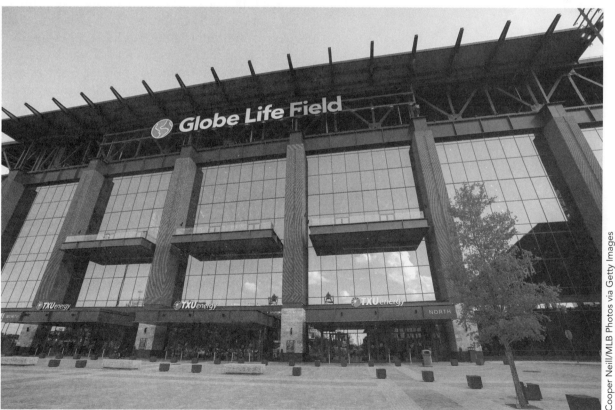

Cooper Neil/MLB Photos via Getty Images

Naming rights generate income for the sports organization or arena and increase visibility for the sponsor.

swimming pools, community gardens, community rooms, and trails.

Print Inventory

Although much of what used to be printed in hard copy is now presented online, some sport organizations still generate revenues from advertisements sold in game programs, recruiting guides, media guides, scorecards, rosters, ticket backs, and credentials. Another important piece of printed collateral is the pocket schedule, which is a small folded piece of paper that contains the team schedule for the year along with various promotions. Most of these print items have space for advertisers. For some fans, the pocket schedule is a collectable. A five-year-old boy from Glenview, Illinois, wrote every MLB team to request a pocket schedule. He heard back from every team except two. Some of the teams simply sent schedules, but others replied with temporary tattoos, magnet schedules for the refrigerator, and personalized letters (Stevens, 2018).

Promotions

Described as the various means through which sport organizations persuade consumers to make a purchase decision, **promotional efforts** include the bundling of tickets with merchandise, on-field contests, premium-item giveaways, and ticket giveaways (Shonk, 2011). In addition, sport organizations may promote buy-one-get-one (BOGO) sales, scoreboard trivia, contests, and raffles. Minor league baseball teams are notorious for running silly promotions. For example, in 2003 the Charleston RiverDogs promoted "Silent Night," during which talking and cheering were forbidden until the fifth inning of the game. Many fans created signs to cheer and boo. Librarians replaced the ushers, and golf marshals held up "Quiet please" signs (Ramsey, 2016). In another promotion, the Lowell Spinners in the New York–Penn League dropped $1,000 in cash from a helicopter on the field after a game. Participants were asked to sign up for the promotion at the guest relations booth as they entered the ballpark.

Signage

You cannot go to any sport venue without noticing various signage throughout the facility. Signage is visible in many areas. For example, printed messages with a sponsor's name and logo are almost everywhere. Before arriving inside the sport venue, you can find printed or electronic messages on street signs, vinyl banners, parking lot street poles, gates, and on the facade of the sport venue as you enter the facility. Within the sport venue, signage is common on billboards, scoreboards, posters, LED displays, and dasher boards. Signage can be found in messages on the field, ice, or courts; in the form of virtual signage; and on signage that rotates. Reliance on this type of signage to generate spectator recognition of sponsors is so commonplace that the concept of sponsorship is equated with the use of signage in sport venues (Maxwell & Lough, 2009).

Taxes

Two types of sport organizations rely primarily on public tax monies. First, governmental recreation agencies such as local parks and recreation departments depend on tax subsidies as part of their operating budget. Second, in a more indirect way, many sport teams operate in facilities that are owned by local governments. The funding to pay for construction of these facilities is partly paid for by public tax revenues.

Parks and Recreation Departments

Parks and recreation departments are predominantly a service provided by local governments and rely on financial support from local governments' general tax funds (National Recreation and Parks Association, 2017). The departments, however, suffer from stagnant or declining budgets because local governments must manage a variety of public services (fire and police protection, education, etc.) that vie for funding from the same limited pool of tax revenues. The typical park and recreation agency in the United States generates $19.38 in revenue annually for each resident in the jurisdiction and recovers 22.9 percent of its operating expenditures from nontax revenues. General fund taxes support 61 percent of operating expenditures (NRPA, 2021).

On average, each park serves 2,277 residents. Most of these agencies run programs related to team sports, themed special events, social recreation events, health and wellness education, fitness enhancement classes, individual sports, safety training, aquatics, racket sports, trips and tours, performing arts, martial arts, and cultural crafts. The typical parks and recreation agency conducts, contracts, operates, maintains, or manages numerous facilities and programs (NRPA, 2021):

- Indoor facilities
- Trails, greenways, and blueways
- Major jurisdiction-wide special events
- Special purpose parks and open spaces
- Nonpark sites
- Outdoor swim facilities and water parks

- Tournament or event-quality outdoor sports complexes
- Tennis center facilities
- Community gardens

Stadium Financing

Most stadiums built today rely more on private funding than public funding. Even so, public funding still factors into many stadium deals. Between 2000 and 2015, over $12 billion of the public's money has gone to privately owned stadiums in the NFL (Florida, 2015). For example, the public paid $325 million of the $1.2 billion price tag for AT&T Stadium in Dallas, Texas, home of the Cowboys. Located in downtown Minneapolis and home to the Vikings, U.S. Bank Stadium opened in September 2016, and the public paid $498 million of the $1.06 billion cost. The public picked up $600 million of the $1.5 billion cost of Mercedes-Benz Stadium in Atlanta, home to the Falcons. Busch Stadium

The new Busch Stadium was constructed with both public and private financing.

Dilip Vishwanat/MLB Photos via Getty Images

in Saint Louis is home to MLB's Cardinals. The financing for the stadium, completed in 2006, included the following (Click, 2014):

- $42.7 million in state funds
- $3.4 million elimination of city ticket tax to pay $42.9 million in bonds
- $90 million paid by the Saint Louis Cardinals
- $200.5 million in private stadium bonds
- $45 million county loan

Tickets and Hospitality

Sales in this category may include inventory related to season ticket accounts, miniplans, premium seating, individual game tickets, and group tickets (Reese & Thomas, 2013). Inventory may include club seating, suites, personal seat licenses (PSLs), parties, special events, parking, and hospitality events. Ticket sales is one of the easiest ways to break into the sport industry. Salespeople must be familiar with the secondary market where tickets are sold on sites such as StubHub, Vivid Seats, Seat Geek, Live Nation, Gametime, and others.

Characteristics of Effective Salespeople, or Revenue Generators

For years, sales trainers have focused on the characteristics of effective salespeople such as a strong belief in the product, belief in oneself, willingness to ask for the order, ability to follow up with clients, preparation, time management, competitive nature, self-motivation, ability to face rejection, and listening skills. Back in the 1960s, Mayer and Greenberg (1964) theorized that a good salesperson must have at least two basic qualities— **empathy** and **ego drive**. They defined empathy as "the ability to feel as another person does in order to be able to sell him or her a product or service" (pp. 119-120). Ego drive makes a salesperson "want and need to make the sale in a personal or ego way, not merely for the money to be gained" (p. 120). Thus, they suggested that a good salesperson

would have the drive and the need to make a sale, and that their empathy would give them a connecting tool with which to do it.

Taking these findings into account, David Kurlan spent four years in the late 1980s and early 1990s seeking to discover the elements that led to sales failure. What he learned was that although successful salespeople had empathy and ego drive, so did many unsuccessful salespeople. Instead, Kurlan (2009) found the following four elements as critical to sales success:

1. *Desire*—Strong desire, how badly a salesperson wants to succeed, is the most important element in sales. When a salesperson lacks strong desire, their incentive to do anything difficult is not compelling and they will often take the easy way out.
2. *Commitment*—Strong commitment is the willingness to do whatever it takes to succeed. Many salespeople had conditional commitment, whereby they will do what it takes but only if it is not too difficult or scary, and only when they agree in principle with what they are being asked to do.
3. *Outlook*—Outlook encompasses attitude about the company, job, career, and self. An outlook that is not strong can affect desire, reduce commitment, and cause excuse making.
4. *Responsibility*—When salespeople take responsibility for their results, or lack thereof, they are being responsible.

Kurlan suggested, "When the combination of strong desire and commitment are present, accompanied by a good outlook, a salesperson will have tremendous incentive to change" (p. 3). Thus, his supposition was that a salesperson with incentive to change would be trainable, and a trainable salesperson would improve. Sales managers have been asked to rate their most important criteria for hiring a candidate for the position of salesperson. The most important criteria were communication skills, negotiation skills, self-discipline, motivation, problem management, teamwork, integrity, change management, and time management (Cvetkoska & Iliev, 2017).

Salespeople: Born or Made?

For many years, debate has been ongoing about whether salespeople are born or made. Are people with certain personality types more successful at sales? Several studies have suggested that people who rated highest in **conscientiousness** are more successful in sales performance (Barrick et al., 2001; Vinchur et al., 1998; Warr et al., 2005). Those who rate high on the conscientiousness dimension exhibit high levels of thoughtfulness, good impulse control, and goal-directed behaviors. They tend to be organized, plan, and be mindful of details and deadlines. Martin (2011) administered personality tests to 1,000 top business salespeople in high technology and business services and found that the following personality traits influenced the top performers' selling style and their success:

- *Modesty*—Stereotypes suggest that salespeople are pushy and egotistical, but 91 percent of top salespeople had medium to high scores of modesty and humility.

- *Conscientiousness*—Eighty-five percent of top salespeople could be described as having a strong sense of duty and being responsible and reliable.

- *Achievement orientation*—Eighty-five percent tested high on this dimension, suggesting that they are fixated on achieving their goals and are continuously measuring their performance in comparison with those goals.

- *Curiosity*—Eighty five percent had extremely high curiosity (i.e., hunger for knowledge and information) levels.

- *Lack of gregariousness*—Gregariousness is a preference for being with people and includes friendliness. Surprisingly, top performers averaged 30 percent lower gregariousness than below-average performers.

- *Lack of discouragement*—Only 10 percent of top performers had high levels of discouragement or were frequently overwhelmed with sadness.

- *Lack of self-consciousness*—Less than 5 percent of performers had high levels of self-consciousness, which measured how easily someone was embarrassed.

Although we have some ideas about the effect of personality on sales performance, it is difficult to claim that one personality trait is conducive to more effective salesperson performance in all cases. Yakasai and Jan (2015) highlight the unending task of trying to understand sales performance, especially now that sales and marketing is a global phenomenon that brings many cultural norms into play as well. With the development of technology, many have claimed that sales professions will become extinct or that people employed in sales will have to develop new skills. As noted previously, technology has significantly changed the landscape of the sport industry from how we purchase tickets, memberships, merchandise, and food and how fans interact with athletes. Although technology is an important component of sales within the industry, sport managers and marketers must never ignore the human element that is important to our industry. According to one study, 88.46 percent of sales people believe that face-to-face is still the best way to do selling (Cvetkoska & Iliev, 2017).

Importance of Influence and Persuasion

Even students who are not interested in pursuing a career in sales need to understand the sales process and be able to influence people. In his book *To Sell Is Human*, Dan Pink (2012) suggests that people now spend 40 percent of their time at work engaged in non-sales-related selling that involves persuading, influencing, and convincing others in ways that do not involve anyone making a purchase. He writes:

> *Physicians sell patients on a remedy. Lawyers sell juries on a verdict. Teachers sell students on the value of paying attention in class. Entrepreneurs woo funders, writers sweet-talk producers, coaches cajole players. Whatever*

our profession, we deliver presentations to fellow employees and make pitches to new clients. We try to convince the boss to loosen up a few dollars from the budget or the human resources department to add more vacation days. (Pink, 2012, pp. 19-20)

"Sales leaders are in the business of influencing others" (DeSena, 2003, p. 103). Cialdini (2007) writes about the idea of influence or the power of persuasion. In his book, he claims that six fundamental principles direct human behavior—consistency, **reciprocation**, **social proof**, authority, liking, and **scarcity**. Each is discussed here:

1. *Consistency*—Cialdini suggests that after we have made a choice or taken a stand, we will encounter personal and interpersonal pressures to behave consistently with the commitment. Thus, consistency is the obsessive desire to be (and appear to be) consistent with what we have already done. For example, a ticket salesperson who promises to follow up with a phone call to help answer a question will be deemed inconsistent when not doing so.

2. *Reciprocation*—Reciprocation suggests that we should repay, in kind, what another person has provided us. Cialdini suggests that the rules of reciprocation are so powerful that it often produces a yes response to a request that would not have been accepted except for the fact the respondent felt a sense of indebtedness. For example, while talking to his sales representative with the Philadelphia Eagles, Jeremy Alberts told the salesperson about a problem that his child was experiencing. Later in the week, Jeremy found an Eagles jersey and hat in the mail. Jeremy wanted to reciprocate by buying tickets the following year.

3. *Social proof*—This principle suggests that we try to find out what others think is correct to determine what is correct. Thus, Cialdini says that we view a behavior as more correct in any given situation based on the degree to which we see others performing it. When consumers

want to know about results or performance, they may ask another to find more information. For example, Allison was interested in buying a new cardio machine she had seen on television that she thought would help her train for a marathon. When she heard that another runner had bought the machine before running a marathon, Allison texted her to find out if the equipment had helped her prepare for the event.

4. *Authority*—Cialdini highlights the power of the deep-seated sense of duty to authority within all of us. For example, a person is more willing to comply with someone with a title such as medical doctor (MD) or someone dressed in attire such as hospital white, priestly black, army green, or police blue. Coaches, athletes, and referees can be considered authority figures in sport. These types of authority figures often appear as commentators on sport broadcasts because they are deemed more credible by fans watching the games.

5. *Liking*—We prefer to say yes to people whom we like. We may like people who are physically attractive, people who are similar to us, those who compliment us, and people who are cooperative and in constant contact with us. Regardless of whether we are talking about sales in sport or any other industry, we want to engage with people we like.

6. *Scarcity*—The scarcity principle suggests that opportunities seem more valuable to us when their availability is limited. People are more motivated by the thought of losing something than by the thought of gaining something of equal value. Scarcity is a common method used in sport sales. For example, a salesperson who tells the fan that only two tickets are left in this section is using this principle.

Baker's Four Strategies

Those who can generate revenue over a sustained period have the ability to influence others. Influence may stem from a person's ability to sell a ticket for a professional or intercollegiate sport team. Selling memberships at a fitness club or merchandise for a sporting goods company also involves influence. Others may exhibit influence by convincing government officials to build a new stadium or approve a recreation budget.

Baker (2015) highlights four strategies for influencing others, which he refers to as investigation, calculation, motivation, and collaboration. According to Baker, the best influencers use a combination of push and pull strategies to persuade. In Baker's influencing framework, the push style is a direct, assertive style, whereas the pull style is an indirect, less assertive style of influencing. Characteristics of the push style include driving, proposing, giving information, blocking or shutting out, and taking the idea to the person. Pull style characteristics include enabling, testing, understanding, seeking information, building or opening up, and getting the person to come to the idea. The framework is based on two influencing approaches that he refers to as logical and emotional. The logical approach is concerned with the rationale of the situation or circumstance, whereas the emotional approach links the proposal to the bigger picture and creates a common and gripping vision of the future. Characteristics of the logical approach include facts, evidence, rationale, structure, and measurement. Emotional characteristics include feelings, perceptions, values, flexibility, and morale.

Investigators (Push–Logical)

Influence using the push–logical strategy involves gathering the facts and presenting them in a logical and convincing manner using a coherent and assertive argument based on well-founded research. Using this strategy, investigators gather facts and prepare a case, generate ideas that are well thought through, assert ideas about pushing a case onto others in an energetic way, quickly spot flaws in opposing arguments, and communicate those faults clearly and convincingly. As you progress through this textbook, you will see how both

sales and fundraising in sport involve a process of collecting information and making a persuasive argument about why someone should buy a sponsorship or ticket, or make a donation.

Calculators (Pull–Logical)

Influence using the pull–logical strategy involves clearly articulating the pitfalls of the status quo and then demonstrating how those pitfalls can be overcome. Calculators weigh their options when contemplating a new direction or making an important decision, and they like to use logic to build an argument (like investigators). Their style, however, is more pull than push. Calculators communicate standards by setting clear and realistic expectations. They are good at providing constructive feedback on whether their standards have been met and offer concessions in the form of bargains or by exchanging favors. Sport salespeople or fundraisers must be calculators; they are constantly listening, weighing the best options for their consumers, and negotiating with the customer. For example, a ticket sales manager might learn that a customer wants her family to be able to attend more games but has a limited budget. The sales manager could present various ticket packages to the customer and help her weigh the pros and cons of each option for her family. If the customer seems to be leaning toward one option, the manager could offer a better price for that package. This effort would be an example of the pull–logical approach.

Motivators (Push–Emotional)

When using the push–emotional strategy, being influential comes from associating an idea, change, or proposal with a clear, compelling, and common vision for the future. Motivators persuade by explicitly pointing out how a new initiative helps others to achieve their goals. These types of people can communicate their vision by articulating a positive and inspiring future. Motivators can generate enthusiasm in others and connect emotionally by putting into words the hope, aspirations, and fears that people may be feeling. Finally, a motivator can build morale by helping others see the benefit and value in pulling together as a team when necessary. Motivation is important in sport because a salesperson is always selling benefits and the value of the product. An example may be a college sport coach who takes over a program with a losing record. The coach may sell the program to potential recruits by highlighting the change in culture. The coach must be good at selling both the new recruits and the players who remain to build morale and a culture of winning.

Collaborators (Pull–Emotional)

Users of the pull-emotional strategy influence through trust building and sharing ownership of the leader's proposal. Collaborators create positive emotional energy and develop a sense of trust and engagement with the people they work with. Collaboration means sharing ownership and communicating openly with their team. Collaborators do not just influence others; they are also open to being persuaded by their colleagues. These types of people actively listen to what others are saying and show empathy and understanding when people become frustrated or upset. Finally, genuine collaboration involves building trust. Collaborators are not only trusted but also display trust in others. Collaboration is key to sport because salespeople work with many stakeholders, from athletes and coaches to sponsors, fans, and many others. The coronavirus pandemic provided many opportunities for collaborators as sport administrators learned how important it was to listen, show empathy, and build trust. This was true for sport managers as they collaborated with health officials, coaches, athletes, family, sponsors, and many other stakeholders.

Summary

This introductory chapter has discussed the vital importance of sales and revenue generation within the sport industry. We hope that you are starting to grasp the broad nature of the sport industry and the many types of inventory it includes. Many employment opportunities are available in the industry if you can sell. Many jobs may reside in a marketing or sales department, but everyone must be willing and able to sell in some respect. Creative salespeople are continuously thinking of new ways to monetize inventory to generate revenue. Effective salespeople have a strong desire to succeed, are committed to success, have a positive outlook, and are responsible for their results. Studies about sales performance highlight the importance of conscientiousness, modesty, achievement orientation, and curiosity. Effective salespeople are good listeners and can persuade others using their influence.

For some students, the idea of selling to someone may be a scary idea. Sales can be learned, however, by following a process to becoming an effective salesperson. Improving sales skills takes time and experience. Consider the first time you made a presentation in the classroom. The second time you gave a presentation, it was probably better because you were able to apply what you learned from the first presentation.

This textbook is designed to equip both students and industry professionals with knowledge of the sales process, but it also provides practical ways to apply this knowledge and help prepare you for selling in the sport industry. Sales is one of the easiest ways to break into the industry, but the ability to generate revenue is the key to staying for the long term. Finally, recognize that reading the textbook is important because it provides a strong base of knowledge on this topic. But if you want to become an effective salesperson, you need to go beyond simple comprehension of the topic to application. In other words, reading the text does not create an effective salesperson. A person seeking to become an effective salesperson applies this knowledge by practicing through role-playing, exercises, internships, volunteering, and other ways when they are actually doing sales. We promise that students who take this to heart, work hard, and apply these principles will be ahead of the thousands of others who are trying to enter this competitive industry. We encourage you to work hard, network, and be competitive and persistent. Finally, do not forget about the importance of relationships. You are running a marathon, not a sprint. Best wishes and enjoy the journey!

APPLIED LEARNING ACTIVITIES

1. The chapter discusses several types of inventory that can be monetized. Choose a segment of the industry (e.g., intercollegiate athletics, professional sport, community recreation, or fitness) and describe all the types of inventory that can be sold. For example, in professional sport you may include tickets and hospitality, promotions, and others. For each type of inventory (e.g., tickets and hospitality) write a short paragraph that explains the inventory.

2. Read the section Characteristics of Effective Salespeople, or Revenue Generators and pay specific attention to Mayer and Greenberg's (1964) idea that a good salesperson must have at least two basic qualities—empathy and ego drive. How did Mayer and Greenberg define each of these qualities? Based on these definitions, type up a one-page document with three paragraphs. In the first paragraph, describe one scenario in your life when you exhibited empathy. In the second paragraph, describe a scenario when you exhibited ego drive. In the final paragraph, explain how these two scenarios can help you to become an effective salesperson.

3. In the section Importance of Influence and Persuasion, Cialdini (2007) suggests that six fundamental principles direct human behavior: consistency, reciprocation, social proof, authority, liking, and scarcity. Read about each of these principles and describe two or three examples that can apply to any combination of the different principles.

CASE STUDY

NCAA INTERCOLLEGIATE ATHLETICS PROGRAMS—WHERE DOES THE MONEY COME FROM?

Two types of revenues are reported by NCAA member institutions. According to Fulks (2017), NCAA revenues that appear on Division I athletics budgets are grouped as either (1) allocated revenues or (2) generated revenues. The allocated revenues include fees paid by the student, direct institutional support (funds transferred from the college or university general fund to athletics), indirect institutional support (i.e., budgeted items like utilities or maintenance fees that are paid by the college or university on behalf of the athletics department), and direct governmental support (e.g., money from state and local governments). Generated revenues are produced by the athletics department and may include ticket sales, broadcasting revenues, alumni contributions, guarantees (i.e., revenue from scheduling and participating in an away game), royalties, distributions from the NCAA, and other revenue sources.

Discussion Questions

1. Guarantees are a type of generated revenue for NCAA member institutions. Type a half-page summary with the following information: (1) provide one example of a guarantee in intercollegiate athletics and (2) explain the benefits and risks of a guarantee to the athletics program.

2. Do some research about the amount of student fees at your college or university that is directly allocated to athletics. Discuss your findings in a small group.

Go to HK*Propel* to complete the activities for this chapter.

Hiraman/E+/Getty Images

CHAPTER 2

The Revenue Generation Process: Selling With the PRO Method

CHAPTER OBJECTIVES

After completing the chapter, you should be able to do the following:

- Understand the difference between selling goods and selling services
- Explain the characteristics and importance of relationship selling in sport
- Demonstrate an understanding of basic prospecting and qualifying of customers
- Use open-ended questions to probe for information
- Match features and benefits of the product with the wants and needs of customers
- Understand the elements of a sales proposal, both written and oral
- Demonstrate an understanding of customer service after the sale

So, you now understand the importance of revenue generation in sport and still want to pursue the career? Great! As the old saying goes, "If you can sell, you will never be without a job." This chapter focuses on the basics of sales and revenue generation. Its purpose is to give you a basic understanding of the sales process, from beginning to end. Although many elements of revenue generation apply to any business, several elements make sport unique.

Selling in the Sport Industry

Sport is different from many other businesses, and those unique elements will shape the way that you connect and communicate with customers. Before you can begin your career in sport sales, you should understand what you will be selling and the fundamental differences between different types of sales.

Selling Goods Versus Selling Services

In some form nearly all businesses generate revenue by selling **products**, which may include both goods and services. Many businesses, such as sport organizations, sell both products and services. Understanding the business's sellable products is important for any salesperson, including why selling goods may differ in approach from selling services.

Selling Goods

Goods are tangible items produced for sale. These are products that we can see, touch, taste, or move. In sport, examples of goods are merchandise, jerseys, and concessions that are available for purchase from a sport organization. Tangible goods that the customer can see and touch are easier for the customer to evaluate. Consider buying an article of clothing in a store. You can see it, feel the material, and try it on before you buy it. You can make your own judgment on the quality of the item or how it looks on you. If it looks great, you will know immediately. If it looks terrible, you

will also know immediately and be able to find something else. The tangible nature of the good usually allows the customer to inspect and assess the quality of the item before committing to buying it. Additionally, customers can often compare different products themselves to find the one that best suits their needs. Because of the customer's ability to gather their own information about the quality of the product, the sales process for such an item is less complex.

Selling Services

Most revenue generated in sport, however, stems from the use of services and does not include as many tangible goods. This chapter (and most of this book) teaches you how to maximize revenue from such services, which requires a different approach from selling goods. **Services** are actions or work done for a person or an organization (Johnson, 1969). For example, the service provided by selling tickets includes the entertainment or emotion of watching the live game. Likewise, the service provided in corporate partnerships includes access to fans and the ability to connect one's business with the goodwill of the team. When the customer buys a service, evaluating quality is difficult because there is nothing to see or touch. The salesperson is therefore responsible for delivering the perceived quality of the service and often helping the customer choose the best option. These responsibilities are amplified when many options are available or the service is complex (Hoffman et al., 1991).

Although many would argue that sport is not a complex service, the addition of varying price levels, views, packages, season ticketholder benefits, and possible donation requirements lead to increasing complexity in attending events. Furthermore, sponsorship and multimedia partnerships can often be confusing, especially considering the depth of inventory available to the modern sport team. Taken together, salespeople who succeed in generating revenue for their team must guide the customer in the decision process.

Additionally, sport is not like a typical service. In sport, every game is different. A customer may attend two games in two days and have completely different experiences because the opponent, emotions, and outcomes can be different. Thus, the real service that the salesperson must sell is not the game itself, but the experience that comes with it. Rather than help the customer "try on" the service, the salesperson must help them envision what the experience and the associated emotions will be like. This occurs regardless of whether the emotions are tied to the attendance of the person themselves or the audience that the salesperson may be selling access to.

Personal Selling in Sport

Envision your stereotypical salesperson. Chances are you were thinking of a highly charismatic, quick-thinking person who talks a lot. In fact, the idea of talking with a salesperson sometimes makes a customer apprehensive because they are expecting to "be sold" or be "talked into" buying something that they do not need. Modern sales philosophies, however, have begun to focus on the exact opposite—listening more, talking less, and trying to find a good fit for exactly what the customer needs.

Recently, the focus has shifted more to relationship-based selling. **Relationship selling** refers to a method of prioritizing the long-term relationship with the customer over the short-term sale. The ultimate goal of relationship-based selling is to find a **win–win scenario** between the customer and the organization. Usually, this means that the customer is paying the organization for their services but is happy with the product they are getting for their money. Keep in mind that this scenario does not always mean the customer gets exactly what they want. For instance, a customer would obviously not be happy about a bad schedule or higher price, but if they still feel that the price is a good value for what they receive, a win–win scenario can be the result. Relationship selling has been connected with increased salesperson performance, revenue generation, customer trust, and customer loyalty (Crosby et al., 1990; Johnson & Grayson, 2000; Arli et al., 2018). When the customer feels as if they have a strong relationship with the salesperson and that they are valued, they are more likely to spend more money.

How do you know if you are practicing relationship-focused selling? Typically, four factors are present in a relationship between the customer and the salesperson (Crosby et al., 1990):

- *Interaction intensity*: refers to how often and under what circumstances the salesperson contacts the customer
- *Customer disclosure*: refers to how much information the customer has willingly offered to the salesperson about themselves
- *Agent disclosure*: refers to how much information the customer receives (and remembers) about the salesperson
- *Cooperative intentions*: refers to the degree to which the customer believes that the salesperson has their best interests in mind

More detailed examples of all of these are discussed in the next section, which describes a relationship-driven sales process in the sport industry.

The Sport Sales Process and the PRO Method

Throughout this book, we will be using the same five-step method to maximize revenue generation for the sport organization. The quick description of each step is described here and in figure 2.1.

- Step 1: PROspect for qualified customers
- Step 2: PRObe for information with open-ended questions
- Step 3: PROvide solutions by matching product benefits with customer information
- Step 4: PROpose an offer that best fits the customer's needs
- Step 5: PROtect the relationship by maintaining contact and customer service

Although these steps are numbered in an order, note that you may not always follow them in that order. Oftentimes, you will uncover new information in steps 3 and 4 that

The PRO Method of Selling

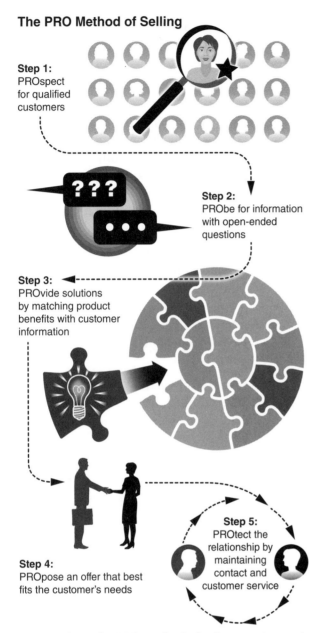

Step 1: PROspect for qualified customers

Step 2: PRObe for information with open-ended questions

Step 3: PROvide solutions by matching product benefits with customer information

Step 4: PROpose an offer that best fits the customer's needs

Step 5: PROtect the relationship by maintaining contact and customer service

FIGURE 2.1   The PRO method of selling can be used in every sector of sport business to maximize revenue generation.

require you to go back and ask more questions (step 2). Likewise, you may propose an offer that the customer declines, which leads to a new objection that you need to solve (step 3) before proposing a new offer. Although all of this may seem like a time-consuming process, you will quickly discover that some conversations with customers include the entire process in only a few minutes, whereas others take dozens of conversations and hours of time. Regardless, the process remains the same.

You may be wondering whether these steps apply most precisely to suite sales, corporate sponsorship sales, or fundraising. The answer is simple: all of them. To be clear, the steps you take in a revenue generation position will remain the same whether you are selling a $50 ticket, a $50,000 corporate partnership, or a $500,000 gift. The only changes between these types of sales are the details involved. To demonstrate this, we will use three distinct examples of sport products throughout this chapter. Keep these basic details in mind:

> Example 1: *Suzie Flynn is a mother of two who has a general interest in attending professional soccer games.*
>
> Example 2: *Sam Schmidt owns a barbeque restaurant located near a professional NFL team.*
>
> Example 3: *Lamar Wilson is a wealthy donor who is contemplating the funding of a sports and recreation facility for under-privileged youth.*

Step 1: PROspect for Qualified Customers

The first step in trying to generate revenue for a sport organization is to figure out whom you should be contacting. **Prospecting** for customers, a vital piece of the sales process, involves making first contact with potential buyers and qualifying whether they are capable or willing to spend money on your product.

Typically, there are two types of contact: inbound and outbound. Inbound customers are some of the easiest (though no less important) prospects you will have. **Inbound sales** includes customers who have actively reached out to the sport organization and expressed some interest in their product. Some common methods of inbound sales include customers who call the organization on the phone, visit in person, send an email, or request help through a web chat feature.

One mistake that many sport organizations make is undervaluing their inbound sales efforts. Although a customer who reaches out to the organization is likely going to be easier to sell to, a sale is never guaranteed and the salesperson needs to be prepared to maximize the revenue for any sale. For instance, Duke men's basketball has sold out every home game at Cameron Indoor Stadium since 1990 (Goduke.com, 2016), and the school certainly has multiple inquiries regarding access to games. Rather than simply allow the customer to hang up after hearing that the game is sold out, sales representatives are trained to inquire about other sports such as football and women's basketball and direct fans to their booster club to get on a waiting list for future tickets. A well-trained and experienced sales force is valuable even when the inbound prospects are considered easy.

In contrast to inbound sales, which refers to customer who reach out to the sport organization, **outbound sales** refers to the sales representatives of the organization reaching out directly to the customers. This activity used to be done almost exclusively over the phone, but modern sales departments take advantage of phone sales, chat features, email, and social media accounts to contact their customers. Most sales representatives do most of their prospecting through outbound sales. This task is the essence of what makes a career in sales difficult; you are talking with someone who did not plan to purchase something that day and trying to get them to spend money. The key to successful prospecting is being positive and having a procedure for structuring the conversation (figure 2.2).

1. Find quality leads
2. Introduce yourself
3. Get past the gatekeeper
4. Qualify the prospect
5. Follow up

Where to Find Quality Leads

Prospect leads are everywhere around us, but seeing them and focusing on quality leads are what make successful salespeople. The salesperson should start with the leads that are most likely to result in an interested customer and work down to the leads that are least likely. The following are some examples of where to look for leads:

Current Customers   The best new customer is sometimes the one you already have. Current customers can be prospected for larger or more expensive offerings. This approach is especially effective if you are calling on less expensive inventory with an opportunity to upgrade. Because active customers are sometimes unaccustomed to being called on, a good tactic is to start the conversation discussing how happy they have been with their current experience. You may gain information regarding how likely they are to increase their investment or remedy a potential issue with a better solution.

> Example 1: *Mrs. Flynn, I saw that you came out to an individual game a few weeks ago. I am calling to talk to you more about the rest of the season.*

1. Find quality leads   2. Introduce yourself   3. Get past the gatekeeper   4. Qualify the prospect   4. Follow up

FIGURE 2.2   PROspecting for qualified customers takes exceptional relational and listening skills.

Example 2: *Mr. Schmidt, I found you on a list of partners who purchased ad space on the official team website. I wanted to talk to you about some other opportunities that are available.*

Example 3: *Dr. Wilson, I wanted to thank you for your tremendous support of the organization and get your thoughts on a new exciting project we are developing.*

Past Customers   Call on customers who used to spend money with the sport organization. Oftentimes, they may tell you why they decided to stop spending or what it would take for them to invest their money in the experience again.

Example 1: *Hi, Suzie, I am calling to talk about the upcoming season. I noticed that we missed you last year. Our schedule was just released for the upcoming season, and we'd love to have you back this year.*

Example 2: *Mr. Schmidt, I see that you were one of our partners several years ago. I was hoping to update you on some of the new opportunities since you left.*

Example 3: *Dr. Wilson, I wanted to thank you for your support a few years ago and give you some information on our campaign for the current year.*

Common Interests   You can also contact people with whom you have a mutual interest or association. This circumstance creates common ground that you can use to make the conversation feel more natural and comfortable for the buyer.

Example 1: *Hi, Suzie, this is Joe. We met at church the other day. I am calling to follow up on our conversation about how big a fan you are and to see if we could get more members of the church out to one of our games this season.*

Example 2: *Sam, I found your business on the Barbeque Brethren Club website. I'm a member and I love your restaurant. I think our fans would, too.*

Example 3: *Dr. Wilson, I got your contact information from the Alumni Association of our alma mater, and I have a project a few other alumni have been involved in. I am hoping to tell you a little more about it.*

Social Media and Web Pages   Now that Internet interactions are a daily part of our lives, it is easier than ever to interact through social media or use the Internet to obtain quality leads. Details about using social media for revenue generation are discussed in depth later in this textbook, but for prospecting purposes, a social media page, Twitter message, or web search can provide contact information as well as information on the customer before you even speak with them.

Example 1: *Mrs. Flynn, thanks for being a fan on Twitter. We have a special promotion right now for our social media fans.*

Example 2: *Sam, I wanted to reach out to you because your restaurant is right next to our stadium, and I think we could really benefit your business. When would be the best time to talk?*

Example 3: *Dr. Wilson, I saw the great work you're doing with the local Boys & Girls Clubs on LinkedIn. It sounds like youth sports are important to you.*

Referrals   **Referrals** are a great way to use your existing fanbase to gain instant credibility with a new prospect. Keep in mind that although referrals tend to be some of the best prospects you can find, they are hard to acquire unless you have a good relationship with the existing customer who would be referring them. People do not generally give out the names of their friends to someone who they think will harass them or whom they do not trust.

Example 1: *Hi, Suzie, my name is Steve. Our mutual friend Tyler gave me your number and said that he brought you out to a game in the past.*

Example 2: *Mr. Schmidt, one of your customers thought you might be interested in hearing more about partnerships with our team.*

Example 3: *Dr. Wilson, you were recommended by one of our donors as a person who is highly active in the local youth recreational community.*

These areas of prospecting are only a few examples. Keep in mind that prospects are everywhere around you; you simply need to determine which are the most likely to be interested in your product. Remember as well that the vast majority of people you contact are likely to tell you no. A good salesperson closes most of their sales from the minority of those prospects who say yes.

Introducing Yourself and Opening Statements

They say you get only one chance to make a first impression. In sales, the opening statement is typically your first impression, so it must be structured well. Keep in mind that on a cold call, the person who answers the phone does not know who you are or why you are calling them. Therefore, you need to give them enough information so that they are not confused, but not so much information that they make their decision before you get a chance to really communicate with them. A good opening statement should introduce yourself and your organization, offer a little bit of information, and gain their attention. Some good opening statements may sound like the following:

Example 1: *Hello, Suzie, my name is Steve, and I work with the Giants Soccer Club. I am calling to talk to you a little about the upcoming season. How was your experience last year?*

Example 2: *Sam, my name is Christina, and I work with the Hawks. I wanted to chat about some ways I think we could benefit your restaurant. When would you be free to meet for 15 or 20 minutes?*

Example 3: *Lamar, on behalf of the Tampa Youth Recreation Association I want to thank you for your previous support. I am reaching out to provide some more information on our initiatives for this year.*

All these statements are honest and transparent. This point is important because when customers think that they are not being given

B2B REVENUE GENERATION

NFL Changes Gears With Prospecting During COVID-19 Pandemic

During the COVID-19 pandemic, many businesses were hesitant to spend funds on sponsorship, and some industries were nearly shut down altogether. Many NFL sponsors, such as travel or hotel businesses, would not benefit from advertising during a time when travel was restricted. Furthermore, because some stadiums did not allow fans and others restricted capacity, the value of in-venue sponsorship decreased significantly. But the NFL made the best of their situation by seeking out partnerships with businesses that were fortunate to thrive because of the circumstances of the pandemic. Postmates, a food delivery app, quickly became one of the NFL's premium sponsors and gained the title "Official Food Delivery Partner of the NFL." Additionally, the partnership included several promotions throughout the year for discounted food during games and secure market share during a time when nearly all fans would be watching the games from home. NFL stars such as Patrick Mahomes and Deshaun Watson piggybacked off the promotion and partnered with Postmates to deliver meals to frontline healthcare workers in their communities. Furthermore, the Super Bowl featured advertisements from similar food delivery services Doordash and Grubhub alongside the freelance worker software company Fiverr. All these sponsors had little to no exposure in the NFL before the pandemic, demonstrating the need to be willing to change plans when business trends change as well as the importance of constant prospecting for creative categories. Fortunately for the NFL, sponsorship revenues rose 10 percent despite the negative consequences of COVID-19 on several prominent sponsors.

all the information, they typically become skeptical and resistant to conversation. Likewise, if they are given too much information and believe they already know the answer, they may not be as open-minded as you would wish. Oftentimes, it is not the intention of the sales representative to be dishonest, but they may appear that way from an eagerness to qualify or disqualify the prospect in the opening sentence. Here are some examples of the most common opening statement mistakes:

- State your purpose without introducing yourself: *"Hi, I'm calling to talk to you about the upcoming season."*
- Ask for the sale in the opening statement: *"Hi, Suzie, I am calling to see if you would be interested in purchasing season tickets for the Giants this year."*
- Forget to mention the organization you are representing: *"Mr. Schmidt, I see that you own a local BBQ restaurant. I wanted to call you about sponsorship opportunities for it."*
- Give the customer an easy decline: *"Dr. Wilson, I wanted to get started on your gift if it is still something that you are interested in."*
- Force a conversation when the customer is busy or distracted: *"I know you are busy, but I promise you are going to want to hear what I have to say."*
- Hang up on a prospect without coordinating a follow-up call: *"Oh, I understand that you are busy. I will call back another time."*

Getting Past the Gatekeeper

Unfortunately, often when you call, email, or visit a prospective customer, the person whom you initially contact is not the person whom you really wanted to reach. In these cases, you find yourself having to get past a **gatekeeper**, who can be anyone who restricts access to the actual prospect—an employee, secretary, personal assistant, spouse, or even a child. A gatekeeper needs the same introduction statement used in a normal call but may be extremely protective of the prospect's time. Because gatekeepers can be the difference between getting a sale and being shut down before you even get started, keep in mind several things when you encounter a gatekeeper.

- The gatekeeper is responsible for managing the prospect's time. If you waste the prospect's time, you make them look bad. Be concise and clear in explaining how much time you need.
- The gatekeeper may be responsible for letting through only the important calls. You can overcome this by explaining why the prospect should want to speak with you, not why you want to speak with the prospect. You are there to help them, not for them to help you. For example, "Good morning, Tony, I am working with local businesses to promote their brands at our games and was hoping to speak with Xavier about a few opportunities we still have left."
- The gatekeeper is a person too! Be polite, use their name, and be sure to thank them for helping you. Having a strong relationship with the gatekeeper can pay off significantly in your relationship with the prospect.
- The gatekeeper can sometimes be the decision-maker themselves. Sometimes they are charged with making purchasing decisions on behalf of the prospect.

Qualifying the Prospect

Once you have contacted a prospect and explained why you are calling, the next thought should be to make sure you got in touch with the right person. A qualified prospect is someone who has the ability and authority to purchase the product that you are selling. Oftentimes, purchasing decisions related to tickets, sponsorship, or donations are delegated to someone else. Although this point is important for ticket sales (especially high-end ticket sales), most issues with qualifying the prospect lie in the business space. Especially when discussing high-dollar sponsorship packages, premium seating, or high-value donations, you can waste time or ruin an opportunity by proposing the sale to the wrong person. Lastly, keep in mind that although qualifying the authority of a prospect can be done early and quite simply, you sometimes must wait before qualifying financial ability. The following are examples of early qualifying questions. Unfortunately, qualifying the customer financially may happen later in the conversation.

> Example 1: *Suzie, who usually coordinates the weekend events for your family?*
>
> Example 2: *Mr. Schmidt, would you be responsible for marketing the business?*
>
> Example 3: *Dr. Wilson, I see that previous donations were made in your name. Who else is involved in the decision-making process for these gifts?*

Following Up

Although a prospect may send you to voicemail or cannot talk with you immediately, the prospecting process may not be over. Successful salespeople have a stick-with-it attitude that helps them even when they are not finding immediate success. Many sales will take four or five calls to complete, but making it to the fifth call without causing the customer to think that you are harassing them can be a challenge.

To get the best results, phone calls are usually recommended because they are the hardest form of communication to ignore. Naturally, people tend to pick up their phone when it rings. But when necessary, following up can take multiple forms. Some customers prefer to communicate by email, video chat (Zoom, Skype, etc.), or text message, so if you are struggling to follow up with phone calls, offering a different method of communication may be more effective. Be careful, however, because emails can be easily ignored or become lost in an inbox full of less personal forms of communication. Additionally, some customers find uninvited text messages intrusive, so be sure to check with the customer. As the world becomes more technologically adept, communication methods are bound to change. Good salespeople are flexible enough to communicate effectively in many ways and always adapt their method to the customer's preference.

Leaving a Voicemail That Gets a Call Back   Unfortunately, not everyone you call will be by their phone when you call them. Even more unfortunately, many prospects may not listen carefully to their voicemails, making it difficult to deliver the information that you are trying to get across. Leaving a good voicemail will help you get back in touch with those missed connections. Good voicemail messages provide content that will interest the prospect into calling back, provide contact information, and confirm that the sales representative would still like to speak with them in person. Consider these sample voicemail scripts:

> Example 1: *Good morning, Suzie, this is Steve with the Giants Soccer Club. I am calling to give you some information on the upcoming season and discuss a few promotions we have available right now. Please give me a call back at 555-1234. I look forward to speaking with you soon!*
>
> Example 2: *Hello, Sam, this is Christina with the Hawks. I am calling to give you some information on opportunities that we have to help your restaurant, and I would love to discuss them with you in person. Please call me at 555-1234 or email me at christina@hawks.com with some times when you may be free. Thank you!*
>
> Example 3: *Good evening, Lamar. My name is Stan, and I am calling on behalf of the Tampa Youth Recreation Association. I wanted to thank you again for your support and discuss our newest project, which I think you may be interested in. Please give me a call back at your earliest convenience. My number is 555-1234.*

Make Appointments to Call Back   If a customer seems interested but is unwilling to complete the sale during the call, be sure to set a specific time when you will reach back out to them. This approach lets the customer know that you are not going to give up and that they need to determine whether they are interested.

Oftentimes, a customer will try to leave an ambiguous commitment to call you back later but may forget or hesitate to do it. Although you want to avoid appearing aggressive or pushy, letting the customer know that you plan to continue working with them helps promote a long-term relationship.

Working Between Calls If a customer asks you a question that you do not know the answer to or presents a unique challenge that you cannot immediately solve, be sure to follow up with that customer when you have relevant information. No one can expect a sales representative to have all the answers, but an honest one will admit when they do not know and provide the information as soon as they get it. Lastly, if something changes that you think would affect the customer positively or negatively, a preemptive phone call or email is a great way to make the relationship feel more personal.

Step 2: PRObe for Information With Open-Ended Questions

After you have qualified the prospect and have their attention on the phone, the next step is to probe for information. **Probing** involves asking targeted questions to gather information. The goal of this step is to gather as much relevant information about the customer as possible and try to understand their wants and needs. Although many people view this step as one that involves a lot of talking to the customer, a good sales representative does the opposite.

The **80-20 rule** states that a salesperson should spend about 80 percent of the conversation listening and only 20 percent talking. The key to gaining the most information about the customer is asking questions that keep the customer talking about their own wants and needs, without the salesperson having to carry the conversation. For step 2 of the PRO method, being closer to 90-10 is desirable. Although the salesperson will do much more talking in steps 3 and 4, this step should focus primarily on inducing the customer to provide information.

Open-Ended Questions

To keep the customer doing most of the talking, salespeople use **open-ended questions**, those that cannot be answered with a simple yes or no. Typically, open-ended questions begin with the words "what," "why," "how," or a phrase like "tell me about . . ." Closed-ended questions often begin with words or phrases such as "is," "do you," "would you," "have you," or "could you." In fact, many typical closed-ended questions can be converted into open-ended questions by changing only a few words. The following are some examples of typical closed-ended questions and their open-ended counterparts:

- "Did you enjoy the game?" can be converted into "Tell me about your experience at the game."
- "Would you be interested in a partnership with our team?" can be converted to "What are your thoughts on partnering with sport organizations to market your business?"
- "How much can you donate this year?" can be converted into "Tell me about your budget for gifts this year."

Prioritizing Wants and Needs of the Customer

In the previous section we talked about customer disclosure, which refers to how much information the customer volunteers to the sales representative. The goal of the second step is to gather as much information as possible, but the sales representative must organize and prioritize this material into what is most relevant to the customer and the sale. For instance, information regarding why the customer is a fan of the organization would be extremely pertinent to the relationship, whereas information regarding where the customer works would be less important (though still valuable). Special attention should be paid to ascertaining the wants and needs of the customer. **Customer wants** are factors of the purchase that are preferable, though not necessarily required. In contrast, **customer needs** are details that must be met for the customer to get reasonable

Effective salespeople listen intently to potential customers.

value from the purchase; this seemingly minor distinction often goes overlooked.

Needs of the Customer   Being clear regarding the wants of the customer can help the salesperson narrow down the options and find the right fit for the customer. Being vague or failing to understand the needs of the customer can waste both individuals' time by discussing options that are ultimately not likely to complete a sale. The following are examples of typical needs of the customer:

• A customer who says that they always attend games with their spouse and two kids is likely to require four seats together. This requirement narrows down available inventory and prevents the salesperson from discussing options in sections where four seats together are not available. This need can identified by asking an open-ended question such as, "Who usually comes with you to games?"

• Customer budget is always a major constraint and is an important need to evaluate.

Typically, customers hesitate to offer their maximum budget, so probing by asking a question such as, "If we found the perfect package for you, what is the most you would be able to invest in it?" is effective. Supplemental questions further clarify budgets when an answer may not be definitive. As an example, a salesperson may say, "OK, so we are going to try to stay at the $500 mark for your budget. How flexible is that number if we find something that provides a better value?"

• Many customers have logistical concerns that dictate additional needs. For example, a customer who lives farther from the facility may be unable to attend day games during the week. Likewise, a customer who travels often and knows that they will miss multiple games may be more interested in a premium minipack than a general admission season ticket. This need can be uncovered by asking, "I noticed that you didn't make it to every game last year. Could you tell me a little more about why you missed them?"

• Businesses often have specific goals they hope to achieve with their corporate partnership packages. Clarifying who the business is looking to target with their partnership is important. For example, a local restaurant may be more interested in in-venue signage that can appeal to a local fanbase rather than advertising on a national television broadcast. A question that almost always yields useful information in these scenarios is "Who is your target audience?" or "Whom are you trying to reach in your marketing efforts?"

Wants of the Customer   Not all customer input will be prioritized into the needs category. After all, most of the inventory in sport is not something that the customer needs to survive. Effective salespeople also track and find solutions for the customer's wants. Typically, a good proposal from a salesperson includes all the customer's needs and at least a handful of their wants. This, of course, depends on the expectations of the customer in providing realistic wants. Here are a few examples of common wants:

• Although pricing and budget is a need of the customer, it can also be a want. This distinction can be confusing for some sales representatives. Although a business's maximum budget for a partnership might be $50,000 for the perfect package, they may prefer to stay in the $30,000 range if possible. A sales representative should then look for options at the lower budget but provide information about the extra value the customer would receive if they increased their investment. Salespeople can clarify this by saying, "I understand that your maximum budget is $50,000, but I am going to try to keep you at the $30,000 range and see if you are happy with how it suits your needs."

• When selling tickets, customer seating preference is usually the best indicator of price. Some customers prefer to pay more and sit closer to the action, whereas others prefer to get the best value and watch the game from a less desirable location. Most customers understand this tradeoff and can clarify where they fall on the spectrum if you ask. For example, you could ask, "How important is the seating location to you, knowing that the best locations are also more expensive?"

• When soliciting for donations and fundraising activities, the wants of the customer may be intrinsically motivated or extrinsically motivated. Intrinsic motivations mean that the donation makes the customer feel good about themselves or that they find a positive emotional response from the gift. Extrinsic motivations mean that the donor may be interested in the recognition, tax benefits, or positive association between themselves and the organization generated by the gift. Keep in mind that some donors may not admit that they appreciate the recognition they receive from their gift, so the salesperson must carefully navigate this issue.

• Sometimes the event itself may not be the motivation behind the customer's interest, but only a consequence. For instance, many families may not concern themselves with the game itself, instead focusing on the atmosphere of going to an event as a family. The customer wants in this case would be the family time associated with a sporting event. Similarly, some customers may enjoy a tailgate or party atmosphere more than the game itself. Asking, "Can you tell me what you enjoy about attending the game?" may be helpful in gathering this information.

Finding the Trigger Statement

Although customers often give the sales representative several wants and needs when being probed for information, one reason is typically paramount in their decision-making process. This motive is known as the **trigger statement**, and the sales representative should note it carefully. The trigger statement evokes a strong positive reaction from the customer and should summarize the customer's biggest wants or needs in a single sentence. This statement will be used later in the sales process when summarizing and closing the sale. When a sales representative thinks they have identified the trigger statement, they should write it down and remember it. Although probing for the trigger statement may seem difficult, oftentimes it can be identified by asking a direct question or seeking clarification as in the following examples:

> Example 1: *Mrs. Flynn, it sounds like time with your family is the most important reason that you attend games. How accurate would you say that is?*
>
> Example 2: *Sam, what is the single biggest marketing problem that you are looking to solve for your business?*
>
> Example 3: *Dr. Wilson, I can tell that it is important to you that we get kids involved in sports who wouldn't normally be able to afford it. How would you say this specific reason ranks among the many reasons you give to the organization?*

Step 3: PROvide Solutions for the Customer's Needs

In the previous step, the goal was to acquire as much information as possible regarding the wants and needs of the customer. In this step, the sales representative applies the wants and needs to the sport product they have available to sell and explains how and why the product can provide a solution for the customer. Figure 2.3 illustrates the tactics used in this step of the PRO method.

Features and Benefits

To provide a solution for the customer, you must first understand your product. Product

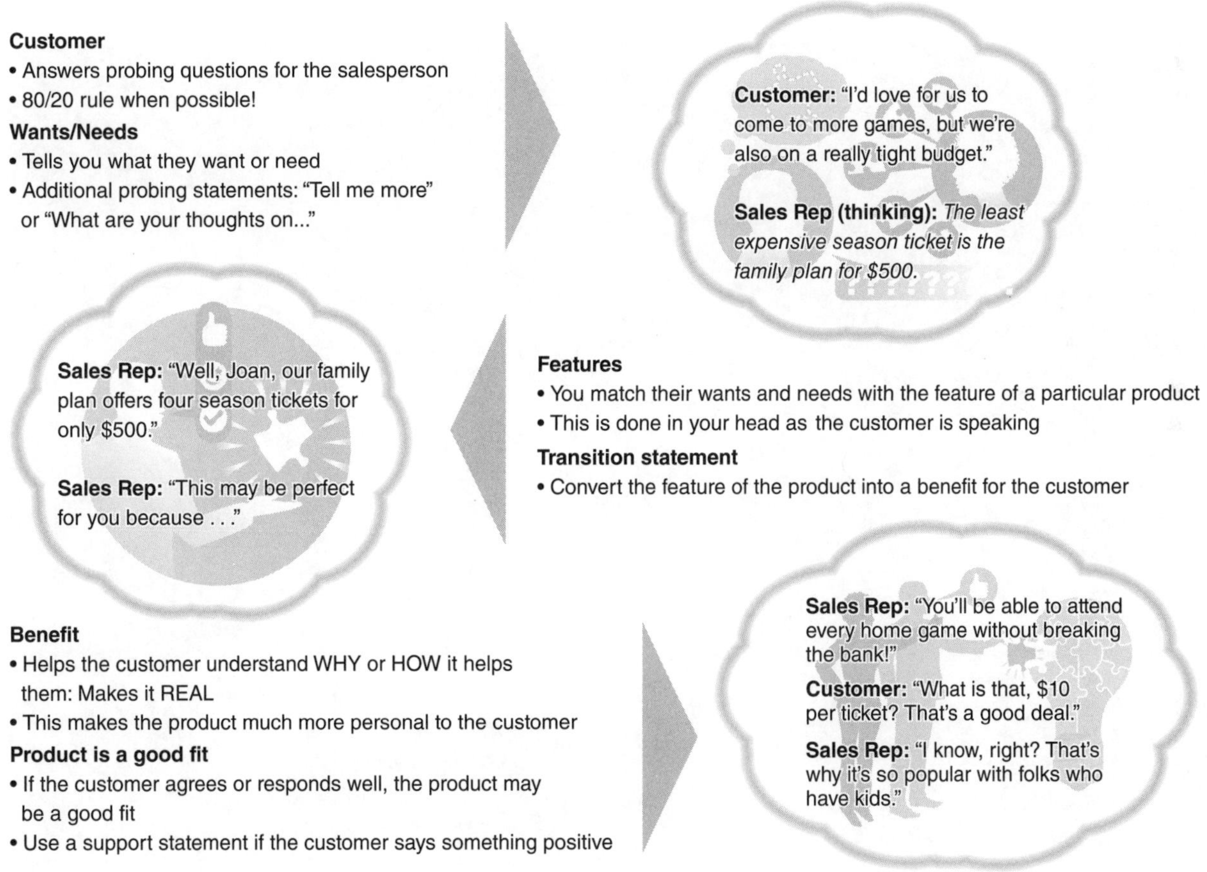

Customer
- Answers probing questions for the salesperson
- 80/20 rule when possible!

Wants/Needs
- Tells you what they want or need
- Additional probing statements: "Tell me more" or "What are your thoughts on..."

Customer: "I'd love for us to come to more games, but we're also on a really tight budget."

Sales Rep (thinking): *The least expensive season ticket is the family plan for $500.*

Sales Rep: "Well, Joan, our family plan offers four season tickets for only $500."

Sales Rep: "This may be perfect for you because . . ."

Features
- You match their wants and needs with the feature of a particular product
- This is done in your head as the customer is speaking

Transition statement
- Convert the feature of the product into a benefit for the customer

Benefit
- Helps the customer understand WHY or HOW it helps them: Makes it REAL
- This makes the product much more personal to the customer

Product is a good fit
- If the customer agrees or responds well, the product may be a good fit
- Use a support statement if the customer says something positive

Sales Rep: "You'll be able to attend every home game without breaking the bank!"

Customer: "What is that, $10 per ticket? That's a good deal."

Sales Rep: "I know, right? That's why it's so popular with folks who have kids."

FIGURE 2.3 PROviding solutions for the customer's needs takes a listening ear and skill in matching the product's benefits with information from the customer.

knowledge is one of the most important skills that a salesperson can have to generate revenue (Sharma et al., 2000). Knowledge of the product usually comes in two forms: features and benefits. **Features** are facts about the product. These points cannot be disputed and typically can be proved. On the other hand, **benefits** are how the features affect the customer. These aspects can often be subjective or debatable. Almost every feature has an associated benefit, either positively or negatively. The following are a few features of various sport products and associated benefits:

- The feature of a ticket may be that it costs $10. The benefit may be that an entire family can enjoy the sporting event for less than the price of a trip to the movies.

- A feature of attending an event may be the stadium in which it is held. The ben-

efit would be the ability to see a historic building or one that is highly sentimental to the customer.

- A feature of premium seating may be that alcoholic beverages are included. The benefit is that the customer does not have to worry about running a tab or even bringing out a credit card at the event.

- A feature of a sponsorship proposal may be signage on the outfield wall. The benefit is that thousands of local attendees will be seeing the local business's logo.

- A feature of a television broadcast may be that it starts at 7 p.m. The benefit is that most people will be home from work, so viewership will be higher.

- The feature of a fundraising campaign may be the construction of a new community basketball court. The benefit is

One feature you might sell is attending a game, and a benefit to the customer could be the adrenaline rush of seeing their team make a great play!

that the facility will provide hundreds of kids the opportunity to play sports without needing to travel.

Understanding the benefit to each feature is important for two reasons. First, the customer can probably find many of the features of a sport product on their own without the need for a sales representative. A good sales representative highlights the benefits, not the features, of the product to make the solution that is being provided more real to the customer. Instead of saying, "Our season tickets include all eight home games," the sales representative can say, "Our season ticket allows you to be a part of the action for the entire year, from beginning to end."

Using Transition Statements

After you understand the wants and needs of the customer as well as the features and benefits of the product, you will begin doing most of the work. Remember, up until this point, the sales representative is supposed to be letting the customer do at least 80 percent of the talking. To help promote the product and increase the likelihood of a sale, a sales representative can match the benefits of the product with the wants and needs of the customer. This task is accomplished most effectively using a **transition statement**, a positive connection between the product and the customer. Essentially, the transition statement shows the customer how the product can be real for them by helping them envision how it will solve a problem for them. Examples of common transition statements include "This is good for you because . . . ," "For you this means . . . ," or "That is great because . . . ." The following are examples of how a sales representative may be able to use a transition statement to take the wants or needs of a prospective customer and highlight a benefit of the product to provide a solution:

> Example 1: *Suzie, I understand that you won't be able to make it to all our games this year. The good news is that we offer a miniplan that still gives you premium seats but for only half of this year's games. This means that you will be able to get a great location without wasting your money on games that you cannot attend.*

> Example 2: *Mr. Schmidt, you mentioned that you wanted to highlight the awards your restaurant has won for its barbeque. I think a live PA read would be perfect because it will allow you to deliver a specific message. This means that fans would hear all your awards listed off during the last timeout right before they leave the stadium.*

> Example 3: *Dr. Wilson, this new recreational facility is going to be only two blocks from the city's largest high school and middle school. This is good news because it means that kids will be able to get involved in our programs without needing a car to get to the facility.*

Support Statements: The Layup of Sport Sales

Although the salesperson is usually responsible for connecting benefits with the customer's needs, the customer will occasionally do it themselves! In these cases, the salesperson gets a free bonus to their sales pitch. Sometimes, however, salespeople are so consumed with providing information to the customer that they fail to notice when the customer does it themselves. At any point in the conversation (even before step 3), the customer may point out a benefit of the product and why it works for them. Rather than allowing the conversation to go on to the next point, the salesperson should use a support statement. A **support statement** is a confirmation that the customer is correct and that you agree with them. This statement not only shows that the customer sees the value in the product but also fulfils the natural desire for the customer to be right.

The best support statements let the customer know that they are correct and that you agree with them, and it reaffirms the benefit that the customer just highlighted. The statement can occur at any point in the conversation, and it allows the salesperson to speak for their 20 percent so that the customer does not feel as if they are doing all the talking. Furthermore, a support statement builds an agreement between the customer and the sales representative without requiring the representative to convince the customer of anything. It really is a win–win for relationship-based selling. The following are examples of a customer bringing up their own benefit and a sales representative stepping in and politely using a support statement to reinforce what the customer just realized.

> Example 1: Customer: *I usually take my family to the game early because of the pregame festivities. My kids love the DJ and the tailgate games that are out in front of the arena.*
>
> Salesperson: *I know! The pregame festivities are one of the most popular things that our team does for families. All the kids seem to have a blast.*
>
> Example 2: Customer: *I was thinking about getting involved with one of the local rivalry games so that I know the home and visiting audiences are both local.*
>
> Salesperson: *I couldn't agree more. By having your promotion run in a game against our local rivals, everyone in the stadium can be a potential repeat customer because no one is traveling from another city! That's a great idea.*
>
> Example 3: Customer: *We already have plenty of basketball courts and parks in the area, but this new recreational facility would be the only free aquatics center around.*
>
> Salesperson: *You know what, you are so right. We don't have any local public swimming pools, so your gift would help support something that is completely new and exciting for young kids who can't afford a paid pool membership.*

Handling Customer Objections and Why They Are a Good Thing!

Many salespeople dread when the customer starts listing the objections and issues they have with a product. This section explains why a customer's objection is not necessarily a bad thing, but can be a good one! Customer objections are opportunities for a sales representative to fix the issue before the customer becomes a nonprospect. The customers who reach out with problems are the ones who care and usually still want to be customers. They just have something that needs to be worked out first. Instead of looking at a customer with an objection as a battle to be won or a fire to be put out, consider it an opportunity to gain a better understanding of exactly what your customer needs. Remember that a customer who has an objection to what you are saying is better than ones who refuse to explain why they are not interested. Here are a few tips for handling customer objections during the third step of our PRO method:

- *Let the customer talk*: Even if the customer is angry or frustrated with what you are telling them, sometimes they just need to voice their frustration and be heard. Interrupting the customer only makes you look combative.
- *Ask them to clarify*: Oftentimes a customer may have multiple objections in the same sentence. Ask them to clarify what is causing the concern.
- *Acknowledge their issue*: Trying to downplay or stage a rebuttal to the customer's concerns almost never works. Instead, acknowledge them and repeat the concern so that they know you understand what is holding them back.
- *Be honest*: No product is perfect, and some features of a product may simply be bad for the customer. Sometimes being honest with them about that consequence and admitting that it is bad for them allows you to move past it and focus on positive features that may be able to overcome the negative aspects.

After you have an idea of what the customer is truly concerned about, the next step is to determine whether their concern is legitimate or whether it is something that can be overcome. If the concern is something that challenges the need category of their wants and needs, overcoming the objection may be difficult. For instance, if a business's maximum budget for marketing is significantly below the price of your lowest priced product, you likely have nothing to sell them. Likewise, a customer who is moving to a different city may simply be unable to attend games anymore. These scenarios are clear in that there is nothing you can do. You may be better off thanking them for their time and moving on to a new prospect.

If the objection is one that is more closely aligned with the wants of the customer, the salesperson can try to increase the likelihood of overcoming the objection by offering a different product or deflecting the objection. **Deflecting** refers to highlighting a different positive benefit to outweigh the negative objection. The following are some examples of addressing the concern and offering an alternative or offering alternative benefits to deflect the objection.

> Example 1: *Suzy, it sounds like you weren't happy with the location of your seats because of the heat and sun in your face. We have a section on the other side of the stadium that puts the sun at your back and is shaded by the building behind you during the weekend games with earlier start times. This location means you wouldn't be as hot and wouldn't have to worry about the sun ruining your view of the game.*

> Example 2: *Sam, I know this package is at the top of your budget, and I don't blame you for being concerned about how much it costs. Unfortunately, it is the only way to get the scoreboard exposure that you mentioned was really important. I'm happy to put together a smaller package for you, but it wouldn't include the football audience that is really a good fit for barbeque.*

> Example 3: *I understand that it is frustrating that we don't accept credit cards for donations. We do this because we want to make sure that 100 percent of our donors' money goes toward providing this new youth facility and not toward paying credit card fees. Perhaps we can break the gift into a series of payments over the next three months.*

Step 4: PROpose an Offer

After you have gathered the information on the customer, provided solutions using the benefits of the project, and identified a product that you believe is a good fit for the customer, it is time to close the sale and propose an offer to them. Although most of the hard work is done at this point, many sales representatives rush through this step and risk losing the sale, despite all

B2C REVENUE GENERATION

College Athletics Offers Creative Solution to Break Up Pricing

Price objections are one of the most common barriers to purchasing tickets in college athletics. Sometimes, season football, basketball, or baseball tickets can mean shelling out thousands of dollars on a credit card in one charge. Although many teams offer payment plans, these can become tricky when dealing with credit card companies who can dispute payments, therefore requiring payments to be complete before a customer receives tickets. But college athletics departments have one advantage. Some of their fans tend to be employees of the college or university, and partnerships with payroll departments can often be a win–win for everyone.

Many schools, such as Vanderbilt and Miami of Ohio, offer a special payment plan in the form of payroll deductions. These deductions are taken directly out of the employee's paycheck before it even reaches their bank. This method provides a few benefits. First, it allows year-round deductions, even if this means that the customer has not fully paid for the tickets by the start of the season! Additionally, it avoids significant credit card fees as well as troubles with canceled accounts or disputed charges. Offering season tickets split up into 12 or even 24 equal payments can help manage a price objection and often increases the potential budget of the buyer who prefers smaller payments.

their hard work. The reason is simple: You are about to ask someone for their money. To be blunt, asking people for their money is the heart of sales and revenue generation. If it is done right, the salesperson should not be afraid of making the offer. Keep three things in mind when proposing your offer to the customer: emphasize the trigger statement, be clear in what you are offering, and ask for the sale.

Summarizing the Offer

The first thing that you must do when making a proposal is to reemphasize the trigger statement that you identified earlier in the conversation or relationship. As a reminder, the trigger statement is the single most important reason that the customer would be interested in your product. By starting your proposal with the biggest, most important benefit to your customer, you are creating a positive impression for the summary and closing statement. This point should be the number one reason that the customer is excited by the product. If the trigger statement was volunteered by the customer during a probing question, it is useful to start by saying, "I know you mentioned . . ." or "You told me that . . . ." If the trigger statement was not directly stated by the customer but gathered by you, you may want to start your proposal by saying, "It seems like . . ." or "It looks to me like . . . ."

The next step in the proposal is summarizing the offer. A salesperson who has been speaking with a customer at length has probably discussed dozens of topics and multiple options for products and pricing. Recap what you are offering and be clear about the cost. This may be a good time to reiterate a good fit or offer your own recommendation. After all, you are the expert in your own product. Ultimately, this leaves no doubt in the customer's mind about what they are getting and prepares them for the closing statement that will follow this step.

Asking for the Sale

The last step in an offer proposal is to ask for the sale. You will finally be asking the prospective customer for their money. Unfortunately, most customers are conditioned to instinctively say no when asked for money, even if they want

to purchase the product and know that it is worth their money. Structuring the question properly is essential to asking for the sale. *Do not* simply ask the customer if they would like to "go ahead and purchase" the product. *Tell* them that they should purchase the product and then *ask* them what their thoughts are on the offer. This technique may sound confusing at first, but it drastically increases the chances of their saying yes. The first part of asking for the sale involves telling the customer that they can have everything you offered if they are willing to commit to buying it. You follow up that statement by asking for their thoughts. A few examples of a trigger statement, offer summary, and asking for the sale follow:

> Example 1: *Suzie, you mentioned that family time is the most important reason you go to games and that you don't care as much about the view. The season tickets that we talked about in section 14 will guarantee that your family will be able to enjoy games together all year. The entire season package is only $2,000, and I can get it taken care of for you right now. What do you think?*
>
> Example 2: *Mr. Schmidt, you said that attracting new customers who have never been to your restaurant is your priority. It looks like the second package with the website impressions, scoreboard signage, and halftime promotion really covers everything you wanted to do, and the message that we deliver will focus on those new customers that you're looking for. The entire package is $30,000 and can be broken down and paid quarterly if you wish. I can have a contract sent over immediately and we can go ahead and get started on helping your business. How does that sound?*
>
> Example 3: *Dr. Wilson, I know having a safe area for kids to pursue positive hobbies is important to you. I want to get this new facility up and running as soon as possible, but we can't do it without help from people like you. A gift of $50,000 would keep us on track to break ground by the end of the year. What are your thoughts on helping us today?*

Step 5: PROtect the Relationship With Continuing Customer Service

After the sale has been closed and the customer has paid for the products, the salesperson's job is not over. One of the biggest aspects of relationship-based marketing involves continuing to communicate with the customer and developing the relationship throughout the year. Each chapter in this book includes several sections and sidebars on continuing customer service, but for the framework of the PRO method, three fundamental pieces are important to protecting the customer. First, a good salesperson stays in touch with their customers throughout the season. This means checking in to see how a customer's experience has been so far, learning whether there are any issues that can be resolved, and continuing to collect information on the customer that may become useful to the salesperson later.

In addition to engaging in general communication, the salesperson should always be looking for ways to add value to the relationship. This activity can take many forms, and it does not always include giving something away for free. Oftentimes, the most valuable things that a salesperson can offer the customer is attention and expertise. If a customer mentioned that they wanted to upgrade their seats and a new location becomes available, the salesperson can contact the customer to let them know that they have something that may better suit their needs. Additionally, value can be added by offering advice on when to arrive for a particularly crowded game or looking into an issue that a customer had and coming back with a resolution the salesperson did not know about at the time. Lastly, many customers appreciate value added by the sales representative by helping them make decisions that they are unsure or unaware of. For instance, a customer may mention that they have some friends coming into town who want to attend a game but they are not sure of the best place for their friends to park. A good salesperson can make the customer's life easier by explaining where the public parking spaces are near the stadium and where their friends can meet them

if the parking lots are different for different customers.

The last way that salespeople can protect their relationship and provide continuing customer service involves cross-selling and upselling. This process not only promotes a long-term relationship and communication with the customer but also typically increases the salesperson's generated revenues! Upselling refers to offering a customer a more expensive or more premium version of the product than they already have. If the customer is particularly enjoying their experience or feels happy with the product, offering an upsell opportunity for the customer to invest more is often worthwhile. The following scenarios are examples of upselling:

> Example 1: *Suzie, I'm glad you are enjoying the general admission seats. How much thought have you given to upgrading your view and getting a reserved seat?*

> Example 2: *Sam, your halftime promotion was a hit. It sounds like it really reached the target market you were shooting for. What are your thoughts on expanding the promotion for each game remaining in the season rather than a one-off event?*

> Example 3: *Dr. Wilson, I wanted to send you some updates and photos on the progress of the new rec center. We are on track to open in the spring but have started a second campaign to finish early and open our doors around Christmas. I have attached some information on how our donors are helping get this ready for the holiday season.*

Upselling is not the only way to generate additional revenue from customers who have already purchased. Cross-selling refers to using a current product to introduce the customer to a different line of products that they may be interested in. Cross-selling may require a strong relationship between the salesperson and the customer because it involves discussing a product that the customer may not have originally been interested in. Done correctly, however, tapping into multiple products can provide significant returns. Examples of cross-selling follow:

Example 1: *Mrs. Flynn, I know that you live near the stadium and love the convenience of watching our soccer club. You may not know this, but a professional lacrosse league will be playing an exhibition in our stadium next month. I can get you tickets for the event, and your family could experience something new and different in the stadium that you are already familiar with.*

Example 2: *Sam, we have been focusing primarily on our college's football packages, but I really think you may want to expand into different sports so that you continue to promote your restaurant in the spring season as well. We have sponsorship packages for baseball that will keep your business in your customers' minds for a lower cost. We may even be able to get your food in our concession stands as a vendor!*

Example 3: *Lamar, I wanted to thank you again for your support of the new youth recreation center. We just opened our doors, and things are looking great. I wanted to reach out and let you know of another opportunity: We are starting to help fund a program for some of our students that will help them improve their grades so that they can continue their athletic careers in college.*

Ultimately, management of the customer relationship is a never-ending process. Customers who are not protected by continuing customer service may lapse or stop purchasing products. Salespeople who continually invest in protecting their customers have the highest chances of generating, maintaining, and even increasing revenue for their sport organization.

Summary

Sales is an integral part of the sport industry, yet sales in sport is different from sales in other industries. In sport, most sales come from the sale of services, which includes things that the customer cannot touch. The customer, therefore, is less able to judge the quality of the product, and the salesperson must find a product that fits the customer, explain the product, and demonstrate the quality. The five-step PRO method suggests that sellers should first prospect for customers, probe them for information, provide solutions for their wants and needs, propose an offer, and then continue to protect the sale with ongoing customer service. The PRO method to selling in sport is not a roadmap to each sale. Instead, it should be thought of as a framework about how to navigate a sale from beginning to end. The method itself is versatile and can be applied to almost every segment of sport business. Each chapter in this book provides additional details about how to use the PRO method in each of these segments of revenue generation. We believe that it provides a thoughtful method of being successful in each of these segments.

APPLIED LEARNING ACTIVITIES

1. Pick a product you recently bought; it can be anything. Next, write down a list of features (facts) about the product itself. Even if a feature seems obvious, write it down. Next, go through your list of features and try to identify the benefit for each feature. What does that feature actually mean? How does it affect the person using it? Lastly, take the feature and benefit and try to connect them using a transition statement such as "What this means for you is . . ." or "This is great because . . ."

2. The yes or no game. Have students take turns trying to find out as much as possible about each other without using closed-ended questions. One student acts as the seller, and another acts as the buyer. The seller must ask the buyer open-ended questions and gather as much information as possible. It helps if the questions are sport related but they do not have to be; carrying the conversation is the hardest part of the exercise. When a student uses a closed-ended question, the other student is instructed to answer it with a simple yes or no. That student then becomes the

new seller, asking questions of the former seller. This rule shows that a yes or no answer to a closed-ended question kills the conversation, and the seller quickly recognizes what has occurred. The game continues until the new seller slips up and asks a closed-ended question, relinquishing the seller role. After five minutes the students compare notes to see who has gathered more information. Students who have asked mostly open-ended questions should have had more time as the seller and gathered more information.

CASE STUDY

Capitalizing on Information From Angry Fans

When Mark Cuban bought the Dallas Mavericks in 2000, the team had not been good in quite a while. Cuban's salespeople told him that morale among fans was low and that many of the calls were quickly becoming negative. Cuban knew that to turn around the attitude of his fans, he needed to understand his new fans' frustrations. One day when Mark came into the office, he instructed his ticket sales representatives to keep a list of the worst customers they called all day—the meanest, angriest, least pleasant ones. After a while, Mark collected the lists and personally began to call the worst, angriest customers in the Mavs' fanbase. What he found was that the angriest fans also tended to be the most passionate, and they loved the team the most. Cuban talked to these fans extensively and gathered information about the worst parts of his organization. He then went to work fixing them. As a result, Dallas broke the NBA streak of consecutive sellouts, which began in 2001, only a year after Cuban took over. The sellout streak lasted for 815 consecutive games.

Discussion Questions

1. Why do you think Mark called the angriest fans he could find?
2. What do you think Mark would have found out if he had talked to the happiest Mavericks fans rather than the angriest ones?
3. What effect do you think Mark's actions had on his ticket sales staff?

Go to HK*Propel* to complete the activities for this chapter.

Billie Weiss/Boston Red Sox/Getty Images

CHAPTER 3

Ticket Sales for Revenue Generation

CHAPTER OBJECTIVES

After completing the chapter, you should be able to do the following:

- Understand the historical importance and significance of ticket sales for sport in North America
- Understand how ticket sales indirectly affects other revenue streams
- Understand the difference between business-to-business and business-to-consumer ticket sales
- Understand inventory options that are available to ticket sales representatives
- Be able to use the PRO method as it applies to ticket sales
- Be familiar with current ticketing trends in the sport industry

Ticket sales is one of the largest departments in most sport organizations, making it one of the most common entry-level sales jobs in the sport industry. Additionally, ticket sales is the most outward-facing sales department for customers, often leading to the mantra that it is the front line of the organization. Therefore, almost every employee of a sport organization can benefit from a basic understanding of ticket-selling strategies.

This chapter first walks you through a brief historical background of ticket sales and operations to gain a better understanding of how ticket sales has evolved. Next, we discuss the nuts and bolts of ticket sales. How does it work? What do you have to sell? What types of customers can you expect? We then move on to applying the PRO method and demonstrating how it can be used to sell tickets. Finally, we wrap up by discussing some of the new challenges occurring in ticket sales today.

Background of Ticket Sales for Revenue Generation

Today, ticket sales and ticket operations are so synonymous with sport and entertainment that it is hard to imagine when the idea of organized seating was considered innovative. Additionally, early ticket operations extend further back than most people would imagine, and the actual processes involved have developed significantly over time. Whether the intentions were to maximize efficiency, maximize revenue, or achieve the more sinister goal of class discrimination, taking a brief look at the origins of ticket operations, and later sales, will clarify how far the industry has developed.

Earliest Ticket Sales: The Roman Colosseum

Some of the earliest known sporting events included ticketing systems that are quite like the ones we employ today! The Roman Colosseum is one of the earliest known sporting facilities in the world, and the Romans were ahead of their time in terms of ticket operations even though revenue generation was likely not the main concern for the games of the Colosseum. After all, admission to the games at the Colosseum was free (Hopkins & Beard, 2011; Platner, 2015). Unfortunately for the Romans, the purpose of ticketing during this time may have been more discriminatory. The Colosseum held several tiers of stadium-style seating, and the "tickets" of the time were called *tessera* and made of shards of pottery. Romans had to wait in line to receive their tessera, which were stamped with an entrance aisle and row number that indicated where the Roman holding it was allowed to sit. This system was not unlike modern ticketing methods, but scholars have suggested that the purpose of this process was to enforce a social class system and keep "undesirable" Romans from sitting outside their class (Platner, 2015; Colosseumrometickets.com, 2018). This seating method created four physical tiers for the games, which correlated with the spectators' social class:

1. The first tier, called the *podium*, was exclusive to the most important Romans: the emperor, senators, and important priests. This section was located closest to the actual games.

2. The second tier, called the *maenianum primum*, was reserved for the noble class, or wealthy elite, and was located above the podium.

3. The third tier was split into two sections and held seating for general Roman citizens. Wealthier citizens were placed in the *maenianum secundum imum*, which were lower, more desirable seats. The poorer citizens were located in a higher section called the *maenianum secundum summum*.

4. The final tier, called the *maenianum secundum in ligneis*, was added during the reign of Domitian and included steep wooden seating for the poorest Romans as well as women.

Although seating in the Roman Colosseum was free, shards of pottery stamped with an entrance aisle and row number were distributed, indicating where the Romans holding the "tickets" were allowed to sit.

Historical Ticket Sales in the United States

Nearly 1,800 years after the Romans introduced the idea of ticket operations, ticket sales began in the United States and rapidly advanced the profitability of U.S. sport. One of the first sporting venues in the United States to require an admission fee was the Union Course in (now) Woodhaven, Queens, which was renovated in 1829 to be fully enclosed. The venue was designed for horse racing, and these new features significantly increased revenues, allowing larger purses and better competition (Reese, 2012). This innovation sparked a trend throughout the United States for the next century and a half as ticket sales rapidly became the largest source of revenue in sport.

Although horse racing in various forms was the most popular sport of the mid-1800s, baseball began to take over in the late 1800s and beyond as "America's pastime." By 1920 the average baseball ticket price had risen from around 25 cents to a full dollar, and, of course, it has only increased since then (Haupert & Winter, 2003). As sport popularity has grown, ticket sales has been a cash cow for sport organizations because until recently attendance often rose regardless of higher ticket price. For instance, despite an increase in ticket price from $1 (1920) to an average of nearly $17 per ticket (2000), total baseball attendance rose from 9 million attendees to nearly 70 million attendees over that time.

Baseball was often the focus of ticket sales in the early 1900s, but other sports would soon follow suit. Boxing was a popular ticket for the majority of the 1920s, and more tickets were sold then than for most modern fights. The rematch of Jack Dempsey versus Gene Tunney drew a crowd of nearly 105,000, who paid total gate revenues of over $2.8 million. The ticket prices capped at a whopping $40 for ringside seats and helped guarantee Tunney's $750,000 purse, or prize money (Cavanugh, 2006). Ticket sales for that fight would help Tunney make roughly as much money as Babe Ruth did in his entire career. Later, football would make similar leaps. The newly merged NFL would average over 50,000 attendees per game in its first year (1967), finishing the season with a World Championship (later named Super Bowl) matchup in front of 61,000 fans (Carroll, 1991). The $12 average ticket price was considered outrageous by fans and was said to have negatively affected attendance (McGinn, 20012).

Are Ticket Sales Careers Still Important?

You may have heard that ticket sales are declining in sport, but that statement is only somewhat true. Many sports, such as college football, have experienced an overall decrease in attendance (NCAA, 2019), but the data may be misleading from a revenue-generating standpoint. Many schools have increased prices of their tickets, which has more than offset the decline in attendance from a revenue standpoint. Additionally, broadcast, multimedia,

sponsorship, and merchandising revenue have all increased more dramatically than ticket sales in terms of percentages. Considering that gate revenues are estimated to account for $18 billion each year (PwC, 2019), the question is not whether ticket sales are still important, but how they compare with other revenues.

Although most major sports have seen a decline in ticketing revenue as a percentage of their total revenue (see figure 3.1 for details), ticket sales are still important for several reasons. First, the decline as a percentage is due largely to the increase in other revenues. The new broadcast agreement signed by the NFL in 2021 will increase broadcast revenues by several billion dollars, diluting the percentage of revenues accounted for by ticket sales. The Green Bay Packers (who are publicly held and must report revenues) showed nearly $77 million in gate receipts in 2019, which represented slightly more than 15 percent of their total revenue. The other reason that ticket sales still have a prominent role in sport sales is that they are easier to manipulate compared with other forms of revenue. For example, the previously mentioned NFL broadcast agreement locks in consistent revenues until the year 2033. No matter how well or poorly a team does, they receive their guarantee. Conversely, ticket sales revenues allow the team to capitalize on success, which will have a direct effect on their bottom line.

Adding to the importance of ticket sales is the fact that it is the most common entry-level

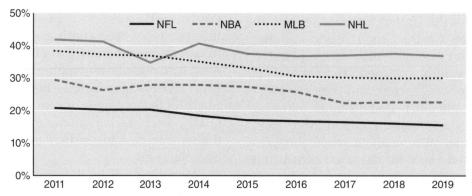

FIGURE 3.1   Gate revenues as a percentage of total revenue by league.
Data compiled from Forbes (2020).

position in sport, making up almost a third of all sales-related job postings in the sport industry (Pierce et al., 2012). Ticket sales is the most common entry-level job in sport because, quite frankly, it is simple. Note, however, that simple does not mean easy. Ticket sales is a grind of long hours and repetitive conversations that result in most people telling you no. But this is exactly the type of position that tests employees' perseverance and professionalism. Thus, although ticket sales is important because of its considerable role in revenue generation for professional sport, it is also important as a test for employees to prove to their employers that they have what it takes to attain a more desirable sales job if that is what the person wants.

Foundation of Ticket Sales for Revenue Generation

Now that you understand the history and importance of ticket sales in the sport industry, let's look at the foundation of what ticket sales for revenue generation means. To develop revenue through ticket sales, you will need to understand the details about how ticket sales work and what is involved in the ticket sales process. This means discussing how ticket sales indirectly affects other revenues, the different types of customers in the ticket sales industry, and the types of tickets that most teams have available to sell.

Effect of Ticket Sales on Other Revenues

The **core product** of a sport organization is the actual game that is played on the field or court. In some way, all forms of revenue generation rely on the sporting event itself, and if no event occurs, there is likely no revenue. Ticket sales, however, has the unique ability to increase the value of other forms of revenue streams.

Sellouts make events more prestigious and valuable: For example, Northwestern Mutual, a financial services company, rewards clients with hard-to-get tickets to NCAA events such as the Final Four or other championships. Likewise, Mercedes-Benz has been a longtime sponsor of the Masters and typically offers exclusive experiences to their VIPs. The exclusivity of these tickets drives the value to higher-end customers looking to attend prestigious events. Aside from the prestige of the events, ticket scarcity also drives up the retail (and secondary) prices of events. Duke University, as of this writing, boasts a 30-year sellout streak to their home basketball games, which dates to 1990. As a result, donation requirements to guarantee season tickets start at $7,000, before the cost of the ticket itself. Likewise, the Boston Red Sox held the title of most expensive season tickets during most of their 820-game sellout streak that ended in 2013. Therefore, although effective ticket sales methods obviously provide revenue in the short term, the result of such sales compounds on itself, creating more desirable and profitable inventory as attendance increases. Conversely, events and stadiums that have historically low attendance decrease the perceived prestige and value of the ticket.

Aside from the effect on ticket costs and prestige by itself, increases in attendance generate revenue by simply increasing the sheer volume of several other revenue streams. For instance, if more people are attending the game, more cars will be driven to the game, so parking revenues will increase. Likewise, more people in the stadium will likely result in increased concessions and merchandising sales as attendees buy more items. Lastly, sponsorship inventory and signage inside the stadium, discussed later in more detail, are often valued based on the attendance at the event. Thus, increases in ticket sales also increase several other forms of revenue, both directly and indirectly.

Ticket sales also affects attendance and other revenue streams because of the impact it has on the atmosphere itself. Researchers have found that spectator stimuli (noise, passion, visual excitement, etc.) are one of three factors that make up stadium atmosphere (Ulrich & Benkenstein, 2010). For instance, the all-day tailgating, community atmosphere, and sheer volume of cheering during Green Bay Packers games is often attributed to the successful gameday atmosphere of Lambeau Field. Likewise in the MLS, Atlanta United has broken national records in attendance, gaining the title "The best soccer atmosphere in the United States" by MLS.com. Fans are known for loud chants, high energy, and standing throughout the entire 90 minutes of the match. Thus, in an even more indirect way, ticket sales has yet another effect on the larger organization.

Business-to-Business Ticket Sales

The basic motivation for attending a sporting event is for the customer to enjoy the experience. But attendance at games is made up of many different types of customers who have various motivations to attend. The majority of tickets in most sports are sold in a business-to-consumer manner. The individual buying the tickets intends to use them mostly for personal enjoyment. Sometimes, however, the individual buying the tickets intends to use them for some sort of business purpose. Companies are interested in tickets for sport

events for several reasons, many of which have already been discussed. Selling tickets to a business would qualify as a business-to-business (B2B) sale.

B2B selling in general business is different from B2B tickets sales in sport for a few reasons. Traditionally, a B2C sale is intended to benefit the consumer directly. In other words, the fans buy tickets because they want to enjoy the sporting event. In traditional B2B sales situations, the purpose is often to benefit the business directly. For instance, buying advertisement space is intended to drive sales by attracting new customers. This is where ticket sales often differ. The purpose of many (but not all) B2B ticket sales is the same as B2C: for the person receiving the ticket to enjoy the event. But B2B ticket purchasers are often looking for a **secondary benefit** of their purchase, which is that the person's enjoyment of the event is likely to result in something positive for the business that purchased it. Some examples of B2B secondary benefits are shown in figure 3.2.

B2B sales differ in their approach throughout the sales process. Remember that people selling tickets with a B2B purpose are often working from smaller prospecting pools, because the

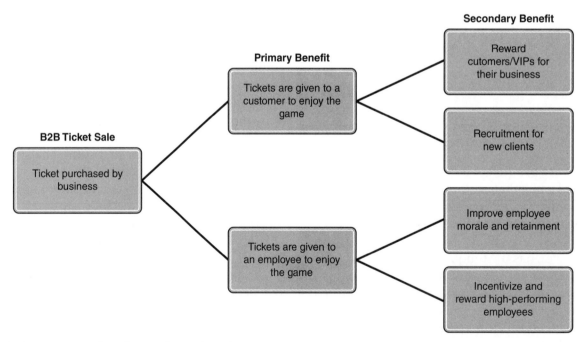

FIGURE 3.2   Examples of B2B ticketing benefits.

B2B REVENUE GENERATION

UPS Delivers on Employee Recognition

Sometimes you do not have to buy tickets for all your employees to recognize hard workers and raise employee morale. UPS rewards a few select drivers with tickets for over 60 college basketball games as part of their partnerships with various NCAA schools. Drivers are selected based on their safety records, and tickets are provided for the entire family (Spanberg, 2012). As part of the promotion, the selected driver gets to deliver the game ball to the referee before tipoff, creating a one-of-a-kind experience. Although UPS is a multibillion-dollar company with hundreds of thousands of employees, the same model works for businesses large and small. Even when a B2B customer may not be able to afford tickets for all their employees, a contest or sweepstakes that rewards only a few can be an effective motivator. The partnership with UPS was formed in 2011 and remains so popular that online chat forums of UPS employees have begun conversations on how to increase the odds of being selected.

leads on businesses are typically less prominent. Also, the sales representative often cannot use emotions such as passion in a B2B sale because the customer may not have the same psychological connection to the team that a fan attending for their own enjoyment would. When trying to judge the effectiveness of a B2B benefit, the salesperson should be aware that B2B customers tend to want more quantifiable measures of success and a secondary benefit can be challenging to measure.

Ticket Sales Inventory

Many sport organizations have several inventory items available for ticket sales representatives to sell. In this case, inventory refers to the types of tickets that a consumer could purchase. Although many people may think that a ticket is a single item available, experienced sales reps know that many more choices are available than one might think.

Season Ticket Packages

Season ticket packages are one of the most common inventory items for sales representatives (especially entry-level ones) to solicit to fans. The season ticket is the lifeblood of many sport organizations and contains some of the best locations in the facility, excluding luxury and club seating. Additionally, season tickets tend to be some of the most expensive

inventory available for the sales representative to offer. Although season tickets may carry the highest price tag for the customer, they are often the lowest price per game, something that may need to be pointed out for the customer to appreciate. Season ticketholders may also receive special benefits such as discounts on concessions and merchandise, priority access to playoff tickets, or invites to exclusive events for season ticketholders only.

Season tickets are almost always divided into two categories for the purpose of revenue generation. **New sales** refer to a customer who has typically not held a season ticket in the previous season. Some organizations may classify a new sale as a customer who has never purchased any sort of ticket at all. New customers are typically the most difficult for the sales representative to go through the PRO sales method with because the person selling to them has no information to work with from the beginning. This means that new customers require the sales representative to do even more listening than they normally would. Although new customers are the most challenging, they are also often the most rewarding for the person selling the tickets because new sales often come with the highest percentage commissions and most valuable sales goals for the organization.

Season ticket **renewals** typically have much smaller (or zero) commissions for the salesperson but are imperative for the sport organization to meet revenue goals. After all, the money received from a season ticket renewal is the same to the team as the money from a new sale, regardless of how hard the salesperson had to work for it. Renewal season ticketholders are often considered easier sales because the customer often volunteers their own sale when calling in to renew their tickets. The salesperson could simply take the sale and move on, but they should still go through the PRO method. Here are some ways that renewal customers can provide additional value:

Customer 1: *Russ, it sounds as if building a tradition of time with your family is important and I see you have GA season tickets.*

If you upgrade to reserved tickets, you and your entire family will be guaranteed the same seat and experience together for years to come. How great would that be?

Customer 2: *Leroy, I love that you've had the same seat for 10 years. We need more fans like you! I noticed the seat next to you is empty; who can you think of who would like to enjoy games with you for the next 10 years?*

Customer 3: *Michelle, you mentioned that your company has gone on events together in the past. Who is in charge of organizing these office events?*

Mark Cunningham/MLB Photos via Getty Images

Group ticket sales, whether for children's birthday parties, employee appreciation, or family reunions, can generate tremendous revenue for a team.

Group Ticket Sales

Group ticket sales involves selling a large block of tickets to a group of people, usually for a single game. Group tickets traditionally require the group to purchase the block all at once, and the sport organization would often give a discount to the group in exchange for selling a large number of tickets at one time. Now, the lines have blurred a bit because sport organizations have allowed group sales to occur through portals or by using promotional codes that lower the price of the ticket down to the group rate. Some organizations do not consider these promotional sales as group tickets for the sales rep and instead consider them individual sales (which usually have lower commissions), so salespeople need to understand the policy when they are hired. Organizations have different standards for what qualifies as a group package, but common benchmarks are usually either 10 or 20 tickets before a group rate can be applied. Depending on the group rate minimum, buying 10 tickets can sometimes be less expensive (with a group discount) than buying 7 or 8 full-priced tickets.

Regardless of how the individuals purchase the tickets, group sales customers typically have different motivations for attending games, and this consideration changes the sales process. First, a group is typically interested in the social atmosphere of attending the game together and they may be less dedicated fans than traditional customers. For teams that are performing poorly on the field or lacking tons of die-hard followers, this can be a sales advantage because the social benefit may be more pressing. Additionally, group sales locations are likely to be less desirable than many other ticket types because they are going to be offered at a discount. Therefore, a group of people who want to attend games together but have a priority on the best location may not be as interested in a group deal because they would be paying full price. Of course, remember that predetermining the motivations of any customer is not possible, so the sales representative must be always listening and asking questions about what the customer is most interested in. Some

group sales may be to die-hard fans. Other group sales customers may be less interested in social motivations and are simply using the group rate for a discount. The following are some probing questions that may help:

> Example 1: *I can seat your entire group together in one block, or I can break up each family individually throughout the section. Do you think your church would prefer to sit together and socialize with each other or enjoy the game only with their family in a slightly better location?*
>
> Example 2: *I know you mentioned that you and your friends need 6 tickets for the game. But if you get 10 tickets, you can qualify for the group rate, which saves you 20 percent. Who can you think of who you might want to enjoy the game with?*

Group sales can also be popular among B2B buyers. As we mentioned earlier in the chapter, employee hospitality is a popular B2B motivation. Although a business may purchase tickets for many reasons, B2B group sales in this area usually fall into one of two categories: employee appreciation or incentives. Some organizations would rather treat their employees to a sporting event than a traditional office party, and group sales is an effective way to accomplish a great experience for a business while requiring far less work. Salespeople talking to a customer about B2B group tickets for an employee event should try to imagine themselves in the shoes of the customer. Group sales are often a turnkey event, which means that the buyer does not have to do much, if any, additional work after purchasing the tickets. Things such as ticket distribution or food and beverage orders can often be handled in the stadium, so the employer is able to offer a great experience from start to finish without requiring a lot of the time of their human resources department. B2B group sales that are not focused on employee hospitality are most often incentives or rewards for high-performing employees. Some examples of employers who purchase tickets for incentives and rewards would be an office party at a ballgame or tickets for a sales department that meets its quota for the quarter.

Partial Plans, Half-Season Tickets, and Miniplans

Partial plans, which were once regarded as a final upsell for buyers who inquired about a single ticket, are rapidly becoming one of the more popular inventory items for sport organizations to offer. Partial plans have many names and designations; they may be called miniplans, minipacks, or ticket bundles. Sometimes they are designated more specifically into half- or even quarter-season ticket packages. These ticket packages are especially popular with sports such as basketball, baseball, and hockey whose seasons include many games. Many fans are not willing to commit the time or money for an 81-game MLB season ticket, but they would be interested in a 10-game partial plan.

One of the key features of the partial plan is the method that the team uses to allocate the games. Many strategies can be used, and certainly more than one way can successfully highlight the benefits of a partial plan. Some teams package their best game with multiple less desirable games and refuse to sell the popular game as a single-game ticket. The customer must purchase the partial plan to get the ticket they want most, but they also pay a discounted price for other games. Although this strategy may be discouraging to a fan who wants to attend only one game, it helps maximize revenue for the sport organization. Additionally, if the fans attend the less desirable games (which they already paid for), ancillary revenue opportunities such as concessions or parking will occur. Other teams decide to allocate their partial plans based on some aspect of the game itself. For instance, the Kane County Cougars (a minor league baseball team) offer a Silver Slugger package targeted to seniors. The 12-game plan includes all daytime games, which the team found was preferable for their older fanbase. Additionally, the package includes a preferred parking pass. Creating targeted benefits such as these allows the salesperson to solve specific needs of a customer. The following are some ways that salespeople can approach these benefits:

> Customer 1: *Linh, I know that you were most interested in the New York Rangers game. Unfortunately, right now those are not available as an individual ticket. But I can sell it to you as a package of 10 games, which saves you 10 dollars per ticket. Which other games might you be interested in?*

> Customer 2: *Tyler, if you plan to come to four or five games this year, I recommend checking out our half-season ticket. As a season ticketholder, you get several other benefits, and the tickets are discounted so that you get many more games for only $100 more.*

Premium Seating

Premium seating has had a relatively short history compared with other forms of seating, although the revenue implications are considerable. The luxury and club-level seating boom began in the 1960s with Dodger Stadium and later the Houston Astrodome. Dodger Stadium was the first to offer an exclusive ticket that included amenities separate from those of other fans and likely defined the future of luxury seating with an enclosed environment and waiter service (Shoemaker, 2011). Later in 1965 the Astrodome followed suit with one of the first definable luxury boxes, which featured 53 smaller, more intimate spaces with higher-end luxuries (Gast, 2014). Now, every modern stadium has some form of higher-end seating for fans willing to spend more.

Premium seating refers to any seating area that includes amenities not available to regular customers. Traditionally, luxury suites tend to be smaller areas that seat 10 to 30 people and have an enclosed environment that allows fans to enjoy the game with a private group. Meanwhile, club-level seating tends to be a larger section of fans, separate from regular fans but not isolated into individual suites. Both are popular revenue generators, but the lines

B2C REVENUE GENERATION

SoFi Stadium's Variety of Premium Seating Options

The SoFi Stadium, home of the LA Rams and LA Chargers, has made high-end seating and revenues a priority. The stadium boasts 13,000 club-level seats, 260 luxury suites, and several brand-specific lounges that fans who pay enough can have access to. The Corona Beach House features a three-story spiral staircase and premium views of the field. The Champagne Bar is part of an exclusive Executive Club that features 19 rows of premium seating. Lastly, the SoFi Social Club is located next to the locker rooms for fans who want to get as close as possible to players leaving the field. It also boasts a glass wall that allows fans to watch postgame press conferences in person (Ramirez, 2020). Because premium seating is often reliant on amenities, SoFi Stadium maximizes revenue by offering vastly different premium experiences that provide something for everybody. Premium-seating salespeople need to be familiar with the (sometimes numerous) perks and benefits of each seating inventory. Probing for the wants and needs of the customer is imperative, as is having intimate knowledge of all features of premium seating.

Keith Birmingham/MediaNews Group/Pasadena Star-News via Getty Images

between the two have begun to blur as teams have increasingly expanded these options. Modern premium seating may include luxury-focused lounges, larger supersuites that can seat 50 to 100 people, or even extremely prestigious field-level suites that may include a price tag of over $1 million per year. One of the most common themes that has begun to emerge from the area of premium seating is the need for multiple options for a variety of fans.

Understanding the purpose and benefits of premium seating is essential to salespeople who are speaking to potential customers. Premium seating typically includes some of the best views of the game, which is likely to be important to customers. But the amenities that come alongside these views may be even more important. After all, for the 2019-2020 season, lower-level season tickets for the Golden State Warriors cost approximately $10,000 to 12,000, depending on location. Meanwhile the courtside lounges at Chase Center have been reported to cost between $1.5 million and $2 million; actual prices are not listed on their website (Dowd, 2019). This pricing should suggest that seating location alone is

likely not the determining factor for premium seating; instead, other amenities play a large role. For example, the Chase Center lounges just mentioned feature an on-site wine cellar and butler service. During step 2 of the PRO method (PRObe), the salesperson should try to identify which features of premium seating are most appealing to the customer, because these benefits may not be the traditional ones that most customers look for. Some examples of probing questions are the following:

> Customer 1: *Rick, what is it about these club-level seats that sounds most exciting to you?*

> Customer 2: *Elizabeth, for your business would it benefit you and your VIPs more for the best possible view of the field or exclusive access to chef-inspired food and beverage?*

Single-Game Ticket Sales

Single-game (or individual) ticket sales is one of the most common forms of sales in the sport world. Obviously, a single-game ticket is valid for only one day or one event. For many annual events, this is the only form of ticket sales available (general admission), but for many other events and organizations, the single-game buyer is the lowest level of investment among many options. A sport organization may sell multiple types of individual tickets and use a different approach for each. The pregame individual buyer is someone who contacted the ticket sales office well before the game but inquired only about a single game. Because they are often the lowest cost (and lowest commissioned) form of inventory available to the sales representative, they are sometimes overlooked by inexperienced sales reps, who will not devote as much time or attention as they would to a larger sale. But remember that single-game ticket sales should not be viewed as undesirable, even if the reward is lower than that for other inventory items.

Pregame individual buyers are great leads for converting to a larger sale. Often, the single-game ticket is one of the lowest price options but is not necessarily the best value. For instance, a team may sell an individual ticket for $60 and a three-game minipack for $99. Buyers who are not aware of the inventory options available to them may be willing to purchase more tickets than just one if they realize they are getting a better deal. Likewise, better seating locations may be available if the customer is willing to invest in more games. The following are some examples of how to upsell individual game buyers into larger packages that may be better for them (and you).

> Example 1: *Rick, I can certainly get you set up for a single ticket to the game. But for only $39 more, you can get a three-game minipack. How would you like to come to two more games this year?*
>
> Example 2: *Danielle, you mentioned that you want the best possible location. Our best seats are sold only as season tickets, so the best way to get you close to the action would be to lock you in for the season or half-season. How many games do you usually come to throughout the year?*

Although it would always be preferable for customers to call and purchase tickets in advance, we know that some customers make last-minute purchases. The more challenging upsell is the walk-up customer. Walk-up customers typically want the transactions to be short and sweet, but upselling is still possible. Walk-up customers are the one scenario when asking for the sale immediately is recommended. The key to this pitch is to respect the customer's time; they probably do not want to have a long conversation while you go through the entire PRO method. The most effective pitch will be a single sentence or two that explains the benefit of the upgrade and asks for the sale at the end. Additionally, this scenario may be the only time that closed-ended questions can be used to close the sale and save time. Here are some examples of short upsell pitches for individual game buyers.

> Example 1: Customer: *Two tickets in the best seats you have, please.*
>
> Sales rep: *The best seats we have would actually be in a three-game minipack for $99. Would you like to get the better seats in the lower level or just two for this game behind the basket?*
>
> Example 2: Customer: *How much for four tickets?*
>
> Sales rep: *Four individual tickets would be $240, or you can get our family season ticket for $999, which includes four tickets to our remaining five games. How would you feel about coming back for more games later in the season?*

Upselling an individual buyer directly before the game is a low-percentage attempt, but it can be effective if done while respecting the customer's time, and some customers will appreciate your giving them a potentially better option. Regardless of whether you can upsell the customer, one of the most imperative tasks for selling to a walk-up customer is collecting their contact information. Far too many sport organizations sell tickets out of a gameday account that includes no way of ever reaching back out to the person who purchased the tickets. These are some of the best leads for future games or seasons! Again, walk-up sales tend to prioritize speed, so at a minimum sales representatives or box office workers should strive to collect a name and phone number, although collecting an email address is an additional bonus. One easy way to do this is to offer to send the receipt to the customer's email address (if supported), which provides a convenience for the customer and data collection for the sport organization.

Selling Tickets With the PRO Method

Understanding the inventory is the first step toward applying the PRO method to selling tickets for a sport organization. As we have mentioned throughout the book, the PRO method to selling can be applied in nearly every form of sales or revenue generation. The next section explains how to apply the specific principles of the PRO method for ticket sales.

Step 1: PROspect for Qualified Customers

Prospecting for qualified customers in ticket sales can be more of a grind than in many other forms of sales. Many organizations expect ticket sales reps to make between 60 and 100 outbound calls per day, and collecting enough qualified leads can become more of a volume game than in many other forms of sales. Ticket sales representatives often make a large quantity of calls with a small likelihood of converting them into sales. For many sales representatives the hardest part of the job is continuing to make outbound calls. Inbound calls are often also part of ticket sales job responsibilities and can provide great leads for customers. Specifically in ticket sales, however, many of the inbound calls are directed toward general information because the box office is the front line for information about a game. For instance, many customers call with

questions regarding parking locations, start times, or complaints that are unlikely to result in a sale. One skill that would be beneficial for all salespeople is the ability to quickly identify whether the inbound caller is a qualified lead or not. Here are some examples:

> Example 1: *Hello, Dave, I can certainly help you with information on general parking. Are you one of our season ticketholders or do you need to purchase tickets?*
>
> Example 2: *Melissa, we won't know the exact start time of the game, so I don't know exactly when you should arrive. But I can tell you that our season ticketholders have a separate entrance if you are worried about standing in line at the gate.*
>
> Example 3: *I am sorry to hear that you had a bad experience with the fans behind you. For your next game, I would be happy to move you farther from the visiting team sections.*

As we mentioned in the previous chapter, phone sales are not the only way to make outbound contact with fans. Email can often be effective when used correctly. Avoid the temptation to use a generic "blast" email and be sure to target specific groups of customers who may be likely to purchase tickets. Additionally, you can use software such as Microsoft Excel's mail merge feature to send an email that personalizes the name and other features to make the email sound more personal. An email that begins with "Dear Joe" instead of "Dear Customer" is always more likely to get a response. Many organizations have this feature built into their CRM (customer relationship management) software as well.

Step 2: PRObe for information With Open-Ended Questions

Probing for information in ticket sales consists of trying to learn as much as you can about the customer's wants and needs at the game. An endless amount of information could be useful, but some of the key things you want to find out include how many games the customer would be interested in attending, what the customer's budget is for tickets, and why the customer enjoys games. The following are some brief open-ended questions that can often quickly uncover a lot of information about the customer:

> *Which games are you most excited about attending this year?*
>
> *How many people usually come with you to games?*
>
> *What is your favorite thing about coming to games?*
>
> *How happy are you with your current seating location?*
>
> *What is the most important thing you look for in buying tickets?*
>
> *How would these tickets help your business?*

These short, quick-hitting questions can often lead to valuable information for the salesperson without having to spend a lot of time talking. Based on the answers to these questions, the salesperson can begin to judge the best fit for different types of ticket inventory. One key tip to remember during this phase is that even if the customer gives you an answer that appears to fit a certain ticket type, you should ask a few more questions before you move on to the next step. For instance, if you ask a customer how many games they plan to come to and they respond, "All of them!" the first instinct of most salespeople is to move straight to pitching the customer a season ticket. After all, the season ticket makes a lot of sense for someone who attends multiple games. But this customer could be a prime candidate for premium seating. If the salesperson does not ask about budget or seat preference, they

By listening to the customer for a trigger statement, you might find that the trigger is the family friendly atmosphere or the special time they have together when they come to the ballpark.

may end up suggesting a regular season ticket to a customer who may have preferred a club seat. Likewise, a customer who says they want to come to only one game may lead the salesperson to suggest an individual or group ticket, when in fact the customer may have friends or family who would also attend and could be qualified for a miniplan or season ticket that could be shared. Even when you think you have found a good fit, you should continue to ask questions and confirm the choice before you move on.

You may remember from chapter 2 that you should try to discover the trigger statement, or the single most important reason that the customer wants to buy the product. When selling tickets, the customer likely has multiple wants and needs, so sometimes the best way to find this information is simply to ask:

> Example 1: *We have talked about a lot of reasons why you come to games. If you had to pick just one, what would you say is the biggest?*

> Example 2: *It seems like there are a lot of ways these tickets can be used to benefit your business. Which one do you think would be most significant?*

Whether the trigger statement is for a traditional customer or a B2B customer, these straightforward questions are typically effective. Later in the sales process, you will be using the trigger statement to reemphasize the benefits of the tickets you are offering.

Step 3: PROvide Solutions for Customers' Needs

Step 3 of the PRO method is usually the most complicated and usually takes the most time because it is also the most important. To sell tickets effectively, you need to be able to provide solutions for your customer. This process involves matching features and benefits of the product with the wants and needs of the customer, as well as helping with issues and objectives of the customer. There is no one way

to be successful in this step, and there is no one-size-fits-all procedure. This section will guide you on some of the most common scenarios and show you multiple examples that you may be able to use or adapt in real life.

Features and Benefits of Ticket Sales

The most obvious feature of a sport ticket is that it permits the holder to watch the game. But a ticket provides many additional subtle features that can be highlighted during the conversation. The location of the ticket, the price, the audience around the ticket, amenities included with the ticket, and even the fact that they are supporting the team are all features that customers may be interested in. Remember to use transition statements such as the ones in the following examples to make the features feel more like personal benefits to the customer:

> Example 1: *These tickets are located right on the 20-yard line. This means that you will be right in front of the action when our Packers score touchdowns this year!*

> Example 2: *Our season ticketholders receive 15 percent off concessions and food at the stadium, including our in-stadium restaurants! This makes it even more affordable for your family to attend games this year.*

> Example 3: *Our group buyers will get a special message on the scoreboard during halftime. That way, you will be able to tell your employees how much you appreciate them.*

> Example 4: *Our club-level seats come with separate restrooms, a catered buffet, and separate cash bar. This setup means that you will never have to miss any of the game while you wait in lines!*

If you have done a good job in step 2 probing for information, you should be able to match some benefit statements like the preceding ones to the wants and needs of the customer. One mistake that many sellers make is emphasizing too many features, especially when they are not matched to wants and needs that the customer identified. Keep in mind that it is not your job to talk the customer into buying something they do not want. Bringing up one or two extra benefits that the customer may not have known about will probably be harmless, but reciting a long list of benefits that the customer never identified as wants or needs for them makes it sound as if you are pushing the product on them.

Handling Objections in Ticket Sales

Objections in ticket sales are bound to be one of the most common hurdles that a salesperson faces. As with all other forms of sales, people will have many reasons to hesitate before spending money on anything. It is simply human nature. When dealing with objections in ticket sales, remember a few key points: Again, you never want to talk people into something they do not want. If the customer is coming up with a list of objections and the salesperson is spending most of their time countering them, then the customer may simply not be interested. In chapter 2 we explained that a customer's objection to a purchase could be considered a good thing because the salesperson then has a chance to fix the problem. The following are some examples of the most common objections specific to ticket sales.

The Price Objection   Price objections are common because they are one of the easiest objections for a customer to admit and articulate. Nobody likes spending a lot of money, especially when the cost of tickets has increased. Although the price objection is a common surface objection, the customer may have a more important objection that they are not mentioning. The key to the sale may be identifying and addressing that objection. The following is just one scenario, albeit a common one, when the price objection is not the real problem.

> Customer: *I don't want to renew my tickets anymore. It is ridiculous that you have increased the price again.*

> Sales representative: *Frank, I'm sorry to hear that. Could you elaborate a bit more?*

> Customer: *I've been a fan for 10 years, and we've only made it to March Madness four times. The prices never went down when we were bad. We finally make it to one Elite Eight, and the prices jump up $100 per ticket.*

In this scenario, the customer is using a price objection to justify not wanting to renew tickets. A good sales representative may suspect that Frank is actually more frustrated with the team's historical performance and feels underappreciated as a fan. Someone who has been a fan for 10 years for a team that is coming off a successful season typically wants to remain a fan, so it may be worthwhile to avoid the price objection and try to address the underlying reason that the customer is not going to renew their tickets.

> Sales representative: *Frank, I understand, and you are right. We did not lower prices over the past few years when we were not quite as successful. Last year was a special year, and while I'm sorry the prices have increased for our team, we still want you back cheering us on for another season like last year. We need more fans like you who have stuck through the bad times and stay with us through the good times.*

Of course, sometimes the price objection really is the biggest problem that the customer has. A significant increase in ticket prices can occasionally change a customer's mind on the potential purchase. In these scenarios, the salesperson can choose from two popular options. First, the salesperson may choose to highlight some of the features of the ticket and try to reinforce the price. This tactic can be used in many situations, and it is the best option if there are no alternatives for a less expensive ticket. A second option is to propose an alternative. Most sport organizations use a pricing strategy known as **price lining**, which involves pricing their product at several different price points, based on location and benefits. Proposing the alternative and being honest with the drawbacks of the less expensive ticket may highlight the value of the more expensive one.

> Example 1: *Yes, I know it is quite an investment to buy season tickets. The good news is that the season ticket saves you 20 percent off the combined costs of individual games, so if you plan on coming, the season ticket will always be the least expensive option on a per-game basis.*

> Example 2: *I understand. It is a lot of money. How much do you use the other season ticketholder benefits such as the member-only invites and early access to playoff tickets? Although they obviously do not help lower the cost, they are some of the best things you get from remaining a season ticketholder.*

> Example 3: *There is no doubt that the club level isn't cheap. If that is above the budget for your business, I can find you some really great season tickets in the lower level. Your VIPs won't get the same amenities such as food, beverage, and air conditioning, but they will still get a fantastic view of the game, which may be most important. Both are great options.*

> Example 4: *It is a lot of money, but you do not have to pay it all right now! We offer a 12-month payment plan that locks in your seats but allows you to spread out your payments over the entire year to make it easier for you than one large payment.*

In the first two examples the salesperson highlighted additional benefits to add perceived value to the ticket. This approach is most effective when the cost does not sound like an absolute barrier, but more of a hesitation as the customer is weighing whether the ticket is worth the cost. The third example shows a sales representative who is providing a less expensive alternative but is also being open about why the tickets would be less expensive. This approach can be effective in multiple ways. First, by highlighting the fact that the view of the game may be most important, the salesperson is giving the customer an easy way to agree with them. But the salesperson is also reminding the customer what comes with the more expensive tickets. The customer will be able to judge the value of both and decide. Note that when discussing options, you may want to avoid showing preference to the more expensive ticket as better. Phrases such as "the lower-level tickets are not as good as club level but . . ." cast a negative light on the less expensive tickets. This statement can cause customers to think they are not getting a good deal unless the choice is a more expensive option. Phrases like "both are great options" or "you can't go wrong either way" leave the choice up to the customer but show both in a positive light. The fourth example is more straightforward. Often, a purchase is more feasible for the customer if it can be split into multiple payments. This plan prevents the charge from being an excessive percentage of their expendable income for the month. This approach is especially common for season tickets with large price tags.

The Performance Objection   Poor team performance is one of the hardest objections for a ticket sales representative to face. After all, they have no control over how the team performs. Most fans are attracted to winning teams, and they may become frustrated when a team does not perform to the level they expected at the beginning of the year. In these cases, the salesperson should never agree or disagree with a fan who is making negative statements about the team's performance. Agreeing with a fan who states, "This team stinks" is just going to reinforce the objection in their mind—even the person selling tickets agrees! What makes this tricky is that you do not want to argue with the customer either. Responding, "I really don't think we're that bad" may make the customer defensive. Unfortunately, sometimes the only way to combat this concern is to acknowledge the customer's objection and try to deflect to something more positive. Here are a few examples:

> Example 1: *I understand the season didn't go how many of us expected. We still need fans like you to show your support behind the team, and if this season goes better I'd like to make sure you are there cheering us on the entire way.*
>
> Example 2: *I know your employees don't want to see the team lose, and I'm sorry that happened last year. Hopefully, they really enjoyed the atmosphere and time socializing with each other throughout the game even if it didn't end the way we hoped.*
>
> Example 3: *I understand why you say that. Some of those games were so close it was heartbreaking for me as well, but the good news is that because of our slower start, we have a lot of great seats that normally would not be considered for a group discount but can be used for the rest of the season! These seat locations will be better than anything we've had in the past few years at this great group discount.*

No matter what, overcoming the objections of a fan who is disappointed in their team's performance will be difficult. Fan passion is what makes interacting with customers so much fun, but it can make them difficult at times as well. The most important rule is to remember to be positive and keep listening. No single way works best to counter a performance objection, but with enough practice a salesperson can be successful even when the team is not.

The Inventory Objection   Many fortunate sport organizations have a limited inventory, which is great for them but not so great for people with smaller budgets or those who want the best locations. The inventory (or location) objection can be difficult because few alternatives may be available to offer the customer. Unfortunately, the customer is placed in a "take it or leave it" situation, and the salesperson must try to soften that sentiment and work with the customer to appreciate the location regardless of its view.

The truth is that the sales representative can do little to improve the location or availability of seats. In these cases, an effective tactic may be to deflect, as with the performance objection, and try to highlight the other features of the tickets. Typically, if the inventory is limited, the stadium or facility should be fairly full, an environment that fans enjoy and that can offer an easy deflection. Additionally, the sales representative may be able to highlight benefits such as atmosphere or exclusivity, or tap into the fan's passion to help them look past their seat location. Some examples that may be helpful are the following:

> Example 1: *Jane, the game is almost sold out, so the only tickets available are behind the endzones. But with a sold-out stadium the atmosphere is going to be amazing, and I don't want you to miss out!*
>
> Example 2: *Nicole, yes, we have only the smaller suites available. All our big hospitality areas are already filled up. But the smaller space is our most affordable suite, and your employees will have the same luxury amenities of our larger, more expensive ones.*
>
> Example 3: *The only seats we have for group ticketing are in the upper level. Yes, it is a little higher, but because we have the available seats, we could seat your entire group together next to each other, which we would never be able to do in the lower bowl. You will be able to socialize and interact with each other all game!*
>
> Example 4: *Sorry, that game is sold out. I still have some tickets left for other games that aren't sold out quite yet if you want to support the team later this season!*

The Logistics Objection   The final objection that we will discuss in this section is a logistics objection. Oftentimes this concern has nothing to do with the team, game, or stadium. This objection is an outside problem that is making a customer hesitate about their choice to buy a ticket to the game. The good news is that these objections tend to be the easiest for the salesperson to handle if a solution can be found. The key to solving a logistics objection lies in the product knowledge of the salesperson. If you are selling a ticket to a sporting event, you should try to know everything about the customer experience, from beginning to end. Traffic, parking, entrances, flow throughout the stadium, and even pricing of concessions are valuable information. Some of this information will come with time and experience, but much of it will come from talking with customers and fans. When countering a logistics objection, an effective approach is to frame the response with information that helps the fan relate to other fans. Additionally, you can offer your opinion in these situations if doing so would help and if you are not disagreeing with the customer. Obviously, the issues that customers face when attending games will vary widely. Here are a few examples:

> Example 1: *Mila, it sounds like traffic right before game time is a big problem for you, and I can certainly understand that. I hate traffic as well. We have some great pregame activities that include yard games, bounce houses for kids, and a chance to meet the mascot. Many families like to arrive early to avoid traffic and enjoy the festivities.*

> Example 2: *Bernard, I don't want you to have any trouble getting from the parking lot to the stadium, and we appreciate our senior fans who have supported us for so long. How familiar are you with our shuttle service? That may be a great solution for you. Additionally, if you have a handicapped parking pass, I can point out the lots that might make it easier for you to park.*

> Example 3: *Quinn, I can certainly appreciate your not wanting to handle the ticket distribution at your office every game. If you want, you can just email me the names of the employee of the week, and I can have the ticket reprinted and left at will call under their name. Just ask them to bring a photo ID.*

> Example 4: *Jay, our tickets are digital, so if you want to transfer them to family or*

> *friends you can do it through Ticketmaster and have the tickets sent to your email. That way you can make sure the tickets are used if you are not able to make it this weekend.*

All these issues were able to be resolved because the salesperson knew their product well and was able to offer help. Of course, not every issue can be resolved as easily, and at times the salesperson would not be able to help. In these scenarios, as with the two previous objections, the best approach is to focus on the positive benefits of the tickets.

Step 4: PROpose an Offer

You will remember from chapter 2 that proposing an offer and asking for the sale involve summarizing the offer and reemphasizing the trigger statement to remind the customer why they wanted the tickets. Additionally, remember that you should avoid asking bluntly whether the customer wants to buy the tickets. That question makes it too easy for the customer to say no. Obviously, you cannot make the customer purchase anything, but you want to be sure that if the customer declines, they do so because an objection still stands, not because of natural hesitation.

Trigger Statements and Urgency Statements in Ticket Sales

One way to ensure that a customer's decline results from an objection and not natural hesitation is to add a bit of urgency at the end of the pitch. You walk a fine line between being pushy or lying and creating urgency, so you should practice and be comfortable with your pitch. You never want the customer to feel uncomfortable, and you certainly do not want to lie to them. The most common ways to create urgency are to mention that locations are never guaranteed until the customer pays for the tickets and that tickets are usually sold on a first-come, first-served basis. In the following examples, sales representatives reemphasize the trigger statement and add an urgency statement.

Example 1: *Buddy, it sounds like you are a good fit for our club-level seats. You mentioned that you like making an entire day trip out of the game, and all the premium amenities of the club level really make that experience much better. Season tickets at the club level are $1,500 each, and of course it comes with the catered buffet each game, a reserved parking space, and a separate entrance so that you never wait in line. If you want, I can get you locked in, and you can get the seats you wanted before anyone else does. What do you think?*

Example 2: *Karen, I know that value is most important for you and your family. The 10-game minipack is one of the best values that we have because your entire family can attend for less than $50 per game. The minipack has been extremely popular, so I would recommend signing up as soon as you can. I can take care of it now if you would like.*

Example 3: *Jorge, I know you want aisle seats so that you don't have to cross over people. Unfortunately, we do not have many of those left, and I cannot guarantee them for you until you sign up for our season ticket membership. The good news is that I can offer a payment plan that doesn't start until next month and breaks up the monthly payments to just under $20 per ticket, per month. How does that sound?*

All these examples show a trigger statement, urgency statement, and ask for the sale without compelling a basic yes or no response. They are designed not necessarily to force the customer into saying yes but instead to probe the customer to explain why if they say no. You cannot be afraid of hearing no! When the customer says no, they will typically repeat an objection or barrier that is stopping them. If the barrier seems like something you can help with, you can address the problem and then come back to asking for the sale again later in the conversation.

Do Not Be Afraid of No

If the customer's reason for saying no is an objection that you do not think you can overcome, or the customer gives you a noncommittal answer like "Let me think about it," traditional sales methods sometimes suggest that you continue to create urgency and repeat asking for the sale. In modern times, many have suggested that this approach is no longer effective and letting the customer go without the sale in the short term may be the better long-term decision. We recommend that whenever a customer seems interested in a ticket but does not want to commit right away, you allow them to leave but ask them if you can follow up with them soon. If they want to be the one to make contact, simply reemphasize your name and contact information. Sending them an email as well is a great idea so that they do not lose it.

Ticket sales is often a volume-based strategy compared with many other forms of sales in sport. You are likely to have many more prospects lined up than you would for other forms of sales, such as sponsorship, which tends to have higher-cost sales with fewer customers (and fewer prospects). Ultimately, this contrast leads to one of the biggest differences between asking for the sale in ticket sales versus many other forms: Letting a customer go is perfectly OK. At the end of the day, ticket sales requires time, and every minute you spend trying to combat dozens of objections from a customer who will never buy is time you should have spent on someone who is truly interested. This concept can be dangerous because it can encourage salespeople to "bulldog" the sale. The **bulldog** sales technique means that the salesperson skips the majority of the second and third steps of the PRO method and asks for the sale shortly after qualifying the customer. This approach is usually an attempt either to get a quick sale or to get off the phone quickly and move on to another prospect. Good salespeople never bulldog the sale, but they also know when to recognize that a sale is not going to happen and politely move on to their next prospect.

Step 5: PROtect the Sale

Step 5 of the PRO method involves protecting the sale. Ticket sales representatives can protect their customers in several ways; some are applicable to all forms of sales, and some are specific to ticket sales. Remember that good salespeople create relationships with their customers, not just transactions. The more the customer feels as if they are in a two-way relationship with their sales representative, the more effective the salesperson will be.

Year-Round Selling and Season Ticket Memberships

One of the fastest growing trends in ticket sales customer management is the idea of year-round communication with fans. Traditionally, sport organizations reach out to their fans once a year to sell them season tickets and then may follow up a few times throughout the season. Rarely did salespeople call on season ticketholders well into the offseason. Recently, organizations have embraced the idea of year-round selling. This activity does not mean that the salesperson is constantly trying to get the customer to buy something, but instead is simply communicating to check in with the customer, answer questions, provide information, or say something nice.

One rule of thumb that some salespeople use is the 3-to-1 ratio. The **3-to-1 ratio** says that you should contact a customer without asking for money three times before you contact them once asking them to buy something. This approach helps build a positive relationship between the seller and the customer because the customer knows that when the seller calls, it is not always just for their money. Sellers can reach out in hundreds of small ways to stay in touch with buyers, some of which are just simple, one-sentence gestures. Here are a few of these gestures:

Example 1: *Hi, Steve. When you bought your tickets you mentioned you were coming out for your birthday. I just wanted to say happy birthday, and I hope you have a great experience.*

Example 2: *Jamaal, I believe you mentioned you had some friends coming with you to last week's game. I just wanted to see how the game went for you all.*

Example 3: *Hi, Brooke. I am just calling to check in on you this season. How has everything gone so far?*

Example 4: *Jason, playoff tickets go on sale tomorrow at 8 am, and I wanted to make sure I reached out and let you know you can call me directly to book them if you need tickets this year.*

Example 5: *Charlie, I wanted to see how you were liking the new seat location this year.*

The idea of year-round selling has become such a common theme that many organiza-

Oakland A's Ditch Season Tickets for A's Access Membership

Although many teams have begun to brand their season ticket packages as memberships, few have embraced the idea as wholeheartedly as the Oakland A's. What started as a pilot idea to fill unsold seats has resulted in the A's completely disbanding season tickets and replacing their season ticket packages with A's Access, a membership program for fans that offers Netflix-style monthly payments in exchange for access to all home games. All plans include general-admission access to home games plus a limited number of games with a reserved view or better location. Fans can pay more for additional reserved games. Fans who choose to use their general admission access can sit in dedicated general admission sections or watch the game in several lounge and standing-room areas. The A's added value to the membership with 50 percent off concessions, 20 percent off merchandise, and discounted or free parking. Although the A's are constantly changing the amenities and structure of the program, the core of it remains the same. Their one-of-a-kind membership allows fans to choose from several different experiences rather than the same one every time.

tions have renamed their season ticketholders "members." The idea of having a year-long **season membership** sounds a lot better to buyers than simply getting a ticket. Teams have begun to reinforce this idea with discounts, members-only events, monthly payment plans, and other special amenities. Season memberships differ in how closely they resemble traditional tickets. For some teams, the change is more about the title and branding, with a few amenities added to make the experience year long. Other teams have completely converted their tickets to memberships, foregoing physical tickets and requiring members to use an app or website to enter the stadium. These unique membership programs may add some additional information for the salesperson to explain, but the constant contact with the team and the additional amenities have produced dividends for many teams.

Upselling in Ticket Sales

Ticket sales might be one of the most promising areas to upsell customers. Typically, plenty of options are available, plenty of customers are out there to upsell to, and the increase in price is not always drastic. Upselling tickets can include taking a single-game buyer to a partial plan or a season ticketholder to a premium seating package. B2B sales can increase in location or quantity as well. The possibilities are endless for ticket sales because many different types and prices of inventory are available. As with step 4, a salesperson can make too many upsell attempts. Many salespeople are trained to finish their calls with a list of a dozen possible upsell opportunities. Bombarding the customer with a long list of possible upsells, a method known as **shotgunning**, is not recommended. Although suggesting one or two upsell opportunities unprompted is usually OK, doing it too much tends to make the seller seem untrustworthy. Good upsells commonly happen for one of two reasons: as a solution to an objection or through some information discovered during steps 2 and 3.

Upsells as a solution to an objection may occur because the customer brought up a bar-

rier that they were unhappy or concerned with, and the solution to the problem involves a more expensive sale. For instance, a customer may not like their view of the field and be intrigued by an offer to upgrade into better seats. Alternatively, a fan who is concerned with the cost of an individual ticket may possibly be more interested in a partial or season ticket that provides a better value per ticket. These upsells can be the most satisfying because they are helping a customer solve a problem and converting an upsell at the same time.

The other common reason for an upsell results from a lead that the customer gave the seller earlier in the conversation. When a customer mentions that they sometimes attend games with friends, the salesperson can ask, "Oh, do they have season tickets as well?" If they do not, the salesperson has a great instant lead for an upsell or referral. Other leads, such as hearing the comment like "Our seats aren't bad" suggests that the customer may be open to moving up to a better location and more expensive sale. If the seller is fortunate enough to have a cross-sell opportunity to a different event or sport, fans who make comments such as "I'm a huge fan and support every event" would create an easy transition. By constantly listening to customers and looking for upsell or cross-sell opportunities, sellers can both maximize revenue for the organization and provide customers with opportunities to upgrade that they may actually be interested in. Mentioning an upsell if the customer gives you a lead that they might be interested is always a good thing.

Protecting the Sale With B2B Customers

Business customers, like traditional customers, need to be protected throughout the season. Keep in mind that even though the name on the account may be a business and the tickets may be used for business purposes, the individual who makes the decision to purchase is a regular person, just like a B2C customer. You should know a few personal touchpoints such as whether they are a fan, how long the business has been operating, and perhaps a piece of personal information like where they went to school. When checking in on how a B2B customer is doing throughout the year, keep in mind that their definition of success may be different from that of a regular customer. Typically, a B2C customer judges success on how they enjoyed the experience. Remember that in B2B situations, the person's experience is only the first motivation of the B2B buyer, and the secondary benefit that results from that person enjoying the game is the true goal. Whether it is employee appreciation, VIP hospitality, or just part of building a more positive culture for the business, the B2B customer is looking for some return on their investment, or ROI. When you are probing for information in step 2, make sure to ask how the customer will be measuring the success of the ticket use. That way, when you check in on them you can be specific and ask how effective the product has been for them. A few examples of service calls to B2B customers follow:

> Example 1: *Emma, it seemed like everyone was having a great time in your party suite. Do you agree? Is there anything we could do to make it even better?*

> Example 2: *Hunter, the single-game tickets for our big rivalry go on sale soon, and I thought of you. I remember that you wanted to bring some extra VIPs to that one.*

> Example 3: *Kiesha, I think your sales team had a really good time. Hopefully, they hit their goals again next quarter, and I get to see them again!*

Referrals in Ticket Sales

The last part of step 5 is to make sure that you ask for referrals. This request can be awkward for some because nobody wants to feel as if they are setting up their friend to be harassed by a pushy salesperson. The key to successful referring in the ticket sales industry is having enough rapport with the customer that they trust you will not make them look bad. If you are asking for referrals on the very first call after talking with a customer for only a few

minutes, your request is probably going to be unsuccessful. If you are a good seller, however, you can have a meaningful conversation with the customer and establish enough trust that the customer knows you will not make their friends or family uncomfortable when you call them. If the customer does not seem willing to give you a phone number, offer to send an email or hand off your information. This contact is not as likely to result in a sale as getting a number, but it is better than nothing. Lastly, do not forget that every regular ticketholder can also be a referral for a group sale from their business or associations that they are a part of. Many customers are far more likely to provide information about their HR department or event organizers than they are friends and family. This approach is a good way to expand a relationship and build leads based on existing customers. Here are some ways to ask for referrals without being pushy:

> Example 1: *Kristin, you have one open seat next to you. Who could you think of who might want to join you for the games this year?*

> Example 2: *Chuckie, how did those extra tickets for last week's game work out? I hope your brother had a great time. I'd be happy to talk to him about joining you for the remaining games if you'd like.*

> Example 3: *I'm glad that you thought the hospitality event went well. I would be happy to do it for any of your other business friends if you know of other companies looking to do something similar.*

> Example 4: *I believe you mentioned you work at American Therapeutics, right? Who is in charge of the company events? I would love to bring your coworkers to a game!*

Future of Ticket Sales for Revenue Generation

The purpose of this chapter is to provide a ton of information, structure, and examples of how to sell tickets in the sport industry. But the sport industry is always changing, and nobody knows what the next big trend will be. As the industry changes, products will change, customer behavior will change, and even the product itself (the game) may change. The best salespeople will be the ones who can adapt and apply the basics using new information and strategies. As we look forward into the next era of ticket sales, several trends are becoming more popular, and sales representatives should monitor them closely.

Flexibility in Seating

We already mentioned that many teams are beginning to sell their tickets on a membership model rather than as traditional tickets. Part of the reason is that consumers want greater flexibility in how they view the game. Lounges and social areas have increased in popularity, allowing continuous interaction throughout the game. Many teams are beginning to offer spontaneous upgrades, or last-minute seating options, for fans in an attempt to fill empty seats and add value to the lower-priced season tickets. Flexibility has been an even bigger focus for younger fans, who are not as attracted to the idea of sitting in the same seats and having the same experience every game. As these fans and options become more prominent, the objections and sales strategies may need to change. Flexibility will become a big selling point, whereas consistency used to be more important.

Another way that teams have added flexibility to ticket plans is by removing the perishability of tickets. Buyers who purchase season tickets or larger packages are often frustrated when a ticket goes unused and is essentially wasted. This concern can become a major hesitation to purchasing a ticket package in the first place, and teams who are willing to help mitigate this fear are creating an interesting new model for ticket sales. Teams who aim to limit perishability are offering programs such as a ticket exchange that allows fans to trade unused tickets for another game. For instance, the Cedar Rapids Kernels' ticket exchange allows fans to trade any unused ticket for any midweek game. Fans who want to trade unused midweek tickets for weekend tickets pay a small $3 fee. The exchange allows fans to take tickets for games that they would normally miss and use them for additional tickets they can give to friends or family. These unique benefits are becoming more common and take a lot of the risk out of buying a ticket package, which is a great benefit for salespeople to offer.

Finally, ticket sales representatives must be prepared to adapt to the unknown. The COVID-19 pandemic resulted in the cancellation or postponement of many professional sport events. Lost gate revenues from MLB may have been as high as $5 billion, and NFL losses approached $4 billion (TicketIQ, 2020). Although many organizations do not publicly reveal their business data, we do know that those who eventually allowed fans back into stadiums did so under significant restrictions. The 2021 season offered entirely new challenges because teams had to recognize that people who lost their jobs would struggle to afford their tickets. In addition, they had to provide customer service for disgruntled fans upset about the cancellation of games.

Merging of the Primary and Secondary Markets

The **primary ticket market** refers to tickets sold directly by the teams or leagues. These tickets are distributed to customers who either use the tickets or occasionally place them back up for sale on a **secondary ticket market**. Originally, the secondary market included people holding "Needs tickets" signs. It later evolved online to sites such as StubHub and Ticketmaster. Secondary sites allow sellers to charge whatever they want for the ticket, leading to an open market that sets pricing based on supply and demand. Although teams long regarded these sites as competitors, they have begun to embrace the secondary markets, which changes the selling strategies for the sellers. Many teams have partnered with secondary markets to obtain the contact information for anyone who purchases a ticket to their games, much to the surprise of the buyer when they get a call from the team!

Aside from trading information, some teams and leagues are creating official secondary markets that allow fans to sell their tickets safely without fear of working through a third party, adding a layer of legitimacy to the transaction. Likewise, other leagues have officially endorsed certain secondary market sites, which adds the same legitimacy. This change has both positives and negatives for ticket sellers. A legitimized secondary market adds more options for the buyer because they can confidently purchase tickets without ever having to speak to a seller. The secondary market limits opportunities for upselling and typically places a large emphasis on the lowest priced ticket in a certain area. Secondary market buyers also miss out on the expertise, advice, and help that a personal sales representative can offer. On the positive side, having a legitimized secondary market allows sellers to endorse that option as a rebuttal to objections when a customer is concerned about whether they will use their tickets.

Dynamic Pricing

A trend that has recently become more prominent has been to include elements of dynamic pricing into ticket operations. **Dynamic pricing** is a pricing strategy that integrates some form of real-time demand. Traditionally, ticket prices have been sold using **fixed pricing**, which means that the price does not change over time. A ticket may go on sale for $50 at the beginning of the year when tens of thousands of them are available. As the event approaches, the ticket is still $50 regardless of how many are left. This strategy was used to encourage fans to purchase their tickets early. Dynamic pricing uses either manual adjustments or computer software to increase or decrease price according to the availability of the ticket. It is most often used for individual tickets in sport. A ticket may go on sale for $25 when tens of thousands of tickets are available but increase to over $100 when only a few hundred remain.

Most sport organizations temper the effects of dynamic pricing by setting limits on how high or how low the ticket price can go, which prevents potential conflict. Teams with little demand could see a truly dynamic model drop their price to the point where it undermines season ticketholders. Likewise, customers may become frustrated when they are buying official tickets from a primary market for several times what other fans paid.

What Do Sales Managers Want in a Ticket Sales Employee?

As we mentioned, ticket sales are the most common entry-level sales job in the sport industry. Chapter 2 gave you a framework about how to sell anything using the PRO method, and this chapter showed you how to apply the PRO method to ticket sales. But the missing link between being educated on sales techniques and getting a job is the skills that the employer wants. What do they want to see? According to a study by Pierce and colleagues (2012), the most transferable (not specific to ticket sales) skills that appeared in ticket sales job postings were communication skills, work ethic, computer skills, and ability to withstand long hours. Obviously, a ticket sales professional needs to be resilient. Combining transferable skills with a good working knowledge of sales strategies provides the best chance of success for a professional looking to work in ticket sales.

Summary

Even though ticket sales revenue has declined as a percentage of total revenue, it is still a considerable revenue generator for almost all sport organizations. Learning to apply the PRO method to ticket sales requires an understanding of the various types of ticket sales inventory, as well as the features and benefits of each. Ticket sales are unique because of the sheer volume of contacts required and the numerous chances to maximize revenue with each customer. The best ticket sales representatives are the ones who can be efficient yet thorough and can properly identify wants, benefits, and upsell opportunities for each customer. Ticket sales is increasingly becoming a year-round process, so the best ticket sellers are the ones who can establish relationships and communicate effectively.

APPLIED LEARNING ACTIVITIES

1. *Working backward*. A typical exercise is for a student to pretend to question a customer and pick a seating type for that customer. Instead, have the customer describe a seating type and ask the seller to describe what type of customer would be interested in that ticket. For instance, the customer might pick an upper-level season ticket with a poor view. The seller may respond, "This ticket would be best for someone who is most concerned with price over everything else but wants to attend multiple games." Switch roles so that both partners get practice in identifying benefits.

2. *B2B practice*. Pick a random business out of a hat from the group your instructor has prepared and research that business to see what type of B2B inventory, if any, these businesses could use. Consider size of company, number of employees, and day-to-day operations.

CASE STUDY

DONATION TICKET SALES. PENN STATE ATHLETICS AND SEATS FOR SERVICE MEMBERS

One of the problems with having a 106,000-seat stadium is that filling it can be difficult when the opponent is not considered a competitive team. Penn State ran into this problem in 2013, noticing that the upper-level seats were going unsold. With one of the largest and most loyal fanbases, Penn State knew that the problem was not a lack of fans, but instead a lack of fans who were able to attend every game. Many fans had relocated to a different part of the country. This thought led to a revolutionary idea that dozens of schools in college football would soon follow: What if Penn State could get people to buy tickets for someone else? Knowing they had a huge fanbase, Penn State started the Seats for Soldiers program. Seats for Soldiers was a program that allowed Penn State fans who were unable to attend games to buy individual tickets (at a discount), which were then donated to military service men and women as well as their families. It was a small way to say thank you. In 2018 over 6,500 military members were invited to cheer on Penn State when they played Iowa. This creative program paired a great way to honor the military with a need to fill unsold seats by tapping into a nationwide network who otherwise never would have been a qualified customer.

Discussion Questions for Case Study

1. If you were selling seats for service members to a Penn State alum, how would you describe the features and benefits of this ticket knowing that the person would not be attending themselves?

2. Discuss how you would prospect if you were making calls for this program.

3. Response: Because this program eliminates the geographic restriction, literally anybody can be a prospect. Savvy students may suggest that prospects would include Penn State alumni groups, wealthier alumni, or those with ties to both Penn State and the military.

Go to HK*Propel* to watch author videos, engage in sales scenarios, and find downloadable sales templates related to this chapter.

Philip Pacheco/Getty Images

CHAPTER 4

Broadcasting and Multimedia Revenues

CHAPTER OBJECTIVES

After completing the chapter, you should be able to do the following:

- Understand the changing nature of broadcasting sport content
- Demonstrate the effect of broadcasting rights on the sport industry
- Explain broadcasting metrics that can be measured by sport properties
- Report how sales is changing in the digital age
- Describe new forms of technology that are affecting the sport industry

Being involved in sales and revenue generation within the sport industry is almost impossible without having a basic understanding of broadcasting and multimedia. The United States is by far the largest sports media rights market in the world. In 2019 the U.S. market was projected to generate $22.42 billion, accounting for 44 percent of the total global sport rights market (Sports Business Media, 2019). Advances in technology have led to dynamic changes in how people consume sport. The average consumer wants access to consume sport 24/7. They want it to be personalized to their wants and needs, and convenient to consume. In 2020 most sport fans could not attend a live sport event because of the coronavirus pandemic. Instead, the broadcasting of games was the primary way in which sport fans consumed the product. The changes have also greatly affected how businesses seek to deliver content to their audiences using multimedia channels.

Although graduates in sport management may never work for a media company, anyone involved in sport sales must understand the intersection of sport and multimedia. Sport consumers are using multiple channels and are moving away from cable and satellite broadcasting to digital formats. Fans travel to live events where they can watch the event on their cell phone after using the mobile applications on those same devices to scan their tickets and buy food. This chapter delves into the economic impact of the lucrative media rights deals for North American leagues like the NFL, MLB, NBA, and NHL. The reader will learn common terms used within the industry and the way in which the PRO method of selling relates to the digital and ever-changing world of the 21st century.

Broadcasting and TV Viewership of Sport Events

Broadcasting is the live or recorded transmission of a sport event through either an analog or a digital method using ground receivers, satellites, or cable networks by a form of media (Tsiotsou, 2011). The broadcast of live televised sports is extremely popular in the United States. In fact, 5 of the top 10 rated television broadcasts of all time are sporting events. The final farewell episode of the popular sitcom *M*A*S*H* in 1983 ranks as the highest-rated television broadcast of all time, but Super Bowl XVI, Super Bowl XVII, ladies' singles figure skating at the 1994 Winter Olympic Games, Super Bowl XX, and Super Bowl XLIX all rank in the top 10 (TV by the Numbers, 2009). Eight of the top 10 leading broadcast and primetime telecasts in the United States in 2020 were sport events. The only top 10 broadcasts that were not related to sport were the post-Super Bowl Masked Singer and the Oscars (Stoll, 2021). Approximately 154.4 million viewers in the United States watched televised live sport content at least once per month in 2019, and this figure is projected to rise to over 160 million by 2024 (Lange, 2020). This statistic reveals how popular live televised content is and why broadcasting companies are willing to pay so much money for the rights to broadcast games.

According to Egan (2020), although traditional TV viewership in the United States is declining, advertising expenditures continue to grow. Many American consumers are **cord-cutting**, which means that they are canceling cable or satellite subscriptions and getting content (sport events, television shows, movies, etc.) by other means. Providers like Hulu, YouTube TV, Sling TV, FuboTV, and others are popular streaming services for cord-cutters. The sport content of streaming services varies, and consumers must decide whether they want access to live sport events or sport content. For example, watching *Real Sports With Bryant Gumbel* or *The Last Dance* on ESPN is very different from watching a live contest between the National Football League's (NFL) Dallas Cowboys and the Philadelphia Eagles. Consumers also demand alternative sports broadcasts like NFL RedZone, an all-in-one channel that allows NFL fans to watch seven hours of live football of various games.

Fantasy sports participation has also added to the viewership of sporting events. Both fantasy sports participants and traditional sport fans follow televised sport contests (Lee

svetikd/E+/Getty Images

What was the last sport event you watched on television? Although the media landscape is changing, viewing live events on broadcast television is extremely popular and, therefore, lucrative.

et al., 2013), but viewing for fantasy sports participants extends to players across an array of teams, rather than just a single team. People play fantasy sports for various reasons, including the competition of managing teams, living vicariously, social purposes, and just having fun. The Fantasy Sports & Gaming Association (FSGA, n.d.) reported that 59.3 million people in North America played fantasy sports in 2017. This figure is up from 57.4 million in 2016 and 18 million in 2006. The most popular fantasy sport is football, which attracts 78 percent of all fantasy players, followed by baseball (39 percent), basketball (19 percent), hockey (18 percent), soccer (14 percent), golf (13 percent), and eSports (11 percent).

Cable television subscriptions have been declining primarily because of cord-cutting. Less than 10 percent of the revenues in the broadcasting industry derive from fees paid by cable television providers to retransmit a broadcast signal. Most major broadcasters are large media companies who have the resources to invest in platforms and have shifted further into digital distribution, which adds to the growth in revenues for the industry. Revenues in the television broadcasting industry increased at an annual rate of 3.5 percent between 2015 and 2020 to $65.2 billion. Industry revenues decreased by 6.7 percent in 2020, mostly because of the coronavirus pandemic, but revenues are expected to continue to grow through 2025. The average industry profit margin, which is earnings before interest and taxes, is expected to expand over the coming years because of the switch to digital distribution by many broadcasting companies.

Move Toward Video on Demand

As sport fans abandon traditional satellite and cable television, 56 percent of sport fans reveal they are willing to invest in an OTT sports channel to watch games and matches over the Internet (USC Annenberg Center for the Digital Future, 2016). **Over-the-top (OTT)** is the productized (i.e., making or developing into a product) practice of streaming content to customers directly over the web (McAdams, 2019). Wilbert (2020) describes OTT video as a broadcasting method that transmits video content over the Internet as a modern alternative to traditional methods of broadcasting, including satellite and cable. With OTT, viewers can easily access videos from any device (smart TVs, smartphones, tablets, etc.) with an Internet connection, thus eliminating the need for cords and other bulky hardware. Increasingly, organizations are looking for ways to monetize OTT videos.

Video monetization in sport refers to the ability to generate revenue from an online sports broadcast. A broadcast can be monetized in three primary ways. The best option depends on the organization's goals and the target audience: transaction video on demand, ad-based video on demand, and subscription video on demand (Small, 2020). The three methods of monetization are described in the following sections. Video on demand (VOD) is uploaded video content that the consumer accesses on demand. You are likely familiar with popular VOD streaming services such as YouTube, Disney+, Hulu, and Netflix.

Transaction Video on Demand

Better known as pay-per-view, transaction video on demand (**TVOD**) is a type of video monetization whereby viewers pay a certain amount of money for what they want to watch. Pay-per-view is a good option when the organization is televising events that occur infrequently and wants to offer viewers a one-off option. Over the years, boxing and mixed martial arts (MMA) matches have been the most popular sport programming using pay-per-view. A good example of a niche sport pay-per-view was The Match: Tiger vs. Phil, a match play golf contest between Tiger Woods and Phil Mickelson at Shadow Creek Golf Course in Las Vegas, Nevada, marketed by Turner Sports in 2009. The purse for the match was worth $9 million.

Ad-Based Video on Demand

A model that is similar to the monetization methods of satellite and cable providers, in which programs are interrupted by commercials, with **ad-based video on demand (AVOD)** advertisers pay a fee for every ad rendered on a video. Rather than paying out of pocket like pay-per-view, viewers pay for the content with their time watching the commercials. Popularized by YouTube, businesses that monetize their content with AVOD often use tools that are built into their website hosts or professional video-hosting platforms (Krings, 2020). Small (2020) suggests that using advertisements to support streaming a Little League baseball game may be a preferred method so that parents and family members do not have to pay out of pocket to see their kids play.

Subscription Video on Demand

Subscription video on demand (SVOD) is a subscription-based (e.g., weekly, monthly, or quarterly) method that allows viewers to have unlimited access to a video library for as long as their subscription lasts. Netflix is a good example of SVOD. An online video platform, also called a video-hosting platform, is used to set up the SVOD. Within the sport industry, the best content for SVOD is live entertainment, exercise and wellness videos, live streaming sports, and online education and e-learning. Video platforms set up using SVOD should have secure paywall capabilities that allow subscribers to pay online.

Broadcasting and Multimedia Rights and Revenues

Broadcasters in television, radio, Internet, and mobile telecommunications buy the rights to broadcast a sporting event to viewers to increase their market share and value (Swayne & Dodds, 2011), take advantage of public relations opportunities that develop in sport, and gain credibility within the industry (Mullin et al., 2007). Multimedia rights refer to a variety of platforms such as television, radio, Internet, and digital rights to broadcast. The broadcasters want to create unique content for their viewers and, at the same time, develop opportunities to generate advertising revenues. Broadcasters also earn royalties by selling their exclusive footage of the sport event to other media outlets, which enables them to cover the costs of organizational and technical infrastructure involved in broadcasting the event (WIPO, 2020). The rights to broadcast a sporting event are purchased by media networks from sport properties, but the network must pay the expenses necessary for producing, distributing, and marketing the event. Tsiotsou (2011) provides details about the three primary parties involved in broadcasting rights in sport: sport rights holders, the licensed broadcasters, and the viewers of the event. The sport rights holders may be classified as either main rights holders or secondary rights holders.

Main Sport Rights Holders

Usually the organizer of the event, the main sport rights holder, controls the broadcasting, as well as the production of the television signal, and has access to the facilities where the event takes place. The main rights holder could be a sport federation (e.g., International Canoe Federation), league (e.g., National Football League), committee (e.g., the International Olympic Committee), association (e.g., NCAA), union (e.g., the Union of European Football Associations), team (e.g., Tampa Bay Buccaneers), or sport club (e.g., Clube de Regatas do Flamengo in Brazil) (Tsiotsou, 2011). The main rights holder can either sell rights to the broadcast of an event to other broadcasters or to secondary rights holders, or combine those strategies by medium or territories. Broadcasters commonly split the rights and sell them to two or more media platforms and broadcasters. Often, this is done to secure revenues, increase revenues, or comply with regulations, such as existing laws.

Secondary Sport Rights Holders

The main sport rights holder, which is the event organizer, may sell the broadcasting rights to an agency that is authorized to sell the rights to broadcasters or advertisers. Using a market-to-market strategy, the Sportfive Group sold the rights to telecast Euro Cup 2008 football matches to more than 60 television channels in 55 countries (Tsiotsou, 2011). IMG, another sport marketing agency, arranges the distribution of more than 45,000 hours of programming annually across all forms of media, such as television, audio, fixed media, in-flight, broadband, and mobile to major broadcasters, channels, and platforms (IMG, 2020). IMG pays an average of $123 million per year for the Football Association's (FA) international broadcast rights (Dixon, 2020). By using a secondary rights holder like IMG, the main sport rights holder maximizes their revenues and avoids separate negotiations with individual broadcasters. Many colleges and universities also outsource their media rights to third par-

B2B REVENUE GENERATION

IMG College and Ohio State University Media Rights

In 2009 Ohio State University sold the media rights for its sports programs to IMG College in a 10-year deal worth $110 million. IMG College is a sport marketing agency that buys multimedia rights from colleges and then resells those rights to corporate sponsors. At the time, the deal was the largest multimedia rights guarantee in collegiate sport. The partnership with IMG College and RadiOhio gives the companies the rights to manage and market publishing related to Ohio State sports, as well as radio game play-by-play and coaches' shows. In addition, the contract covers television not included in contracts with the Big Ten Conference and NCAA.

Jamie Sabau/Getty Images

ties such as sport agencies. For example, West Virginia University sold their television, radio, and multimedia rights to IMG College in 2013 for at least $80 million over 12 years (Staples, 2016).

Licensed Broadcasting

Broadcasters of television, radio, Internet, broadband, and mobile telecommunications may buy, as well as sell, broadcasting rights. A broadcasting company can sell the rights to a broadcast in two ways. First, they may sublicense all or part of the broadcasting rights to a different media platform. Second, the broadcasting company can sell the advertising time for the event. Most broadcasters sell advertising time. For example, a 30-second commercial spot during the 2020 Super Bowl broadcast by Fox cost $5.6 million.

The Congressional Research Service (CRS) (2013) report about laws governing the broadcast of professional sporting events describes the uniqueness of broadcasting professional sport:

> *The licensing rights for the telecast of professional sports programming are treated in a somewhat unique way under federal law. There are special provisions that apply only to sports programming that exist in order to support a number of policy goals. Some of these goals include ensuring the availability of the games of local teams to local audiences and preserving the competitive nature of professional sports leagues. However, these statutory and regulatory provisions come under fire occasionally. They are cited as the cause for certain games being "blacked out" (i.e., unavailable on television) in some areas of the country when certain conditions are met. They are also cited as a reason that licensing professional sports programming has become so expensive that it may be partially responsible for the rising prices of cable and satellite bills. (p. 1)*

As noted by the CRS, the fees for licensing professional sports are expensive. Leagues, teams, and events put the rights for their broadcast up for bid in exchange for guaranteed payments over an agreed-upon number of years.

The broadcast helps to expand their audience, revenues, and reputation within the minds of viewers (Mullin et al., 2007). For most sport properties (e.g., NFL), the sale of broadcasting and media rights is the largest source of revenues, thus helping to finance major sporting events, refurbish stadiums, and develop the sport at the grassroots level. NFL rights are already costly. Steinberg (2020) reports that CBS, NBC, and Fox all have an agreement with the NFL and are paying a combined $3.1 billion per year for Sunday games. ESPN pays $1.9 billion per year for the rights to broadcast *Monday Night Football*, and Fox's *Thursday Night Football* deal is worth more than $650 million per year (Tainsky, 2010). The National Broadcasting Company (NBC) pays over $4 billion to the International Olympic Committee (IOC) to televise the Olympic Games. In 2018, Fox Sports and MLB signed an agreement on a contract extension through the 2028 season for exclusive broadcasting rights to televise the World Series and the All-Star Game. The deal was worth $5.1 billion (Daniels, 2018).

Revenues for media rights in North American Leagues such as the National Football League (NFL), Major League Baseball (MLB), National Basketball Association (NBA), National Hockey League (NHL), and Major League Soccer (MLS) increased from $14.6 billion in 2014 to $20.2 billion in 2018 and were projected to increase to $25.3 billion by 2023. In this case, media rights included fees paid to show sport events on broadcast and cable television networks, television stations, terrestrial radio, satellite radio, the Internet, and mobile devices (PwC, 2019). According to Gough (2020), the top broadcasting rights revenues from various leagues in 2019 across the world included the following:

- National Football League (USA)—$4.52 billion
- English Premier League (UK)—$3.83 billion
- National Basketball Association (USA)—$3.12 billion
- La Liga (Spain)—$3.12 billion
- Major League Baseball (USA)—$1.65 billion

- Bundesliga (Germany)—$1.57 billion
- Serie A (Italy)—$1.51 billion
- Ligue 1 (France)—$1.37 billion
- National Hockey League (USA)—$220 million
- Major League Soccer (USA)—$110 million

Leagues operate in various ways when it comes to media rights revenues. For example, revenue sharing within the NFL is quite different from the model used in MLB, in which each team signs their own local television contracts. Revenue sharing has a significant effect on competitive parity between leagues. In MLB, 49 percent of local revenues is distributed equally among all 30 teams. MLB is well behind the NFL in terms of revenue because each team receives only 3.3 percent of the total sum of revenues generated (Baseball Reference, 2020). In terms of competitive parity, note that in the 2020 MLB World Series the National League's Los Angeles Dodgers, with a payroll of $107.9 million, played the American League's Tampa Bay Rays, with a $28.3 million payroll. In the NFL, each team receives approximately $255

million a year from revenue sharing of television and streaming contracts from broadcast companies like ESPN, CBS, and Fox, who broadcast the league's games. In 2013 the Los Angeles Dodgers signed a 25-year, $8.35 billion contract with Time Warner, now Charter Communications, to televise games in southern California (Hendricks & Vockrodt, 2019).

Most teams in baseball, hockey, and basketball broadcast their games on regional broadcast networks related to Fox Sports, NBC Sports, AT&T Sports, Spectrum, Sportsnet, and others. As shown in table 4.1, total television viewership is astronomical. **Regional broadcast networks** are cable broadcasting channels that provide sport programming in local markets. In 2018 the New York Yankees averaged 277,000 viewers per game, and they have a $3.47 billion deal with the YES Network that allows them to have programming with a footprint in both broadcasting and OTT (Ozanian, 2019). Broadcast rights for specific sport events also demand big money. For example, CBS and ESPN broadcast the Masters golf tournament. The Masters is different from most sport events in that it has about a third of the commercial interruptions

TABLE 4.1 Approximate Total TV Viewers by Sport in 2020

League or sport	Total TV viewers
NFL	120 M
MLB	82.2 M
College Football	82.6 M
NBA	64.5 M
College Basketball	53.4 M
Golf	45.8 M
Minor League Hockey	5.8 M
NHL	43.9 M
Tennis	38.4 M
NASCAR	33.6 M
MLS	27.7 M
Mixed Martial Arts	27 M
Soccer (non-USA)	26.6 M
IndyCar	23.6 M
eSports	17.9 M

*M denotes millions.

Data from SBRnet, *TV Viewers: Total TV Viewers by Major Sport Category* (2020).

of most other events. Augusta National charges their partners like Mercedes-Benz, IBM, and AT&T $6 to $8 million each. At the end of the tournament, CBS sends Augusta a bill for $30 million (Kerr-Dineen, 2017).

Although media rights within professional sport are lucrative, the same can be said for intercollegiate athletics, especially for Division I institutions in the NCAA. According to a report from the Center for Research in Intercollegiate Athletics (CRIA) (2018) at the University of North Carolina, the total amount of guaranteed rights fees paid to Power Five (ACC, Big 10, Big 12, Pac-12, and SEC) and Group of Five (AAC, Conference USA, MAC, Mountain West, and Sun Belt) institutions during the 2017-2018 academic year totaled more than $515 million, with more than $400 million allocated to the Power Five institutions. Maestas (n.d.) reports that approximately 40 percent of the value of multimedia rights deals in the Power Five derives from football-related exposure (in stadiums, during broadcasts, etc.), 30 percent is from men's and women's basketball events, and the remaining 30 percent comes from all sports collectively. More than 40 percent of the exposure for sponsors at these events comes from in-venue signage that is seen in person and on television. Rights holders traditionally share anywhere between 50 and 70 percent of the revenue with the institutions. Maestas suggests that two primary types of multimedia rights models are used in intercollegiate sport: a guarantee model and a revenue-sharing model.

- *Guarantee model*—Somewhat risky for the multimedia partners (e.g., agencies selling the media rights), in this model the revenues achieved by the school on their own or with a previous agency are guaranteed upfront to the school. When that same revenue grows at a rate slower than what the agency can generate on their own, the school is able to keep the remaining revenue and achieve profits in later years.
- *Revenue-sharing model*—Rather than guaranteeing revenue to the school, the multimedia partner shares revenue percentages at different revenue thresholds,

such as sharing 50 percent of the first $3 million in revenue, 40 percent of the next $3 million, and then 35 percent of all revenue beyond a certain limit.

Radio Broadcasting

The first commercial radio broadcast in the United States took place in Pittsburgh, Pennsylvania, on station KDKA in 1920 (Lippman, 2007). That same year, station WWJ in Detroit began broadcasting the final scores of World Series baseball games through public radio (Harvey, n.d.). The first play-by-play sports radio broadcast occurred on August 5, 1921, in Pittsburgh when a KDKA staff member passed notes to a broadcaster to provide an in-depth overview of a Pittsburgh Pirates game at Forbes Field. The golden age of radio in the United States was from 1935 to 1950 (Leblebici et al., 1991). National networks promoted the stability of radio and controlled entry of new radio stations by taking over programming from advertising agencies. New innovations addressed two uncertainties in radio: the relationship between the networks and their affiliates, and the relationship between advertising agencies and the networks. Through the years, these networks and affiliates, along with the advertising agencies, have proved vitally important to sport. It is through regional affiliates that professional and intercollegiate sport teams have traditionally reached out to larger audiences with their broadcasts. For example, MLB's Baltimore Orioles (2020) Radio Network broadcasts all 162 regular season baseball games over 40 stations in six states and the District of Columbia. This radio network allows the Orioles the opportunity to expand their brand and advertising opportunities to a larger audience in multiple states. Traditionally, radio has been the medium that sports fan use to stay connected to their team while traveling. Mobile technologies and live streaming, however, are changing the way that fans connect with their team. The Oakland A's were the first team to switch permanently from radio to a full-time audio streaming platform.

Radio broadcasts of football, baseball, and boxing date back to the early 1900s (Harvey, n.d.). In 2020 more than 241 million people aged 12 years and over listened to terrestrial radio each week (Radio Advertising Bureau, 2020). **Terrestrial radio** is broadcast by a land-based station to a limited geographic region; therefore, the content is broadcast and received locally. Terrestrial radio (also called HD) simultaneously broadcasts both traditional analog and digital signals. HD is a digital extension of terrestrial broadcasting (Laukonnen, 2020). According to the FCC (2020), digital signals process sounds into patterns of numbers, or digits (i.e., digital radio), whereas analog processes sound into patterns of electrical signals resembling sound waves. Reception for digital radio is less likely to experience interference compared with traditional analog, but some interference can occur in areas that are far away from a station's transmitter. In contrast, **satellite radio** uses satellites to transmit content, covers an entire continent instead of a local geographic region, and requires a compatible head unit or a portable satellite tuner as well as a monthly subscription. Terrestrial radio, on the other hand, does not require a fee or monthly subscription (Laukonnen, 2020).

Listeners enjoy radio because they can listen to it while on the road, in the car, at the beach, and as they travel. Traditional terrestrial stations are now using online and podcast for radio broadcasting. Sport fans enjoy listening to radio because the broadcaster paints a picture in their mind of what is happening on the field, court, or ice. Every pass, dribble, and hit are described in detail. Great American broadcasters like the late Vin Scully of the Los Angeles Dodgers are iconic in sport because so many fans grew up hearing their voices. Radio is inexpensive and can be listened to without having your eyes open. Many people go to sleep listening to the radio. A good broadcaster can sear images into the mind of the listener. Fans remember where they were when listening to the broadcast of iconic events like the World Series, Kentucky Derby, and Super Bowl. Radio creates these lasting impressions on the mind, but more importantly it appeals to the emotions of the listener.

According to Petersen (2019), advertising in radio is generally seen as cost effective and allows a company to target specific audiences. It allows the advertiser to reach a local audience with their message. Because you cannot see a product, radio is not as effective for ads that need to show a visual. But the advantages of radio advertising are that it allows a person to multitask and can capture the attention of the audience while at work, in the car, or on a smartphone while exercising.

Broadcasting Return on Investment Metrics

Several metrics or forms of measurement are used in multimedia. Multimedia inventory has drastically changed over the years in terms of media forms that can be sold to advertisers. The term **rate card** has been used for many years to describe a document or brochure listing the various inventory for sale in newspapers, television, and radio, including pricing. Although the term is outdated, reference is still made to rate cards despite the fact it is often mysterious to the salespeople selling the inventory.

Advertisers place traditional advertisements with broadcasters normally as a 1-minute or 30-second spot, but the average television ad continues to decrease in duration. For example, the average ad in 2018 was 26 seconds in length, whereas it was 24 seconds in 2019 (MediaRadar Blog, 2020). Beyond placing traditional advertisements, brands also place what are called live reads. You have probably listened to a broadcast in which the broadcaster reads the advertisement. Whereas a traditional ad is produced and delivered by the brand owner, a **live read** occurs when the presenter or announcer talks about the product or service live and on air. Used primarily in radio, a live read offers three advantages (Phala, 2019):

- *Impact on the audience*—A live read can have a larger impact because the broadcaster has already developed trust and a bond with the audience.

- *Greater engagement*—When placing an ad with a certain demographic, ads on networks with a similar demographic can lead to greater engagement with this audience.

- *Greater investment*—A live read requires only an effective written message, making it more cost efficient than a traditional advertisement that has greater production costs.

The pricing of advertisements in the broadcasting industry is primarily based on ratings points or the number of viewers who watch a commercial (Bollapragada & Mallik, 2008). Throughout a broadcasting year, the ratings points are sold through two processes: (1) the upfront, which occurs before the broadcast season, and (2) the scatter, which occurs during the broadcast season. About 80 percent of the advertising inventory on an annual basis for a broadcast company is sold during the upfront, whereas cable networks sell around 50 percent in that period (Blattberg, 2015). The term **gross ratings points** is a measure of the size of an audience reached by a specific media vehicle or schedule (Peters, 2017). It is calculated by multiplying the target audience reached by an advertisement times the frequency percentage of the ad's exposure during the schedule. The calculation for a commercial that runs on the air 10 times and reaches 50 percent of the target audience is the following:

gross ratings points (500) = frequency (10 times) × percent reach (50 percent)

Perhaps the most important and most talked-about form of measurement is **ratings**, which is the percentage of households tuned into the medium (e.g., television or radio) at any given moment. Ratings have helped particularly in understanding patterns of use and expectation for both radio and television (Hurwitz, 1984). Ratings help to shed light on who was exposed to broadcasting content and advertising along with the percentage of a specific population that was exposed to content and ads by using various metrics such as reach, frequency, and averages (Nielsen, 2020). Normally expressed in percentages, **reach** measures the number of viewers that can view an ad during a given period. Another metric is **share**, which refers to the percentage of televisions tuned to a program among those in use. Shares and ratings are similar. The rating is the product of the number of homes that have a device (e.g., television or radio) and the number of homes with the device turned on, whereas the share is limited only to those households where a device such as a radio or television is turned on (Sarokin, 2017). If 120 million homes have a television, 50 million have their television turned on, and 10 million are watching a particular show, then the rating and share are calculated as follows:

rating (8.3 percent) = homes watching show (10 million) ÷ homes that have a device (120 million)

share (20 percent) = homes watching show (10 million) ÷ homes with device turned on (50 million)

Metrics like ratings and shares are best used as comparison tools. There is no universal good rating. For example, a rating of 5.1 may be good for one show and poor for another. Share gives you a good idea of how you are competing against other shows. You might have a low rating and a high share for a broadcast on a late Friday night because most people are asleep.

Advertisers who are looking to place ads targeting certain markets or certain demographic characteristics within their audiences often consider the more than 200 **designated market areas (DMAs)** in the United States. A DMA (also referred to as a media market) is a geographic area that represents a specific television market. DMAs comprise several counties in a metropolitan region (or rural area) that receives the same programming. DMAs are normally identified by the largest city in that region. Markets with larger populations and thus more viewers naturally have higher costs of advertising. For example, an ad in Los Angeles, California, will cost more than one in Hartford, Connecticut. DMAs are determined by the Nielsen Company, an organization that is recognized and commonly used for its measurement of broadcast audiences (Tainsky et al., 2014). Nielsen uses what they call a **panel**, which is a group of people they choose to represent a larger universe of people. A panel is like a sample. The population of viewers is normally included if they are viewing a particular program for at least 6 minutes within a given 15-minute period (Tainsky et al., 2014). Because Nielsen cannot retrieve information from everyone in a specific geographic area (e.g., a country or city), sophisticated sampling and statistical techniques are used to ensure that the panel chosen is representative of the larger population (Nielsen, 2020).

Set-top boxes or set meters are placed in the homes of those chosen to serve on the panel. When connected to a television, these boxes provide Nielsen with results that can be categorized by demographics such as race, gender, age, and income. Nielsen can then distribute this type of information to broadcast networks and advertisers with data on reach, percentages of viewers in specific demographic groups, weekly and monthly averages, and the estimated total number of viewers (Lane, n.d.). Although Nielsen started by measuring radio and then television, they have recently been implementing "total audience measurement" to provide measurement across multiple devices and platforms (Pallota, 2014). Nielsen has moved beyond collecting data from private residences to measure places like bars, dormitories, and other public areas with televisions. Nielsen uses various methods to collect information and measure audiences.

Digital Media

Sport organizations use digital media to reach across multiple channels to distribute content. For B2B companies, most of this content is consumed on desktops (83 percent), followed by smartphones (13 percent) and tablets (4 percent), whereas the majority of B2C business searches take place on smartphones (Quicksprout, 2018). Sport properties are increasingly developing their own media platforms and companies, like NBL TV and AFL Media, that bypass traditional news media to broadcast their own games and break their own news. As media continues to change, sport properties along with athletes can tell their stories directly to fans through their own social or digital channels, thus making it more difficult for traditional news journalists to get access to athletes or coaches (Harris, 2020).

Digital media has fundamentally changed the sport industry with social media, live tweeting, platforms like Facebook Live, and virtual teams. Virtual teams are made up of a group of people who interact with each other through electronic means and are often in different geographical locations. The 2017 International Cricket Council (ICC) Women's World Cup in England and Wales had 100 million global viewers, 100 million video views on ICC digital, 1 billion Facebook impressions, and a global reach of more than 180 million. The viewing hours in 2017 were almost 500 percent higher than for the previous World Cup, which occurred in 2013 (Ganekar, 2018). Digital is being embedded in every aspect of the sport business by transforming people, processes, and technology (Deloitte, 2020). The change can be witnessed in four fundamental ways.

- *Broadening content reach*—Sport properties have partnered with broadcasters to create new distribution platforms that provide fans with new experiences and capture viewership across multiple devices. Although live game attendance has declined, smartphones and tablets have provided a broader reach and more people are switching to live streaming. Over-the-top (OTT) platforms are emerging, and sport organizations are leveraging digital media to build direct connections with fans.

- *Driving the fan experience*—Sport fans want shareable experiences that can be amplified by technology, and sport organizations are growing stadium attendance using immersive technologies such as augmented and virtual reality. Finally, sport properties are increasing fan engagement by leveraging loyalty and customer relationship management (CRM) data to tailor experiences to individual fan preferences.

- *Engaging sponsors*—As fans increasingly interact with digital media, audio consumption, television viewership, and application use are increasing across the board. Increasingly, sport properties are personally engaging with fans through targeted advertisements, which are twice as effective as nontargeted ads. For example, millennials are more likely to share their data for coupons or promotions. These types of analytics help sport properties better understand what excites fans, thus providing sponsors with information about what types of ads and engagement models work for individual audiences. Digital tools also help sponsors understand fans so that they can tailor the timing, content, and delivery of messages.

- *Generating new revenues*—With analytics, sport properties can mine fan data to increase their understanding of fans' habits, preferences, and demographics. They use data to improve core business operations and build and solidify partner relationships. They have also monetized anonymous data; one-third of all companies are commercializing or sharing their data to create new revenue streams.

Key performance indicators (KPIs) are metrics (e.g., click-through rate, engagement rate, bounce rate) used to track the performance of social media campaigns (Sherman, 2019). KPIs are central to the well-being of the organization and indicate how well the organization's goals are being served (Sterne, 2010). More than 2.56 billion people use mobile social media globally, and 1 million new and active mobile social users are joining every day (Sherman, 2019). Popular for advertisements on online platforms like Facebook and Google, **cost per acquisition (CPA)** measures the cumulative expense of acquiring one paying customer on a specific marketing campaign or channel. Under this pricing model, the buyer of a digital advertisement pays for a consumer taking an action that leads to a conversion, such as a sale, click, a submitted form, or an app download. Often used when the end goal is sales, CPA can be calculated by dividing the total cost of the marketing campaign by the total number of new customers through the campaign (Social SEO, 2018).

Cost per impression (CPI) is the measurement of how many times an advertisement appears on a site regardless of whether the user actually sees or interacts with it. Impressions help build brand recognition (Brandi, 2020). Click-through rates and engagement rates are other important metrics. For social media campaigns, the **click-through rate** measures how many times an ad was clicked on by users. Click-through rates can be measured in the following way:

click-through rate = total number of clicks that the ad received ÷ number of times that the ad was shown (impressions)

Websites often use a method called **cost per click (CPC)** when billing advertising based on the number of times a visitor clicks on an advertisement. When placing online advertisements, many advertisers take into account the **cost per thousand (CPM)**. The *m* in CPM stands for *mille*, which is French for "thousand." So CPM is an advertising term that stands for cost per thousand. The cost is often denoted as CPM; therefore, when the price is listed as $6 CPM, the advertiser will pay $6 every time the ad is seen 1,000 times. The cost varies from industry to industry and between social media platforms. For example, in 2019 the average cost was $5.76 for Twitter, $6.05 for LinkedIn, $6.70 for Instagram, and $9.06 for Facebook. CPM refers to the number of impressions, or viewers, in thousands, regardless of whether the viewer clicks on the advertisement. The advertiser must understand the differences between CPC and CPM when making purchasing decisions. Advertisers who have the goal of bringing in traffic more than getting the word out are more likely to use CPC, whereas those interested simply in displaying their ad to a wide audience are more likely to use CPM (Faris, 2019).

Brands looking to generate awareness and ensure that every eyeball viewing a website is looking at their advertisement can do what is called a **website takeover**. To do this, the publisher of the website allows an advertiser to place creative content in every available ad spot in the layout, put content into the site background, or provide interactive content. A good example of a website takeover occurred in January 2015 when Adidas and Miami University, a longtime Nike school, announced their new 12-year contract by taking over ESPN's website so that everyone was aware of the new agreement.

Sports Illustrated Monetizes Subscriptions Using a Metered Paywall

On August 16, 1954, you could buy a *Sports Illustrated* (*SI*) magazine at a newsstand for 25 cents (Wulf, 1989). In February 2021 *SI* announced they would implement a metered paywall that charges readers to access content from its website for $7.99 per month billed monthly or $5.83 per month billed annually (Shultz, 2021). Most digital publishers have turned to subscription programs like metered paywalls to generate revenues. A metered paywall allows website visitors to access only a certain number of articles for free before having their access cut off. To read additional articles, the reader pays a subscription price. Often what happens is that casual readers start reading articles, get hooked, and then subscribe. Some readers, however, have found ways around metered paywalls through various widgets, private browsing apps, and extensions (Miles, 2019).

Posts on Facebook, Twitter, Instagram, and blogs have **engagement rates**, which measure how much users are interacting with a brand by considering factors like the number of comments on a post or the number of shares received. Engagement rates can be measured in several ways depending on social media goals—by views, impressions, or posts (Sehl, 2019). The best content normally has the highest engagement rates. Search engine marketing metrics can use Google Analytics to provide a **bounce rate**, which measures when a user lands on a website and views only one page. As users view and spend time on a site, the site moves higher up in search rankings.

Another common term used in website design is the term **above the fold**. Knowing where the term came from furthers our understanding of how it factors into website advertising. The term goes all the way back to the invention of the printing press and newspaper publishing (Brebion, 2018). Newspapers were printed on large sheets of paper, folded, and then placed on newsstands. Therefore, only the top half of the paper was visible to people walking by. The most important headlines were placed on top, and this principle was carried over into website design for digital content. But because websites do not have a fold per se, the concept **above the fold** refers to the area immediately visible at the top of the page that does not require a user to scroll down. Advertising at the top of the page that does not require scrolling obviously costs more than placements below the fold. Many websites are moving away from putting any content below the fold, which refers to the fact that a website user would never have to scroll on a page (Brebion, 2018).

Live Streaming of Sport

You have likely benefited from the streaming of a live sport event by watching the event on your mobile phone during a work break, wedding reception, or while out shopping. Almost every intercollegiate athletics program now streams contests of their athletics programs. This access is wonderful for parents, fans, or friends who cannot make it to the live event, and the cost is low. High school games are now commonly streamed in many states through the NFHS Network. Parents can even live stream various youth events using platforms like Facebook Live or YouTube Live streaming services. The benefit of streaming for most organizations is its affordability, but ease of use and convenience are also selling points. Streaming allows the sport fan to engage in dialogue and analysis on their mobile devices during live events. It also allows a team to interact directly with their fans. Equipment for streaming continues to become more affordable (Quinn, 2019). Kariyawasam and Tsai (2017) provide a succinct explanation of streaming:

> Streaming involves "any audio or video content delivered over a network based on Internet protocols" and is different from the traditional process of downloading. A download requires a computer to copy an entire file onto a hard disk before it can be accessed. Streaming, however,

does not require content to be saved as users view or listen to the digital work in real time. A couple of seconds of data is buffered at a time and subsequently deleted once played. (p. 268)

Platforms like Twitch offer live video streaming and video game livestreaming of popular sport games such as Madden, FIFA, and NBA2K. In 2019 revenue in the video streaming segment amounted to $24.7 billion (Shilina, 2019). Television is the most popular type of live video content accessed, and 70 percent of consumers who livestream do so at least once a day (IAB, 2018). Livestreaming continues to grow. The streaming market is projected to grow to $184.3 billion by 2027 and to expand by 20.4 percent from 2020 to 2027 because of increased demand for blockchain technology and **artificial intelligence (AI)** (Grand View Research, 2020). AI is a branch of computer science that is concerned with building smart machines capable of performing tasks that typically require some form of human intelligence. Anyone can become a broadcaster, run a streaming server, store data, or share bandwidth using **blockchain technology** (Shilina, 2019). Used for transactions made for cryptocurrencies, a blockchain is a digital record of transactions whereby individual records, called blocks, are linked together in a single list, called a chain.

As digital delivery evolves, several promising technologies will enhance quality and provide new and innovative ways to experience streaming. Examples include high dynamic range (HDR), virtual reality (VR), augmented reality (AR), and mixed reality (MR). HDR, the ability to capture detail in both bright and dark areas of an image, can be supported by a variety of streaming services such as Amazon Prime, Netflix, YouTube, and others (Green, 2020). Tokareva (2018) provides a good explanation of the differences between VR, AR, and MR. VR is a technology that immerses users in a completely virtual environment that is generated by a computer. To experience VR, you need to wear a headset that is usually connected to a computer or game console (e.g., PlayStation VR). Also in use are standalone devices (e.g., Google Cardboard) that work in combination with smartphones. Although VR is totally virtual, AR allows users to see and interact with the real world while digital content is added to it. In other words, virtual objects are overlaid on a real-world environment. Pokémon Go is a good example of AR. Anyone who owns a smartphone can download an AR app and see content on the screen using special AR headsets, such as Google Glass. Finally, with MR, virtual objects are not only overlaid on the real world but also can interact with it.

Pixellot and Automated Intelligence

Pixellot is an Israeli company that produces more events than any other sports broadcaster in the world. From soccer and basketball to hockey and handball, Pixellot produces approximately 100,000 hours of sport events every month using artificial intelligence (AI) and automation. Founded in 2014, Pixellot systems are installed in more than 6,500 venues around the world. Their cameras provide a panoramic broadcast of a sporting event that can be livestreamed with various angles, and additions like live stats are also available. Using AI, the broad-

Courtesy of Pixellot www.pixellot.tv

casts do not require human camera operators or production staff (Kidd, 2020). This type of technology has been utilized by amateur leagues and semiprofessional leagues in multiple countries. For example, in the United States, fans can watch high school games on the NFHS Network using Pixellot cameras. This provides sport leagues who traditionally were not able to provide game content with a new revenue stream that can be sold to viewers.

Leagues and teams across all sports continue to venture into the new world of using technologies like VR, AR, and MR. For example, in partnership with an Australian company called Unbnd, the NBA is offering mixed reality broadcasts presented to NBA-TV subscribers located in Australia and Singapore. Using mixed reality broadcasts, the VR will display live game statistics and interactive content overlaid on live NBA games. In essence, users will be immersed in a 360-degree virtual theater (Johnson, 2019). Innovative teams, such as the NHL's Washington Capitals, are also involved in offering these types of technologies to their fans. The Capitals have launched AR experiences such as the Tilt the Ice game and Ovi O's. The Tilt the Ice game, which allowed fans to download an app to scan barcodes on coasters in and around pubs located near Capital One Arena to play, was highly successful; each fan played the game on average nine times. The second AR experience involved Ovi O's, a cereal that features Capitals superstar Alex Ovechkin. The cereal is sold by regional grocery chain Giant Food. For this game, fans had to scan barcodes on the Ovi O's cereal boxes to unlock a mini hockey game in which users could shoot the cereal at targets with Ovechkin (Santana, 2019).

PRO Method Sales in the Digital Age

Students have numerous opportunities to pursue broadcasting and multimedia-related sales jobs in sport. One example would be a job selling multimedia rights with a sport marketing agency like Learfield IMG College, Wasserman Media, or Legends. For example, in 2020 Georgia Tech announced what they called a multifaceted partnership with Legends in which the agency sells multimedia rights, premium seating, ticketing, fundraising, corporate hospitality, data analytics, business intelligence, and ecommerce, and provides an analytics platform to help the Georgia Tech athletics department better understand their fans (Carp, 2020). Many college athletics departments outsource broadcasting and

multimedia rights because they do not have expertise in those areas. Minor League Baseball recently hired Octagon to help sell its media rights (Ourand, 2019). In-house opportunities are available with professional teams to be involved in selling broadcast and multimedia rights. For example, although the rights for broadcasting games in Minor League Baseball typically belong to a local radio station, the radio broadcaster for some teams sells radio ads. Of course, another option for students is to work in sport communication with various broadcasting networks (e.g., ESPN, Fox Sports), radio stations, and websites (e.g., Bleacher Report). The titles for these jobs may vary, including titles related to multimedia, sales, broadcasting, and communications.

Sales in sport broadcasting and multimedia is primarily focused on B2B, but it also involves an understanding of B2C. Many jobs focus on selling digital marketing, social media, and broadcasting commercials to local or national businesses. These types of jobs require the salesperson to be persuasive in their communications and have an excellent understanding of the PRO method, including prospecting for new business, asking good questions, listening, and matching multimedia benefits with business goals to make an offer that best meets the company's needs. But salespeople must understand the B2C component because sport properties seek to deliver content through social media, livestreaming, broadcasting, and other forms of multimedia. The salesperson must understand their customer's needs and wants. In the case of teams, that would be the fan base. Event properties must understand both active participants and spectators. Although most of the sales may come in the form of broadcast or digital or social media advertisements, some content is delivered directly to the consumer. For example, the National Federation of State High School Associations (NFHS) is headquartered in Indianapolis, Indiana. Both live and on demand, the NFHS streams high school sport contests by subscriptions to the end consumer, through their NFHS Network. Consumers may include parents, friends, local fans in the community, and others who are likely to buy a subscription to watch their local team play. The

NFHS Network became a handy way for high school sport fans to watch their favorite teams during the COVID-19 pandemic because most schools were not permitted to have spectators in attendance.

Broadcasting and multimedia sales requires an understanding of all five steps of the PRO method. The salesperson also needs to understand how technology can affect the sales process. In his book *Digital Selling: How to Use Social Media and the Web to Generate Leads and Sell More*, Grant Leboff (2017) explains how sales has changed over the years. Because people have access to a great deal of information because of technology, the salesperson who once possessed most of the knowledge about a certain product or service is less powerful because the consumer can access much of the same information. In many ways sales has changed, but Leboff claims that "good selling" has never changed because salespeople add value when they are able to influence the customer's criteria of purchase. Today the problem is that the salesperson often does not even engage the customer until after the potential buyer has already collected a lot of information about the product or service, most likely online through communication channels such as websites, videos, and social media platforms. Therefore, when the customer reaches the salesperson, they already have existing impressions of the product or service. In this case, the salesperson must challenge the customer's preconceived assumptions about the product or service to influence the criteria of purchase.

The percentage of U.S. businesses that used a social media presence for marketing was 86.2 percent in 2013, and this number increased to 91 percent by 2019 (Guttman, 2020). Undoubtedly, this number will continue to increase as technology penetrates further into the fabric of society. With this said, Leboff (2017) claims that technology becomes more imperative because the salesperson must have a presence earlier in the consumer's decision process where many of the assumptions of the product or service are formed. To gain this presence, the salesperson must engage the consumer online through blogs, websites, and social media platforms. Because of technology, the traditional sales process is also challenged. For example, consider the first two steps in our PRO method of prospecting for qualified customers and probing for information with open-ended questions. As noted by Leboff, the traditional sales funnel of trying to create awareness by the largest number of potential prospects is challenged. Because of the constant bombardment of information, prospective customers are less likely to respond to an unsolicited email, LinkedIn invitation, or phone call. Further, these types of requests come across as forceful or intrusive to most consumers. Therefore, selling in a digital world is less about prospecting the largest number of consumers and more about using what is called web scraping to help identify prospective consumers by looking at demographics, mining information on LinkedIn, and joining various social media networks. Sport organizations employ analysts to perform web scraping using what is called sport analytics to explore key data points related to marketing or business performance, consumer behavior, player performance, stadium capacity, and similar topics. These data help sport managers make important decisions such as pricing and personnel decisions.

Web scraping is a way for a salesperson to ensure that the leads being contacted are in fact interested in buying (Octoparse, n.d.). **Web scraping** (also called web data extraction or web harvesting) refers to a set of techniques used to get information from a website automatically instead of manually copying it (Vargiu & Urru, 2013). The goal is to extract certain kinds of information and aggregate it into new web pages. Web scrapers focus on transforming unstructured data and saving it into structured databases. Octoparse is just one company that provides a web scraping service. They suggest using the following three stages in web scraping:

1. *Sourcing*—The first part of lead generation is to identify what sources will be used, so the customer must be defined and located on the Internet. You must clarify who you are trying to reach out to and whether you want customers or influencers to help grow your business. One way to approach this stage is to

scrape demographic information from competitors' websites and then gather information from their public forums to learn what their customers are like and what they are talking about. An example would be for the MLB's New York Yankees to go through and source the website of the NHL's New York Rangers for prospective sponsors.

2. *Data extraction*—The process of retrieving unstructured data for further processing is data extraction. Normally, data can be retrieved in three ways: writing the code on your own, using scraping software, or hiring a third-party service to provide you with customized data. For example, a league, event property, or team could extract information (e.g., demographics, avidity) from a broadcast that would help them understand their viewers better. In turn, the information would help guide decision-making for the sport property as well as target future advertisers.

3. *Cleansing and structuring*—Cleansing refers to the process of detecting and correcting corrupt or inaccurate records; structuring is a process in which the data is reformatted and reorganized. Simply put, data is organized and formatted by replacing, modifying, or deleting some captured data. An example would be the Raiders, who moved from Oakland, California, to Las Vegas, Nevada, in 2020. The Raiders likely cleansed some of their records of company sponsors located in Oakland from their databases.

The third step in the PRO method is to provide solutions by matching product benefits with customer information. Leboff (2017) suggests that to keep prospective buyers engaged in both the top and middle of the sales funnel, the salesperson and company must provide them with value. To sell the benefits of any product or service, the prospective buyer must perceive its value, which describes what something is worth. When any prospective buyer considers whether to purchase a product or service, they go through a transactional process that considers what it is worth in exchange for the amount they are willing to pay. Leboff (2017) suggests, however, that creating value is not enough in our digital world. Rather,

salespeople must have a keen understanding of the content that is likely to attract prospective buyers. In a world where we are constantly bombarded with all sorts of information, Leboff claims that 90 percent of the information transmitted to the brain is visual. Therefore, the brain processes images much faster than text, and images cut through the noise and convey a lot of information quickly. Traditionally, print mediums like newspapers incorporated photos because editors understood that more than 90 percent of subscribers were likely to look at a photo but only 30 percent would read the text. What does this mean from a sales perspective in our digital world? Visuals are vitally important to the sales process. Visual content comes in numerous forms:

- *Blog headers*—Marketers care about the header because it gives visitors their first impression. When developing a blog header, consider what the header communicates about the purpose of the blog and what mood it sets to attract a certain target audience. Yahoo Sports, SB Nation, Bleacher Report, and the Athletic are sport blogs that use effective headers.

- *Cartoons*—A fun and engaging way to make a concept easier to understand, cartoons put people into the shoes of the character. Cartoon characters can help present the harsh reality of disturbing topics in a softer way. Cartoon characters can make your brand more recognizable and human (Pavlova, 2017). The Oregon Ducks mascot is modeled after Disney cartoon character Donald Duck.

- *Charts*—Graphic representations of data that may include project management tools (e.g., Gantt charts), timelines, representations that describe similarities and differences between concepts (e.g., Venn diagrams), maps, process diagrams, and other graphic displays of information. Sites like Vizzlo and Infogram can be used to create various types of charts.

- *Cinemagraph*—A GIF that contains subtle motion that plays in a short, never-ending loop, while the rest of the image remains still.

- *GIF*—Stands for graphical interchange format, a series of images or soundless video that loops continuously without anyone needing to press play. A GIF is a great way to create visually engaging content and is useful when you do not have enough time to record a video. Teams like Manchester City and Liverpool FC in the Premier League use GIFs to share a lot of their fun moments (Danjou, 2018).

- *Infographics*—A collection of imagery, charts, and minimal text that covers a complex topic but provides an easy-to-understand overview of the topic. Numerous online sites (e.g., Canva, Piktochart, and Venggage) allow a user to create an infographic. Infographics are used by professional and intercollegiate teams on Twitter. You can also find several sport-related infographics on Pinterest.

- *Meme*—An image, video, or piece of text that is copied, slightly altered, and spread rapidly by Internet users. Often, memes are humorous, and thus should be used with caution in business communications. Cut4 on Twitter is a good example of an account that has a lot of MLB memes.

- *Photos, images*—As noted earlier, readers are more likely to pay attention to a photo because most people look first at a photo before reading any text. Among the various places to find images are your own images, stock photos, public domain images (i.e., no copyright images), and creative commons images (free source of images). When using social media images, ask for permission. Before posting any image, ask yourself whether you have permission, if the photo might offend someone, whether the place where the photo was taken allows photography, and if anyone would be placed in danger if the photo is posted.

- *Presentations*—Help to tell a story about a product, service, or organization. Tools like Powerpoint, Prezi, Visme, Canva, and others help marketers create presentations.

- *Quote cards*—Allow the marketer to take a quote and make it part of a visual. Quote cards can be used to show a consistent branding image for an organization, product, service, or event.

- *Screenshots*—An image of data displayed on the screen of a computer or mobile device that can help communicate complex ideas. Screenshots capture exactly what a person is seeing on a screen and can add value to an article. Social media and search-optimized screenshots often go viral and are eagerly shared. Common tools include Snaggy and ShotPin.

Summary

Broadcasting plays an important part in the production of the sport product. Millions of people consume sport through various platforms. Traditional forms of viewing a sport event continue to change as younger people consume content in new forms of media. As fans abandon traditional satellite and cable television, major media networks have embraced OTT, which allows the consumer to view content directly over the web. Revenues for media rights in North American leagues is a multi-billion-dollar business, and sport properties spend a lot of time negotiating contracts with various networks. Streaming offers many sport properties a cost-effective avenue to deliver content to consumers all over the world.

Throughout the chapter, we discuss various metrics for measuring ROI. Although a sport management student may not plan to work in radio or television broadcasting, understanding the interactions between sport properties and media companies is important. Equally important is an understanding of the economic impacts that media rights play within the sport industry. Professional sport teams and intercollegiate athletics departments often outsource the sales of media rights to sport marketing agencies. If you work for one of these companies, you should understand terms like ratings, share, and reach, and KPIs like engagement rate, bounce rate, CPC, CPM, CPA, and others. Selling in the 21st century continues to change because of technological innovations. Using the PRO method, you need to understand how to engage customers who arrive to the salesperson having already formed numerous impressions about a product from searching online. Therefore, you will want to know how to engage these types of consumers using various digital media, including the use of visual content. Finally, technologies like HDR, VR, and AR will continue to affect the industry, and sport management professionals will need to learn how to leverage them.

APPLIED LEARNING ACTIVITIES

1. Look at a social media platform (e.g., Facebook, Twitter, Instagram, Snapchat) or digital marketing platform (e.g., YouTube) for your college or university athletics program. Provide three different examples of ways that the platforms are engaging sponsors and driving the fan experience.

2. List some digital visual content (e.g., blog headers, cartoons, charts, cinemagraphs, GIFs, infographics, memes, photos, images) that you have viewed within the last two weeks. Was the visual content part of the larger story? If so, go back and write a paragraph that talks about the larger story. Within the paragraph describe the platform where you found the visual content and how visual content incentivized you to engage with the organization posting it.

CASE STUDY

OAKLAND A'S BECOME FIRST FULL-TIME AUDIO STREAMING PLATFORM

The Oakland Athletics (A's) in Major League Baseball became the first team to switch permanently from traditional radio broadcasting to a full-time audio streaming platform (Bengel, 2020). Moving away from KTRB 860 AM, the team announced that A's Cast will become the new exclusive audio home of all A's content, including spring training, regular and postseason games, podcasts, and daily sports shows. All the games are available in the Bay Area and most of Northern California for free on TuneIn, a live global streaming and on-demand audio service. Tune-In also broadcasts all regular-season Spanish-language broadcasts. A's Cast was the most popular downloaded MLB team podcast in 2019. Claiming they have streamlined the process, team officials suggest that making A's Cast a one-click process makes it simple and easy for fans. Officials point out that this type of audio streaming is the way that sport is being pushed out to people. Fans outside the area continue to listen to games on the A's Radio Network, including KHTK AM 1140 in Sacramento. In addition, 11 other radio affiliates throughout Northern California broadcast the games, and fans can listen to A's Cast on-demand for free (Gallegos, 2020).

Discussion Questions

1. Based on reading the case, what do you believe is the most important reason that the A's have moved away from traditional radio broadcasting to A's Cast?

2. The case study reports that the A's will continue to broadcast games on the A's Radio Network. What are the advantages of broadcasting the games on radio and why?

Go to HK*Propel* to watch author videos, engage in sales scenarios, and find downloadable sales templates related to this chapter.

Mark Cunningham/MLB Photos via Getty Images

CHAPTER 5

Sponsorship Sales and Revenues

CHAPTER OBJECTIVES

After completing the chapter, you should be able to do the following:

- Define sponsorship and understand the importance of generating sponsorship revenues within the context of sport
- Demonstrate the broad and diverse nature of the sport industry
- Explain the sponsorship inventory available to sell in the sport industry
- Describe the various sponsorship platforms available in the sport industry
- Understand sponsorship activation and fulfillment
- Develop an effective sponsorship proposal
- Apply the PRO method to sponsorship sales and revenues

Figuring out why sponsorship sales are important to sport is not difficult. All you have to do is look at the statistics to understand the financial implications of sponsorship within the sport industry. Annual spending for sport advertising and sponsorship is around $60 billion. Television advertising accounts for $22 billion, sponsorship for $17 billion, and print media advertising, radio advertising, and online advertising for the remaining $21 billion (Miller & Washington, 2020). Verizon, Geico, Ford, AT&T Mobility, and Chevrolet were the top five companies in 2018, collectively spending more than $1.45 billion on sport advertising (Miller & Washington, 2018). Anheuser-Busch alone spends $299.7 million on sport, which makes up 66 percent of their total advertising spending. Sponsorships are vitally important to many sport organizations. In NASCAR, for example, 75 percent of team revenues derive from sponsorship. The number of Fortune 500 companies investing in NASCAR increased 29 percent from 2008 to 2018, and 140 Fortune 500 companies had sponsorship agreements throughout the sport in 2018 (Brown, 2018). Note that Anheuser-Busch did not spend money on Super Bowl advertising in 2021 to focus instead on COVID-19 relief efforts.

If you are a creative person, sponsorship sales can be one of the most empowering and enjoyable ways to generate revenue for your organization. Sport marketers spend numerous hours brainstorming ideas for sponsorships. The *Activate Annual 2018/2019* report provided an example of a creative sport sponsorship campaign that addressed an important problem by using technology. Nike's Juntas Imparables (which means "Together Unstoppable" in English) contest invited Mexican women to create teams of four and track their exercise on Nike's training app. By tracking their exercise, each member could do a different sport while logging minutes in the app to measure the team's combined efforts. Nike used a film to promote the contest, and each team was added to a WhatsApp chat group that connected them to a Nike ambassador coach. Although the contest clearly served the purpose of increasing the number of app downloads, it also served to address a more fundamental problem. The issue that Nike was addressing was that 47.8 percent of adult Latina women never engage in any leisure time physical activity. They do not receive encouragement and, in fact, are usually discouraged from being active in their leisure time.

Sport sponsorship has evolved over the years. Logos on jerseys is one example. The concept of jersey sponsorships was started in the 1950s by Peñarol, a soccer club in Uruguay (Allen, 2014). Most European leagues at that time opposed the idea and prohibited member teams from featuring names or logos other than their own on their shirts. The same was true of North American leagues. It was not until 2006 that the first major professional team in the United States had a jersey-front sponsorship when Major League Soccer's (MLS) Real Salt Lake announced a deal with XanGo, which produces nutritional supplement products. Shortly after MLS embraced jersey sponsorships, other leagues, such as the WNBA and the NBA's Developmental League (D-League), joined in. Jersey sponsorship has become commonplace with North American professional teams. The Phoenix Mercury were the first team in the WNBA to use the idea when they replaced their logo with that of their sponsor LifeLock, a company specializing in identity-theft protection.

Because sport has the amazing capacity to tap into human emotions, sponsorship is a highly effective tool for reaching people. Companies are becoming increasingly creative in how they share and place their brands in sport. Sponsorships are effective because the brand becomes subconsciously ingrained in a sport fan's brain in a way that both increases brand awareness and changes the perception of that specific product or brand (Koerber, 2019). The technological savvy and digital nature of our society now make sponsorship more appealing to the biggest and best brands. For example, brands may use sport events like the Olympics to promote inspiration, pride, and excellence, whereas Super Bowl ads are more likely to make consumers laugh (Waterhouse, 2017).

Our digital society allows brand marketers to use sponsorship to tell a story about their company and use influencer marketing to reach their targeted audience (Thieringer, 2018).

Adidas used their own platforms and app to reach their targeted audiences during the 2018 World Cup. **Influencer marketing** is a recent trend in sport sponsorship that uses not only celebrity endorsements but also influencers, people who would never be considered famous in an offline setting. Brands create collaborations with influencers because they have the power to affect purchasing decisions of others because of their authority, knowledge, position, or size of their social media following.

Sponsorship Defined

Sponsorship can be defined as the "acquisition of rights to affiliate or directly associate with a product, person, organization, team, league, or event for the purpose of deriving benefits related to that affiliation or association" (Mullin et al., 2014, p. 231). Sponsorship has also been defined as "an investment, in cash or in kind, in an activity, person or event, in return for access to exploitable commercial potential associated with the activity, person or event by the investor" (Quester & Thompson, 2001, p. 34). It entails a wide array of activities within a communication process that uses sport and entertainment to send messages to a targeted audience (Dees et al., 2021). Sponsorship is one of the elements of the promotion mix within sport marketing. **Marketing** consists of "all activities designed to meet the needs and wants of sport consumers through exchange processes" (Mullin et al., 2014, p.13). Promotion has to do with persuading defined user groups, which are the target markets for the sponsor. Within marketing, sponsorship is so prevalent in sport that sometimes the term *sponsorship* is used instead of *marketing*. Sponsorship can be regarded as both a method, or way, of carrying out the act of donating resources that is mutually beneficial to the sponsor (donor) and sponsee (recipient), and an activity, or way, to improve the attitude or influence purchasing behavior to enhance sponsor sales (Demir & Söderman, 2015). Another way of describing sponsorship is to say that a sponsor pays money to a property to communicate to fans who are attracted to that property (DeGaris et al., 2015).

Although sponsorship is a form of advertising, the two differ in several key ways (Shin et al., 2018):

- As an indirect and subtle marketing communication, sponsorships are generally perceived as more favorable compared with advertising.
- Advertising is more oriented to short-term objectives, such as sales, whereas sponsorships are more concerned with long-term benefits, such as awareness and image.
- Unlike advertising, sponsorships are assumed to benefit society with a good-will factor.

A **sponsor** is the party that pays or provides compensation to be officially associated with a specific property, whereas the **sponsee** is the property providing value by virtue of that association (Fullerton, 2007). Visa is an official sponsor of the Olympic Games and serves as the exclusive payment technology partner of the Olympic Games. In this case, Visa is the sponsor, and the Olympic Games is the sponsee. The term **partner** is used interchangeably at times with the term *sponsor*. Although the term *sponsor* involves payment, a partnership, although it may include payment, implies working toward a common goal or having common interests at heart (Lynde, 2007). A **sport property** refers to a league, team, event, venue, governing body, or association that sells sponsorship rights. For example, a sport property could be the National Basketball Association, New England Patriots, Kentucky Derby, Madison Square Garden, USA Lacrosse, or National Collegiate Athletic Association.

Our simple definitions of sponsorship do not adequately describe the complexity of understanding sponsorships in sport. What many refer to as a relationship between a sponsor and a sport property is in reality more of a "relationship between a portfolio of partnerships held by a brand and a roster of partnerships held by the sport property" (Cornwell, 2017, p. 172). When seeking to sell a sponsorship, representatives of the sport property seek to develop strong relationships with representatives of the potential sponsorship organization. Often this arrangement entails correspondence through email, phone calls, and letters. Initial phone calls are often intercepted by a **gatekeeper**, the person who answers the phone, directs phone calls, and usually protects decision makers from the constant barrage of phone calls from salespeople. The goal of the salesperson is to reach the **decision maker**, the person who has the ultimate authority to decide on a sponsorship purchase. Ultimately, the goal of the salesperson is to close the sale through developing a relationship with the person or persons making the decision.

Economics of Sponsorship in Sport

Sponsorship spending continues to increase on both a global basis and within North America. In 2018 total global sponsorship spending was over $65 billion, and total North American sponsorship spending was over $24 billion (IEG, January 16, 2018). In North America, sport accounted for $17.05 billion in 2018, up from $16.26 billion in 2017. Sponsors of the four major U.S. pro sport leagues spent an estimated $1.25 billion on the NFL, $892 million on MLB, $861 million on the NBA, and $505 million on the NHL (IEG, December 18, 2017). NFL sponsorships increased by 103 percent between 2006 and 2017, while MLB sponsorships increased by 76 percent, NBA sponsorships by 74 percent, and NHL sponsorships by 80 percent during the same time (Brown, 2017). Meanwhile, sponsorship spending within college athletics departments, bowl games, and related proper-

ties was estimated to total around $1.24 billion during the 2017-2018 season (IEG, March 19, 2018). Revenues by each league can be found in table 5.1.

The most popular channel for activating sponsorships is social media, and Facebook is the media platform most often used (95 percent of sponsors), followed by Twitter (80 percent of sponsors) and Instagram (66 percent of sponsors). Two of the most common forms of sponsorship evaluation are **return on investment (ROI)** and **return on objectives (ROO)**. ROI can be determined by taking the bottom-line profit attributed to a sponsorship and dividing this number by the total sponsorship investment (Maestas, 2009). ROI is an educated approximation of how much additional profit the company has earned based solely on the sponsorship. ROO uses metrics based on company objectives to measure the value of a sponsorship. Companies must clearly define their objectives for the sponsorship, including factors like sales, site visits, and margins. Although companies like MetLife prefer to use ROI during long sales cycles, an easier approach is to have specific measurable objectives such as whether the sponsorship drove a consumer to their website or whether a consumer prefers the brand because of the sponsorship (Greenberg, 2010).

As suggested, sponsorship has a large effect on the sport industry. Words cannot describe the devastating effect that COVID-19 had and may continue to have on the sport industry as it relates to sponsorship. Two Circles, a sport marketing agency, projected that sponsorship rights fees decreased by 37 percent from $461

TABLE 5.1 2019 Sponsorship Revenues of Teams by League

Dallas Cowboys	New York Yankees	Philadelphia Flyers	LA Galaxy
AT&T	Anheuser-Busch InBev	Chick Fil A	Barefoot
American Airlines	Bank of America	Comcast	Chevrolet
Bank of America	Canon Inc.	Dunkin Donuts	DoubleTree by Hilton
Ford	Delta Airlines	Kia	
Keurig Dr. Pepper	Hess Corp.	Toyota	
PepsiCo			
NFL sponsorship revenue: $1.47B	MLB sponsorship revenue: $994M	NHL sponsorship revenue: $559M	MLS sponsorship revenue: $78M

billion in 2019 to $28.9 billion in 2020 (Cutler, 2020). Although the sport industry was projected to generate $75.7 billion in 2020, it instead potentially lost a third of its value. Television ratings declined, 1.3 million jobs were potentially eliminated, and $28.6 million in earnings were projected to be lost (Drape et al., n.d.). Of course, these figures are just estimates, and it may take some time to understand the ramifications of the pandemic on the industry and sponsorship in particular. As Cornell (2021) suggests, costs to the sponsorship segment will not end after 2020, and among the continuing effects will be the delaying of contract renewals.

Types of Sponsorships

Sport properties can sell four primary types of sponsorships (Lynde, 2007). These include title sponsor, presenting sponsor, official status, and naming rights. These types of sponsorships are described in the following sections. People who sell sponsorship packages need to understand the differences and nuances between these four types of sponsorships.

Title Sponsor

An organization that contracts to be the **title sponsor** of an event provides money, goods, or services in exchange for the exclusive right to have their name appear prominently before the title of the event. A title sponsorship is also referred to as a name-as-title sponsorship. Research suggests that higher level sponsorships like this are likely to lead to greater returns for the sponsor because consumers more accurately recall the title name (Jensen & Cornwell, 2018). Most sport properties will ask the title sponsor to commit to spending money with the networks televising the event for commercials that air during the event. In 2019, Valspar extended their title sponsorship through 2025 of their PGA Tour event played annually on the Copperhead Course at Innisbrook Resort in Tampa, Florida. The most successful title sponsorships are those that preclude fans or attendees from thinking of the event without thinking about both the corporate name and the event. For example, fans rarely separate corporate names and event names for NASCAR's Coca-Cola 600 at Charlotte Motor Speedway or the McDonald's All-American High School Basketball Game. A less prominent example is the sponsorship of the South Atlantic League All-Star Game in 2019, hosted by the West Virginia Power, a single-A affiliate of the Seattle Mariners. The title sponsor for the game and all surrounding activities was Segra, a fiber bandwidth company.

Presenting Sponsor

Like a title sponsor, a presenting sponsor has the corporation's name in the title, but it is included after the name of the event. Thus, these types of sponsorship are also referred to as name-in-title sponsorships. Good examples include ESPN's College GameDay Built by The Home Depot, the Rose Bowl Game presented by Capital One, and the College Football Playoff National Championship Trophy presented by Dr. Pepper. Presenting sponsors are traditionally asked to commit minimum marketing rights and media spend commitments like those of title sponsors. They also receive benefits similar to those of title sponsors. Some companies use these name-in-title sponsorships (Jensen & Cornwell, 2018) to both recruit and retain customers. For example, in the banking industry, JPMorgan Chase created and launched Chase Freedom Weekends as part of their presenting sponsorship of Madison Square Garden (MSG). Current customers received a $5 gift card for use at an MSG concession or merchandise stand when they entered the facility at the Chase entrance (Jensen, 2017).

Official Status Sponsor

Official status is typically used by high-profile leagues such as the National Football League, Major League Baseball (MLB), the National Basketball Association (NBA), and the Olympics. These properties provide the sponsor with exclusivity within their product category. Sprite has been the official soft drink of the NBA since 1994. Pepsi is the official soft drink of the NFL. Visa is the exclusive payment technology partner and the only card accepted at the Olympic Games. The Holiday Inn Elmira is the Official Sponsor Hotel of the Elmira Enforcers, a professional ice hockey team that plays in the Federal

Prospects Hockey League (Elmira Enforcers, n.d.). Rawlings is the official baseball of MLB. An official product or service sponsorship is similar to a title sponsorship in several ways (Cornwell et al., 2004). First, official status sponsorships can be as expensive as title sponsorships. For example, Gatorade is paying $500 million for eight seasons to be the official sports beverage of the NFL. Second, these types of sponsorships must be leveraged or activated by collateral advertising and promotion for the value of the sponsorship to be fully realized. Lastly, official product sponsorships are like large-scale event sponsorships that offer national coverage, which is important for marketers seeking to have media exposure that parallels their national product distribution.

Naming-Rights Sponsor

Naming rights for various facilities are commonplace now in both sport and recreation. **Stadium naming rights** are defined as "a transaction in which money or consideration changes hands in order to secure the right to name a sports facility" (Thornburg, 2002, p. 2). In 2018 the Air Canada Centre in Toronto, Canada, was renamed Scotiabank Arena in a 20-year sponsorship agreement between Maple Leaf Sports & Entertainment and Scotiabank worth about C$800 million (Sports Business Journal, 2018). But naming-rights deals are common not only in professional sport but also in amateur sport, within both intercollegiate and interscholastic athletics. For example, in 2017 Kroger signed a 12-year deal with the University of Kentucky worth over $22 million and $1.85 million per year to name their football stadium. Likewise, SHI International Corporation signed a contract with Rutgers University in 2019 worth $7.25 million over 5 years for naming rights to their football stadium. Two lucrative naming-rights deals in high school sport are in the Dallas-Fort Worth area in Allen, Texas ($59.6 million Eagle Stadium), and McKinney, Texas ($69.9 million McKinney ISD Stadium).

Traditionally, most venues were named after an individual or a geographic location.

For example, the National Football League (NFL) team in Washington played their home games for many years in RFK Stadium, named in memory of U.S. Senator and presidential candidate Robert F. Kennedy. In 1953 Anheuser-Busch wanted to buy the naming rights for Sportsman's Park, home to MLB's St. Louis Cardinals, and rename it Budweiser Stadium. National League President Ford C. Frick did not allow the company to name the stadium after Budweiser beer, but he did allow Anheuser-Busch owner Augustus Busch to use his last name, and in 1954 the Cardinals opened Busch Stadium (Trex, 2008).

Since the start of the 21st century, naming rights has become a common practice for sport governing bodies. City governments, transportation authorities, hospitals, universities, environmental conservation groups, and other nongovernmental organizations are now selling the rights to name everything from convention centers and sport arenas to public parks (Burton, 2008). Naming-rights deals raise revenues without raising taxes, but the practice has generated some criticism. Some have suggested that naming-rights sponsorships commercialize urban public spaces and create urban namescapes that remain in a constant state of flux as one corporate sponsor's name replaces another when naming-rights contracts expire (Rose-Redwood et al., 2019). Fan backlash against commercialization is a possibility, which may manifest particularly from critics of amateur sport such as intercollegiate and interscholastic athletics (Eddy & Cork, 2016).

Sponsorship Assets

Sponsorship proposals outline various assets. These **sponsorship assets** are the benefits and rights that the sponsor negotiates with the sport property (Lynde, 2007). Most sport properties have a complete listing of every salable asset, and the sales representative must understand not only the breadth and scope of every item for sale but also the details of each. The cost of not understanding your assets is the potential for leaving money on the table (i.e., not making

B2B REVENUE GENERATION

Types of Sponsorship Asset Inventory

Table 5.2 lists some types of sponsorship assets and the inventory that a sponsee (team, league, or other sport property) might sell as part of that asset. These are described further in this chapter. This list is not all inclusive, and as a salesperson, you need to be familiar with the available inventory of your sport property.

TABLE 5.2 Examples of Sponsorship Assets and Inventory

Type of asset	Inventory for each category
Category exclusivity	Official product status
Couponing	Tickets, rosters, programs, other print materials
Digital or electronic	Blog, email, radio, mobile applications, online streaming, social media, television, website
Direct marketing and databases	Ticket mailers, demographic information
Event sponsorships	Game-day sponsors, hospitality, hole sponsors, in-event sponsorships, presenting sponsorship, title sponsorship
In-game sponsorship	On-field promotion, scoreboard contests, live interviews
Intellectual property	Logo, trademark, or other marks
Media	Radio, television, live streaming, rights fees
Pass-through rights	Media, marketing
Premium giveaways	Authentic jersey, ball, bam bam sticks, bobblehead, rally towels, trading cards
Print advertising	Magnet schedules, pocket schedules, rosters, scorecards, souvenir programs, tickets, posters, pocket schedules
Signage (digital or print)	Banners, scoreboards, LED, billboard, concourse, dasher board, dugout, end zone, on-deck circle, sideline, signage on jerseys and cars, video board
Special event marketing	Autographs, exhibits, half-time shows, and so on
Tickets, couponing, product sampling	Advertising and coupons on back of tickets, buyout ticket nights, buy-one-get-one free (BOGO) coupons, sampling kiosks

sales from lack of knowledge), simply not making the sale, or even worse, losing a sale to a competitor.

Category Exclusivity

Almost every sponsor would like to have and will ask for exclusivity, which means that their competitors cannot have an official sponsorship affiliation with the sport property. If you represent the sport property, you must be careful when negotiating exclusivity. By careful, what we mean is that granting an organization exclu-sivity can limit the ability to sell to other orga-nizations within the category. As an example, imagine that 25 different pizza restaurants do business in the area and that the sport property grants Domino's Pizza category exclusivity. By doing so, the sport property eliminates their ability to partner with and gain revenue from Papa John's, Pizza Hut, Little Caesars, and 21 other local pizza restaurants. In contrast, if you represent the sponsoring organization, you want to push for this asset. Normally, an official designation (e.g., the official baseball of MLB, official soft drink, official bank, official credit card) comes with category exclusivity. Because of the importance and demand for exclusivity, the property can demand significantly more money for this asset.

Couponing

Coupons can be incorporated into sport events in several ways. Coupons or sponsor advertisements can be found on the back of tickets, rosters, programs, and other types of print materials that are distributed to fans or participants. Many sport properties have moved away from offering coupon opportunities for sponsors on tickets or game programs for big events (e.g., a championship game) because fans are more likely to want to keep the item for nostalgic purposes. Sport properties also work with sponsors of an event and use them to assist with distributing tickets or coupons for admission to the event. The sponsor underwrites the cost to provide consumers with either free tickets or coupons for discounted admission to an event. For example, Kroger grocery stores may buy the rights to a night with a sport team and use their various retail outlets to distribute free tickets to their customers. Buy-one-get-one-free coupons are popular ways for companies to advertise their product. Sponsors will also be charged for the rights to sample their products with event attendees.

Digital or Electronic Sponsorships

Digital or electronic advertising and sponsorships deliver content through electronic or digital means. Examples of sponsorships here include advertising on social media pages such as Facebook, Twitter, Instagram, SnapChat, and YouTube channels. A survey by the Association of National Advertisers (2017) of marketers who spend money in sport revealed that social media and technology for sponsorship activations were identified as topics of keen interest. The five top reasons for using social media were to

1. generate awareness,
2. connect with customers during the event,
3. improve brand perception,
4. connect with consumers before the event, and
5. distribute content.

Content can also be delivered through mobile application using a phone. Other examples include advertising on blog posts and email mailings for upcoming events or through means of radio and television or online streaming. Few sport properties nowadays do not use their website to engage customers. In terms of the efficiency of marketing on the web, the sport industry has some benefits over other industries (Koronios et al., 2020). These benefits relate to the "stickiness" of sport sites in engaging a visitor on a website for a longer time. A website is considered **sticky** when a user visits the site repeatedly and spends more time browsing than the average user (Hsu and Liao, 2014). This activity is important because the longer a customer spends on the site, the more likely they are to make purchases and be exposed to ads, thus resulting in greater profitability (Hu et al., 2020).

Direct Marketing and Databases

For some sponsors, reaching fans with their message through mail or email is important. Direct mail allows sponsors to learn more about customers and then tailor specific messages to them. Sport properties use several ways to reach out to fans and learn more about them. Direct marketing mail can be sent out to current or prospective consumers (e.g., season ticket or plan information). When a fan purchases a ticket, information such as name, address, phone number, email, number of games they will attend, and other pertinent information is included. Credit card, address, and other billing information is also provided when a fan purchases merchandise. Some fans also provide information about themselves when they enter a contest or sign up for fan clubs. This kind of information tells the sport property more about their customers and provides an opportunity to create a robust database of information about their fans. This type of information is helpful in sharing messages about sponsorships.

Event Sponsorships

Events need numerous sponsors to help offset the costs of expenses. Therefore, event planners must stay in contact with potential sponsors. Sponsorships often vary based on the type of event being planned. In 2020 the London Marathon announced that plant-based margarine brand Flora had signed a four-year deal to sponsor the race. As part of the sponsorship agreement and activation, Flora agreed to donate UK£1,000 every week leading up to the race to one marathon participant who was fundraising for a smaller charity. Many events cover costs using either a title or presenting sponsor. A title sponsor is more likely to be the main partner for a team, whereas a **presenting sponsor** is often the key sponsor for an event (Tafà, 2017). Both title and presenting sponsorships offer the sponsors benefits such as the use of the team or event's name or image, prominent positioning of the sponsor's logo, increased brand exposure, access to attendee data, speaking opportunities at the event, discounted event tickets, appearing on the team or event's website or social media channels, and being involved with hospitality packages. Many event planners offer sponsors multiple tiers of sponsorship based on the sponsor's investment amount in the event. Examples of sponsorships include Red Bull Rampage, a free mountain biking event, and the Bank of America Chicago Marathon, an event that each fall attracts runners from all 50 states and over 100 countries.

In-Game Promotion

Promoting a sponsor during a game is a great way to get fans involved. Typically, breaks

B2B REVENUE GENERATION

In-Game Promotions

Table 5.3 shows some in-game promotions run by intercollegiate and professional sport properties. Sport marketers can create many more ideas for in-game promotions besides the four listed. A little imagination and creativity can create in-game promotions that can be a lot of fun for fans.

TABLE 5.3 Examples of In-Game Promotions

In-game promotion	Sport property	Description
In-N-Out Lucky Section of the Game	Texas State University (2020)	One lucky section of football fans is randomly selected and gets free burgers. Each fan receives a coupon good for any burger on the menu.
Apple Federal Credit Union T-Shirt Toss	George Mason University (2020)	Fans at the basketball game are asked to get on their feet as T-shirts are tossed into the stands.
Bermo	West Virginia Black Bears (Wolfe, 2018)	Similar to *The Price is Right* game Plinko, in Bermo a lucky fan is chosen to roll a bowling bowl through wooden pegs down a steep hill toward boxes at the bottom of the hill. Each box has a sponsor that awards prizes to the fans.
Neymar roll cam sponsored by Triad Foot & Ankle Center	Greensboro Grasshoppers	Fans at the Grasshoppers game are caught on camera as they pretend to be hurt like soccer star Neymar and roll on the ground.

occur during games when fans can be on the field, ice, or court. Baseball has a break between innings, and football, basketball, and hockey have breaks at halftime or after quarters or periods. An example of a good in-game promotion during a baseball game that can be sponsored is the dizzy bat race, in which two or more fans twirl around a bat until they are dizzy and then race to a finish line. Other types of in-game promotion include a contest on the scoreboard or a live interview with a fan. This promotion is always fun and is completed on the field in a relatively short time. These types of promotions encourage sport involvement and thus allow fans to progress through Funk and James' (2001) four stages of involvement from awareness of the sponsor to attraction, attachment, and then allegiance.

Intellectual Property

One of the primary reasons that sponsors want to attach themselves to a sport property is to gain access to intellectual property rights. The intellectual property rights consist of the right to use a logo, trademark, or other marks that can be granted only by the property. Registered trademarks are the property's legally owned logos or marketing slogans. Because many sport organizations are well-known brands, sponsors seek to associate themselves as sponsors with the marks of the International Olympic Committee, Major League Baseball, Manchester United, and the New York Yankees. For example, the sponsor may have access to use the Olympic rings marks or Major League Baseball's World Series logo.

Media

In the United States, total media ad spending is predicted to be $322.11 billion by 2024 (emarketer, 2020). Many sport properties include minimum media spend requirements as part of their sponsorship package (Lynde, 2007). These sport properties collect rights fees from media outlets such as television and radio networks for the rights to broadcast games and events. Sponsors place ads with these media companies at which time the networks refer to their

advertisers as sponsors of the sporting event or program. As an example, Chevrolet is an official sponsor of Major League Baseball, and Fox Sports may run a Chevrolet ad, referring to them as a sponsor of the game.

Pass-Through Rights

Pass-through rights are those that the rights holder is allowed to transfer to another company; in essence, they "pass through" the rights holder and give the sponsorship rights to a third party (Lynde, 2007). Pass-through rights often allow sponsors to use business partners in their activation efforts. Pass-through rights are important to consumer packaged goods companies, such as Pepsi and Frito-Lay brands, that do not have stores. Instead, they can partner with retailers such as Kroger that help bring their products to life. Another example is 7-Eleven, who received pass-through rights from the Dew Tour. The pass-through occurred when 7-Eleven received advertising spots on NBC and NBC Sports Network along with on-site activation at the three Dew Tour events (Mickle, 2013). Because they create more options and potential revenue for the sponsor, pass-through rights are normally in a sponsor's interest (Kte'pi, 2011), but this is not always true for the sport property because they lose some control over the situation. Specifics are laid out in the contract about who can or cannot have rights passed through to them.

Premium Giveaway Sponsorships

Perhaps you have been to an event where you received a T-shirt, bobblehead, trading card, or other item as you entered or left the sport venue. Many sport organizations offer premium items to incentivize customers to attend a game. Among the numerous and varied premium items that can be handed out at a game are jerseys, balls (e.g., football, baseball), player trading cards, bobbleheads, T-shirts, rally towels, bam bam sticks, and pom poms. These types of items are normally given away on nights when dynamic ticket prices are not in effect. **Dynamic ticketing** refers to the concept whereby the price of single-game tickets fluctuates based on a range of supply and demand market factors such as the opposing team and the night of the week. For example, on a night when the New York Yankees play the rival Boston Red Sox, incentivizing with a premium item is unnecessary because fans will come to the game regardless. Traditionally, weekend games involve less need to incentivize, but a game on a Monday night against an opponent that generates less fan interest may require incentives such as premium items.

Print Advertising

Print advertising consists of physically printed materials used by sport organizations. Although print advertising and sponsorship increasingly go online, some sport organizations and events continue with traditional forms of printed products that can be sponsored. Examples of printed products within sport include magnet schedules, pocket schedules, rosters, scorecards, souvenir programs, tickets, and posters. As organizations continue to focus on issues concerned with efficiency and sustainability, selling the value of print advertising becomes increasingly challenging. The key here is understanding that some consumers still prefer a tangible ticket or want to have a tangible item that serves a nostalgic memory of the event.

Signage

Signage depends on the sport venue and can include billboards, concourse, video board signage, dasher boards, scoreboard signage, concourse signage, banners, sideline and endzone signage, dugout signage, and on-deck circle signage. In addition, signage appears on jerseys and all over race cars. For sport marketers, signage is often a premium item that has a perishable inventory. For example, a minor league baseball field has only so many places on the outfield fence for signage, and the costliest signs are located in areas that have high eyeball traffic, such as the scoreboard. Therefore, most sport organizations are less likely to barter with organizations on signage inventory. Although signage technology has made it much easier for sponsors to communicate with fans,

sport properties must constantly balance their revenues from sponsorship with various public-relations factors (Steinbach, 2005). For example, in 2004 Major League Baseball proposed a $3.6 million deal with Columbia Pictures that called for *Spider-Man 2* movie logos to appear on the bases, the pitcher's mound, and on-deck circles in every MLB park for three days in June. When details of the deal became public, however, opposition to the idea was so great that the league-wide promotion was dead within days.

Special Event Marketing

Sport properties own the rights for many special events. Some of these special events are tied to a larger sport event. For example, during the Super Bowl, the National Football League runs the NFL Experience, which is often held in a convention center. The event includes autograph signings, ice carvings, exhibits, and other interactive exhibitions. These interactions allow sponsors time to interact with fans, demonstrate and sample their product, and provide more information about their services. Although the special event is often not the main event, events like the Super Bowl halftime show can come with tremendous cost. In 2020 the NFL Super Bowl between the San Francisco 49ers and the Kansas City Chiefs was the main event, but the 13-minute halftime show sponsored by PepsiCo and starring Jennifer Lopez and Shakira cost $13 million (Brown, 2020). In conjunction with the NFL, Roc Nation was the entertainment company that produced the highly complex show. The production required 2,000 to 3,000 people to produce, lots of lights and dancers, and special effects. Almost 500 people were needed to move the stage, which was wheeled on 38 separate carts, and the audio equipment took 108 people to move another 18 carts. Setup for the halftime show lasted 8 minutes, the actual show was 13 minutes long, and removing the stage took another 6 minutes. Needless to say, special events like the Super Bowl halftime show are a big part of the event and a critical part of the sales package for the NFL property.

Sponsor Identification

Often, the higher the cost of a sponsorship, the greater the number of rights and benefits the sponsor has access to for the purpose of attaching their name, logo, and marks. This is especially true for sponsors who own the naming rights to the event or venue. For example, the 2017 World Tennis Association (WTA) Hawaii Open included some of the following rights and benefits for the title sponsor:

- Exclusive naming rights, including being the exclusive title sponsor from 2017 through 2019 and tournament category exclusivity

- Marketing exposure, such as promotional exposure, host city campaign, local newspaper and television coverage, and signage

- On-site tournament benefits, such as player appearances, display booth, entertainment-like hospitality lounge, concert, and so on

- Media integration, including worldwide news service, interview backdrop, and award ceremony

- Souvenir program, including advertising pages and official welcome page

- Digital integration, including website, phone app, and media initiatives

Tickets and Hospitality

Tickets and access to hospitality with food and entertainment are highly sought-after commodities at many events. Rights holders like the NFL make it difficult for the public to obtain tickets to some events at the Super Bowl. Instead, the NFL offers access to these events to their sponsors. Corporate sponsors can reward their employees with tickets to these VIP events. For example, access to a private concert by Justin Timberlake during Super Bowl XLVII in 2013 between the San Francisco 49ers and Baltimore Ravens was limited to only 200 attendees. Because these private, exclusive events are difficult for the public to gain access to, sponsors feel special and cared for by the rights holder.

Sponsorship Platforms

Sport sponsorship can be leveraged on several platforms. These platforms are based on various stakeholder groups, including governing-body sponsorship, team sponsorship, athlete sponsorship and endorsement, media channel sponsorship, facility sponsorship, and event sponsorship. Information about each of these types of sponsorship is presented in the following sections.

Governing-Body Sponsorship

Governing bodies are sport organizations that have regulatory and sanctioning authority with wide-ranging responsibilities that may include updating and enforcing rules; settling disputes; coordinating and organizing individual events, championships, or leagues; and generally promoting the development of a particular sport (Hoehn, 2006). Examples of governing bodies include the International Olympic Committee (IOC), United States Olympic Committee (USOC), Fédération Internationale de Football Association (FIFA), National Collegiate Athletic Association (NCAA), National Association of Intercollegiate Athletics (NAIA), and the National Federation of State High School Associations (NFHS). Regardless of whether the governing body relates to a corporation, school, university, religious organization, charitable institution, nation state, voluntary association, nonprofit organization, or professional sport franchise, effective governance is vitally important (Hoye & Cuskelly, 2007).

Each of these governing bodies has a host of sponsorship partner organizations. The IOC has what is called the Olympic Partners (TOP) program that grants category-exclusive rights to the Summer, Winter, and Youth Olympic Games to a select group of global partners. Created in 1985, the program attracts well-known multinational companies from around the world. Coca-Cola, Toyota, and Visa are just a few organizations that are part of TOP (International Olympic Committee, 2020). Coca-Cola and Visa are also FIFA official sponsors. Corporate sponsors for the NFHS receive the rights to use their logo and category exclusivity when applicable as sponsors of inventory such as advertising schedules, exhibit shows, event marketing, education initiatives, and award programs (National Federation of State High School Associations, 2020).

Team Sponsorship

Although organizations may spend funds to sponsor a governing body such as the NCAA, they also sponsor specific teams that play under the authority of the governing body. For example, the Duke Blue Devils play in the NCAA in the Atlantic Coast Conference (ACC). In 2008 Nike signed a 10-year sponsorship agreement to supply all 26 of Duke University's athletics teams with uniforms, footwear, apparel, and equipment. In the contract, Nike agreed to pay cash compensation annually to the Duke Department of Athletics, to fund local charities of Duke's choice, and to provide an opportunity for one Duke student-athlete to complete a paid internship at Nike's headquarters in Beaverton, Oregon, each year (Duke Sports Information, 2008). During the 2019-2020 season, Chevrolet was a shirt sponsor of the Manchester United team in the Premier League. Other shirt sponsors included Emirates Airline for the Arsenal team and Yokohama Tyres for the Chelsea team. Although the sponsorship money for professional sport teams is certainly more lucrative, sponsorship is also quite common in youth sport. For example, many youth league teams in various sports contact local business organizations for sponsorship to help pay expenses related to uniforms, equipment, travel, and food.

Athlete Sponsorship and Endorsement

Although the terms *sponsorship* and *endorsement* may sometimes be used interchangeably, the two are somewhat different. A sponsorship is used by a company to reach a target audience, whereas an endorsement is more personal and allows an athlete to talk to consumers. An **athlete endorsement** is defined as "an agreement between an individual who enjoys public recognition (an athlete) and an entity (e.g., a brand) to use the celebrity for the purpose of promoting the entity" (Bergkvist and Zhou, 2016, p. 644). Athletes can be sponsored, and they can also endorse a product. Many athletes who are sponsored compete in Olympic sports. For example, snowboarder Shaun White landed a sponsorship with snowboard manufacturer Burton at the age of seven. Some athletes have large endorsement deals that provide them greater income than their annual playing contract. In 2013 Steph Curry signed a shoe contract with Under Armour through 2024 worth $42 million, which exceeded his $34.9 million playing contract. Christiano Ronaldo's $1 billion lifetime contract made him the richest of all Nike athletes in the world.

Media-Channel Sponsorship

Sponsorship in this category includes numerous examples, including connection with local television, radio, newspaper, or other media outlets. A media sponsor such as a television station may present an opportunity to provide ads, public service announcements, interviews, or public appearances related to an event. Media sponsorship may also entail social media, such as Twitter, Facebook, Instagram, Snapchat, and others. Almost four billion people around the world use social media, suggesting why it is a critical component in sport marketing (Enoch, 2020). Enoch describes the following trends in social media sports marketing.

Livestreaming

Fans watch on platforms like YouTube TV, Amazon Prime, and Hulu. Sport organizations partner with social media platforms like Facebook and Twitter to broadcast real-time sport content. One of the advantages to sport properties when using livestreaming is the relatively low cost of using these platforms. A common form of livestreaming sponsorship occurs before the start of the sport event when the user is required to view a commercial.

Live Tweeting

Twitter is now used, especially for big sporting events, to keep fans updated on games in real time. Teams and broadcasters use the concept of live tweeting to keep their audience engaged. Fans can follow the game by receiving Twitter notifications on their computer or mobile device. Sponsors can be incorporated into live tweets using a branded hashtag. For example, live tweets of the Rose Bowl game may include a hashtag such as #CapitalOneRoseBowl.

Sponsorship Activation and Fulfillment

Earlier in the chapter, the concept of sponsorship was introduced, including the acquisition of rights, affiliation with an entity, investment in cash or in kind—all for access to exploitable commercial potential. In the end, the goal of sponsorship is to achieve specific business objectives, but the mere signing of the sponsorship deal does not help to achieve the objectives. In large-scale partnerships between the sponsor and the rights holders, a large sum of money can be spent on leveraging the contractual relationship. **Leveraging** is defined as "the investment in communicating about and through the sponsorship that is in excess of the sponsorship deal" (Cornwell, 2017, p. 173). During the 2018 Olympic Games in Pyeong-Chang, Intel leveraged the Games with their drone show during the opening ceremonies, which provided the company with global brand awareness (Hookit, 2018). Resources need to be allocated to communicate with the target audience about the sponsorship and its relevance to the target market (Lynde, 2007). Therefore, the question often asked within sport marketing is how a sport organization can connect their fans with particular brands. Here, sponsorship has been replaced by **sponsorship activation**, which has been defined as "communications that promote the engagement, involvement, or participation of the sponsorship audience with the sponsor" (Weeks et al., 2008).

Activation, defined by IEG (2017, p. 132) as "the marketing activities a company conducts to promote its sponsorship," is the money spent over and above the rights fee paid to the sponsored property. Deriving from sponsorship marketing, activation can also be defined as an operational method of sponsorship implementation in events organized with the objective of connecting fans (or the direct audience) to sponsors' brands (Chanavat et al., n.d.). Activation is a form of leveraging that is engagement oriented (Cornwell, 2017). This idea suggests that the objective of connecting club fans, events, or athletes to sponsor brands is important and that activation is integrated into programs designed by advertisers to develop an interaction with those who are exposed to sport competitions (Chanavat et al., n.d.). In 2020 Subway restaurants signed a long-term deal with the NFL as the quick-service restaurant sponsor after McDonald's exited. To create interactions, the activation plan for Subway included in-store promotions and advertising with NFL on-air talent. More information about the activation can be found in the B2C sidebar.

The benefits of sponsorship must be activated into an effective sponsorship program, which can be leveraged to achieve the desired marketing and business outcomes for the orga-

---

B2C REVENUE GENERATION

Subway Sponsorship Agreement and Activation with the NFL

In July 2020 Subway Restaurants signed as the exclusive official sandwich sponsor of the National Football League as part of a multiyear sponsorship agreement. By doing so, Subway has exclusive marketing rights and opportunities for activation at various NFL events. Part of the sponsorship agreement is for Subway to sponsor NFL Flag and NFL Play 60 along with television commercials with Bill Belichick, J.J. and T.J. Watt, and Deion Sanders. As part of the promotional campaign, digital, print, out-of-home, and social media marketing was included. The activation for consumers included "Buy 2 Footlongs, Get 1 Free" at participating Subway restaurants.

nization (DeGaris, n.d.). The communications within activation may include advertising, sales promotions, public relations (DeGaris et al., 2009), and other forms of brand marketing that supplement a sponsorship (Olejniczak & Aicher, 2012). An activation plan includes several important steps. Before activating a sponsorship, a corporation must (1) spend above and beyond the cost of the sponsorship to maximize the value of the investment; and (2) know and understand the idea for the sponsorship plan before finalizing negotiation (Lynde, 2007).

Developing the Activation Plan

To develop the activation plan, Lynde (2007) suggests the following steps should be implemented:

- Define quantifiable objectives and measurement methods
- Develop ideas
- Test ideas with the target audience
- Implement the sponsorship activation plan
- Measure the results of the plan

Define Quantifiable Objectives and Measurement Methods

The company's sponsorship objectives should trickle down from company-wide objectives regardless of whether the objective is to generate sales, build the brand or image, or enhance awareness. Most important, the objectives must be clear before beginning the activation plan. Without clearly stated objectives, measuring the success of the sponsorship will be next to impossible. Several questions should always be asked regarding sponsorship objectives:

- Are the objectives quantifiable with a numeric goal?
- Did we include measurement methods and benchmarks in advance?
- Are senior executives on board with the objectives and the way they will be measured?

Develop Ideas

Ideas for sponsorships usually start with brainstorming. The following information should be collected and understood before starting: (1) take an inventory of the company's sponsorship assets, (2) gain some insights into the sport property and its fans or customers, and (3) determine the company's objectives for the sponsorship (Lynde, 2007). As an example, the Hawaii Tourism Authority (HTA) has been the title sponsor of the WTA Hawaii Open, mentioned earlier. An inventory of some of the assets identified by the HTA includes category exclusivity, appearances with a defined number of tennis players, access to a defined number of tickets, signage with the HTA name on the court, a defined number of HTA radio ads, and television coverage with HTA ads.

Peter Larsen/Getty Images for Dr Pepper

Sponsorship can take on many forms, and a solid activation plan can be developed by brainstorming ideas and testing them with the target audience.

Some insights about the sport property may include that the event is inclusive for the local community and attracts fans from all over the world. Finally, an objective for the event was to attract a defined number of fans from around the world who can appreciate a sport event and the incredible setting and culture.

Test Ideas With the Target Audience

A prospective sponsor can test some of the ideas with their target that were generated in the earlier step. The testing of these ideas may come in the form of focus groups or interviews of people in the target audience. It could also include mailing or emailing a survey to the targeted audience or making phone calls. After brainstorming ideas in the earlier step, now is the time to have members of the target audience rank the best ideas. If the objective for the HTA was to attract visitors from around the world for an event, they could have chosen any of several events in Hawaii to sponsor, such as the Honolulu Marathon, Maui Marathon and Half Marathon, Hawaiian International Billfish Tournament, or the Queen Liliuokalani Long Distance Canoe Races. The HTA could conduct a focus group with current visitors in Hawaii to ask them which of these events they would be most likely to attend.

Implement the Sponsorship Activation Plan

After receiving feedback from the target audience, the next step is to implement the activation plan (Lynde, 2007). As the plan is implemented, representatives of the sport property must be aware of all the deliverable assets. In addition, the sponsor, especially if it is a large corporation, must inform and educate all departments and functional areas about the sponsorship and their acquired assets so that they can best leverage the sponsorship.

Measure the Results of the Activation Plan

Every corporation measures their activation plan differently. The results of each part of the activation must be quantified and then com-pared with the objectives stated earlier. Based on measuring these results, the corporation can tell what worked best and what did not work. This type of information can be used to make informed future decisions. Representatives of the sport property need to understand the objectives of the sponsor and be in communication about what worked well and what did not. Without constant communication, the sponsor may simply pull away from the sponsorship because they do not think that representatives of the sport property care about helping them achieve their objectives.

Fulfillment

"The implementation, or fulfillment, as it is often called in practice, of a sponsorship involves three main activities: activation, evaluation and servicing" (O'Reilly & Huybers, 2015, p. 155). Whereas activation is the investment of additional resources to maximize the impact of the sponsorship (O'Reilly & Huybers, 2015), fulfillment is the delivery of benefits promised to the sponsor in the contract (IEG, 2017). Fulfillment is used to describe an activation plan of a sport property honoring contractually obligated components of a sponsorship agreement (Irwin et al., 2008). With this said, fulfillment ranges from collecting print inventory for a program ad to posting banners or writing the sponsor into a public address announcement. Fulfillment staffing and reporting is essential (Irwin et al., 2008). Staff members assigned to fulfillment duties are responsible for fulfilling the sponsorship agreement and should be able to assist sponsors with the execution and leveraging of ideas.

Fulfillment staff is also responsible for reporting. These proof-of-performance reports often include several components. This activity involves measuring the impacts of a sponsorship against previously set benchmarks. It should start with an introduction and executive summary that includes basic facts about the property and provides an overview to the reader. The report should include demographic, psychographic, and behavior information about attendees. Visuals should document on-site signage, programs, and activities that occurred during the sponsorship. Off-site exposure, such as newspaper clips or television publicity, should be reported. Advertising and editorial media exposure, such as property broadcast ratings, are also important to report. Finally, sponsor product samples provided to event attendees along with other sport property tracked promotional results may be included (Irwin et al., 2008).

Sponsorship Programs and Proposals

Sponsors develop programs that seek to leverage their target markets so that the organization achieves their objectives and return on investment. The process of developing a sponsorship program starts with developing objectives, followed by budgeting, acquisition, and finally implementation and evaluation (Miller, 2020).

Stage 1: Sponsorship Objectives

The first stage of the sponsorship program process is the development of sponsorship objectives. **Sponsorship objectives** should be linked to a broader promotional planning process and objectives, which will help to achieve marketing goals that derive from objectives of the organization (Miller, 2020). Objectives can be both direct and indirect. **Direct sponsorship objectives** focus on increasing sales for the sponsor and have a short-term effect on the behavior of the consumer. In contrast, those objectives that ultimately lead to the goal of enhancing sales are **indirect sponsorship objectives**, such as reaching new target markets, generating awareness, handling competitive threats, improving image, and building relationships.

A sponsor can achieve indirect objectives in several ways, but these objectives are sometimes more difficult to measure or see. For example, sport events provide a natural platform to reach out to new markets that target or reach consumers with similar activities, interests, and opinions (Miller, 2020). Sponsors can also seek to raise awareness of their products, services, product lines, or corporate name. In some cases, corporations sponsor sport events because of the competition. Consider, for example, the number of soft drink and beer companies that sponsor sport events. Exclusive sponsorships are prevalent with soft drink companies; Coca-Cola and Pepsi often compete to have their product in a certain venue or event. With ballparks empty because of COVID-19, Major League Baseball sought to leverage its partnership with sports betting as one of the few sources of incremental revenue. To build exposure and their image, the Detroit Tigers developed a sportsbook sponsorship by signing PointsBet (King, 2020). The concept of building image works as a strategy for both the sponsoring organization and the sport entity, but the sponsoring organization in particular wants to associate itself and its brands with the positive images generated by the unique personality of the sporting event. Finally, as you have seen as a consistent theme throughout this text, building relationships is a vitally important indirect objective of sponsorship. **Relationship marketing** is a term often used to describe how sponsors build long-term relationships with customers.

Stage 2: Budgeting and Sponsorship Programs

The second stage for developing a sponsorship program is to budget for it. Sponsors use several strategies for budgeting, including competitive parity, arbitrary allocation, percentage of sales, and the objective and task method. To achieve a decent position as compared with competitors in the market, **competitive parity** is a top-down strategy whereby a company sets a budget of marketing activities at par with their competitors or the industry average. **Arbitrary allocation** is a top-down approach whereby the budget is set solely based on what decision makers believe is necessary. Another top-down approach to budgeting is **percentage of sales**, whereby decision makers determine advertising and promotion budgets based on product sales. The amount is determined in one of two ways. The first method is simply to take a percentage of sales dollars. The second method is to assign a fixed amount of the unit product cost to promotion and multiply this amount by the number of units sold. The final strategy for determining the allocation for sponsorships is the **objective and task method**, a bottom-up approach to budgeting in which funds are allocated based on sponsorship objectives.

Stage 3: Sponsorship Acquisition

The third stage in developing a sponsorship program is sponsorship acquisition, a reactive process in which organizations receive a multitude of sponsorship possibilities from sport entities looking to secure sponsors. During this time, potential sponsors receive proposals from sport properties that may include information such as (1) fan attendance and demographic profile of fans at the event, (2) cost or cost per number of people reached, (3) length of contract, (4) media coverage, (5) value-added promotions, and (6) sponsorship benefits (Miller, 2020). Arthur and colleagues (1997) developed a model that describes the decision-making processes undertaken by corporations to evaluate sponsorship proposals submitted by sport properties. The model suggests that sponsors receive proposals from sport properties (stage 1, sponsorship acquisition); screen the proposals to discard undesirable ones or use an outside agency to screen (stage 2, composition of the buying center); make a decision to purchase, which is influenced by both rational and emotional factors (stage 3, the purchase decision); and finally select a sport property for implementation (stage 4, selection of the preferred sport sponsorship party).

Stage 4: Implementation and Evaluation

The final stage is implementation and evaluation (Miller, 2020). This stage occurs after the sponsorship decision is finalized. The actual sponsorship must be implemented and eventually evaluated for effectiveness. Unfortunately, many organizations spend considerable money on sponsorships but do not effectively evaluate the sponsorship to ensure that objectives were met. Some key questions to ask during the evaluation process are the following:

1. Did the sponsorship achieve the objectives set for it?
2. Did the sponsorship enhance the image of the sponsoring organization?
3. Did the sponsorship produce a return on investment?

An organization that works with corporations by using the power of sponsorship to enhance their brands and grow their business should use image enhancement and revenue generation to measure sponsorship. Measurement of whether a corporation's image has been enhanced by the sponsorship can be accomplished in the following ways (Charge, n.d.):

- *Exposure of property*—exposure that a corporation received as a result of being a sponsor of the property, including television viewership and event attendance data
- *Brand impact measures*—change in brand awareness, opinion, or affinity
- *Differentiation with competitors*—differentiation of products and services from competitors
- *Consumer voice*—evaluation of comments from consumers
- *Employee engagement*—engagement of the sponsoring organization's employees with the sponsorship

Likewise, sponsors can evaluate the effectiveness of a sponsorship by measuring revenue generation, although direct measurement of revenue is often difficult. Leads, opt-ins, and conversions are ways to evaluate revenue generation (Charge, n.d.). Sponsors may generate consumer leads through promotions such as experiential displays on-site or sweepstakes. They may also generate B2B leads that can be tracked through activities such as invitations to hospitality events. Because of the sponsorship, consumers may opt into a sponsor's email marketing list that can subsequently be converted to sales. Conversion refers to the time needed to convert a prospect into a sale.

Writing the Sponsorship Proposal

The actual writing of the sponsorship proposal is important for a sport property during the process of selling a sponsorship. The proposal should describe how the sponsor can leverage the sport property's event, program, initiative, or campaign and drive their business goals (Bower, 2019). The salesperson must get the proposal into the hands of the decision maker. Often, salespeople meet with lower-level representatives (e.g., a brand manager) who do not have final authority to make the sponsorship purchase. Therefore, the proposal should be designed to help these lower-level managers sell the sponsorship internally (Skildum-Reid & Grey, 2014). Although there is no standardized way to write a sponsorship proposal, several important components are often included, such as an executive summary; introduction or overview; information about the sport property; a description of the event, program, or initiative and the targeted market; benefits provided to the sponsor; leveraging opportunities for the sponsor; and terms of the agreement. The proposal should always focus on the goals of the prospective sponsor, the benefits of the proposal, and the way that it creates value and meets sponsor goals.

Many sport properties develop **boilerplate proposals**, which are templates that refer to standardized documents and include general information about the property. Using boilerplate proposals saves time when drafting the proposal, but the key components unique to each prospective sponsor must be revised and changed to meet the needs of the prospect. Proposals that come across as boilerplate are not likely to be considered for funding. When writing the proposal, keep in mind that decision-makers are busy and will not take a lot of time to read it. Most proposals will need at least 7 to 12 pages to give the prospect enough information, but they should not be so lengthy and complex that they will not be read.

Many companies employ an in-house group to evaluate proposals and select those with the most merit or that meet the criteria set by the organization. Proposals that are poorly written or do not meet the objectives of the organization are eliminated from consideration (Fullerton, 2007). Making it more difficult is the fact that many companies receive hundreds or even thousands of proposals. Statistics suggest that only 10 percent of proposals are given serious consideration and less than 1 percent receive funding. Fullerton (2007) suggests two key takeaways. First, companies with many sponsorship opportunities will only select proposals with events, initiatives, or programs that meet their needs. Second, the 1 percent that do receive funding are normally selected not because of the proposal but because of direct communications between the salesperson and the prospect.

Executive Summary

Some proposals have the executive summary at the beginning of the proposal, and others have it at the end (Fullerton, 2007). We recommend putting it at the beginning of the proposal because decision makers are more likely to read that section. The executive summary should be limited to three to four paragraphs and be no longer than one page. Often, writing this section is easier after completing all other parts of the proposal. The most important parts of the proposal are then simply copied, revised, and pasted into the executive summary.

Sport Property

This section should include information about the sport property such as the mission, vision, activities, achievements, and other relevant information. It should also address how the sport property event, initiative, or program aligns with the mission and vision of the organization.

Sponsorship Inventory Components (What Is Being Sold)

Of course, the proposal must include information about what is being proposed (i.e., inventory) for the prospective sponsor to fund.

This inventory may take many forms. Detailed information should be included about the event, program, or initiative, such as objectives, date, time, location, timeline of activities, the target market, and the marketing, media, and public relations that will reach the target market.

Sponsor Benefits

This section should include a comprehensive list of all the benefits to the sponsor. These benefits may include key sponsorship assets such as category exclusivity, direct marketing and databases, special event marketing, in-game promotion, intellectual property, media, pass-through rights, sponsor identification, tickets and hospitality, and venue signage. This section should also highlight how these benefits meet the goals of the prospective sponsor and how the sponsor can leverage the relationship with the sport property. Ultimately, this section

should demonstrate the value of the sponsorship opportunity and the potential it has to produce an ROI for the prospect.

Terms of the Agreement

Sales should always focus on meeting the needs and objectives of the prospect. Price should not be a major topic of discussion because most prospects will agree to it when they are convinced that the item being sold aligns with their business objectives. At some point, however, the cost of the sponsorship must be discussed, and it is in this section where financial implications are disclosed. Therefore, this section includes the sponsorship fee, terms and termination of the agreement, right of renewal, trademark information, cancellation, and other legal implications of the prospective agreement. The amount of legal information contained in this section varies between sport properties. Larger sport properties may have

People magazine's in-game contest at a Philadelphia Phillies game.

more detailed legal language in comparison with smaller ones. Some properties use the proposal as a binding contract and thus have more legal language. Most proposals, however, are simply a suggested idea or recommendation to meet the sponsor's goals. In this case, the property is simply trying to sell the sponsor on the idea and will send a more formal contract to the prospect for signature after a purchase decision has been made.

Applying the PRO Method to Sponsorship Sales

Sponsorship sales involves all the steps outlined in our PRO method described in chapter 2. The application of each of these steps is important to success in sponsorship sales. We discuss each step of the PRO method and its application to sponsorship sales in the following sections.

Step 1: PROspecting for Qualified Sponsors

Many sport properties offer extensive training that covers prospecting, step 1 of the PRO method. Younger salespeople are often involved in cold-calling and must prospect for qualified customers, whereas salespeople established with the sport property have long-standing sponsors up for renewal. Methods for prospecting for new corporate sponsors vary from one sport property to another. Some properties distribute new leads equally between sales reps, some use a lottery system to distribute leads, and some find other creative ways to distribute leads. Prospect leads may derive from data mined from the sport property's database that lists organizations that booked an event, purchased tickets, ran an advertisement, or spent money with them in another way. Typically, these types of prospect leads are generally considered **qualified leads** because the prospect has shown some interest or had contact with the sport property by attending a game or running an advertisement. Referrals from a current sponsor may also be considered a qualified lead. A qualified

lead becomes a **hot lead** when the prospect has high interest in purchasing the product and simply needs to be contacted. Other forms of lead prospecting, such as Internet searches, LinkedIn searches, and searches in printed publications, are less likely to lead to closing a sponsorship sale.

Step 2: PRObing and Asking Prospective Sponsors Open-Ended Questions

As we have noted, many corporations receive numerous proposals for sponsorship funding. Often, the challenge for the sport property salesperson is to get through the gatekeepers to talk to decision-makers. Getting to the final decision-makers entails some probing and asking numerous open-ended questions along the way as outlined in step 2 of the PRO method. All too often, the salesperson asks closed-ended questions that allow gatekeepers, brand managers, or decision-makers to reply with a simple yes or no, thus shutting down communication. Questions like "What are your organization's goals?" or "What are the most important priorities for the sponsorship" are much more effective than "Was your last sponsorship effective?" The salesperson should ask questions of the prospective sponsor that help identify a fit between the sponsor's needs and the inventory being offered by the sport property. After asking questions, the salesperson should stop talking and simply listen. Listening is important because active listening and understanding after asking open-ended questions in step 2 help the salesperson match features and benefits in step 3.

Step 3: PROviding the Sponsor With Solutions by Matching Benefits and Information

Step 3 of the PRO method suggests that the salesperson must listen to the prospective sponsor, understand their needs, and provide solutions to meet those needs by matching them to the features and benefits of the inventory being sold. Sales is always about developing relationships, and learning about the customer is key. A good salesperson mixes small talk with excellent questions that provide information about how to align the product and its benefits with the needs of the customer. Step 3 of sponsorship sales is all about listening closely to the prospective sponsor and having comprehensive product knowledge, which means knowing everything necessary about the sponsorship assets available for sale. As noted earlier, sponsorship assets may include items such as category exclusivity, couponing, digital or electronic, direct marketing and database, event and in-game sponsorships, intellectual property, media, pass-through rights, premium giveaways, print advertising, signage, special event marketing, tickets, couponing, and product sampling. Each of these assets has benefits, and the salesperson must know how to align those benefits with the needs of the prospective sponsor.

Step 4: PROposing an Offer to the Prospective Sponsor

After the salesperson has learned about the needs of the prospective sponsor and aligned their needs with available assets, then moving on to step 4, when a proposal is developed and sponsorship ideas are presented, is much easier. We outlined the steps in the process for developing a proposal. This step can be fun because the salesperson is outlining some of the activities that are part of the sponsorship. For example, the proposal for sponsorship of an event may include detailed descriptions of assets like exclusivity, naming rights, and tickets that are included as part of the sponsorship.

Step 5: PROtecting the Sponsor Through Activation and Fulfillment

The final step in the PRO method for sponsorship entails a lot of follow-up and service to the sponsor. The follow-up and service are what we call activation and fulfillment in this chapter. As described earlier, activation is the investment of additional resources to maximize the impact of the sponsorship, whereas fulfillment is the delivery of benefits promised to the sponsor in the contract. This activity may mean following up with the sponsor to let them know how many consumers viewed their name or logo or advertisement. It may entail offering some statistics that outline their ROI or providing qualitative comments from consumers that highlight how they used the sponsor's product. In the end, the sport property needs to service each sponsor. Never should a salesperson sell an asset to a sponsor and then fail to communicate with the sponsor until the following year when they are trying to get them to renew the sponsorship. Continuous follow-up and service show that the sport property cares about the sponsor.

Summary

Sponsorship sales is a big business that continues to grow, and students who want to work in sport can break in by understanding this type of sales. Sponsors are constantly looking to advance their brand, and sport is a lucrative way to reach a targeted audience. After reading this chapter, you should have a better understanding of sales terminology and sponsorship assets. Assets like digital or electronic event sponsorships, premium giveaways, print advertising, signage, tickets, couponing, and product sampling are sold on various platforms that may include governing-body sponsorship, team sponsorship, athlete sponsorship and endorsement, media channel sponsorship, and facility sponsorship. Sponsorship programs start with developing objectives. Budgeting and acquisition come next, and implementation and evaluation follow. Salespeople working in this area need to be able to write solid sales proposals and have insight on sponsorship activation and fulfillment.

APPLIED LEARNING ACTIVITIES

1. The chapter discusses several different types of assets (category exclusivity, couponing, digital or electronic sponsorships, direct marketing and databases, event sponsorships, in-game sponsorship, intellectual property, media, pass-through rights, premium giveaways, print advertising, signage, special event marketing, tickets, couponing, product sampling, and venue signage) that can be monetized. Choose one of these assets and create an infographic with examples that demonstrate how a sport property could use the asset.

2. Activation in this chapter is partly defined as the idea of connecting fans to sponsor brands. Choose a popular brand and, taking into account the principles shared in this chapter in the section Developing the Activation Plan, create ideas for activating a sponsorship for the brand. Write a one-page summary of this activation plan.

CASE STUDY

SPONSORSHIP AND MLB'S BALTIMORE ORIOLES

The Baltimore Orioles in recent years have been a below-average team on the field, generating low fan attendance and a subpar winning percentage. Orioles Park at Camden Yards is owned by the Maryland Stadium Authority and therefore does not have any naming-rights sponsors. The Orioles themselves, however, have several major sponsors, such as Bank of America, Geico, and State Farm (Forbes, 2020). During the 2019-2020 season the Orioles had the second worst record in the American League and the third lowest average attendance. The team experienced an injury to Mark Trumbo, who sat out the entire season, and poor performance by Chris Davis, their star first basemen. Low fan attendance led to smaller revenues from ticket sales and concessions. Orioles sponsors also experienced decreasing return on investments.

Discussion Questions

1. As described in the case, the Orioles have experienced some challenges on the field. Discuss some ways that the Orioles could use sponsorship to enhance fan attendance at their stadium.

2. The case talks about some of the Orioles sponsors (e.g., Geico). Go online and look for various examples of how the Orioles sponsorship with Geico has been activated.

Go to HK*Propel* to watch author videos, engage in sales scenarios, and find downloadable sales templates related to this chapter.

Aaron Davidson/Getty Images for Sprite

CHAPTER 6

Corporate
and Foundation Revenues

CHAPTER OBJECTIVES

After completing the chapter, you should be able to do the following:

- Understand the financial scope of corporate giving
- Discuss corporate social responsibility (CSR)
- Explain the different ways in which corporations give
- Understand why corporations donate
- Describe the diverse types of foundations
- Know how to research possible corporate and foundation funders
- Apply the PRO method to corporate and foundation fundraising

ndividuals, bequests, foundations, and corporations gave an estimated $427.71 billion to U.S. charities in 2018 (Giving USA, 2019). Of this amount, the funds donated by corporations in 2018 totaled $20.05 billion, which was 5.14 percent more than the amount given in 2017. A survey by the *Chronicle of Philanthropy* of the top 150 of the Fortune 500 companies in 2016 revealed that the industries most represented were pharmaceutical, technology, and financial services organizations (as cited by O'Leary, Olsen-Phillips, & Daniels, 2018). Using this data, *Fortune* magazine identified the top 20 companies and calculated that those organizations donated cash in the amount of $3.5 billion in 2015 (Preston, 2016). As we write this book during the COVID-19 pandemic, these statistics most likely provide a relatively false narrative moving forward.

The COVID-19 pandemic had an effect on corporate giving and corporate social responsibility (CSR) in the year 2020. As noted by Manos (2020), the pandemic was unprecedented for many reasons, most importantly that businesses quickly shifted their corporate giving for the good of workers, customers, and society. He noted a few examples of companies' immediate responses to COVID: Target announced pay raises, bonuses, and a new paid leave policy; Shopify paid employees a $1,000 stipend to work from home; Starbucks offered all employees access to therapy; Anheuser-Busch shifted to producing and distributing hand sanitizer; Netflix created a $100 million coronavirus relief fund; and Disneyland donated leftover food to food banks.

The longer-term effect of COVID-19 on CSR is hard to predict, and the ultimate implications for sport are even more difficult to determine. In all likelihood, however, COVID will continue to affect CSR. Ultimately, the implications of how much CSR within sport is affected will probably be determined by the economic conditions as we move forward post COVID-19 and by the lingering effects of the pandemic over the long term. Issues like social justice permeated the sport landscape in the United States in 2020. Regardless of the pandemic and social justice unrest, one issue that does not change for sport organizations is the importance of continuing to develop relationships with corporations considering their mission, goals, and programs.

Corporate Social Responsibility

Although the prevailing view of business during the 20th century and earlier was that the only responsibility of business was to make a profit, in the 21st century organizations began to focus more on making a positive contribution to society. The principle behind the idea of social responsibility is that those with power should help those in need (Parent, 2018). Therefore, the leaders of corporations understand they have "responsibilities beyond profit maximization" (Babiak & Wolfe, 2006, p. 215) and thus have shifted from simply providing charitable donations to implementing a more strategic corporate social responsibility (CSR) model that integrates corporate donations and community service activities with business operations and interests (Dean, 2002).

Today, almost every professional sport team has some form of community affairs, community outreach, or foundation that gives back to various causes. CSR initiatives are integrated not only into teams but also into virtually every sport organization (e.g., sporting goods manufacturers, college and university athletics programs, and even youth sport) within the broadly defined sport industry. The organizations have adopted some form of activities that reach out to bring messages and resources to underprivileged members of society (Babiak & Wolfe, 2006). What is interesting about sport is how it differs from other types of business. For example, teams are valued based on their revenues and built equity rather than cash flow and assets, and leagues share revenue streams at different levels, including gate receipts, marketing and broadcast rights, concessions, luxury boxes, club seats, advertising, and membership fees (Sheth & Babiak, 2010).

Unique Power of CSR in Sport

Almost every corporation in every industry has some form of social responsibility initiative in place. But what makes the concept of CSR so powerful within sport? What forces contribute to the importance of CSR in sport? Parent (2018) suggests that social responsibility in sport is distinct from and more powerful than CSR in other industries because of the following four factors.

Passion

The level of passion generated by sport fans at both an individual and collective level is unique. Sport not only helps individual fans express their identity to a team but also, on a collective level, cuts across all social strata whereby members of different races and ethnicities, religions, socioeconomic status, and gender experience a commonality. Furthermore, sport teams represent their host cities, and there is a reciprocal relationship whereby team success is often contingent upon fan attachment and loyalty.

Economics

The visibility, and ultimately the power, of sport exceeds that of other industries because sport is less dependent on simple market-driven economics. In other words, the close ties between teams, leagues, local host-city government entities, tourism providers, and many other stakeholders all factor into the economics of sport. Unlike other industries, professional sport leagues operate as monopolies that are often immune from external competitive forces.

Transparency

Expectations, particularly from fans and the media, for sport teams to be transparent is more widely scrutinized than in most other industries. Team and athlete outcomes are constantly monitored, personnel decisions (e.g., player salaries) are announced through public statements and press conferences, and off-court or off-field behavior of athletes and sport employees is subject to much greater public attention

than in other industries (Parent, 2018). These factors make the effective implementation of social responsibility in the sport industry more challenging than in other industries.

Stakeholder Management

Stakeholders are vitally important within the context of sport. Although an organization operating within most industries has a high degree of control over matters of production, sport leagues are more dependent on the cooperation of many stakeholders, such as the media, teams, fans, leagues, sponsors, and athletes.

Forces That Make CSR Important in Sport

Two primary forces drive the importance of CSR within the context of sport (Djaballah, 2016). These forces include internal resources and external pressures.

Positive Internal Resources

First, sport offers unique internal resources. One example is the youthful appeal of sport and its positive health and social effects. Issues like sustainability awareness, the fostering of cultural values in sport events, and factors such as admiration, passion, and identification that people assign to teams, athletes, sport associations, and facilities are key components of these resources.

Strong External Pressure

Second, sport organizations face strong external pressure that compels them to act more responsibly (Djaballah, 2016). Many sport organizations are economically structured in such a way that they rely on public subsidies or infrastructures. For example, many sport facilities are publicly financed using taxpayer monies and are therefore expected to give back to the community. Also, media attention and fan support often focus on the external performance of sport organizations. In addition, corporations increasingly use sport as a vehicle for carrying out their CSR initiatives to the public.

Examples of CSR Initiatives in Sport

Sport organizations invest in giving to numerous different causes such as community programs, education, environment, health, poverty, youth, and many others. An example of one team who regularly gives back to the community is Major League Baseball's Boston Red Sox. In 2002 the Red Sox were sold to out-of-state owners who agreed to sign a contract with the Massachusetts attorney general promising to raise $20 million for area charities over the succeeding 10 years. Ten years later, in 2012, the Red Sox Foundation reported they had raised $52 million for local charities over that period, more than twice the promised amount (English, 2012). The following are just a few examples of how organizations or sport leagues are giving back within both professional and intercollegiate sport.

National Football League

The National Football League (NFL) launched the Head Health Initiative, a four-year, $60 million collaboration with General Electric Co. and Under Armour Inc. The collaborative initiative aimed to improve concussion research, diagnosis, and treatment among athletes, members of the military, and society. In 2006 the NFL also combined with the American Heart Association to create the NFL Play 60 Challenge with a goal for kids to be physically active and improve their overall health. NFL Play 60 is an in-school curriculum designed to teach educators and students the importance of engaging in 60 minutes of physical activity a day. It provides fun and engaging ways for students, teachers, and parents to integrate physical activity into their daily lives. The Play 60 Challenge has helped more than 5.5 million students in various communities engage in physical activity (American Heart Association, 2020).

Denver Broncos wide receiver Cody Latimer works with children during the Fall 2016 NFL Play 60.

John Leyba/The Denver Post via Getty Images

B2B REVENUE GENERATION

Washington Football Team and the FITT initiative

Calvin Parson Jr. is the Director, Community and Charitable Programs, for the Washington Football Team. The Washington Football Team Charitable Foundation, in partnership with District of Columbia Public Schools, created FITT (frequency, intensity, time, and type), a youth health and wellness initiative, to empower and assist middle school students in developing their personal fitness goals. The program includes three key elements: the FITTbook, FITT workshops, and instructional online videos. During the 2017-2018 school year, Aquafina became the presenting sponsor of the program, helping to offset some of the programmatic costs associated with facilitating the program at each participating school. In addition to having the Aquafina logo included on all program collateral and having naming rights to the program, PepsiCo staff were invited to participate in the team's FITT Special Events with the team's staff and players and to become involved in other volunteer opportunities with the Washington Football Team Charitable Foundation.

Major League Baseball

Major League Baseball (MLB) created a league-wide effort to raise awareness for childhood cancer. On the league's designated Childhood Cancer Awareness Day at ballparks, Major League players and on-field personnel wear gold ribbon decals and wristbands to promote awareness for childhood cancer, which is the leading cause of death by disease in children aged 15 and under in the United States.

National Hockey League

Through their NHL Green initiative, the National Hockey League (NHL) seeks to keep both the outdoors and water habitable, sustainable, and usable. Omar Mitchell, the NHL's vice president for corporate social responsibility, suggests that the roots of hockey are tied to playing outdoors on frozen fresh water and that the league is therefore focused on these environmental sustainability issues (Benjamin, 2017).

National Basketball Association

NBA Cares is the National Basketball Association's global social responsibility program that addresses social issues in the United States and around the world. NBA Cares works with internationally recognized youth-serving programs that support education, youth, family development, and health-related causes, including Special Olympics, Boys & Girls Clubs of America, UNICEF, the Make-A-Wish Foundation, Share Our Strength, and GLSEN. The Charlotte Hornets are a team within the NBA. According to their website, the Hornets teamed up with Food Lion and established Food Lion Feeds as its Official Hunger Relief Partner. The Hornets and Food Lion started the partnership by distributing more than 9,500 meals to 300 local school families with the help of a local food bank. Food Lion Feeds committed to provide more than 300,000 meals to members of the local community over three years.

Teams like the Milwaukee Bucks in the NBA have made structural changes; what used to be called the Community Relations Department is now called CSR. Teams in the NBA are leading the way in CSR. The Milwaukee Bucks suggest on their website that they are committed to positive change around Wisconsin, including youth education, youth health and wellness, community betterment, and mentoring. On their website, the Bucks highlight community betterment by stating that they

are committed to revitalizing and enriching our Wisconsin culture, one neighborhood at a time. From physical renovations to neighborhood safety programs to workforce development and social equality issues facing our communities, the Milwaukee Bucks Foundation aims to improve outcomes for residents across the state of Wisconsin. (Milwaukee Bucks, 2020)

Therefore, it was no surprise in August 2020 that the Bucks decided not to play their playoff game against the Orlando Magic because of the police shooting of Jacob Blake, a black man in Kenosha, Wisconsin. What followed will continue to revolutionize sport in America. All three NBA playoff games were postponed, three games in Major League Baseball were postponed, as were games in Major League Soccer. After canceling the game, Bucks players George Hill and Sterling Brown read the following statement to reporters:

The past four months have shed a light on the ongoing racial injustices facing our African American communities. Citizens around the country have used their voices and platforms to speak out against these wrongdoings. Over the last few days, in our home state of Wisconsin, we've seen the horrendous video of Jacob Blake being shot in the back seven times by a police officer in Kenosha and the additional shooting of protesters. Despite the overwhelming plea for change, there has been no action, so our focus today cannot be on basketball.

When we take the court and represent Milwaukee and Wisconsin, we are expected to play at a high level, give maximum effort and hold each other accountable. We hold each other to that standard, and in this moment we are demanding the same from lawmakers and law enforcement. We are calling for justice for Jacob Blake and demand for the officers to be held accountable. For this to occur, it is imperative for the Wisconsin state legislature to reconvene after months of inaction and take up meaningful measures to address issues of police accountability, brutality, and criminal justice reform. We encourage all citizens to educate themselves, take peaceful and responsible action and remember to vote on November 3. (Goldman, 2020)

CSR initiatives like those of the Milwaukee Bucks are now commonplace in professional sport. Players like George Hill and Sterling Brown may work in collaboration with front office representatives in CSR and the ownership to effect change. NBA Cares launched in 2005, and the goal of the league was to address societal needs through philanthropy, service, and legacy by raising and contributing $100 million to charities, providing 1 million hours of hands-on service, and creating 100 places in which people could live, learn, or play, all within the first five years (King, 2019). According to Todd Jacobsen, the NBA's senior vice president of social responsibility, the numbers were exceeded and quickly extended. The NBA realized that "creating places" was important. Therefore, the NBA's goals quickly changed from a focus on revenues to ways in which they could take action. Jacobsen gave the following best practices for managing CSR that can work across sports:

- Develop a social impact strategy and plan that everybody believes in from the top down.
- Select a strong leader and give them day-to-day access to leaders across other departments.
- Incorporate internal volunteer programs, which are increasingly important as the workforce becomes mostly millennial and Gen Z.
- Leave space to innovate and evolve, and work with the community organizations that do the best job of addressing changing needs.
- Integrate by making sure that the social responsibility group includes strong leadership that does day-to-day work with that leader on the business side (King, 2019).

English Premier League

Primary Stars is a program in the English Premier League (EPL) available to every primary school in England and Wales. It uses the appeal of the Premier League and professional football clubs to inspire children to learn, be active, and develop important life skills.

Colleges and Universities

At North Carolina State University (2020), the campus-wide Sustainability Council exists to advance sustainability at NC State. Their Zero Waste Wolfpack initiative leverages the power of sport to champion sustainability. More than 340,000 fans visit Carter Finley football stadium each season. This program provides recycling bags in tailgating lots; helps fans sort their stadium waste into recycling and compost bins; and educates visitors in fan guides, on the jumbotron, and on ribbon-banner ads.

Environmental initiatives dealing with waste management are important to the athletics department at the University of Oregon. In 2011 all vendors in the Moshofsky Center, an indoor football practice facility, switched to biodegradable service wares. Items like beverage cups, plates, silverware, and napkins are diverted from the landfill. Local community volunteer groups are paid a base salary each game to collect beverage containers in the tailgating parking lots. The groups are then refunded the five-cent deposit on all the beverage containers collected and returned to the Oregon Beverage Recycling Cooperative (OBRC). Since 2002 the University of Oregon athletics department has contracted with local youth groups and athletics teams as a fundraiser for their programs with the hope of 70 percent waste diversion.

Corporate Giving

Organizations within the sport industry are not the only companies who are carrying out CSR initiatives. Corporations in almost every industry now employ CSR in some way or another. Corporate giving varies in terms of why the corporations choose to give and what they are giving. A corporation may choose to be socially responsible for seven reasons: (1) consumers demand it; (2) employees want to work for companies with world-positive missions; (3) employees perform better when engaging in socially responsible activities and reporting; (4) CSR develops new markets, helps the company improve operations, and strengthen partnerships; (5) social good fosters innovation and collaboration; (6) CSR can increase access to capital; and (7) CSR is a moral imperative (Horoszowski, 2015). Corporations may choose to give away money for numerous reasons (Ciconte & Jacob, 2001):

- Build a positive public image
- Increase revenues
- Get tax deductions
- Reward employees
- Improve the communities in which they operate
- Support certain causes or events
- Be in good favor with the public and be perceived as exuding good will
- Create an environment of community responsibility
- Be good corporate citizens, which may help them attract new customers

The differences between corporate giving and foundation giving are sometimes difficult to identify. For example, some corporate giving stems from the company's foundation. In other cases, the corporation refers to their funding arm as a corporate giving program, community affairs, or community relations. A corporation may have a giving program for various reasons, but most see the advantages of a positive image, better relationships with customers, engagement from employees, and a greater feeling of community (Kain, 2019). Most corporate giving programs are directly tied to corporate profitability, so most gifts are not spread out over more than one year (Scanlan, 1997). Some companies may offer a matching gift program for employees. Companies may take either a "soft bottom line" approach or a "hard bottom line" approach to giving. Companies taking a soft bottom line approach focus on intangible benefits to the company, such as image in the community or increased goodwill. In contrast, companies using the hard bottom line approach place greater emphasis on showing direct and measurable benefits to the company's profitability. A good fundraiser will be able to talk about both benefits. Most companies are likely to take a hard bottom line approach, especially as budgets become tighter. Among the various types of corporate giving programs are community grants, employee volunteer grants, employee matching gifts, corporate sponsorships, and noncash contributions (Weinger, 2012).

Many corporations have a foundation that distributes grant funds to nonprofit organizations. Companies can gain several advantages by creating a foundation (Foundation Source, 2019). These advantages include tax benefits, avoiding capital gains taxes, reduced staffing and overhead costs, and simplified recordkeeping. Corporate foundations can engage in various charitable activities that would not be tax deductible if handled directly by the company, such as the following:

- International grants directly to organizations outside the United States
- Employer-related scholarship programs
- Grants to individuals for disaster relief and economic hardship
- Loans for a charitable purpose that are paid back to the foundation
- Grants to for-profit entities for a charitable purpose

The foundation is a legal organization separate from the corporation and often serves as a vehicle for building up reserves during higher profit years that can be given away during the years in which the company is not making as much profit. Companies can contribute cash to the foundation to establish an endowment, or they can donate appreciated assets. The two types of corporate foundations are corporate foundations with yearly funding and corporate foundations with permanent assets (Scanlan, 1997).

Corporate Foundations With Yearly Funding

The distinguishing factor in corporate foundations with yearly funding is that each year the corporation transfers some of its pretax profits to the foundation, which has a separate board of directors (Scanlan, 1997). The foundation board, however, may also include the company's existing board members or senior management. Family-owned or closely held companies may have foundation boards that consist entirely of family members or owners of the corporation. Funding decisions are usually made by the board of directors, but in some cases foundation staff may make decisions on all requests up to a certain amount. Like a corporate giving program, yearly funding may be tied to corporate profitability. The foundation may also have its own limited assets (e.g., company stocks) from which it can distribute income.

Corporate Foundation With Permanent Assets

In a foundation with permanent assets, the corporation gives the foundation permanent assets (usually stocks) at some point in time or over the course of time (Scanlan, 1997). The earnings on these stocks are then used for distributing grants and operating the foundation. This type of foundation may have part- or full-time professional staff and a board that makes final grant decisions. Because this type of foundation is less dependent on corporate profits, concerns of stockholders, and senior management, funding is often allocated in more bottom-line areas such as community services, improvement, and enhancement.

Earlier, we highlighted some of the reasons why corporations may give. In many cases the corporation's justification may include more than one reason. When approaching any corporation for purposes of asking the company to engage in philanthropy, a sport fundraiser must understand why the corporation may give because the reasoning may vary between individuals, companies, and industries. Equally important to the why is what corporations can give. The tendency for any sport fundraiser is to approach a corporation with the expectation of asking for a cash donation. But just as the reasons why a corporation gives varies from company to company, likewise what a company can give may also vary. Examples of what corporations may donate include more or less of the following.

Cash or Product Donations

Corporations work with nonprofits to donate cash or products. An example is the way that Chicago Cubs Charities partnered with Good Sports to donate $90,000 worth of equipment for baseball and softball programs on the South and West Sides of Chicago (Good Sports, 2017). In 2020 during the COVID-19 outbreak, technology companies pledged more than $1 billion for relief along with products such as free video conferencing software and free ads. Google and Cisco donated $800 million and $220 million, respectively, in response to the pandemic (Schleifer, 2020). Within a month of the shutdown for COVID-19 in the United States, corporations and foundations had accounted for 63 percent of the nearly $7 billion in private funding. Some businesses reconfigured their operations to help make face masks, hand sanitizer, and other supplies (Gannon, 2020). Restaurants donated meals, and companies offered various free products and services to hospital workers and essential frontline personnel. During the coronavirus outbreak even professional sport teams got involved. Shortly after the onset of the pandemic, Mark Cuban, owner of the NBA's Dallas Mavericks, committed to pay all arena workers inside American Airlines Center. Cuban made the following comments to reporters:

I reached out to the folks at the arena and our folks at the Mavs to find out what it would cost to support, financially support, people who aren't going to be able to come to work. They get paid by the hour, and this was their source of income. So, we'll do some things there. We may ask them to go do some volunteer work in exchange, but we've already started the process of having a program in place. I don't have any details to give, but it's certainly something that's important to me. (Wimbish, 2020)

Cuban followed through with his comments, and the Mavericks announced they would pay hourly employees at the American Airlines Center for the first six postponed games in 2020. In an effort to spur economic recovery in the community, Cuban also implemented a Mavericks policy that reimbursed all employees who purchased breakfast at independent, local restaurants and coffee shops. To extend these efforts, the Mavericks also partnered with DoorDash (Rader, 2020).

Company-Wide Day of Service Events

Many companies have created large volunteer events that impact the local community and often bring together multiple partners. The benefit is often a larger group of skilled employees who come together and are funded by the company. For example, in 2012 the Comcast Cares Day had volunteers at more than 600 sites in 39 states and the District of Columbia that contributed more than 450,000 community service hours. In collaboration with nonprofits such as Boys & Girls Clubs of America, United Way, and other nonprofits, volunteers at this event planted gardens, beautified schools, and connected computer labs at community centers. Here are some ideas that corporations can use as service events for their employees (Tiny Pulse, 2020):

- Food pantries and donation distribution centers
- Park or beach cleanups, which get employees outdoors for a good cause
- Mentoring, which allows employees to mentor students or members of underserved communities
- Volunteering for events such as a 5K race, festival, or speaker series
- Hosting a fundraising public event in the nonprofit's office space
- Crowdfunding, which allows people to raise money on behalf of a nonprofit through social media or other public-facing donation platforms

- Collecting donations such as a canned goods drive or collecting items of clothing, toys, or hygiene items at the company's office
- In-office activities such as writing letters, making animal toys from donated materials for a local pet shelter, or performing other activities that support the mission
- Health events such as hosting a blood drive or immunization day to support wellness and engage a company's employees in promoting the event in coordination with other organizations

Checkout Charity Campaigns (Point-of-Sale Donation Programs)

You have probably had the cashier at a grocery store ask if you want to contribute $1 for a certain cause. Sometimes the cashier asks if you would like to round up your change to the nearest dollar in support of the cause. Children's health is a big beneficiary, and causes such as Children's Miracle Network Hospitals and St. Jude Children's Research Hospitals received almost half of all donations at the register in 2016 (Fritz, 2019). In 2018 the five top retailers using checkout charity campaigns

Sarah Crabill/Getty Images

Company-wide volunteer events, such as the annual Comcast Cares Day, involve employees in carrying out CSR.

included eBay, who raised $69 million for tens of thousands of consumer selected charities; PetSmart, who raised $42.1 million for animal welfare organizations; Walmart, who raised $36.5 million for Children's Miracle Network Hospitals; Petco, who raised $32.6 for animal welfare organizations; and Costco, who raised $28 million for Children's Miracle Network Hospitals (Hessekiel, 2019). A good example of a sport-related campaign was the $2.1 million raised at the checkout by Publix grocery stores in 2013 that went toward Special Olympics ("Donate a Dollar at the Register?" 2013).

Corporate Grants

Corporate grants are nonrepayable funds or products that are disbursed or given by a corporation. The B2B sidebar Causes and Corporate Grants depicts a list of various causes and the corporations that give grants for each cause. Corporations may award grants through their foundation, trust, or CSR office. Grants are normally awarded to nonprofit 501(c)(3) charitable organizations. Corporate philanthropy is often overlooked as a strategy because it is less traditional than asking for contributions and many nonprofits do not think of it when trying to raise money (Weinger, 2017). Corporations often include a listing of various organizations, activities, or purposes that are not supported. When applying for a grant, fundraisers need to pay particular attention to these guidelines. Like many other corporations, Wex (2020), a financial company, does not provide grants for certain types of programs:

- Residents of communities outside the company's geographic footprint
- Private individuals or foundations
- Political campaigns, political candidates, and lobbying or advocacy organizations
- Organizations with a limited constituency, such as fraternal, labor, or veterans' groups; religious organizations; athletic teams or social groups
- Organizations that discriminate based on race, national or ethnic origin, color, religion, age, sex, sexual orientation, gender

identity or expression, marital status, family status, veteran status, disability, or other characteristic protected by law
- Trips and tours by groups or individuals

Corporate Matching Gifts

Matching gifts are a type of philanthropy whereby companies financially match the donations that their employees make to nonprofit organizations. Companies normally match an employee's donation at a 1:1 ratio, but some will match at a 2:1, 3:1, or even 4:1 ratio (Double the Donation, 2020). The first matching gift program was created in 1954 by General Electric (GE), and the company has donated over $1 billion since that date (Weinger, 2016). The program has a minimum of $25 and a maximum of $5,000 with a 1:1 match ratio. GE employees like the program because it has a fairly long deadline and gives employees the time needed to research whether their donation and the charitable nonprofit they are donating to are eligible to receive a matching gift. Companies that agree to match a gift normally provide employees with a deadline. Most corporations specify one of three deadlines: (1) matching the gift up to 3, 6, or 12 months following the initial donation; (2) matching the gift by the end of the calendar year; and (3) matching the gift by the end of the calendar year with an extended grace period, perhaps an additional month or two for employees to submit their matching gift request (Weinger, 2015).

In-Kind Contributions

Donations made in-kind can consist of goods, services, or time, in place of cash. Donated in-kind goods may be tangible (e.g., equipment) or intangible (e.g., advertising). Examples of services may be transportation (e.g., busing or rental car) or technology (e.g., free cell phone). The time component occurs when people give their time free of charge or for payment by a third-party (Engelhardt-Cronk, n.d.). The advantage for nonprofits receiving in-kind donations is that they can access goods and services otherwise unaffordable or free up resources to spend on something

B2B REVENUE GENERATION

Causes and Corporate Grants

Table 6.1 provides a listing of some of the causes supported by various corporations. Although the list is not exhaustive, it provides some context of the many causes supported by corporations. Note that many organizations support more than one cause. Fundraisers in sport should understand the causes that are important to the organizations when considering how to partner. For example, think of some ways that a nonprofit like Special Olympics could partner with the Safeway Foundation on causes related to disabilities. Youth sport organizations like Boys & Girls Club may consider collaborations with corporations that support youth development, civic and community, education, health and human services, well-being and nutrition, and workforce development. Each of these corporations provides guidelines, which the sport fundraiser will need to consult when approaching a corporation for funding.

TABLE 6.1   Examples of Causes Supported by Corporations

Cause	Corporations
Arts and culture	Emerson, Fidelity, Founders Brewing, M&T Charitable Foundation, McCormick Corporation, MetLife, PNC Foundation, Sony, Southern Company, US Bank
Civic and community	3M, Duke Energy, Emerson, Enterprise, Fidelity, Ford, GM Foundation, Goldman Sachs, IBM, JP Morgan Chase & Co., Kimberly-Clark, M&T Charitable Foundation, Merck, Nationwide, Polaris Foundation, Prudential, Shell, Southern Company, Tyson Foods, Union Bank, United Health, Waste Management, Walmart, Westinghouse
Disabilities	OMRON Foundation, Safeway Foundation
Disaster relief	OMRON Foundation, Topgolf
Disease prevention	Bristol Myers Squibb, Gilead, Johnson & Johnson
Economic	Cisco, MetLife, US Bank, UPS
Education	3M, Alcoa, BASF, Chubb, Cisco, Coca-Cola, Duke Energy, Emerson, Enterprise, Exxon Mobil, Ford, GE Foundation, General Mills, GM Foundation, Goldman Sachs, Halliburton Foundation, Kohl's, McCormick Corporation, Merck, Safeway Foundation, Shell, Southern Company, US Bank, UPS, Wells Fargo, Westinghouse, Wyndham
Environment	3M, Alcoa, BASF, Chubb, Duke Energy, Enterprise, Founders Brewing, GM Foundation, Hilton, Kohl's, McCormick Corporation, Polaris Foundation, Shell, Sony, Southern Company, Tyson Foods, Waste Management, Wells Fargo
Families, basic needs, poverty	Chubb, Family Dollar, Ford, General Mills, Harold Simmons Foundation, Payless ShoeSource, Prudential
Health and human or social services	BASF, Chubb, Emerson, Exxon Mobil, Fidelity, GE Foundation, GM Foundation, Halliburton Foundation, Hilton, Johnson & Johnson, Kohl's, M&T Charitable Foundation, McCormick Corporation, MetLife, Merck, Safeway Foundation, Stanley Tools, Topgolf, Tyson Foods, United Health, Walt Disney, Wawa

Cause	Corporations
Housing	Bank of America, General Mills, Union Bank
Hunger	Bank of America, Safeway Foundation, Tyson Foods, Wawa
Jobs	Bank of America, Goldman Sachs, Prudential
STEM	Intel, Lockheed Martin, OMRON Foundation, PNC Foundation, Sony, Stanley Tools, Westinghouse
Social justice	Founders Brewing
Sustainability	PepsiCo Foundation, Walmart
Veterans and military	Goldman Sachs, Lockheed Martin, Newman's Own, OMRON Foundation, Stanley Tools, Topgolf, United Health
Well-being and nutrition	Coca-Cola, General Mills, Newman's Own Foundation, Wyndham
Women	Coca-Cola, Exxon Mobil, Kohl's
Workforce development	Duke Energy, JP Morgan Chase & Co.
Youth development	Coca-Cola, Emerson, Nordstrom, Office Depot, Polaris Foundation, Walt Disney

Data from Corporate Grants Guide (2020); Fundraiser Help (2020).

else. Disadvantages occur when a nonprofit receives unsolicited in-kind gifts they have no need for, cannot use, or that create issues with physical storage space. Certain gifts, like real estate or vehicles, can cause some of these problems and are often a hassle for nonprofit organizations (Morand, 2020). A common good used as an in-kind donation by sport properties is merchandise. For example, the Tampa Bay Lightning within the NHL support various charitable events through the donations of in-kind merchandise. They try to donate to as many organizations as possible (Tampa Bay Lightning, n.d.).

Volunteer Time Off (VTO)

Many companies provide their employees with paid days off to work with charitable organizations. Volunteer time off (VTO) is a way to encourage employees to participate in socially responsible activities that foster meaningful relationships in both the community and the company. These types of programs allow a company to support the causes that matter most to their employees. Instead of VTO, some employers sponsor a nonprofit, match

employee donations, or engage in some other type of philanthropic initiative. VTO is sometimes called a dollars for doers or volunteer grant program. The grants occur when the company donates cash to charities based on the number of volunteer hours that each employee contributes. Perhaps the largest driving force behind VTO is that 75 percent of millennials expect their employer to engage in some type of social corporate responsibility (Schiavo, 2019). How may this apply for a fundraiser with a sport organization like Special Olympics that runs many events in many places? As an example, Special Olympics representatives may work with a grocery retailer like Safeway that supports people with disabilities. With approximately 1,300 grocery store locations, Safeway would be capable of providing employees to volunteer with running Special Olympic events.

Pro Bono Service

The term *pro bono* should not be mistaken for volunteerism in the sense that it is different from volunteering to work at a marathon for free. The Latin term *pro bono* means "for the public good" and refers to situations where services are offered for free or at a cost but benefit a specific cause or the public good (Weinger, 2019). The American Bar Association requires lawyers to continue their pro bono work throughout their careers and asks them to perform, without fee, at least 50 hours of pro bono legal services per year (Stetson University College of Law, n.d.). Although the term *pro bono* traditionally applies within the legal profession, examples of pro bono service may go beyond legal services. For example, an accountant may provide pro bono services to a local sport- or recreation-related nonprofit by doing their tax work at no cost.

Philanthropic Foundations

Foundations and their corresponding giving are widely misunderstood in philanthropy. During the period between 1988 and 1998, the number of foundations in the United States grew from 28,000 to over 44,000 and their assets expanded from $115 billion to more than $300 billion (Lee, 2019). Foundations are difficult to define fully because they differ from country to country and assume several forms. For example, foundations in European countries (e.g., Germany and Switzerland) are defined by civil law, whereas in the United States they are a creation of tax law and can be regarded as a subcategory of 501(c)(3) organizations (Bethmann et al., 2014). In the United States, a fundraiser within the sport industry must have an understanding of the types of foundations who may donate money. We can categorize these foundations into the following types (Scanlan, 1997):

1. Private foundations
2. Community foundations
3. Operating foundations

Private Foundations

A **private foundation** is a 501(c)(3) organization that is established to fund charitable activities through grants and other gifts (Foundation Group, n.d.). A private foundation typically has a small number of donors and is categorized as a 501(c)(3) organization that the IRS does not recognize as a public charity. Norton (2013) describes the following consequences of being treated as a private foundation in contrast to a public charity:

- The foundation must comply with additional restrictions on operations, most notably what are called self-dealing rules that prohibit a private foundation from providing any benefits to, or entering into transactions (such as sales, leases, or loans) with, significant contributors and others (so-called disqualified persons) who have certain insider relationships to the organization.

- The foundation is subject to an excise tax on investment income.

- Donors to a private foundation receive a less generous tax deduction when contributing than when contributing to public charities.

- A private foundation may be further classified as a nonoperating foundation or an operating foundation.

A private foundation is governed by its board of directors, and unlike a public charity, its board can be a relatively closed group of individuals. Foundation Source (2020) suggests that private foundations have many advantages, including tax savings, helping people in need, linking a family name with good works (legacy), passing on values and skills to younger generations, controlling foundation governance assets and spending, and providing a sense of fulfillment to the giver.

According to Norton (2013), most private foundations are classified as nonoperating foundations that function as grantmakers and do not directly provide services or conduct other charitable activities. Each is required to disburse a minimum amount of funds each year (equal to 5 percent of the foundation's assets) in the form of qualifying distributions.

Qualifying distributions may consist of a grant, gift, or what are called program-related investments along with reasonable administrative expenses incurred by the private foundation in carrying out its charitable purposes and amounts paid to acquire assets used in carrying out the foundation's exempt purposes. The **program-related investments** may be loans or equity investments made by a private foundation or public charity, primarily for charitable purposes. Private foundations that do not distribute this minimum amount within a specified period are subject to an excise tax. The Council on Foundations (n.d.) suggests that private foundations may fall into one of the following categories: independent or nonoperating foundations, family foundations, corporate foundations, international foundations, and private operating foundations.

Independent or Nonoperating Foundations

An **independent foundation** is funded by endowments from a single source (e.g., individual or group of individuals). The term *nonoperating foundation* is used interchangeably with independent foundation. Usually, these types of foundations are funded through the bequest of one person. But unlike other types of private foundations (e.g., family or corporate foundations), independent foundations are not governed by the benefactor, benefactor's family, or a corporation. Members of the founding family, if any, have minority representation on the board and do not control the board. Instead, these types of foundations are normally run by community, business, and academic leaders (Wisconsin Philanthropy Network, 2020). An example of an independent, or private nonoperating, foundation is the Bill & Melinda Gates Foundation. In their 2020 letter, Bill and Melinda Gates claimed that the foundation had spent $53.8 billion over the last 20 years, allocating 45 percent to global programs, 29 percent to global health, 16 percent to U.S. programs, and 10 percent to other charitable programs (Gates & Gates, 2020).

Family Foundations

Often the term *family foundation* is used interchangeably with the term *private foundation*, thus making it difficult to distinguish the two. The term *private* suggests that the foundation possesses no constituents or shareholders and only a slight connection to the stock market. A **family foundation** is an independently governed institution that has large private assets used to promote public benefit. The assets are typically in the form of permanent endowments, and family members have substantial roles in governance (Leat, 2016). According to Fidelity Charitable (n.d.), approximately 50 percent of private foundations in the United States are categorized as family foundations and they meet all the IRS guidelines for private foundations. Family foundations must disburse a minimum of 5 percent of their assets each year, and their grants are publicly viewable. These types of foundations are funded with assets such as cash, private stock, real estate, publicly traded securities, or other assets. They are often managed by the family or a professional manager.

Corporate Foundations

Corporate foundations (or company-sponsored foundations) are separate legal entities that are created and financially supported by a corporation. Corporate foundations are often staffed by employees of the corporation, and the board is normally controlled by the corporation. Most corporate foundations are classified as private because they are created by a single corporation, funded by their money, and controlled by the company's board of directors. But a smaller number can be classified as public charities (Valor, 2017). Many corporate foundations depend on allocations from the corporation; thus, they do not have an endowment or build assets. The amount that the foundation can disburse is therefore highly dependent on the financial health and success of the corporation (Smith, 2016). As an example of a grant from a corporate foundation, inspired and informed by their employees, the Starbucks Foundation disbursed community service grants in the form of Neighborhood Grants totaling over $1 million to more than 400 local organizations across the United States and Canada in response to the COVID-19 epidemic (Starbucks Foundation, 2020). See the B2B sidebar Initiatives Supported by the Starbucks Foundation.

International Foundations

Typically, an **international foundation** is based outside the United States and makes grants to their own country and overseas. The term *international* can also refer to any foundation in any country that engages primarily in giving across borders. But giving across borders can be tricky. When a private foundation in the United States makes a grant to a foreign organization not deemed to be a 501(c)(3) charity, the foundation must take extra steps to ensure that the grant will not trigger an excise tax as a taxable expenditure (Norton, 2013). This issue is just one of the legal complexities that these types of foundations encounter when working outside the United States. Some practical complexities can also come into play. For example, these foundations may want to consider working with intermediary organizations that provide funds and monitor programs in one or more foreign countries. The advantages of working with an intermediary are not having to deal with the cultural complexities of hiring in a foreign land, taxes, and a host of local laws. These types of foundations may want to provide funds to organizations operating their own programs in foreign countries (Norton, 2013).

B2B REVENUE GENERATION

Initiatives Supported by the Starbucks Foundation

An example of a corporate foundation, the Starbucks Foundation supports communities by providing grants to nonprofit organizations. The foundation supports the initiatives shown in table 6.2.

TABLE 6.2 Starbucks Foundation's Efforts

Initiative	Description
Access to clean water	For every bottle of Ethos water sold in the United States, the foundation gives 5 cents to a water fund that helps finance water programs around the world.
Community service	Supports employee engagement in the local community through matching grants to nonprofits where employees made personal monetary and time contributions.
Opportunities for youth	Invests in programs for young people (ages 16-24) to equip them with skills required for a changing global economy.
Supporting coffee, tea, and cocoa communities	Supports programs that strengthen local economic and social development by working collaboratively with nongovernmental organizations that have experience and expertise in working with farming communities in countries where coffee and other agricultural products are raised. Projects include improving access to education and agricultural training; microfinance and microcredit services; improving biodiversity conservation; and increasing levels of health, nutrition, and water sanitation.

Data from Starbucks (2020).

Private Operating Foundations

A **private operating foundation** is another type of private foundation that operates as a 501(c)(3) organization and does not qualify for public charity status because of limited sources of support. A private operating foundation is subject to some, but not all, of the restrictions that apply to nonoperating foundations. To qualify, an organization must not only be involved in charitable activities beyond grantmaking but also meet certain technical tests. The key difference between a private nonoperating foundation and a private operating foundation is how they distribute their income. A private nonoperating foundation can grant money to other charitable organizations, whereas a private operating foundation distributes funds to its own programs that exist for charitable purposes (Coffman, 2001).

The private operating foundation is different from most family foundations because it directly conducts activities, such as providing charitable services, rather than functioning solely as a grantmaker. Each year, the *Chronicle of Philanthropy* produces their Philanthropy 50 list of the people who gave the most to charity. In 2020 the top five donors, giving mostly through the use of private operating foundations, included Michael Bloomberg, Barron Hilton, Eric and Wendy Schmidt, Jim Walton, and Thomas Lord. Their donations amounted to more than $9 billion to a variety of causes (Di Mento, 2021). Three years earlier in 2017, the top 50 donors had given a median amount of $97 million, which was almost double what it was in 2000 (Di Mento & Lindsay, 2018).

A private operating foundation is a legal classification by the IRS whereby those foundations operate their own charitable programs (although some also make grants) and are required to spend a certain portion of their assets each year on charitable activities. The Internal Revenue Service (n.d.) classifies a private operating foundation as a private foundation that devotes most of its resources to its exempt activities and is subject to taxes on net investment income. A private operating foundation must annually meet an income test

and one of three other tests (assets, endowment, and support test) to qualify for and retain its status (Alexanderson, 2017):

- *Income test*—Although the calculation can be complicated, in its simplified form this test suggests that the amount of qualifying distributions for the foundation must be equal to substantially all (i.e., 85 percent or more) of the lesser of the foundation's adjusted net income or minimum investment return (Alexanderson, 2017).

- *Assets test*—The foundation passes this test if 65 percent of the value of its assets is devoted to one or both of the following: (1) active conduct of exempt-purpose activities or (2) business activity that is functionally related to its exempt purpose.

- *Endowment test*—This test measures qualifying distributions and minimum investment return, which means that (1) a foundation must make qualifying distributions directly in support of the active conduct of the charitable activities for which the foundation was established and (2) the foundation must make qualifying distributions in excess of two-thirds of its minimum investment return.

- *Support test*—This test requires the foundation to receive at least 85 percent of their support from the public and five or more exempt organizations, not including disqualified persons. In addition, not more than 25 percent of support can be from any one of the five exempt organizations and no more than 50 percent of total support can be received from gross investment income.

Community Foundations

Community foundations are tax-exempt, nonprofit, publicly supported philanthropic organizations that the Internal Revenue Service (IRS) recognizes as public charities partly because of support from the public through endowment funds and individual, family, or business donations (National Council of Nonprofits, n.d.). A **community foundation** maintains and administers funds on behalf of multiple donors primarily to meet the needs of the geographic community or region where it is based (Foundation Center, n.d.a).

According to Mazany and Perry (2014), community foundations have always defined themselves as institutions of "communal good" that seek to respond to and define the community. Furthermore, Mazany and Perry suggest their mission is not restricted to the interests of any individual donor or individual grant recipient, nor constrained by a certain type of philanthropy, interests of one political party, or a particular initiative.

More than 750 community foundations operate in both urban and rural areas in every state in the United States. For example, the Community Foundation of Harrisonburg & Rockingham County (TCFHR) serves a relatively rural area in the Shenandoah Valley of Virginia. This community foundation organizes and administers an initiative called the Great Community Give, which is one day of philanthropy held each year. During the 2019 event, held from 6:30 a.m. to 8:00 p.m. on April 17, the foundation engaged with 59 partners, raised $73,500 in sponsorship prizes, trained 46 nonprofits in social media, and raised $536,300 from 5,725 donations given to local nonprofit organizations (Community Foundation of Harrisonburg and Rockingham County, 2020). For small nonprofits in sport and recreation, community foundations like TCFHR can provide excellent resources and help them to raise funds.

Operating Foundations

The National Center for Family Philanthropy (NCFP) (n.d.) describes an **operating foundation** as a special form of private foundation that uses the bulk of its income to run its own charitable programs or services. Examples include the operation of a museum, library, research facility, or historic property. In its most basic form, an operating foundation is set up to make grants to itself—to its own programs, projects, and services (Scanlan, 1997). This type of foundation has a narrow purpose (e.g., cancer research), and it holds permanent

assets that produce income for its operation and specific programs and projects. Operating foundations are required to spend the major portion of their investment income (85 percent) each year directly on the active conduct of their charitable operations (Foundation Source, 2020). The primary advantage of the operating foundation is that a founding donor or family can invite others to contribute to its endowment while receiving the same tax benefits as they would for gifts to a public foundation. In addition, donors and families may choose to establish a private operating foundation for the following reasons (NCFP, 2020):

- Interest in managing activities that are directly aligned with their philanthropic mission
- Desire to engage directly and regularly with the community they serve
- Interest in encouraging others' investment in their philanthropic mission and in leveraging the family's investment

Applying the PRO Method to Corporate and Foundation Fundraising

The PRO method can be applied within the context of corporate and foundation fundraising, as described in the following sections.

Step 1: PROspect for Qualified Customers by Researching Funding Partners

A large amount of research goes into determining which corporations best match the needs of the initiative for which you are seeking funds. This process of determining which companies to approach is called prospecting, which is step 1 of the PRO method of sales discussed in chapter 2. Unlike other forms of prospecting, one of the advantages of researching a foundation is that you already know the entity from which you are requesting funds is philanthropic in nature. Whether you are looking to approach a foundation or a corporation, it is smart to see if you know anyone who has contacts with the funding agency. In addition, you always want to make sure to check the website of the foundation or corporation to ensure that you have the most recent guidelines. Of course, you need to analyze and research corporations that align with the needs of your sport organization. Scanlan (1997) provides some tips for researching prospective corporate funders. For example, he suggests checking the mission of the foundation because some are clear, whereas others are not. You may need to interpret the population or group (e.g., children, people with disabilities) served by the foundation by reading mission statements and guidelines or by looking at the grants they have awarded. In addition, reading the funder's annual report and their guidelines will help you learn more about what they will fund. Reviewing past grants can help you understand who is on the board for the funding organization, which will tell you about their interests (Scanlon, 1997).

Determining the best corporation or foundation to fund your initiative is not an exact science, and the process can be extremely time consuming and intricate. Researching the best match for your organization's initiative may involve the use of multiple computer database directories, online resources, print media resources, IRS forms, and other sources of information. For example, the Foundation Directory, Foundation Source, LexisNexis, GuideStar, Foundation Center, Grants.gov, and GrantForward all provide information about potential funders. Today, almost all research is done online, but printed materials from the foundation or corporation can also provide important information. Financial information about a foundation can be found from IRS forms. You can also find important information by going to online publications such as the *Nonprofit Times* or *Chronicle of Philanthropy* and by visiting nonprofit sites such as the Association for Fundraising Professionals (AFP) and the National Society of Fundraising Executives. Other sources that may be helpful include the Council on Foundations, *The Wall Street Journal*, Dow Jones News, and, of course, the websites of individual funders.

To find more information about foundations, numerous online sources are useful for conducting research. If you are looking for a particular foundation, you can always Google the name of the foundation and go straight to their website. But finding prospective funders is not always so easy. Here are some free and paid resources:

- GuideStar (www.guidestar.org)
- Foundation Center (https://fconline. foundationcenter.org/)
- Foundation Search (www.foundation search.com/)
- Council on Foundations (www.cof.org/)
- iWave (www.iwave.com/)
- Wealth Engine (www.wealthengine. com/)
- Social media sites
- Search engines like Google and Bing

Step 2: PRObe for Information With Open-Ended Questions

Before your meeting with the client, you can begin to probe for information using some important open-ended questions that you can ask both yourself and the client. For example, using your previous research, you should understand the issues involved in the following questions before talking to the client:

- What are the most important priorities for the funding organization?
- What do the funder's guidelines fail to tell you about what they fund?
- Do you know any board members of the funding organization?
- What does the funding organization value the most?
- What is the strategic fit between your organization and the client's organization?

- What are the important questions that you need to ask the client that you cannot learn online or from previous research?

According to Scanlan (1997), fundraisers use several approaches with corporate donors and foundations (beggar approach, superior–inferior approach, and negotiated partnership approach). We highly recommend only using the negotiated partnership approach. In principle, we never recommend the beggar approach that says, "Anything you can do will help." Instead, we believe that the most productive approach is to seek to create a long-term partnership in which both parties recognize that they may have different but complementary goals. Both parties will change roles in the relationship, but trust and commitment to the relationship are vitally important.

Step 3: PROvide Solutions by Matching Program Features With Funding Guidelines

Finally, in keeping with step 3 of the PRO method, the fundraiser must match features of the program or initiative with the funding guidelines. Remember, you are the expert (i.e., the pro) when it comes to your organization and the prospective initiative for which you are seeking funding. Therefore, do not ever shortchange yourself or your organization. Instead, speak to the funder in a positive, enthusiastic manner and with confidence. Koenig (2019) suggests that the best way to create long-lasting connections is to practice, practice, and then practice some more before talking to the prospective client. You should practice aloud

The Boston Bruins Foundation making a special donation to the Franklin Youth Hockey Association.

Patrick McDermott/NHLI via Getty Images

(perhaps using a tape recorder or practicing with a friend, colleague, or family member) and in front of a mirror. According to Koenig, you should rehearse the following:

- What are some potential objections from the funder, and how will you graciously address each objection? Objections from a funding organization may include statements like "We don't fund those types of initiatives" or "We fund only certain types of organizations."

- How will you structure the in-person meeting? Where will it be held? At the funding organization's offices? Will you be speaking to one person or a group? Will the meeting possibly be virtual instead of in person?

- How long will you allow small talk in the beginning? What do you know about the person or persons you will be speaking with? What are their interests (e.g., sports, travel, hobbies, etc.) that may lead to small talk?

- How will you transition smoothly from small talk to making the ask for funding? From your first conversation, the funder should be aware of why you scheduled the meeting. One of the best ways to transition from small talk is to use stories that lead to talking about the funding initiative. If you are in the funder's office, you may be able to ask questions about certain photos or other artifacts that lead to talking about the funding initiative.

- What are your most important talking points? Make sure they align with important priorities for the funder.

- Exactly how will you frame your ask for funding? The ask may take time, and sometimes it may be best to bring in someone else to help make it. In some cases, the appeal can be personal; at other times, you may need to be specific about how your program aligns with the funding organization's priorities. Stories are always effective, especially when they come from the population being served. For example, if a nonprofit is asking for funding to provide equipment for a team in a low socioeconomic community, hearing from the players and coaches about how the equipment helped would be beneficial.

Step 4: PROpose an Initiative That Fits With the Funding Client's Priorities

Step 4 of the PRO method is to PROpose an offer that best fits the customer's needs. In the case of working with corporations and foundations, we recommend that the fundraiser propose an initiative that fits with the funding client's priorities. At some point, the fundraiser will need to talk to the funder in detail about the dollar amount needed for funding the initiative. At this point, most potential funders will ask for a letter of inquiry.

Letter of Inquiry

Many funding organizations will ask for a one- to three-page letter of inquiry (LOI), and full proposals will be by invitation only. The process depends on the funding organization and their guidelines. Funding organizations often ask for LOIs because they put less of a burden on the organization applying and assure that only projects of interest to the funding source are invited to submit a full proposal. The **letter of inquiry** is "a non-legally binding document that includes an introduction to your project, contact information at your agency, a description of your organization, a statement of need, your methodology and/or an achievable solution to the need, a brief discussion of other funding sources and a final summary" (Hikind, 2020). The LOI is like a miniproposal that normally includes a description of a proposed program, initiative, or project. When writing the LOI, the fundraiser must be persuasive in building the case for why the organization should receive funding (Scanlan, 1997).

The LOI should be clear, concise, engaging, and tailored to each foundation. Your initial research about the mission and program areas at the foundation are essential when writing it (Northwestern University Foundation Relations, 2020). The goal of the LOI is to move to the next stage of the process, which is to submit the full proposal.

The LOI is the fundraiser's chance to get representatives from the funding organization excited about funding the idea. Reaching this goal is why writing is an important skill for sport fundraisers. According to the Foundation Center (n.d.b), the LOI can be the deciding factor for funding organizations, and it should include the following sections:

- *Introduction section, which serves as the executive summary*—Include the name of the organization requesting the grant, a description of the project, qualifications of project staff, a brief description of evaluative methodology, the amount requested, and a timetable. You should highlight the need for the project in this section and the way in which it meets the funding organization's guidelines and interests.

- *Organization description*—Briefly discuss your organization's ability to meet the stated need, include a brief history and description of your current programs, and clearly show a direct connection between what you do now and what you want to do with the requested funding.

- *Statement of need*—You must convince the reader at the funding organization that your project can meet an important need. You should include a description of your target population and geographic area along with quantifiable facts about what you are doing and hope to do.

- *Methodology*—In this section you should present a clear, logical, and achievable solution to your earlier stated need. Describe the project briefly, including major activities, names and titles of key project staff, and your desired objectives. You may also include other funding sources in this section.

- *Final summary*—In this section, restate the purpose of the project and let the potential funder know that you are willing to answer any

questions. Finally, do not forget to thank the potential funder for considering your project.

The LOI is a business letter and should be written on a business letterhead with the company's address on the right-hand side and the funder's address on the left-hand side of the paper. When addressing the funder, use the name of the recipient and avoid general terminology such as "Dear Sir" or "To Whom It May Concern" (Hikind, 2020). Carlson and O'Neal-McElrath (2008) suggest that you state the name of the project and amount of money being sought in the first paragraph. The second paragraph should elaborate about the project. The LOI should talk about the organization's mission, the need for the project, project outcomes, implementation of the project, and the fit with the foundation's priorities. The LOI should also discuss whether any funding has already been committed and provide contact details of a person who can answer questions.

Full Proposals or Letters?

When requesting funds from corporations and foundations, the question is often asked whether they both require full proposals. The answer to this question is "It depends." Foundations normally require a full proposal, but when requesting a donation or a gift-in-kind from a corporation, a two-page letter instead of a full formal proposal is usually best. In some cases, the corporation may have an application process. For example, the Dick's Sporting Goods (n.d.) Community Program supports leagues, teams, athletes, and outdoor enthusiasts by donating to and providing sponsorship for youth sports and outdoor recreation organizations in communities surrounding their stores. Organization representatives must go to their website where they are asked whether they are requesting a donation or sponsorship, years in existence, IRS classification, type of event, dates, total attendance, and participants. In the case of Dick's Sporting Goods, organizations can apply online. But if you need to write a letter, it should be written in a way that explains the need for the funding, outlines the request, and shows how the request will help your organization.

B2B REVENUE GENERATION

Follow-Up Report

Many funding agencies require a follow-up report by the nonprofit that addresses some or all of the following:

1. Project name
2. Amount funded
3. Date when the project started and ended
4. Total number of people served
5. Description of the outcome or results from the program
6. Reactions of the participants
7. What the organization learned from running the program
8. Description of the program's success

Step 5: PROtect the Relationship With a Corporation or Foundation

Building and cultivating relationships are important in fundraising, as is true in sales. Maintaining contact with funding representatives through continuous communications by email or phone is important to cultivating the relationship with a funding agency. Fostering the relationship is important because the funder is more likely to consider the nonprofit when other initiatives align with their priorities.

Some foundations will ask the nonprofit agency to file a follow-up report. This type of report is important because it lets the funding organization know that the nonprofit is spending the funds as planned. The report also helps the funding agency understand the effectiveness of the programs and the way in which their funds are impacting their target audience.

Summary

Corporations and foundations donate hundreds of billions of dollars each year. The fundamental principles of giving back are ingrained in almost every company and corporation, and their employees expect that the organization will be engaged in promoting the social good. CSR is vitally important within sport, and almost every sport organization is engaged in being socially responsible in one way or another. These initiatives range from national initiatives like NBA Cares and NFL Play 60 to more localized initiatives in which players volunteer at a local food bank. Corporations outside sport engage in many forms of giving. Some donate through corporate giving programs, and others have a corporate foundation. Corporations may give away cash or product or raise funds through company-wide service events or checkout charity programs. They may make corporate grants, matching gifts, or in-kind contributions. They may offer volunteer time off for employees or pro bono services.

Corporate giving programs are important ways that companies give back. The three basic types of foundations are private foundations, community foundations, and operating foundations. We discussed the differences among them and some of their advantages and disadvantages. Private foundations include independent or nonoperating foundations, family foundations, corporate foundations, international foundations, and private operating foundations. More than 750 community foundations in the United States play a key role in identifying and solving community problems by distributing funds for a variety of nonprofit activities. Finally, operating foundations use the bulk of their income to run their own charitable programs or services.

Fundraisers in sport must understand how to research and correspond with corporate giving programs and foundations. This chapter provided guidance about how to research funders using resources like the Foundation Directory, Foundation Source, LexisNexis, GuideStar, Foundation Center, and Grants.gov. The PRO method can be applied effectively when soliciting corporate and foundation funding. Unlike some other areas of revenue generation, written skills come into play when writing inquiry letters or letters of requests for funding. Funding from corporations and foundations can be lucrative for sport organizations, and applying the knowledge and skills presented in this chapter provides a good foundation for seeking such funding.

APPLIED LEARNING ACTIVITIES

1. Do some surfing on the Internet to find out if you have a community foundation in your local area. Find contact information for the foundation and contact them. Either call or email representatives of the foundation and ask the following questions: (1) What is the primary mission of the community foundation? (2) What are the most important initiatives for the foundation? Create a one- to two-minute YouTube video describing what you learned.

2. Based on reading the chapter, describe the differences between receiving funds from a corporation versus a foundation. Write a short essay with a minimum of 250 words that highlights these differences.

CASE STUDY

NFL'S CRUCIAL CATCH PROGRAM AND SOCIAL RESPONSIBILITY

Corporate social responsibility is the idea that corporations with power should help those in need and recognizes that corporations have responsibilities beyond profit maximization. One of the most popular and relevant corporate social giving initiatives is the NFL's Crucial Catch program. Crucial Catch is a fundraising initiative that helps fight cancer through early detection and risk education. Many NFL players get involved by donating money and time. Athletes like Stephon Gilmore and Kyle Rudolph are even recognized as Crucial Catch regional ambassadors. The NFL's investment in helping save lives has reached hundreds of thousands of people through cancer screenings and raised tens of millions in funds since 2009 (NFL, n.d.). In 2020 the cancer diagnosis of Washington Football Team (WFT) coach Ron Rivera resulted in an increase in fundraising and support. The NFL rallied to support Rivera and created new merchandise with colors that represent Crucial Catch. The NFL and the WFT created a special surprise for Rivera before a game against the Ravens. The surprise consisted of several cardboard cutouts of Rivera's family and friends that were placed in the stadium. The cutouts helped raise $33,000, which was donated to Crucial Catch.

Discussion Questions

1. Imagine that you are the senior director of social responsibility for the NFL. You want to create a new social responsibility program and must present your idea to the owners to get it passed and turn your idea into reality. Do some research and identify a marginalized group that is struggling or needs help within the United States. Create a headline for the program and a brief description like the one provided for the Crucial Catch program.

2. Corporate social responsibility is the idea that corporations with power should help those in need. It emphasizes the idea that corporations have responsibilities beyond profit maximization. This notion carries over heavily into the sport industry. Beyond the case with the NFL described earlier, describe initiatives of two other sport organizations involved with CSR.

Go to HK*Propel* to watch author videos, engage in sales scenarios, and find downloadable sales templates related to this chapter.

Robert Laberge/Getty Images for Masters Grand Slam Indoor

CHAPTER 7

Fundraising
and Development in Sport

CHAPTER OBJECTIVES

After completing the chapter, you should be able to do the following:

- Define fundraising and the difference between sales and fundraising
- Explore the ethical challenges of sport development
- Explain fundraising in the context of the sport industry
- Describe the many types of giving
- Understand the various ways to raise money in interscholastic sport
- Discuss fundraising issues and challenges in youth sport
- Explore how to create a development plan
- Apply the PRO method of selling to fundraising from individuals

Whereas chapter 6 focused on corporate and foundation revenues, this chapter focuses on fundraising from individuals. Fundraising, also called development, is a type of sales that has its own terminology and is used more predominantly in some segments of the sport industry than others. For example, fundraisers are needed in intercollegiate and interscholastic athletics to advance their sport programs and provide scholarships for student-athletes. Nonprofit sport organizations such as Special Olympics, Girls on the Run, Soccer Without Borders (SWB), and the Boys & Girls Clubs of America raise funds to help advance their mission. Organizations take a variety of approaches to generating revenues, from soliciting larger donations and smaller gifts to using events and various forms of technology. One of the best ways to progress to the top of any organization is to have the skills necessary for generating revenues. Fundraising and development generate essential income for nonprofit organizations, but they also measure the degree to which the purpose of an organization is affirmed (Fogal, 2005). Throughout this chapter we use the words *fundraising* and *development* interchangeably.

Raising funds is one of the most important business skills for any higher-level manager or administrator. Fundraising is the most important skill and experience that Power 5 Conference athletics directors can have (Kirkpatrick, 2018). Students who not only understand the importance of fundraising and development but also are able to develop transferable skills in those areas will be well positioned to advance and prosper in the sport industry. Matt Goff (personal communication, October 19, 2020), the associate director of major gifts at Virginia Tech, advises college students to develop those skills while in college and make the effort to talk to and be comfortable around people. Goff explains that development is a form of sales and recommends that students reach out to their college or university's athletics department or even the business office to do an internship in fundraising or marketing.

Fundraising is instrumental to sport at every level, and professional fundraisers are critically important to nonprofit organizations. But fundraising is done not just by professionals but also by youth, parents, and friends to allow youth sport and recreation programming to happen. Jeff Brooks, a fundraising professional who has written books on the topic, suggests that the kind of fundraising that changes the world is about connecting a cause with the donor's values and putting action in their hands (Jeff Brooks Fundraising, 2020). Brooks claims that if you need to raise funds from donors, then you are going to have to study them, respect them, and build everything you do around them (Hansen, 2017). Regardless of whether you are a professional fundraiser working within the sport industry or nonprofit sector, or are simply raising funds for a youth program, you need to understand the fundamentals of fundraising and development. You also need to be aware of ethical issues in fundraising.

Ethical Considerations in Development

Although development is critical to the long-term success of any organization, raising funds is not easy. Increasingly, corporations are analyzing where, how, and why they are contributing money. In a post-COVID 19 era, such contributions will become even more highly scrutinized. But it is not only corporations that are reviewing their contributions but also individual donors. Therefore, ethics is critically important for people who are raising funds. How much money you spend on fundraising is an important issue. Donors want to know that most of the money given is being spent on important issues they support. Perhaps you have heard a story about a nonprofit that was misappropriating funds or spending it on salaries and administrative costs instead of important programming. Some nonprofit organizations provide a **donor's bill of rights**, which was created by a number of associations to highlight various ethical issues germane to philanthropy. The bill of rights helps to foster respect and trust in the public and build donors' confidence in the organizations they support.

Today's development professional is not only being asked about the amount of money raised but also responding to these equally important questions (Ciconte & Jacob, 2001):

- How much did the fundraising campaign cost?
- Is that cost reasonable?
- How do your costs compare with those of similar organizations?
- How do you measure performance?
- Can you estimate how much will be raised next year?

The Association of Fundraising Professionals (AFP) developed five universal principles for fundraisers, which include honesty, respect, integrity, empathy, and transparency, as outlined here (as cited in Rohrbach, 2013, pp. 142-143):

- *Honesty*. Fundraisers shall at all times act honestly and truthfully so that the public trust is protected and donors and beneficiaries are not misled.
- *Respect*. Fundraisers shall at all times act with respect for the dignity of their profession and their organization and with respect for the dignity of donors and beneficiaries.
- *Integrity*. Fundraisers will act openly and with regard to their responsibility for public trust. They shall disclose all actual or potential conflicts of interest and avoid any appearance of personal or professional misconduct.
- *Empathy*. Fundraisers will work in a way that promotes their purpose and encourages others to use the same professional standards and engagement. They shall value individual privacy, freedom of choice, and diversity in all forms.
- *Transparency*. Fundraisers will write clear reports about the work they do, the way donations are managed and disbursed, and their costs and expenses in an accurate and comprehensible manner.

As an example of these principles, the United States Olympic and Paralympic Foundation (2018) makes the following promises in their donor bill of rights: (1) donor being informed of the intended use of the gift; (2) identity and stewardship of the board of directors; (3) right to see audited finances; (4) funds will be used for the purposes for which the gift was given; (5) the right to receive acknowledgment and recognition of the gift; (6) information will be handled with respect and confidentiality; (7) relationships with organizational representatives will be handled in a professional manner; (8) informing donors about who is seeking donations; (9) ability to delete the donor's name from the organization's mailing lists; and (10) the donor can ask questions and receive answers.

Sport development professionals must consider other various ethical considerations when raising money. The fundraiser must understand the types of funds being donated (Fritz, 2020). As noted by Fritz, the two types of funds are restricted funds and unrestricted funds. **Restricted funds** are set aside for a particular purpose normally because the donor has requested the funds be used for this purpose. These types of funds can be temporarily restricted or permanently restricted. Temporarily restricted funds may allow the restriction to end after a specified time or at the completion of a project (e.g., construction of a facility). Permanently restricted funds are normally meant to be saved or invested in an endowment fund. An endowment fund is an investment made by or on behalf of a foundation that uses the earnings from the investment to fund operations. The largest endowments are normally held by universities with wealthy alumni who donate money to the institution's endowment each year. In contrast to these restrictions, **unrestricted funds** can be used by a nonprofit organization for any purpose they deem necessary, often toward normal operating costs. When talking to a donor the sport fundraiser must determine whether the donor has certain restrictions on how the funds are used because the donor helps to determine whether the funds are restricted or unrestricted.

Development professionals should also understand the two types of charitable solicitations (McRay, 2017). McRay suggests when a nonprofit organization asks an individual or corporation to donate for a particular cause, this donation is deemed a **solicited designation**. Therefore, when a nonprofit organization directly solicits for a particular cause, these funds must be dedicated for that purpose. But when an individual or organization approaches a nonprofit without having been solicited by the charity, the donation is considered an **unsolicited designation**. In unsolicited cases, where the donation is designated depends on what the nonprofit tells the donor at the time of the gift. If the donor requests that the money be used for specific purposes and the nonprofit charity does not notify the donor that it may be used otherwise, then the funds should be restricted. If, however, the nonprofit charity informs the donor of what the funds will be used for or provides a disclaimer (e.g., our organization reserves the right to use donated money as we see fit) at the time of the donation, then the restriction does not apply.

Types of Giving

Development jobs are often categorized by the type of giving. For example, a nonprofit organization may have positions with job titles within the organizational like development director, director of annual giving, capital campaign manager, athletics major gifts officer, manager of fundraising events, and planned-giving offi-

cer. We discuss each of the various categories in the following sections.

Annual Giving

An annual giving program uses a great variety of fundraising techniques to introduce the programs, services, and needs of an organization to the widest audience possible (Ciconte & Jacob, 2001). The term *annual giving* is often used as an all-encompassing term for fundraising such as direct mail, email appeals, online solicitations, special events, and others. Regardless of what the gift funds, the hope with annual giving is that the donor will support the organization each year (AGN, 2017). An **annual fund** is an organized effort to solicit regular donations from donors that support the daily operation of a nonprofit organization and its ongoing programs. Its primary purpose is to cultivate a large group of active donors who share an interest in the organization's mission. Many donors are invited to renew their investment each year, and payments may occur in the form of a one-time payment or in an agreed-upon number of installments (Sargeant & Shang, 2017). Building a strong annual fund is an important part of any effective fundraising program. Although the terms *annual giving* and *annual fund* are often used interchangeably, the latter is often considered simply a financial term, whereas *annual giving* is a much broader term (AGN, 2017).

B2C REVENUE GENERATION

Annual Campaign for the Boys & Girls Club of St. Lucie County

The Boys & Girls Clubs (B&GC) of St. Lucie County in Florida uses an annual campaign to support their programs that seek to enrich experiences for youth. On their website, B&GC suggests that donors can contribute tiered amounts, and they provide investment levels that indicate what the donated amount funds. For example, B&GC suggests that $20 provides one child membership for a year; $50 funds a one-week scholarship for a child to attend a summer program; $100 funds homework help for a child for one month; $250 funds a five-week summer program scholarship; $500 funds 25 B&GC club memberships; $800 funds an entire summer program for a child; and $1,000 funds 50 B&GC club memberships.

When considering an annual appeal, fundraisers within a sport organization should plan out a year's worth of appeals aimed at particular segments of their database. For example, these segments may include past contributors, affinity groups, and nondonors. The fundraiser should develop a yearly appeals schedule that includes the date when the appeal will be sent, audience, number of persons in each category, funding goal, and the project for which they are asking for funding. Many sport organizations build their donor base by asking for small gifts from new prospects and by sending direct mail appeals to nondonors at least three times during the year. Sharing a list of items that donors could potentially fund is useful, and using matching challenge gifts can increase the response rate of the appeal. Asking sponsors to underwrite the total cost of one or more or even all the appeals during the year is a common way that many organizations pay for the cost of direct mail (Stevenson, 2009). Table 7.1 shows an example of an annual appeals schedule that a fundraiser in youth sport may put together.

Many intercollegiate athletics departments use annual giving to reach out to donors. For example, at the University of Colorado, the goal of the Buff Club (2020) annual fund in 2020 was to raise $6.5 million and to grow their member base exponentially. As with most intercollegiate athletics departments, funds contributed to the Buff Club Annual Fund support athletics scholarships, the academic experience of student-athletes, and various sport-specific pro-grams. The following advice can enhance an appeal to an annual fund donor (Jarvis, 2018):

- Be clear about what you are asking the funder to do. If you want them to contribute, then ask specifically.
- Tell a story by putting a face to the problem you are asking them to help fund.
- Choose your words carefully. Use words like "you, your, yours" instead of "we, our, ours," and use "because" language.
- Check the formatting of your letter and remember that people will look first at the photo, followed by the salutation, postscript, signature, and then the body of the letter.
- Make sure to personalize your appeal and ensure that it is easy to scan because most people will not read the entire letter.
- Make it easy for someone to donate by including a link to the donation form. Find out how many clicks it takes you to get to the donation form.
- Stay away from standard number 10 envelopes if mailing the appeal. A larger envelope with the company's logo or a slogan may be more eye catching. Also, when emailing you should use a short, positive subject line that stands out to donors.
- Inactive donors should be monitored and removed, and the annual appeal should speak differently to different types of donors.

TABLE 7.1 Example of an Annual Appeals Schedule

Date	Type of appeal	Audience	Number of donors	Funding goal	Project
1/20/2022	Letter	Organizations	200	$30,000	Youth Fit-for-Life (ages 6-18)
2/10/2022	Telephone	Organizations	200	$30,000	Youth Fit-for-Life (ages 6-18)
6/15/2022	Email	Parents	50	$5,000	Cardio Plus
7/01/2022	Telephone	Parents	50	$5,000	Cardio Plus

Capital Campaign

A **capital campaign** is an organized effort to raise funds for a relatively large project within an existing organization with a fixed budget and timeline (Sargeant, 2017). A capital campaign is often the strategic means that an organization uses to achieve their major funding requirements (DeWitt, 2011). Capital campaigns traditionally pay for projects such as new buildings and their expansion or for large-scale equipment and supply purchases. For example, on September 28, 2018, the University of Arizona Wildcat Club announced the approval of four athletics department facility projects with a combined cost of $66 million: the east side of Arizona Stadium, Hillenbrand Aquatic Center, Hillenbrand Softball Stadium, and the Cole and Jeannie Davis Sports Center. These facility projects were part of the University of Arizona's Capital Improvement Plan, and the funding stemmed from their capital campaign (University of Arizona Wildcat Club, 2020). Capital campaigns normally occur over multiple years, and most of the costs are typically incurred in the initial months of the campaign (Sargeant, 2017).

The methods chosen for the capital campaign provide the organization opportunities such as raising major gifts for facilities and endowments, renewing enthusiasm in the mission, training new leadership, broadening the base of supporters, and raising the organization's visibility (DeWitt, 2011). Development professionals need to create a timeline for their capital campaign. The timeline for a campaign may vary, but it usually includes three stages and two important phases within the implementation stage (Donor Search, 2020):

1. *Planning stage*—In this stage, an organization must assemble a team that may consist of board members, staff, and volunteers. Goals and deadlines are set, and a feasibility study is conducted. In addition, the organization screens potential prospects.

2. *Implementation stage*—After careful planning for the capital campaign, it is now time to put it into practice. The implementation stage contains both a quiet phase and a public phase.

   a. *Quiet phase*—In this phase the committee starts to solicit major gift donors, corporations, or government agencies. Approximately 50 to 70 percent of the funds for the capital campaign will be raised during this time, which may take up to a year to complete.

   b. *Public phase*—The public phase includes a kickoff, or launching, of the campaign. It may include a press conference or launch party. In the public phase, the committee begins to solicit a large number of smaller donations from various members of the community.

3. *Follow-up stage*—This stage wraps up all the efforts put forward in the capital campaign. The primary activities that occur in this stage are saying thank you to donors and updating them on the project by sending emails and newsletters, conducting special events, making phone calls, and using other forms of communication.

An organization can tier their giving by using a giving funnel during the public phase of the capital campaign. Table 7.2 illustrates an example of an organization with a $1,000,000 goal using a giving funnel. A giving funnel can be useful in motivating donors, and it tells the development professional how many gifts at various amounts are needed to reach various goals. The funnel also helps donors better understand how their gift can contribute to the greater goal. Not everyone can give a large gift, but development professionals should strive to keep everyone involved, regardless of the amount they give. Someone who may not be able to give a large gift at one point in time may be able to contribute a larger gift at another time. With the giving funnel, a development professional is building a culture of giving for all.

TABLE 7.2   Capital Campaign Funnel During Public Phase to Raise $1M

Individual gift amount	Number of gifts and amount	Subtotal raised
$100,000	1 gift of $100,000	$100,000
$50,000	2 gifts of $50,000	$100,000
$25,000	12 gifts of $25,000	$300,000
$15,000	2 gifts of $15,000	$30,000
$10,000	15 gifts of $10,000	$150,000
$5,000	22 gifts of $5,000	$110,000
$2,500	30 gifts of $2,500	$75,000
$1,000	60 gifts of $1,000	$60,000
$500	150 gifts of $500	$75,000
		Total raised: $1M

Event Fundraising

Raising funds through various types of events and causes is popular. Such activities are not only a great way to raise a lot of money but also help to enhance an organization's brand awareness. Some of the largest and most common types of fundraising events include A-Thon events, art exhibits, auctions, banquets with food and beverage, bike races, concerts, fun runs and walks, galas, nonsport competitions, sport competitions and tournaments, and many others. Event fundraising has four primary purposes: (1) raising money by providing a social opportunity for a donor to make a gift; (2) identifying prospects by inviting the participation of individuals, corporations, and foundations who have an interest in the cause; (3) educating and cultivating supporters; and (4) recognizing others by acknowledging volunteers or individual donors who donated significant gifts (Sergeant & Shang, 2017).

Perhaps you have participated in a fundraising event like American Cancer Society's (n.d.) Relay for Life event, which is designed to bring communities together to raise funds for the fight against cancer. The overnight event consists of teams of 8 to 15 people formed by businesses, clubs, families, friends, hospitals, churches, schools, and service organizations who have the common purpose of supporting the mission of the American Cancer Society. Team members take turns walking on a track and camping out overnight. Each participant is encouraged to raise at least $100 for the American Cancer Society.

Worldwide, about 56 percent of all donors attend some type of event fundraiser (Double the Donation, 2020). In the midst of the global pandemic in April 2020, the NFL raised more than $100 million during their Virtual Draft, which was donated to organizations such as the Salvation Army, American Red Cross, Meals on Wheels, United Way, Feeding America, and the CDC Foundation (Young, 2020). The following tips are helpful when using an event to fundraise (Heyman & Brenner, 2016):

- Identify specific goals for the event by having a clear purpose that drives and focuses all the fundraising efforts for the event.

- Create a calendar and a budget that lists all necessary tasks.

- Recruit an event committee to assist with organizing the event at least six months before the event. Duties should be divided and assigned.

- Secure sponsors and start reaching out to past event sponsors and the organization's largest supporters at least six months in advance.

- Build a strong event page with the goal of maximizing the **conversion rate**, which is the percentage of people who visit the page and then sign up to attend.

- Promote your event by recruiting event attendees through email and leveraging your existing networks, social media, public relations, newsletters, and mailing lists.

- Launch ticket sales six to eight weeks before the event that provides a 10 to 20 percent discount for the first two weeks.

- Create an agenda that maps out a detailed timeline that may include a welcoming reception, autograph session, meet and greet, luncheon or dinner, welcoming remarks, live auction, or other activities.

- Maximize your ask by explicitly and directly inviting people to donate.

- Follow up and debrief by thanking people as soon as possible after the event for their attendance and donations. Follow-up phone calls or handwritten notes are excellent ways to communicate gratitude.

One of the biggest challenges of event fundraising is the sheer amount of coordination that goes into planning an event (Cherico, 2014). With this said, fundraisers need to have the full support of the nonprofit board of directors, staff, and upper-level managers along with a host of volunteers. Furthermore, all those involved in planning the event will be frustrated if they work hard and fail to raise significant funds. Fundraisers should consider the efficiency of the event to measure and communicate its success. To measure event efficiency, first determine net revenue by adding up costs and subtracting the total costs from total revenue. Next, divide net revenue by total revenue and multiply the result by 100 (Rosen, 2012).

$$\text{net revenue} = \text{revenue} - \text{cost}$$

$$\text{event efficiency} = (\text{net revenue} \div \text{revenue}) \times 100$$

After you determine event efficiency, the next issue is determining whether an event is successful. Most organizations that depend on volunteers and seek full or partial donations of event merchandise should be able to attain at least 70 percent efficiency (Rosen, 2012).

Event Fundraising and the Duke Club Golf Classic

At James Madison University in Virginia, the Duke Club Golf Classic is a signature event for the athletics department that raises funds for student-athlete scholarships and the general operating budget. The event raised over $38,000 in 2019. In 2020 the 35th annual Classic took place in fall rather than spring because of the COVID-19 pandemic. Typically, the tournament is maxed out at 200 golfers in a captain's choice USGA style of play. The golfers register for one of two flights, morning or afternoon. Pre- and postflight food and beverages are included in their registration. Along with their greens fees, golf cart rental, and pre- and postflight hospitality, the golfers receive a registration bag with a gift and items from sponsors. On the course, golfers enjoy unlimited beverages and snacks while interacting with coaches and student-athletes, the beneficiaries of the tournament.

Courtesy of JMU Athletics

Major Gifts

Major gift fundraising is considered one of the most cost effective and efficient forms of development because it allows an organization the opportunity to inform people with financial means about their programs and services (Weinstein & Barden, 2017). Major gifts, also known as gifts of significance, may include substantial contributions of cash or assets such as gifts of appreciated securities or in-kind gifts such as valuable art or personal property (Tempel et al., 2011). Major gifts can be used for sponsorships, special projects, pacesetting operations contributions, and capital and endowment campaigns.

How much must a person give for the gift to be considered a major gift? The answer depends on the organization. For example, for a small organization, a gift of $1 million might be a major gift; for another organization, a gift of $25 million might be considered major. A good rule of thumb for determining a major gift within an organization is to set it at a level where approximately 5 percent of donors can and will give at that level (Einstein, 2020). Major gifts are 10 to 25 times larger than an annual gift, are infrequently requested, and require considerable thought by the donor before commitment (Dunlop, 2000). Although cash contributions are always great to receive, the truth of the matter is that most major gifts are in the form of a prospective donor's assets.

Planned Giving

Planned giving refers to charitable donations made with some level of professional guidance (Weinstein & Barden, 2017), which normally involves a process of making a significant charitable gift during a donor's life or at death that is part of their financial or estate plan (Prince, 2016). Some authors have defined planned giving more broadly by suggesting that it refers to any donation requiring a lot of thought by the donor, whereas others regard it more as a synonym for charitable gifts that are made at the time of the donor's death (Beem &

Sargeant, 2017). Various terms are often used in place of the term *planned giving*, including deferred giving, charitable gift planning, and legacy giving. According to Giving USA (2019), bequests given by individuals to charities amounted to $39.71 billion of the $427.71 billion given to charities in 2018, thus amounting to 9 percent of total giving for the year. Beem and Sargeant describe planned giving as having the following characteristics:

- Planned gifts are created now for the future benefit of an organization.
- The future benefit of a planned gift could occur later in a donor's life, at death, or at some point after the donor's death.
- The benefit of the planned gift could be a one-time distribution, regular payment of a specific amount, or regular payment of a variable amount.
- The commitment to a planned gift is revocable in some cases and not in others. Donors can change the specific nonprofit organization that benefits from revocable and some irrevocable gifts.
- Donors may receive tax benefits because of their planned gift.

Several instruments or vehicles can be used within planned giving. Beem and Sargeant (2017) and Weinstein and Barden (2017) define a variety of planned-giving vehicles used by fundraisers for engaging donors, including bargain sales, bequests, annuities, and trusts. Sport organizations vary in terms of their level of commitment to seeking planned gifts. For example, many universities and larger nonprofit sport organizations have specific staff members who work in planned giving. In these cases, the planned-giving officer talks with potential donors about the various giving vehicles. These types of organizations have already set up a system that helps in administering these types of gifts. Development officers talk with the donor about potential tax issues and any risks to the donor. Some sport organizations, however, do not have a specific staff member assigned and instead may be

Planned Giving With the Women's Sports Foundation

On their website, the Women's Sports Foundation (WSF) (2020) suggests that a donor may receive financial and tax benefits while also supporting the needs and mission of the organization. For example, in the form of various types of bequests, donors may include the WSF in their will, retirement plan, living trust, or estate plan in the following ways:

© Human Kinetics

- *General bequest*—The donor specifies a specific dollar amount left to WSF.
- *Naming a specific property*—The WSF would receive specific assets, such as securities, a piece of real estate (such as a residence), or tangible personal property (such as artwork).
- *Residuary bequest*—In this case, the WSF receives all or a percentage of the remainder of the donor's estate after the payment of general and specific bequests and estate-related expenses.
- *Contingent bequest*—The WSF is given a bequest only in the event of the death of other beneficiaries.

---

approached by a donor asking if they can set up a vehicle like a bequest or bargain sale. In this case, the organization may work with a legal expert to make this happen. The following sections describe each of the various giving vehicles that may be used in planned giving.

Bargain Sale

As the name suggests, a bargain sale occurs when a donor sells something for less than its worth. For example, a donor may sell stocks or bonds to a nonprofit for less than their real worth. The amount paid by the nonprofit is the sale, and the bargain is the difference between the sale and the true purchase price. Donors can claim the bargain amount as a charitable deduction when filing their taxes.

Bequests

A donor can make a simple provision in their will, trust, or codicil whereby they allocate a gift (bequest) to a designated charity. A bequest

allows donors to perpetuate their values and support the work of an organization of their choice. The formal language used in a will may be something like the following: "I give, bequeath, and devise the sum of one million dollars to Sports for Kids, 156 King Street, Herndon, Virginia." The gift amount may be stated in several ways, including a specific amount, a percentage amount (e.g., 15 percent), or a remainder amount, also called the residue amount (i.e., the remainder of the donor's estate after all specific bequests have been paid).

In their first ever planned-giving report, FreeWill (2020) shed some interesting insights germane to the more than 50,000 users who completed wills on their website between 2017 and 2019. Their findings suggested that the mean size of all giving made in wills with bequests was $108,482 and that adults aged 44 and older represented more than 75 percent of the wills and greater than 80 percent of the total value of all charitable bequests. In addition, although almost 80 percent of those writing a will were parents, the remaining 20 percent did not have children, and they were far more likely to include a charitable bequest in their wills and at a higher monetary value. A key finding from their report suggests that a person's net worth does not drive their planned giving; more important was their level of passion for the issues and causes they most care about.

Charitable Gift Annuities

Another fundraising option is a **charitable gift annuity**, which is a legal contract between a donor and a nonprofit organization that involves the irrevocable transfer of property (cash, real property, or securities) in exchange to pay the donor or donor's designee an annuity for life. In essence, the donor severs ties to his or her assets over the entirety of life and gives the assets to the nonprofit in return for payments for life (or payments to a designee) that have a present value less than the value of the assets. The benefits to the donor include the following:

- The donor cannot outlive the source of income.
- The donor receives an immediate income tax deduction equal to the present value of the future gift.
- The annuity reduces the donor's taxable estate, and the donor avoids probate.
- The gift continues after the donor's death.

Charitable Remainder Trusts

With a charitable remainder trust (CRT), a donor can transfer cash or other valuable assets to the trust and receive income for life. The irrevocable trust pays a specified annual amount to one or more people for a fixed period of years. The remaining trust assets are distributed to the nonprofit charity at the end of the term of the trust. The donor can avoid capital gains taxes because the trust can sell those assets tax free, which can be beneficial for assets that have appreciated in value.

Charitable Remainder Unitrusts

The most versatile of the planned-giving instruments, a **charitable remainder unitrust** (CRUT) allows the donor and other designated beneficiaries to receive income over either the donor's life, donors' joint lives, or for life plus a stated term of years. The balance of the trust assets is transferred to one or more charitable remainder nonprofits after the life income beneficiary obligation has been met. The CRUT is a standalone entity that must meet strict Internal Revenue Service (IRS) code requirements and cannot be changed by its donor or beneficiaries after it is set up. CRUTs can take any of the following three forms:

- Standard, whereby annual payments of a fixed percentage of the trust's annual value are made, regardless of whether earnings from the trust's assets are sufficient to make the payments. When the earnings are insufficient, the difference comes out of the trust's principal.
- Net income, whereby annual payments of a fixed percentage of the trust's annual value are made but are never more than the amount earned by the trust in any given year.
- Net income with makeup provisions, whereby annual payments are made with an added provision. The added provision states that when earnings exceed the percentage that must be paid, the excess earnings must be used to make up for any payments less than the fixed percentage in earlier years.

Charitable Remainder Annuity Trusts

With a **charitable remainder annuity trust** (CRAT), the amount paid to the donor each year is a fixed percentage of the value of the trust at the time it is established. A CRAT is essentially the same as a CRUT with the following exceptions:

- The annuity trust may take only one form, whereas the CRUT may take three forms.
- The CRAT must make annual payments regardless of the trust's earnings in any given year.
- The CRAT must pay a fixed amount established at inception of the trust, and it can never vary.
- With a CRAT, additional contributions can never be accepted.

Charitable Lead Trusts

The opposite of a CRT, a lead trust makes annual payments (i.e., lead interest) to the charitable nonprofit and pays the remainders (i.e., the assets) to the donor. Following are some ways that donors can contribute to CRTs.

- *Current gifts*—Also referred to as outright gifts, current gifts include funds that are tax deductible for the donor and immediately available for use by the nonprofit organization (Weinstein & Barden, 2017). Current gifts may include any or all of the following: cash and checks, life insurance policies, personal property, real estate, or securities (e.g., stocks and bonds).
- *Life insurance gifts*—Donors can irrevocably donate an existing life insurance policy to a charity or purchase a policy on their life and irrevocably transfer its ownership to the charity.
- *Real estate gifts*—A donor can make a current or deferred gift of real estate. Current gifts offer immediate tax savings and relieve the donor of incurring the expense and burden of managing the property. Deferred gifts are often called life estate reserved, and donors retain a life estate in their personal residence while transferring the remainder interest to charity.
- *Wealth replacement trusts (WRT)*—Also called an asset value replacement trust, a WRT is an insurance trust that is established to benefit the heirs of the donor.

It is set up in tandem with a CRT and is funded with the money saved through tax deductions and the increased cash flow associated with the CRT.

Models of Fundraising in Various Types of Sport Organizations

This chapter has focused on fundraising, which is used in some, but not all, segments of the sport industry. So far, we have focused on the various types of development or fundraising, such as annual giving, capital campaigns, event fundraising, major gifts, and planned giving. The terms *fundraising* and *development* are primarily used in segments of the sport industry such as nonprofit sport organizations, intercollegiate and interscholastic athletics, and youth sport. Each of these segments has various types of models for raising funds.

Nonprofit Sport Organizations

Fundraising is vital to nonprofit sport organizations throughout the world, whatever their mission or purpose. These types of organizations are often classified by the IRS as 501(c)(3) charitable entities. Students who plan to work in one of these organizations need to understand the various types of fundraising and the process for raising funds because as development professionals they will implement the fundraising process for annual and capital campaigns, event fundraising, major gifts, and planned giving. Another important way that nonprofit sport organizations raise funds is through grant writing, which is covered in detail in chapter 8.

Although we could cite numerous examples of the types of gifts solicited by nonprofit organizations, we mention just one or two organizations for each. For example, a donor can contribute to the annual campaign for the Boys & Girls Clubs, fund the building or renovation of a facility through a YMCA capital campaign, donate a major gift to the United States Olympic and Paralympic Foundation, or donate to an organization through a planned-giving vehicle. Special Olympics (2020) suggests that a gift in a donor's will or trust is an easy way to create a legacy at no cost. The donor has the flexibility of altering their gift or changing their mind while making a lasting impact. The North Carolina High School Athletic Association (2020) uses an external partner to guide potential donors in terms of planned-giving opportunities such as donations of cash or stock, beneficiary designation, charitable remainder trusts, charitable lead trusts, and pooled income funds.

Intercollegiate Athletics

In 2019 American University in Washington, DC, which plays in the Patriot League, received a $3 million major gift to build a new athletics facility that provides competition and practice space for their NCAA varsity teams as well as club and intramural sports. In 2005 oil pioneer T. Boone Pickens made one of the largest major gifts ever to an athletics department when he gave the Oklahoma State athletics department $165 million, much of which went to football facilities. In 2014 the 48 schools in the Power 5 conferences in the NCAA spent $772 million combined on athletics facilities (Hobson & Rich, 2015). Where do all the funds come from to pay for these lavish facilities? The answer is that most of these funds come from major gifts that are donated to the athletics departments.

Almost every college or university in the United States has some form of development department that raises funds for their athletics program. Of course, fundraising and development vary from institution to institution based on factors like size and level of athletics competitiveness, conference affiliation, culture, budgets, and structure. For example, a Division III institution like American University in Washington, DC, will have a smaller fundraising staff than an institution competing in a Division I Power 5 conference like the Big Ten. American University is more likely to have one or two staff members raising funds in multiple specialty areas from fundraising

events (e.g., a tailgate, golf tournament, or virtual 5K) to annual campaigns and major gifts. A smaller fundraising department like this provides the fundraising professional with a lot of experience in multiple areas. In contrast, larger Division I institutions may have 18 to 20 staff members who specialize in annual or major gifts. Annual gift fundraisers often make cold calls and must have a keen understanding of the need for philanthropy. This side of the fundraising office often focuses on first-time gifts and casts a large net as they try to bring in as many gifts as possible. Development officers in major gifts often focus on gifts over $100,000 for scholarships, endowments, and capital support. In some cases, major gift officers reach out to prospective donors for seven-figure principal gifts. For many fundraising professionals in intercollegiate athletics, the traditional career path is to start as an annual gift fundraiser and climb the ladder to become a major gift officer.

Depending on the college or university, fundraising in the athletics department will be more or less integrated with the larger academic institution. A fundraiser working in the college or university's development office may move into an athletics fundraising position and vice versa. Some development officers are former athletes or coaches, and almost all of them have a passion for athletics. Regardless of the job, fundraising professionals must be self-starters who are highly motivated and have a strong work ethic. People in these positions must be resilient and optimistic, allowing them to handle rejection on a regular basis. Communication is critical. Fundraisers must be excellent writers and presenters, researchers, listeners, and collaborators because they work with a diverse pool of people in numerous disciplines and departments across campus.

People who possess the necessary skills and can apply the fundamental concepts of fundraising are likely to be successful regardless of the institution or level of athletics competition. Some minor differences are present among institutions, however, as already noted in the example highlighting staffing sizes at larger and smaller schools. The following are some of the differences between fundraising at the Division II level in comparison with Division I (Elliott, 2010):

- Division II programs have a higher percentage of large donors who support athletics along with other significant university causes.
- Division II programs have smaller donor bases, thus allowing development professionals the opportunity to build closer and more intimate relationships with donors.
- Development professionals at the Division II level have a better opportunity to match their donors' desires and interests with the greatest needs of the university because they develop more intimate relationships with donors and work closely with other development professionals at the school.

Note that although NCAA Division III institutions do not offer scholarships, Division II programs use a partial athletics scholarship model that permits the athletics department to divide a scholarship that counts toward a program's limit among multiple student-athletes. Therefore, these types of institutions can fund several student-athletes through one scholarship. For example, a $6,000 scholarship can be offered to a basketball player as a 0.25 scholarship equivalency of the institution's tuition (Hanson, 2019). Partial scholarships are also awarded at Division I institutions.

Technology is important within development because of the amount of time spent researching donors, making presentations, and writing proposals. Considerable time is spent using word-processing programs, spreadsheets, and databases. As researchers, fundraisers need access to as much information as possible concerning prospective donors. The three most common customer relationship management (CRM) programs across intercollegiate athletics are Blackbaud-Raiser's Edge, Paciolan, and Salesforce. Some institutions, such as the University of Pennsylvania, use their own proprietary database (National

Association of Collegiate Directors of Athletics, 2020). At the University of Notre Dame, located in South Bend, Indiana, the Athletics Advancement department uses a tool called FastAccess that provides greater stewardship with their alumni and donors through personalized video messaging. FastAccess allows the department to deliver personalized and customized content to alumni and donors through text messages or email (FastModel Sports, 2019).

Interscholastic Funding Models

Like intercollegiate athletics, high school sport relies on revenue generation. Donations given to secondary schools help advance the athletics programs. The way in which revenue is generated depends primarily on whether the school is public or private and its tradition of athletics. Athletics directors and administrators at secondary schools use four primary funding models: pay to participate, corporate sponsorship, gate receipts, and booster club donations.

Pay to Participate

The pay-to-participate model is a reactionary tool to combat tightening school budgets (Bucy, 2013) whereby student-athletes must pay to participate in a school sport (Lee, 2018). A total of $3.5 billion was cut from high school budgets in the United States between the years 2009 and 2011 (Golden, 2015). Previously called pay to play, this model is now called pay to participate because the school does not guarantee the student-athlete any actual playing time. The amount charged per athlete varies from school to school or school system to school system. As an example, for the 2010-2011 academic year, the Charlotte-Mecklenburg Schools (n.d.) system in North Carolina voted to implement a pay-to-participate fee of $125 for high school students and $75 for middle school students for each sport season (fall, winter, spring) played. The Walled Lake Consolidated Schools (n.d.) in Michigan charges $212.50 per high school athlete per season or a $425 maximum per family. For middle school students, the cost is $100 or a $200 maximum per family.

The pay-to-participate model helps fund athletics departments and pays for important expenses such as equipment, team meals, uniforms, and travel. But numerous criticisms against this model should be considered. Many public schools or school systems choose not to implement a pay-to-participate system because of socioeconomic factors (Lee, 2018). Public schools are supposed to offer equal access, and many think that implementing this type of fee creates a barrier for many students (Ridpath, 2016). Some states are more likely to have this model than others.

Corporate Sponsorships

Corporate sponsorship is typically viewed within interscholastic athletics as a way to avoid implementing participation fees, raising ticket prices, reducing the number of scheduled games, or eliminating certain sports (Pierce & Petersen, 2011). As the professional model of sport continues to push its way into youth sport, the pressure to raise funds continues to increase and corporate sponsorship becomes increasingly important. ESPN broadcasts of high school football and basketball showcase top college recruits. In 2019 ESPN broadcast 11 games of the top high school recruits in football across various ESPN channels (Elchlepp, 2019a). Eleven basketball games were broadcast on ESPN, ESPN2, and ESPNU, and 26 games were available digitally on ESPN3 (Elchlepp, 2019b). Texas boasts several of the most expensive high school football stadiums, each costing as much as $70 million. This type of spending on high school athletics coupled with funding reductions and cuts in education has further elevated the need for corporate sponsorship and naming rights in interscholastic athletics.

Although these examples demonstrate the significant commercialization of high school sport, most interscholastic athletics programs are much more modest. They may place great emphasis or little to no emphasis on corporate sponsorship. In addition, in many cases the athletics director may be limited in their ability to sell corporate sponsorships. Often, these limitations may be due to limited sales skills as well as the time required to schedule and run events; hire, supervise, and evaluate coaches; attend meetings; and perform other administrative duties. One study of corporate sponsorships found that 89 percent of schools solicit corporate sponsorships, most often initiated by the athletics director, booster club, or coaches; and most sponsorships involved stadium signage, game program recognition, and advertising on promotional items (e.g., schedule cards and calendars). Banks (87 percent), car dealerships (54 percent), insurance companies (54 percent), food companies (52 percent), and medical centers (50 percent) were the most represented types of organizations (Sherman, 2012). Another study (Pierce & Petersen, 2011) found that local companies (especially medical, legal, financial, and educational companies) tend to be the most prevalent sponsors of interscholastic sport along with food and beverage companies like Coke and Pepsi, which heavily invest in trade-out agreements for items such as scoreboards and score tables.

Gate Receipts

Gate receipts, or ticket sales, for sport events can be a significant source of income for interscholastic athletics departments. For example, the rival football game between Henrico High School and Highland Springs High School in Virginia can account for 10 percent of the athletics department revenue for the year (Kolenich, 2018). A notable high school rivalry football game each year is a contest between Trinity and St. Xavier in Louisville, Kentucky. In 2008 the attendance for the game held at the University of Louisville's Cardinal Stadium was 38,000. But attendance has declined for various reasons over the years; in 2017 the game drew only 24,000 spectators. At $10 a ticket, this decline accounts for $140,000 in gate receipts per school (Frakes, 2018). Gate receipts for larger events, such as rival football games, are important because these monies often help pay for other sports at the school.

Increasingly, athletics directors are using technology to sell tickets for their events, especially larger events when they expect a big crowd. Software platforms like ThunderTix and GoFan are used by various schools across the country. For example, GoFan provides a platform whereby a spectator can buy and share tickets using a credit card. Financial reporting of revenues is easy for the school and school district (GoFan, 2020). These types of digital ticketing solutions allow parents and other spectators to enter the event without having to pay cash, which can be convenient for those who are running from work to attend events.

Booster Clubs

The National Federation of State High School Associations (NFHS) defines a booster club as "an organization that is formed to help support the efforts of a sports team or organization" (Myran-Schutte, 2020). Proceeds collected through booster clubs are another source of income for many high school athletics programs. The booster club is normally organized as a nonprofit organization that has the purpose of advancing the athletics programs through financial assistance and providing an excellent athletics experience for athletes. Booster clubs often help pay for necessities such as sport-specific equipment for players, as well as field maintenance, meals, scholarships, travel, uniforms, training supplies, and other needs. Booster clubs may be responsible for managing concessions at sport events, producing athletics programs, managing booster club memberships, selling athletics apparel, overseeing various types of fundraisers and fundraising events, and organizing other initiatives that help accomplish the mission. Parents who serve on the booster club also help to promote the school and encourage sportsmanship and school spirit. They work closely with the athletics director and school administration to represent the school.

Technology is increasingly playing a bigger part in revenue generation for high school athletics. Traditionally, high schools have used Admit One hard tickets that could be bought from a local office supplies store. But digital is now becoming the norm. High schools are increasingly using mobile applications like GoFan for digital ticketing and FanFood for cashless food and beverage operations at stadiums. Digital ticketing not only provides instant gate receipts and attendance data but also reduces the risk of theft because less cash is involved. It offers increased opportunities for advertising revenue on the mobile application and can serve as a communications platform for the athletics program. Although the ticketing software is free to the school, a small convenience fee and surcharge is often added to the price of tickets (Karkaria, 2017). Mobile applications like FanFood offer athletics programs the opportunity to provide contactless delivery, keep fans from having to wait in long lines, and make it easy and convenient for fans who did not have time to get cash before arriving at the game. Mobile applications can lead to increased profit margins and provide insight into the wants and needs of fans. These types of contactless ticketing and food and beverage operations will be increasingly popular in the post-COVID era when consumers have greater expectations of convenient, contactless purchasing. Schools like Spotswood High School in Virginia have implemented mobile applications. Fans attending a game at Spotswood can purchase tickets in advance using their mobile phone and bypass the ticket line when they arrive at the game. While sitting in the stands, the same fan can purchase food and beverage from their phone using their mobile application and then pick up their order from a tent set up separately from the long lines at the concession stand. Volunteers at the tent use an iPad to fulfill the order.

Athletics directors must work closely with the booster clubs within their respective schools. Often, the booster club has parents who serve on an executive board that includes a president, vice president, secretary, and treasurer. Parents may become members of the booster club by paying a membership fee. Booster clubs may differ slightly from area to area and between schools and school systems. Financial transparency is vitally important, and the athletics director should work closely with executive board members to ensure that funds are not misappropriated and to educate parents about how finances flow within athletics. A good booster club can help the community understand the value of athletics, and its members can serve as role models concerning the expectations of parents and athletes. In addition, a healthy booster club helps the athletics director accomplish a lot of time-consuming work that helps to advance athletics within the school. One of the biggest challenges facing booster clubs is gaining parent involvement. Too often, the 80–20 rule applies whereby 20 percent of the parents do 80 percent of the work.

Youth Sport Fundraising

Sports ETA, a leading advocate for the sport events and tourism industries, estimates the youth pay-to-participate sports segment in the United States to be approximately $11.8 billion (Greenwell et al., 2020). Many of these costs can be attributed to team travel from one nonfixed youth sport event to another. The average athlete on a traveling team spends $957 per event, and between 2011 and 2018 the average daily rate for U.S. hotels rose 27.6 percent (O'Connor, 2019). In their *State of Play Report*, the Aspen Institute (2019) reported that in 2018 only 22 percent of youth between the ages 6 and 12 in households with incomes under $25,000 played sports on a regular basis, compared with 43 percent of kids living in households earning $100,000 or more. The Aspen Institute also reports that families spend $693 per child on average for just one sport each year and that the average child spends less than three years playing a sport before quitting (because of lack of enjoyment) by age 11.

The increasing cost of participating in youth sport can place a burden on administrators, athletes, parents, and coaches. These costs have resulted in greater emphasis placed on fundraising. But youth sport fundraising has traditionally been characterized by children and parents pushing products like candy, merchant-discount coupon cards, and prepaid debit cards into the community in an unor-

ganized manner (Kelley, 2012). Parents, children, and community members have become increasingly wary of these types of fundraisers because of the cost and the frequency of donation requests. Further, these fundraisers can cause aggravation within the community and often fall short of their intended goals (Kelly, 2012). Among the myriad challenges facing youth sport are the following:

- Increased sport specialization at younger ages
- The professional model sinking into the lower levels of youth sport
- Increasing cost to participate in sport
- Lack of qualified and trained coaches
- Parents placing greater performance pressure on children, coaches, and officials
- Greater reliance on travel sports and the related costs
- Declining budgets of local and community sport and recreation organizations

Often, the people who are fundraising for youth sport programs are parents or other volunteers. Fundraising in this way involves many challenges. Parents and volunteers, although often well intentioned, may not have enough information about the team or sport program to approach corporate funders. Multiple parents may be talking to the same corporations, and they often lack any sales experience or training. Therefore, youth sport fundraising should use a planned approach that includes some important training and organization. Here are some tips to assist with youth sport fundraising:

- Have one person coordinate the fundraising effort to ensure consistent communication between coaches, athletes, and parents. This person may be the coach, a parent, or other volunteer.
- Avoid having the coach send home a brochure asking kids to raise money without any direction for the athletes or the parents. Kids often leave the brochure in their backpack, and parents may not be

Jeffrey Greenberg/Universal Images Group via Getty Images

Youth sport fundraising relies on offering a significant benefit to donors so that they become loyal donors.

aware of the fundraiser. Without some direction, parents may not know what is expected. Ultimately, the result is a lack of motivation on the part of both the young athletes and the parents. Instead, have the fundraising coordinator set up a meeting to talk with parents and athletes specifically about the expectations and details of the fundraiser.

• Use an app to communicate with parents and athletes about the fundraiser.

• Set some fun goals and challenges that make the experience enjoyable for parents and athletes.

• Explain to parents, coaches, and athletes why the fundraiser is important. Talk about what is funded (e.g., uniforms, specific equipment, or travel expenses) and how the funding helps the team or

program.

• Talk explicitly about the collection of money to avoid any misappropriation of funds, uncollected bills, or other problems.

One of the biggest challenges with youth fundraising is that children and parents become tired of doing the same fundraisers year after year. The same candy bar fundraiser may become stale and lead to a decrease in donations. But when the product being sold is unique and offers significant benefits to the donor, a level of loyalty develops and donors look forward to purchasing the product. Girl Scout cookies are a good example of a product that funds programs for an organization. Annual sales for this product total up to $800 million annually (Schmidt, 2020).

Applying the PRO Method to Development and Fundraising

An adage in development is that success occurs when you have the right person asking the right prospect for the right amount for the right program or project in the right way and at the right time (Weinstein, 2009). Regardless of the level (i.e., youth, interscholastic, intercollegiate) of sport, developing a plan for fundraising is imperative. Strategic planning for fundraising is essential and should address the fundraising goals, mission, tactics, and timeline. Planning builds a spirit of ownership within the organization's leadership, provides a framework that guides day-to-day decisions, focuses attention, and sets goals and objectives that promote organizational growth (Ciconte & Jacob, 2001).

Just as a coach would not enter a sport contest without developing a plan, neither does a fundraiser try to solicit funding for a program or project without one. The fundraising plan should build a case for support, identify supporters and prospects, and develop the strategies that will be used (Chung, 2020). An organization needs to answer the what, who, how, and why questions to build a case for support. The fundraiser should start with a clear articulation of what the organization does and what sets it apart from other organizations. Next, the organization must understand what problem is being addressed, how is it being addressed, and how the fundraising campaign is helping the organization achieve larger goals. Finally, building the case includes understanding how the donor can get involved and why the donor should support the fundraising campaign.

The fundraising plan should discuss how every part of the campaign will be executed by including internal start and end dates, pre- and postcampaign outreach, and campaign dates to promote to the public. It should also detail what the financial goals are, how many donors are being sought, when and how supporters will be contacted, when phone calls are scheduled, and when the campaign will be launched. The fundraiser needs to determine the various communication channels that will be used, such as email, social media, and phone calls. The fundraiser needs to decide what content will help tell the story of the organization, such as infographics, photos, and videos. Another aspect to consider is how to incentivize or create a sense of urgency in donors, along with how they will be recognized (Chung, 2020). The development of the fundraising plan is based on understanding the fundamental process of fundraising, which includes prospecting, cultivation, solicitation, and stewardship. These terms can be applied within the context of the PRO method.

Step 1: PROspect for New Qualified Donors

Prospecting is a term used in both sales and development. Fundraisers may use the term *donor prospecting*, or identification, to refer to the step when the fundraiser is identifying those who are capable of making a gift to their organization. The fundraiser creates a specific list of prospective donors who care about the organization and the specific campaign. Identification should be as specific as possible and potentially include various donor segments (Chung, 2020). This question should be asked: Who are the organization's most dedicated supporters who have donated money in the past? As with the sales funnel, identification of supporters starts with those in the inner circle. This inner circle is what Weinstein and Barden (2017) refer to as the primary market, which consists of those closest to the organization with the most resources who can be solicited early with a personalized approach. Next, Weinstein and Barden suggest looking at less affluent supporters, the secondary market, followed by those not yet associated with the organization but who have shared values, which is the tertiary market.

Also, in this step, the fundraiser is researching various aspects of these people to determine their capability to give based on factors such as their finances, how they made their money, family background, and other interests. To find this type of information, fundraisers use **data mining**, the process of selecting, exploring, and modeling raw data to uncover trends and patterns (Dollhopf-Brown, 2013). The fundraiser should consider looking for the following seven traits when identifying prospective donors (Tedesco, 2020):

- Have they given to your organization?
- Have they donated elsewhere?
- Are they involved in nonprofit work?
- What real estate do they own?
- What about their stock ownership?
- Have they made donations to political campaigns?
- What are their business affiliations?

When it comes to research, the most important information that a development professional wants to know about a prospect is their net worth. By determining the person's net worth, a fundraiser can better estimate how much the prospect can donate. Simply put, net worth is someone's assets minus liabilities. The problem with trying to determine a prospect's net worth is twofold. First, not all the information about a person's assets is easily obtainable. Fundraisers can search for clues like company sales, real estate values, public company insider stock holdings, and the amount of the prospect's donations to other organizations to estimate net worth (Lamb, 2011). Although a search may take some time, a development professional can obtain this type of information in various ways, including databases (e.g., Bloomberg), websites (e.g., SEC, Zillow), newspapers, company documents (obtained online or through public tax filings), industry publications, and personal sources.

Second, no exact formula is available for determining net worth. Although no formula exists, the IRS provides the following averages for households whose net worth is between $1.5 million and $10 million (Lamb, 2011):

- About 25 percent of household net worth is tied up in real estate.

- About 17 percent of household net worth is tied up in publicly traded stock.
- About 9 percent of household net worth is tied up in private company investments.

The best way to identify prospective donors is to consider those who are currently involved or were previously involved with the organization (Ciconte & Jacob, 2001). Examples of groups where you may find these types of donors include board members of a nonprofit, current donors, volunteers, alumni, staff leaders, affiliated groups, advisory council members, special event attendees, and those known to believe in what the organization does.

Step 2: PRObe for Information

A term used primarily in fundraising, **cultivation** is the process by which the fundraiser starts to build a relationship with the prospective donor. In this stage, the fundraiser also starts to develop strategies that connect the donor to the organization and an initiative that the donor can fund. Cultivation should concentrate on growing the number of giving opportunities over the course of a donor's lifetime (Polivy, 2014). Cultivation starts with the first gift, continues with retaining the gift, and is followed by motivating the donor to continue giving and to join other core supporters in helping to identify other prospective donors over the long term. The term *moves management* has been used in place of cultivation to suggest a process and plan for how to grow the relationship and give a person various opportunities to become a more engaged and passionate donor. During this process, fundraisers need to record their activity with the donor, make notes after the donor responds, assess the prospect's readiness to donate, and make note of next steps (Weinstein, 2004). The development professional is constantly asking open-ended questions of the donor to learn more about them. The fundraiser may ask various questions to learn more about the donor's job, interests, family, and hobbies. But development professionals may also ask donors to provide feedback on their work, solicit professional advice (e.g., legal, financial), or help with solving a problem (Eisenstein, n.d.).

Developing donors who give repeatedly is vital because research suggests that maintaining and increasing giving from existing givers is cost effective (Nichols, 2004; Sargeant, 2013). A key factor to keep in mind in the cultivation process is that many donors do not necessarily give because of the organization, but because of the fundraiser (i.e., the person doing the fundraising). This tendency holds true within the context of both sales and fundraising. In a study of 14 nonprofit organizations, the primary gift-giving relationship was found to exist not between the giver and the beneficiary, but between the giver and the fundraiser (Alborough, 2017).

Steps 3 and 4: PROvide Solutions and PROpose an Offer

As we move from probing for information to providing solutions, the development professional transitions from cultivating the donor to solicitation. During this phase, the fundraiser or fundraising team or committee can start to prepare any necessary presentation materials for a face-to-face meeting with the prospective donor. By this point, the development professional has been asking questions, already knows that the donor is interested, and has a good idea about the appropriate amount of funds to request. Materials prepared for the presentation should always include a personalized case for support, and the development professional should stress the major points that resonate with the donor (Weinstein & Barden, 2017). For example, if you know that Mr. and Mrs. Hayes support organizations with initiatives that help at-risk youth, then all your materials should not only address them by name but also focus on the benefits of your program for at-risk youth.

In the world of fundraising, step 4 of the PRO method, which is to propose an offer that best

fits the customer's needs, is often referred to as solicitation. The primary form of solicitation with major gifts is face-to-face contact. In this step, the fundraiser invites or asks the donor to make a major gift or investment in the organization. Terminology commonly used in this step by fundraisers is **making the ask**, referring to asking the person to donate a certain amount of money to the organization. A fundraiser should never fail in the solicitation phase because they should know they are talking to a person who has the necessary resources and cares about the project being funded (Sargeant & Shang, 2017). Unlike sales, solicitation is less about persuasion or charm and more about stirring the donor's moral obligation and appealing to the donor's passions and the organization's needs (Gattle, 2011).

Generally, fundraisers should solicit a board member, alumni, or other person who is close to the organization (Weinstein & Barden, 2017). In addition, the fundraiser should know that their organization has the capacity to carry out the project as promised to the donor. If the sport organization is a nonprofit, a development team or committee is often assembled, consisting of full-time staff members, board members, volunteers, and friends of the organization. Before any of these people make the ask, each of them must be already fully committed not only to the mission of the organization but also to giving to the organization themselves. The following guidance regarding fundraising solicitation is useful (Weinstein & Barden, 2017):

- Solicit board members and people close to the organization before approaching those who are not as close to the organization.
- Never delay approaching a prospect who has stated that they expect to be solicited.
- Carefully time your funding request to when a donor's stocks or assets are valued at a high level; avoid making a request after a sharp decline in the value of the prospect's holdings.
- Approach prospective donors only after they have had an opportunity to attend

one or two informative relationship-nurturing gatherings or events.

- Be mindful and sensitive to any milestones or major events coming up in the prospective donor's life, such as a family wedding or change in employment.

Development professionals have no magic formula to use when asking for donations. Here are a few ways to ask:

- Tell the donor a story about how they could help serve a specific population of people, individuals, or groups. For example, you could say, "Last year was the first year that Mia played basketball, and she developed a lot of enthusiasm for the sport. In fact, she loves it so much that she tried out for her junior high school team and is now a starter on the eighth grade team." State the urgency of the need. For example, you might say, "Kids between the ages of 6 and 12 will not have access to playing any organized sports or activities after August 1 without your support."

- Suggest how easy it is to donate to the cause. For example, you might say, "A gift as little as $30 not only feeds a child but also gives them all the equipment and support they need to be successful."

- Show your creativity in asking for the donation. For example, you may invite the donor to visit the playground they are funding or to play at the basketball court with some players who would benefit. You may ask them while attending a game with their favorite team, eating their favorite food, or reading their favorite poem.

Step 5: PROtect the Relationship

In step 5 of the PRO method, you protect the relationship with continuing customer service. After you have made the ask and the donor has agreed, you need to steward the relationship. Stewardship refers to the step in which the fundraiser thanks and recognizes the donor's generosity. It also refers to a continuous personal interaction with the donor that paves the way for the donor to make repeat larger gifts (Fredricks, 2001). Stewardship can be thought of as an hourglass whereby the top few people are making very large gifts and many people at the bottom are making small gifts. The middle of the hourglass becomes increasingly narrow (with fewer donors overall) if you fail to steward your base and ensure that those relationships blossom (see figure 7.1). Without

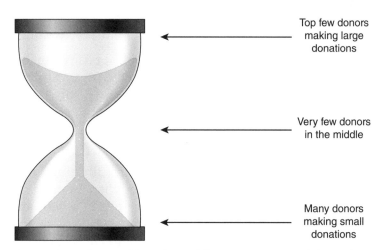

Top few donors making large donations

Very few donors in the middle

Many donors making small donations

FIGURE 7.1 The hourglass analogy of stewardship: The middle gets narrower, with fewer donors, if you do not properly maintain a relationship with your base.

University of Cincinnati Thank-A-Thon

Each year, the University of Cincinnati Department of Athletics, in collaboration with the University of Cincinnati Athletic Team Support (UCATS), holds a public outreach to all donors. The thank-a-thon uses student-athletes to thank donors for their contributions to the program. In 2019 student-athletes made over 4,000 calls and wrote more than 600 personal thank-you letters to donors (UCATS, 2019). The student-athletes thank donors for support of scholarships, capital projects, and various strategic initiatives.

the stewardship of existing donors, your only option is to bring in new donors constantly, which only gets harder over time (Heyman & Brenner, 2016).

Effective stewardship entails relationship building, including recognition when appropriate, and is one of the best ways to reduce donor attrition and increase revenues while decreasing costs (Metrick, 2005). Relationship building should include feedback to the donor and an understanding of donor needs. Regular feedback to the donor concerning the way in which the gift has been used, its effectiveness, and regular communications (e.g., annual reports, newsletters, and invitations to participate in a range of events) are important factors (Heyman & Brenner, 2016). Many nonprofit organizations within the sport industry create a stewardship program that provides a framework for acknowledging and thanking donors in a systematic way. Brown University uses their Loyal Bears Program to recognize alumni, parents, and friends who have given any amount to Brown athletics for two or more fiscal years (Brown University, n.d.).

The concept of stewardship is imperative for the development professional in terms of providing customer service to donors. One way to provide superior customer service is to develop a stewardship program, which includes several important steps (Marcus, 2013). From the first gift, the fundraiser needs to get the donor involved. Messages to the donor should be alternated, and a certain budget should be allocated specifically for stewardship activities. Stewardship must be appropriate to the amount of the gift and in line with the budget and image of the organization. Major gift and planned-gift donors may be busy with other organizations or their profession, so the fundraiser must determine how they will be involved. Outreach must be coordinated so that donors can convey their commitment and enthusiasm to prospective donors. Stewardship must be tied to the organization's mission, and it should focus on intangible benefits. Maintaining stewardship programs with long-time and generous donors is important even if they cannot give as much. Finally, establishing relationships between donors and program staff whenever possible is important.

Summary

Many nonprofit sport organizations use fundraising both to generate income and to affirm the purpose of the organization. Fundraising occurs at every level of sport. This type of sales is carried out not only by professionals but also, at the youth level, by parents, youth-athletes, and friends. This chapter discussed the nuance of fundraising within various nonprofit organizations, intercollegiate athletics, and youth sport. Fundraising professionals need to be sensitive to ethical considerations in development. Types of giving include annual giving, capital campaigns, event fundraising, major gifts, and planned giving. An annual fund cultivates a large group of active donors and regularly solicits donations that support the daily operation of a nonprofit organization. Capital campaigns raise funds for large projects such as new buildings, and they have a fixed budget and timeline. Event fundraising not only helps an organization to raise money but also raises an organization's brand awareness. Major gift fundraising allows an organization the opportunity to inform people with means about their programs and services. Finally, planned giving allows a donor to make a significant gift during their life or at death as part of their estate plan.

Fundraising begins with a clear articulation of what an organization does and what sets it apart. The fundraising process should discuss how every part of the campaign should be executed. The first step of the process, prospecting for new qualified donors, occurs when the development professional identifies those people who are capable of making a gift to their organization. The approach involves data mining, which is the process of selecting, exploring, and modeling raw data. Next, when the development professional probes for information in the cultivation phase, they begin to build a relationship with the prospective donor and develop strategies to connect the donor to the organization and initiative. In the solicitation stage, the development professional provides solutions and proposes an offer by inviting or asking the donor to make a gift or invest in the organization. Finally, after the gift is secured, customer service becomes imperative. The development professional stewards the donor by thanking them and recognizing their generosity. Stewardship programs must continually maintain the relationship with long-time and generous donors.

APPLIED LEARNING ACTIVITIES

1. Go to the athletics department website for both a Division I and a Division III college or university and view the athletics staff directory. Look for information about how many development and fundraising officers are on the staff. How does athletics development and advancement differ between the two schools? Write a paragraph that contrasts these differences.

2. Imagine that you have started a new nonprofit sport organization. You can choose the mission of the organization. How would you go about raising funds for this new organization? Develop some strategies and discuss them in a short two- to three-minute video.

CASE STUDY

MAJOR GIFTS FOR UNIVERSITY ATHLETICS

A major gift is a type of fundraising in which a substantial contribution of cash or assets is gifted to an organization. In many cases major gifts are given to organizations or schools anonymously. Nonprofit organizations within sport, such as college and university athletics programs, benefit from major gifts that are often given to help create a new facility or improve an existing one. Virginia Tech Athletics (2017) was the beneficiary of a gift from an alumni couple who donated $15.2 million to construct a new Student-Athlete Performance Center. The facility incorporates all collegiate athletics offered at the school and provides student-athletes a competitive advantage in balancing academics and sports. Another example of a major gift can be seen at San Jose State, where an alum in the transportation and logistics industry donated $100,000 to help build a new practice facility for the Spartans baseball team (Waltasi, 2020). Georgia Tech Athletics (2020) has received major gifts from alumni Ken and Trish Byers that are used to fund scholarships, faculty, research, student life, cooperative engineering, and even the Einstein monument on campus. They also gave a major gift to create the Ken Byers tennis facility.

Discussion Questions

1. Look up information online about each of the gifts from Virginia Tech, San Jose State, and Georgia Tech. What are the primary purposes of these gifts, and who are the primary donors?

2. After learning about these examples of major gifts at colleges and universities, imagine that you are a wealthy alum at your college or university and have decided to give a major gift to the school. Do some research and discover an area of need on your campus. After discovering the need, implement a plan about what the major gift will be and how much money you will donate.

Go to HK*Propel* to watch author videos, engage in sales scenarios, and find downloadable sales templates related to this chapter.

CHAPTER 8

Grant Writing in Sport

CHAPTER OBJECTIVES

After completing the chapter, you should be able to do the following:

- Highlight segments of the industry that write the most grants
- Identify key resources used for writing grants
- Understand the process for researching grants
- Demonstrate how to write a needs statement
- Explain how to develop and submit a grant proposal
- Discuss the various sources of grant funding
- Review methods for evaluating grants

Grant writing is a form of fundraising undertaken by many nonprofit sport organizations. The three most common types of organizations within sport that need grant writers are intercollegiate athletics departments, nonprofit sport organizations, and government organizations (e.g., community recreation departments). Development professionals in intercollegiate athletics may work in an advancement office within the university or, more often, in the development arm of the athletics department. For example, the Iron Dukes, the fundraising arm for Duke University Athletics, provides an opportunity for alumni, friends, and other people or groups to support the athletics department (Iron Dukes, 2019). Interscholastic athletics directors or booster clubs may also write grants. Numerous nonprofit organizations in sport (e.g., Special Olympics, YMCA, and sports commissions) write grants. Many nonprofits within sport are small, so the job title for a grant writer varies. For example, the YMCA may hire a grant writer, development associate, grant compliance manager, development director, or other title. Nonprofit organizations need writers who can persuade funders to support their causes. Students who are willing to start at a small nonprofit with a relatively modest salary can gain valuable on-the-job experience they can transfer to higher-paid positions. Finally, government agencies within sport such as tourism departments, community recreation departments, and others may apply for grants. The federal government offers more than 1,800 grant programs administered by federal departments and agencies, and all of them are published in the Catalog of Federal Domestic Assistance (Kachinske & Kachinske, 2010).

Understanding Grants

A **grant** is an award of money to an organization or individual that is normally tied to a specific activity. Sometimes grants are described as awards. Grants have specific budgets, timelines, and reporting procedures throughout the grant period or at the conclusion of the project or activity. Browning (2014) describes a grant as a cooperative agreement and defines it as an award of financial assistance that has the purpose of transferring funds from a funding agency (grantor) to a recipient (grantee) who undertakes to carry out the proposed activities (set forth in an application). The **grantor** (sometimes called the grantmaker, funder, or funding agency) is the organization or agency that receives the funding request and consequently decides whether to fund or reject the request. The **grantee** is the individual or organization designated to receive the funds from the grantor. One helpful criterion for determining the appropriate funding source is to determine the type of grant, the most common types of which are described in table 8.1 (Hall & Howlett, 2003).

TABLE 8.1 Types of Grants

Grant type	Description
Capital award	Funds that help to build or remodel a facility or equipment.
Challenge grant	Funds that are matched by either the applicant or another source.
Endowment grant	An investment whereby some of the annual income is used for a specific purpose. Universities are the most common type of organization that uses endowments and regularly withdraws money for purposes such as granting scholarships to students.
Operating or general-purpose grant	Funds that are donated to an organization with no expectation that the funds will be used for any specific purpose or activity.
Project or program grant	Funds that are awarded to achieve specific outcomes within a specified timeframe. Activities that are fairly limited in scope are often referred to as projects, whereas programs are wider in scope.
Start-up award or seed grant	Funds given to an individual or organization to help begin the process for an initiative. Activities taken during the initial steps will help to determine the feasibility of moving forward with the initiative.

Based on Hall & Howlett (2003).

The type of grant is normally spelled out in the guidelines provided by the grantor, or funding source. In some cases, the grantee has an idea and sends an unsolicited project idea to the funding source. Most grants, however, are solicited project ideas, meaning that the idea (specific or general) was proposed by the funding source. Solicited project ideas are normally distributed in two ways. A common way that funding sources inform potential grantees about grants is called a **request for proposal (RFP)**. An RFP outlines information such as the type of program, geographical areas or targeted groups to be served, range of acceptable costs, timeline, criteria for selecting recipients, and acceptable procedures or methods. **Program announcements** are another method that funding sources use to provide information about grants that are more flexible in terms of the procedures, methods, timeline, and targets to be served by the grant. Announcements are often listed on the funding source's website or in its annual catalog (Hall & Howlett, 2003).

Learning about and finding funding agencies can be challenging, especially for inexperienced grant writers. The Foundation Center (n.d.) claims that 90 percent of all foundations do not even have a website. This fact is astonishing for any entity operating in the 21st century. The takeaway here is that finding funding is kind of like a scavenger hunt that involves some secrecy and planning but also takes time, research, and help from others to succeed. Every year, the federal government awards about $40 billion in grants to eligible organizations. Most grants are awarded to government organizations (e.g., state, county, and city agencies, and Native American tribes), education organizations (e.g., public schools, school districts, public and private institutions of higher education), and nonprofit organizations classified as 501(c)(3) or other nonprofit status by the IRS, a category that includes faith-based organizations (Price, 2018). The two primary types of grantors are public sector and private sector. Both sources of funding have advantages and disadvantages, and each type has restrictions about what they fund, where they fund, what populations they serve, and so on.

Public Sector Grants

Public sector grants are funded by government agencies at the federal, state, county, or local level with money that is subject to congressional approval, federal pass-through programs that may or may not be funded by federal money, and taxpayer dollars. Some of the important advantages and disadvantages of public sector grants are listed in table 8.2.

TABLE 8.2   Advantages and Disadvantages of Public Sector Grants

Advantages	Disadvantages
Have the most money and are more likely to award large grants or contracts.	Much more bureaucratic in nature than private sector grants.
Grant awards have an impact on large groups in society.	The requirements for the proposal can be lengthy, with complex application, administration, and compliance procedures.
More likely to cover indirect costs and to pay all project costs.	The grants often require institutional cost-sharing and matching.
Because the grants are public information, finding information about application processes and deadlines is easier.	More established applicants are often favored by those reviewing the grant.
Proposals use prescribed formats, and many use common application forms.	New ideas and riskier methods can be more difficult to sell to reviewers.
The possibility of renewing the grant is known from the beginning, and the funds are available to both for-profit and nonprofit organizations.	Because of the expensive application and compliance procedures, the cost to the applicant is much higher.
Most projects have a specific contact person, staff resources, and technical assistance, and staff are accountable to elected officials.	The availability of funds can change rapidly because of changing political trends, which may affect the security of the grant.

Based on Hall (1988); Ohio Literacy Resource Center (2018).

State and local governments received approximately $750 billion in grants from the federal government in 2019. The grants were used to fund public policies in areas such as health care, transportation, income security, education, job training, social services, community development, and environmental protection (Congressional Research Service, 2019a). Various nonprofit organizations rely on public sector grants, which are typically used to fund building projects, administrator costs, or other types of expenses. Community recreation agencies are a good example of organizations who rely on this type of funding. State government agencies in recreation are often eligible for federal funding that can be found on the Grants.gov website. Within sport, college or university athletics programs may be recipients of public sector grants.

Private Sector Grants

Private sector grants are funded by foundations or corporate grant makers that use funds from private sources (e.g., investments, contributions, grants, or donations) to fund eligible grantees (BarCharts, 2012; Browning, 2014). As with public sector funding, a grantee needs to consider several advantages and disadvantages when seeking private sector funds, which are outlined in table 8.3.

Foundations exist to fund projects, causes, and areas of interest as defined at the time they were established and that reflect the aims and goals of the founders. More detailed information can be found in chapter 6, Corporate and Foundation Revenues. The following are a few examples of private sector grantors in sport:

- MLB-MLBPA Youth Development Foundation, a joint initiative between Major League Baseball and the Major League Baseball Players Association, considers requests for funding capital projects (e.g., field renovations), baseball and softball programs, and education initiatives.
- The U.S. Soccer Foundation awards Safe Places to Play grants on a rolling basis to support field-building initiatives nationwide.
- The Bill Belichick Foundation (BBF) grants a $10,000 stipend to recognize deserving athletics communities or organizations in need of financial support. The grantee must (1) be an educational institution or qualifying sport organization, (2) have been in existence for two years or more, (3) be based in the United States, (4) illustrate the need for funding or plans for growth, and (5) have not received a BBF grant in the prior year.

TABLE 8.3   Advantages and Disadvantages of Private Sector Grants

Advantages	Disadvantages
Private sector funders are willing to pool resources with other funders.	The average grant size is often smaller and less likely to cover all project costs, and many do not cover indirect costs.
Grants range widely in size; some provide large awards, and others are geared toward small projects.	The priorities of the funding source can change unpredictably and suddenly.
Private sector funders are more willing to award start-up funds.	The applicant's influence on the decision-making process is limited.
Complex, full-length proposals are often not necessary.	Researching information about policies and procedures can be time consuming.
Private sector funders attract fewer applicants, are more flexible in responding to unique needs and circumstances, and are much less bureaucratic.	The limited staff often means that grantees have fewer opportunities for personal contact or site visits.
The process is a more informal process, and staff are more likely to help with the proposal process.	Reviewers offer less detailed feedback, making it more difficult to revise proposals.

Based on Hall (1988); Ohio Literacy Resource Center (2018)

- The N7Fund is an initiative of Nike that makes grants of $15,000 or $20,000 (USD or CAD) and is committed to inspiring and enabling participation in sport for Native American and Aboriginal communities in the United States and Canada. U.S. applicants must be 501(c)(3) public charities, a federally recognized Indian Tribe, or a school with a fiscal sponsor who has tax-exempt status.

- The Challenged Athletes Foundation provides grants for equipment, such as sport wheelchairs, handcycles, monoskis, sport prosthetics, and resources for training and competition expenses for physically challenged athletes.

You are probably aware of the many foundations created by professional athletes in various sports. For example, J.J. Watt, a defensive end with the NFL's Houston Texans, created the Justin J. Watt Foundation (n.d.) with a mission of providing after-school athletics opportunities for middle-school-aged children. The foundation donates items such as game jerseys; safety equipment like helmets, pads, and wrestling and cheerleading mats; equipment like balls and bats; and some storage equipment to schools that meet the following criteria:

- Have a planned or established after-school sports program in the United States, meeting between 3:00 and 5:30 for kids in grades 6 through 8

- Have over 60 percent of students in the school eligible for the free or reduced-lunch program

- Are using outdated, worn-out uniforms and equipment that need to be replaced and will be reused year after year

- Have a secure place to store uniforms and equipment

- Have staff, transportation, and space for the after-school program

Equally notable is the LeBron James Family Foundation (n.d.), which focuses on education and invests time, resources, and attention to kids in LeBron James' hometown of Akron,

Ohio. The foundation serves more than 1,400 Akron-area students by providing them with the programs, support, and mentors needed to succeed in school and life. LeBron wears a bracelet on his wrist that symbolizes his love and commitment to the common bond and the promise that students make to themselves, their families, and each other to be the best they can be in everything they do. Steph Curry and his wife Ayesha have the Stephen & Ayesha Curry's Eat. Learn. Play Foundation (n.d.), which has a mission to end childhood hunger, ensure that students have access to quality education, and provide safe places for all children to play

Tim Boyles/Getty Images for Up2Us

Milwaukee Bucks forward John Henson lifts a young girl for a dunk at the John Henson Experience, benefitting Up2Us at the Tampa Bay Youth Sports Expo. The event raises money to put coach-mentors in the Tampa community.

and be active. Curry has also donated to numerous causes, including a donation of $118,000 of his own money to Hurricane Harvey relief in 2017, an unspecified amount of money to Howard University in 2019 to establish a golf team, and $25,000 to a golfer who was battling cancer in 2018. Other athletes have created private foundations. For example, Tiger Woods has donated millions of dollars to the Tiger Woods Foundation for at-risk youth, and Eli Manning has donated millions to support the Eli Manning Children's Clinics at the Blair E. Batson Hospital for Children.

The number of athletes is too long to list, but almost every high-profile professional athlete either has a charitable foundation or had one in the past. But not all athletes have the business acumen or time to run these types of organizations. Furthermore, a lot of paperwork, tax filings, and day-to-day operations go into creating these types of 501(c)(3) charitable organizations. Therefore, these types of foundations are opportunities for capable sport management students to find jobs and to offer expertise in running the organizations. The following are just a few of the athletes who failed to operate their foundations correctly or misappropriated funds while running them (Ford, 2019):

- Former Major League baseball player Alex Rodriguez did not file a tax return for several years for his two foundations, so the IRS revoked their tax-exempt status.
- A foundation started by former NFL linebacker J.T. Thomas stopped operating because it became too much for his mother to run.
- Former NFL player Chris Zorch had to pay back over $300,000 in unspent funds from his charity that were not accounted for.
- Kermit Washington, a former NBA player, was sentenced to prison for spending hundreds of thousands of dollars in charity donations on luxury items like vacations, shopping sprees, and plastic surgery for his girlfriend.

As you can see, giving away money is not always as easy as it looks. Foundations are sophisticated nonprofit organizations that are time consuming to run and must be operated in a professional manner. Because of this challenge, instead of creating a foundation some athletes are now turning to what is called a **donor-advised fund (DAF)**, which is an account administered by a third-party sponsor, such as a community foundation, who handles all the business and legal matters, thus freeing the donor from those responsibilities (Ford, 2019). Most important, this type of fund allows individuals, families, and businesses to make an irrevocable gift and take an immediate tax deduction. In 2018 a total of 728,563 DAF accounts held $121.42 billion in assets, had $37.12 billion in annual contributions, and distributed grants to charities totaling $23.42 billion (National Philanthropic Trust, 2020).

Steps in Writing the Grant Proposal

Now that you have a better idea of the terminology used in writing grants and know about the various types of grants, we can turn our attention to the key elements in writing and submitting a grant proposal. Grant writing is both a science and an art. Grant writers must follow a process that will be discussed in the following sections. The actual writing, however, is more art than science. Much of the work of a grant writer involves the crafting of the proposal, which entails doing research, speaking with clients, producing illustrations, and writing and designing the proposal (Pain, 2020). Grant writers must be organized, understand who needs to be involved in the process, persistent because they will experience many setbacks, detail oriented, creative, and able to work with various technologies. Grant writers must understand their audience. Often, it consists of a few readers who are only going to skim the first page and then look at some figures in the rest of the document. Therefore, page after page of text does not work as well as telling the story with pictures (Stanford Medicine, 2020).

Applying Steps 1 and 2 of the PRO Method to Grant Writing

Because grant writing is a form of sales, the PRO method can be applied to its application. For example, we suggest that steps 1 and 2 of the PRO method include prospecting for customers and probing for information. In the same way, the grant process includes considerable research by grant writers to probe for suitable grants. The grant writer is also probing for information from the grantor or primary funding.

Grants research is the systematic collection and analysis of information that will lead to the submission of a proposal. The idea is to match a nonprofit organization's need for financial support and the grantmaking entity's stated interest in that need. But the success of a proposal depends as well on the organization's eligibility to apply for the funding based on the stated guidelines by the grantmaking entity. Prospective donors are not individuals, but rather grantmaking entities such as private companies, foundations, or government agencies (Kachinske & Kachinske, 2010).

Writing a proposal without ensuring that the project matches the goals of the funding agency is not a good idea. A good grant writer will contact the **program officer (PO)** with the funding agency before writing the grant. The PO is the point of contact for understanding the funding agency's response to the grant submission (Tufts Office of Research Develop-

What Are Grantors Looking For?

Grant-making agencies receive many applications each year. What are they looking for, and how can you make sure that your grant is taken seriously? Funding agencies consider all the following when evaluating a project (Newman, 2017):

- Has the organization run similar programs in the past, and does their previous experience set them up for success with the current program?
- What is the financial health of the organization? The funding agency will likely look at the nonprofit's financial records for red flags that may indicate that funding the project would be an unwise investment.
- Is the nonprofit seeking funding working with partners? If so, are these partners experienced with the programs, activities, and targeted community? What specific roles will partners play, and how will their activities be tracked?
- The description of the program being proposed should describe in detail how the program will be executed, how the pieces fit together to reach outcomes, and what phases are involved in running and implementing the program.
- The proposal should include a timeline that indicates when various parts of the program will be executed so that the funding agency can monitor the progress of the grant and ensure that it stays on track by hitting various goals and milestones.
- Does the nonprofit agency include an appropriate plan for monitoring and measuring program outcomes? Does the staff tasked with evaluating outcomes have the appropriate knowledge and experience to do so? Or does the grant include an experienced independent evaluator to administer the outcomes measurement plan?
- Does the nonprofit include a specified plan to obtain continued funding or have the ability to self-sustain the program after the grant period has ended?
- Does the proposal outline a communications plan to promote awareness and gain buy-in from the targeted population?
- Does the proposal include a detailed line-item budget?

ment, 2018). For many grant writers, especially those without much experience, the idea of contacting the funding agency can be daunting. Remember that the job of POs with funding agencies is to give away money and talk about grant initiatives.

Porter (2009) suggests the most important relational skill in securing a grant is the ability to initiate and maintain contact with the grant PO. This dialogue should help to (1) determine whether the nonprofit project is a good fit with the program's goals and objectives and (2) seek advice concerning the project design. First, the grant writer should put together a preabstract using accessible language that describes the proposed project in concise terms and lists the main objectives, methods, and expected outcomes. The grant writer should stress the novelty of the project along with how its outcomes will address an important problem or issue. Next, the grant writer should send the PO an email that includes the preabstract outlining how the project will achieve the objectives of the grant program. The email should end by asking if the project is a good fit that the agency would consider funding. A positive response from the PO opens the door for the grant writer to make contact over the phone. The phone call should start with another description of the project and proceed by discussing the issues raised by the PO in the earlier email. After the phone call, sending a quick thank-you email or note is a courtesy that keeps the line of communication open and summarizes the conversation.

Applying Steps 3 and 4 of the PRO Method to Grant Writing

Steps 3 and 4 of the PRO method suggest that the salesperson should provide solutions by matching product benefits with customer information and then proposing an offer that best fits customer needs. As the grant writer starts the process of writing the grant, they follow a somewhat different yet similar process.

Many grant writers start by writing the problem statement, goals and objectives, methods, evaluation, program sustainability, and budget. Next, they focus on the background section and then finish with the summary and cover letter. A rule of thumb is to focus 70 percent of the time on program planning and the other 30 percent on writing and packaging the proposal (O'Neal-McElrath & Carlson, 2013). Writing a grant can be challenging and time consuming. Grant writers must follow the guidelines provided by funding agencies for applying for their funds. As noted in the chapter Corporate and Foundation Revenues, funding organizations often ask for a one- to three-page letter of intent (LOI), and if the grantor is interested in the project, the grantee will be invited to submit a full proposal.

From a broad perspective, O'Neal-McElrath & Carlson (2013) suggest that there are three primary types of proposals. First, an LOI is sent when a funding agency wants to see a brief description of the project before requesting a longer, more detailed full proposal. The LOI is normally two or three pages in length. Second, a letter proposal is a three- to four-page description of the project plan, the organization requesting the funds, and the actual request. The difference between the LOI and the letter proposal is that the letter proposal requests the funds, whereas the LOI is only introducing the idea and finding out whether the funding agency has interest. The third type is the full proposal. A grant seeker who sends a full proposal is akin to a job seeker getting a job interview. The resume introduces the applicant, but the interview closes the deal. The full proposal can be from 5 to 25 pages in length, but most funders are interested in receiving only 7 to 10 pages plus attachments. The full proposal should include a detailed description of the program or project, and the funding request should be clearly stated in the body of the proposal and in a cover letter sent to the funding agency. The following are the primary sections that most funding agencies require in a full grant proposal, although they may differ among funding agencies. We discuss each section in more detail throughout the chapter.

- Executive summary or abstract
- Needs statement
- Goals and objectives
- Methods and implementation

- Evaluation
- Timelines
- Budget
- Sustainability

Executive Summary or Abstract

An executive summary provides an overview of the larger project for which the grant writer is seeking funding. It should describe the problem to be addressed by the grant and its impact on society. It provides a description of the project, expected results, a brief timeframe, contact information, expectations of the funder, and the organization's investment in the project. A grant writer should always include an executive summary when requesting funds from a corporation or foundation unless it is specifically prohibited or a page limitation prevents its inclusion (New & Quick, 2003).

Sometimes the funding agency requests an abstract, which, like the executive summary, is a brief overview of what the funder will find in the full grant proposal. In education, many research proposals use the term *abstract* instead of *executive summary*. You may want to write the executive summary or abstract after writing the entire grant application because you can often copy and paste key sentences from various sections of the proposal (Browning, 2014). For example, you can copy and paste the name of the project and the full name of the funding competition for which you are applying. You can also copy and paste one or two sentences about the target audience that the program serves, the goals and objectives, and key activities from the methods and implementation section.

Needs (Problem) Statement

The needs statement should clearly and concisely define the need. It should be simple, contain no jargon, be easy to read, and be supported with evidence such as statistical facts and data (Harvest Foundation, 2020). It answers the question about why the funder should care while simultaneously demonstrating that a particular problem is important, significant, and urgent. The focus of the needs statement should not be the organization, but

rather the population to be served. Use strong words to describe the important problem and the reason that the organization needs the requested funds (Browning, 2014). The following elements should be included in the needs statement (Harvest Foundation, 2020):

- *Description and recognition of the problem.* Who sees it as a problem and why? What are the views of the problem from various stakeholders?
- *Implications of the problem.* If the problem is not solved, what will happen to the population being served? What is the effect on the larger society?
- *Challenges and urgency of the problem.* Describe the gap between what exists now and what ought to be, as well as the challenges to solving the problem. In addition, talk about why the problem has not already been resolved and the urgency of the problem.
- *Meaning of solving problems.* Why should outside funding be used, and why is outside funding needed? Is the proposed action achievable and measurable?
- *Human interest stories.* Use real-world examples to demonstrate the need for the proposed action and the way that it has helped or can help a person within the target population.

Before we move forward, we should take a step back and talk about the needs statement in more detail. Perhaps the biggest problem with the needs statement is that the grant writer does not connect with the funding agency (New & Quick, 2003). Funding agencies such as corporate giving programs and foundations must submit bylaws that specifically state why they are in business to give away money as a nonprofit. Often this reason has its roots in some life event or personal philosophy that drives the problem that the individual or corporation wants to solve. For example, the person may have lived in poverty as a child or had a family member or friend with a debilitating disease. Or the person or organization may have a philosophical position related to education (e.g., reaching at-risk youth), politics

B2B REVENUE GENERATION

Sample Needs Statement

Research suggests that almost half (47.8 percent) of adult Latinas, or Latino women, report they never engage in any leisure-time physical activity. Therefore, they have the highest rates of inactivity of any subgroup in the United States (Larsen et al., 2013).

Antonio_Diaz/iStock / Getty Images

The Latin Studio is a fitness center in Southern California that features activities focused on cardiovascular health and well-being. We offer a variety of classes that are associated with cardiovascular health, flexibility, muscle strength and toning, and wellness education. Our classes include multiple types of yoga, boot camps, tribe team training, Pilates, martial arts, spin classes, step, dance, and strength training. One of the key components of our classes is the educational focus on the benefits of fitness and wellness. More than 60 percent of the population in this community identifies as Hispanic, and more than 30 percent of them are Latina women. Many of these women are single mothers who are classified by the Census Bureau as earning below the poverty line.

Recently the Latin Studio ran a pilot program focused specifically on offering a couple of fitness classes for single mothers in the area. The class was so popular that we simply could not accommodate the demand. Isabella was one of the single mothers who was able to attend the class. Here is what she had to say about attending the boot camp:

> I have never had an opportunity to be involved in a fitness class such as the Latin Studio boot camp because I could not afford it. However, I am very thankful for a friend who paid the registration fee for the boot camp. It was difficult for me to make it to all of the classes because of my busy schedule and family obligations. I have three children and they keep me busy. However, the program was able to provide childcare for one hour while I exercised. I have never felt so good and my children had a great time playing a variety of games while I was in class. This has changed my life. I only wish that I had the resources to be able to continue to attend these types of courses. In my two weeks of attendance I not only lost seven pounds but also learned so much and ultimately was more productive in other areas of my life. Even better was how much fun my children had during this time.

The mission of the Latin Studio is to provide an affordable, educational, and inviting environment for Hispanics within the local community to learn about the benefits of fitness and motivate them into action. Time after time, we see stories like Isabella's, and they have inspired us to reach out to more Latina women like her. Our current facility, however, does not allow us to move beyond our current user capacity because our two classrooms can accommodate only up to 15 people each. In a recent survey we sent to 40,000 Hispanics in the local community, we learned that up to 30 percent of Latina women with children would like to be involved in this type of program. But 28.7 percent of those who expressed interest fall under the poverty line and simply cannot afford the classes.

The Latin Studio has access to experts who can help us with fitness programming to meet the needs of the increasing demand. But our estimates suggest that we need to add three classrooms and expand our current childcare facility. In addition, we would like to provide grants-in-aid to Latina women with children to attend various classes at no charge to them. Experts all agree that these types of programs can enhance not only the physical well-being of people but also their mental health. Furthermore, statistics show the dearth in fitness centers appealing to Latina women. We would like to change that by expanding our fitness center.

(e.g., sustainability or nuclear disarmament), or religion. Therefore, the need, or problem, statement should align with why the funding agency is giving away money.

The grant writer should recognize that the needs statement is by far the most critical component of the proposal. It is here that the grant writer must convince the funding organization that an important problem is being addressed. The needs statement sets the framework for the entire proposal by describing a critical condition or important social need that affects certain people or things in a specific place at a specific time. The need should align with the organization's mission, focus on those people or groups whom the organization serves, and be supported with evidence. A good needs statement may include quantitative data along with a qualitative personal illustration of the need in the form of a story. The needs statement must demonstrate that the organization applying for the grant has the ability to respond to the need. Finally, it should be easy to read. This type of compelling approach is more likely to motivate a funding organization to give serious consideration to the funding request (O'Neal-McElrath & Carlson, 2013). A sample needs statement appears in the sidebar.

Goals and Objectives

Goals address the big picture ideas behind the program for which you are seeking funds, whereas the objectives quantify or measure how you will reach your goals. Another way to put it is to say that a goal is what the program aspires to achieve and objectives are how an organization will know if it is meeting those goals (O'Neal-McElrath & Carlson, 2013). Browning (2014) suggests to start the goals with the word *provide* and then include words like *plan, develop, educate, create,* and *build* as starter words. Each goal should be one sentence, be clear and concise, specify the target audience, and should not include measurements and timelines.

You should include an objective for each goal. Goals should never be measurable, but the objectives should be SMART, that is, specific, measurable, attainable, relevant, and time bound.

- *Specific*—Tell how much (e.g., 100 percent) or what is to be achieved (what behavior or what outcome) by when (e.g., 2026).
- *Measurable*—Information about the objective that can be collected or obtained.
- *Achievable*—The funding agency wants most of all to know whether the organization can achieve the objectives.
- *Relevant to the mission*—The organization needs to understand how the objectives fit within the mission.
- *Timely*—A timeline has been developed that clearly states when activities will be achieved.

Objectives should be focused on outcomes rather than process (O'Neal-McElrath & Carlson, 2013). Therefore, the grant writer must understand the difference between outcome-based objectives and process-based objectives. An outcome-based objective is focused on the change or the results of an organization's actions. The grant writer should ask what the program or organization is trying to accomplish, what will be different, and how it will be better or improved because of the existence of the program. The sidebar offers good examples of objectives that focus on outcomes; thus, objective 1 is to have 50 percent of schools registered by year 1, objective 2 is to have 75 percent of all participants recognize the importance of fitness, and objective 3 is that 80 percent of schools will see a reduction in obesity rates by the end of the second year of the program. To write process-based objectives, the grant writer may ask the following process-based questions: What services do we offer? What is it that the organization does? What are the service needs that the organization meets? To write outcome-based objectives, the grant writer may ask the following outcome-based questions: What results that benefit the targeted audience do we hope to accomplish through our services? What is our organization striving to achieve? What is the change in condition or behavior that we are attempting to accomplish in our target audience for the program? (O'Neal-McElrath & Carlson, 2013).

B2B REVENUE GENERATION

Sample Goal and Objectives in a Grant

Goals are what the organization hopes to achieve and can be set at the organizational, program, or individual employee level.

Objectives are smaller steps that help the organization reach the goal. Objectives should always be stated by the grant writer in such a way that they can be measured. The following is a stated goal and its corresponding objectives:

Goal 1: Develop a fitness program targeting children enrolled in K through 6 schools in Los Angeles, California.

Objective 1: A total of 50 percent or more of all public schools in Los Angeles will be registered for the program by the end of year 1.

Objective 2: At the end of the program, 75 percent of all participants will recognize the importance of fitness.

Objective 3: Up to 80 percent of all schools will experience a reduction in obesity rates by the end of the second year of the program.

Methods and Implementation

In this section, the grant writer needs to describe the specific activities that directly support all the goals and objectives outlined earlier. Grant applications may call this section procedures, methodologies, activities, or work plans. This section provides details about the activities that will take place and elaborates how each objective will be attained. The grant writer should list how the project is organized and who is involved in making it happen. The description should clearly articulate what will be done over the course of the project, what resources the grant writer's organization will contribute, and what role the funding organization is expected to play.

This section should be clear and concise, contain no jargon, include major project events in logical order, show that budget requests are necessary, and include time charts and organization charts. Remember that grantors do not just fund good ideas; they fund good ideas that are developed into well thought out and workable projects that articulate every detail about how the project works (New & Quick, 2003). When working on this section, the grant writer should consider elements of the program that are not flexible and the activities that are essential to meet the objectives (O'Neal-McEl-

rath & Carlson, 2013). The length of the methods section will vary depending on the type of grant and the number of activities that need to be explained. When approaching this section, the grant writer should be detailed enough that the grant could be replicated.

Evaluation

Project evaluation is critical for the following reasons: (1) It helps to determine how effective the project has been—the level, or amount, of success or failure—and (2) it provides feedback for course corrections during the operation of the project as it goes along (New & Quick, 2003). Most federal agencies require some form of program evaluation conducted by an internal staff member of the nonprofit, an evaluation firm, or both. Evaluation can accomplish several objectives (Fritz, 2019):

- Determining if the hypothesis was right. Did you do what you set out to do?
- Determining if the specified methods were used and if the objectives were met.
- Learning what type of impact was made on the need that was identified.
- Obtaining feedback from the people served and other members of the community.

- Maintaining control over the project.
- Making changes midstream, if necessary, to ensure the program's success.

Two types of evaluation can be used: formative and summative. **Formative evaluation** provides immediate feedback that monitors a group to determine where problems may be emerging (Orlich & Shrope, 2013). Formative evaluation is done during the program rather than at the end. Using formative evaluation, problems can be quickly identified and corrected. For example, Romeo-Velilla and colleagues (2014) used formative evaluation to inform future implementations of a multidimensional community-based intervention called SmokeFree Sports, whereby five youth clubs in Liverpool, United Kingdom, were used as settings to deliver sport coaching sessions for 12 weeks. Formative evaluation was used to test concepts, test program materials and methods, and understand whether the intervention was accepted and appropriate in the target population. Formative evaluation revealed that coaches may need practical tips and creative ideas to incorporate smoke-free messages within sport activities. Formative evaluation helps to identify whether resources are being allocated appropriately as well as whether areas require program improvement. To identify areas for improvement, formative evaluation considers inputs (e.g., cost, time, and resources like personnel), activities (e.g., training programs, workshops), and outputs (e.g., participants, number of people and their characteristics) (Stombaugh, 2013).

Summative evaluation is a final or concluding task, or the final formative evaluation of a project (Orlich & Shrope, 2013). Summative evaluation is sometimes referred to as impact or outcomes evaluation. Its purpose is to determine whether the program is effective in making meaningful change for participants over the short and long term. It often looks at changes in knowledge, attitudes, or behaviors among the participants of a program or community conditions. Often, summative evaluation uses a logic model that helps to illustrate the relationship between program activities and intended outcomes. A logic model can provide direct and systematic ties between the goals, inputs, participants, and meaningful outcomes (Stombaugh, 2013). Evaluating the goals, objectives, and activities of every grant at the end of the grant period is important, and both formative and summative evaluation are useful.

Timelines

Many grant guidelines ask the grantee to prepare a PERT diagram (program evaluation review technique) or a Gantt chart, which uses timelines to illustrate who is responsible for what and when specific events are scheduled (Orlich & Shrope, 2013). Both PERT diagrams and Gantt charts analyze projects, but PERT diagrams are more detailed and therefore more helpful for complex projects (Bryant, 2019). With complex programs, one event often represents multiple activities. A **PERT diagram** highlights the interdependence of activities by diagramming their network. The key components include activities, events, time, the critical path, and cost (Lussier & Kimball, 2014). A project in a PERT diagram is plotted on a flowchart where the nodes are deadlines or milestones that mark important dates. The most important date is the final due date. Project managers move backward and identify tasks that must occur in sequence, known as serial, or dependent, tasks. Arrows in a PERT diagram represent dependent tasks, and these dependencies are represented by linked pathways that move from left to right (Redbooth Team, 2018).

Using bar graphs, **Gantt charts** displays the progress on a project by showing activities vertically and time horizontally (Lussier & Kimball, 2014). Gantt charts help managers break down a project into manageable pieces of work, stay organized, and visualize dependencies between tasks (Gebicz, 2020). Creating a Gantt chart can help you see how tasks overlap and visualize whether the workload for each period is realistic. Using a Gantt chart offers the following benefits (Gebicz, 2020):

- By breaking projects into manageable chunks of work, a Gantt chart helps to establish a project schedule by setting start and end dates.
- Gantt charts establish roles, responsibilities, and resources that help the project manager ensure that resources are sufficient for the amount of work to be done.
- Using progress bars, Gantt charts help to monitor progress.
- Gantt charts help to identify milestones.
- Using a Gantt chart, a project manager can find and report problems.

Table 8.4 and figure 8.1 illustrate using a Gantt chart to map out timelines. Table 8.4 lists the various activities and their priority, the person responsible for completing the activity, whether they have reviewed the activity, and its status, date, and notes. Figure 8.1 shows these tasks in the form of a Gantt chart.

Budget

A budget is a key element of most grant proposals. Depending on the source of the funding, the presentation of the budget may vary slightly. The budget requirements for a grant from the National Institutes of Health (NIH) may be slightly different from those of a corporate foundation. The most important point is that the grant writer must follow the budget guidelines from the funder. The budget should serve as a blueprint for spending project funds and provide information about planned project activities. Most budgets include elements such as direct costs, indirect costs, cost sharing, and a budget justification (Dartmouth College's Office of Sponsored Projects, 2020).

A budget should clearly state to the funding agency how much the entire project will cost and specify the specific cost categories. Direct costs are directly linked to carrying out the project and include the following: salaries and wages, fringe benefits, consultants, equipment, materials and supplies, travel, subcontracts, and other services that relate to activities performed to support the project. Indirect costs represent the expenses that are not readily identifiable with the grant or the project.

Another way to look at indirect costs is to say these are those costs that are not classified as direct. Like indirect costs, **facilities and administrative costs (F&A)** are sometimes the label used, especially by federal agencies, to describe expenses that are difficult to assign to a particular project but are at the same time required by the project. For example, at some universities, sport and recreational programming take place in the same building. The programming that is supported by the grant funding, however, does not use the entire building. Determining how much of the utilities, maintenance, and janitorial services apply to just the part of the building where programming is taking place would be difficult. Therefore, the federal government allows institutions to negotiate a flat rate for facilities and administrative expenses that is applied to all projects (Licklider, 2012).

Developing a budget for a grant proposal takes considerable time and careful thought along with knowledge of technical budget terms and an understanding of both the funding agency and the applying agency's budgetary requirements and restrictions. Begin developing a budget for a proposal as soon as the project idea and its specific aims have been identified (Gitlin & Lyons, 2014). The agency applying for the grant will need to supply the funding agency with the organization's 12-month operating budget for the current fiscal year. Some funding agencies may also request the operating budget for the period that the grant would cover (Browning, 2014). Again, the grant writer should always follow the guidelines outlined by the funding agency regarding the budget. Budgets may include both hard and soft money (Orlich & Shrope, 2013). **Soft money** is obtained by grants or contracts and has a deadline date, whereas **hard money** is a regular appropriation.

Sustainability

Some funding agencies require a section of the proposal that addresses the issue of sustainability. This section is important because the funding agency wants to know and needs assurances that the organization seeking the funds has a plan beyond the scope of their

TABLE 8.4   Tasks and Time Frames for Example Activity: Spiders Travel Baseball Showcase, August 24, 2022

Task	Assigned to	Reviewed?	Status	Date	Notes
High Priority (2)					
Call sponsors about upcoming event	Sofia	No	Start soon	2/7/22	Call 30 on list
Finalize budget	Jayden	No	In progress	3/7/22	Add brochures
Medium Priority (4)					
Schedule ticket sellers and ticket takers	Richard	Yes	Not started	6/13/22	Rich emailed Mia
Schedule umpires	Amy	Yes	Not started	6/27/22	Tim is not available
Write sponsorship script	Sofia	No	Not started	6/18/22	Insert Pepsi
Field maintenance day	Roger	No	Not started	6/23/22	
Low Priority (2)					
Fix fan	Roger	No	Not started	8/23/22	Sometime prior to event
Post-event evaluation meeting	Sofia	No	Not started	8/29/22	Invite coaches
Completed (2)					
Sponsorship brochure	Sofia	Yes	Completed	1/21/22	Same printer
Close out Jan budget	Jayden	Yes	Completed	2/1/22	

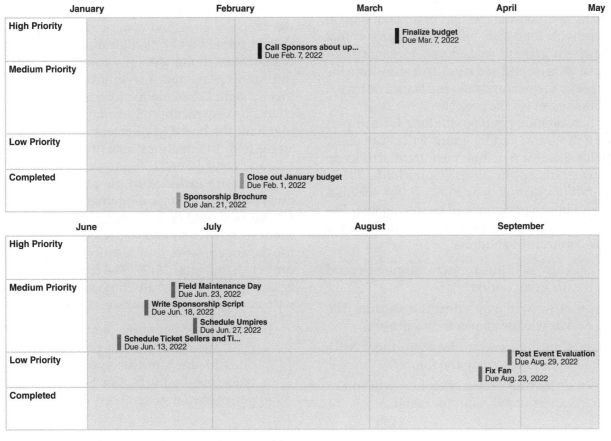

FIGURE 8.1   A Gantt chart of the tasks shown in table 8.4.

time-limited funding. If the money is not there next year, will the organization keep the program alive? (O'Neal-McElrath & Carlson, 2013). Writing this section is tricky because the grant writer must demonstrate that the organization both needs and does not need the grant money (Neilson, 2018). The funding agency does not want to assume the responsibility of being the only hope, so the grant writer must show accountability for ensuring the continuation of the project (Johnson, n.d.). In addition, the agency seeking the funds should send the message that they have community support from local organizations and other grant-making organizations.

Grant-making agencies normally support projects only for a specified period and operate under the assumption that the applying organization will continue to fund the project as long as it is successful and needed (Kachinske & Kachinske, 2010). In this section, the organization applying for the grant needs to demonstrate the steps that the organization will take to sustain positive change after the initial project is completed. Some sustainability plans mention the creation of an endowment to provide long-term funding for a project that has been granted seed money. Organizations need to be careful and need to demonstrate the capacity to raise funds and maintain a restricted endowment for the project.

Sustainability outlines the long-term impact of a program, and the grant writer can show evidence of it by citing past grant activity in new grant applications (Gottschalk, 2019). Funding organizations may ask for specifics about how a program will be sustainable. The following are some questions that funders may ask applicants to address:

- How will this project continue beyond the grant period?

- How will you continue sharing the knowledge gained in this project?

- Can the program be reproduced with little or no cost in the future?

- After your project ends, how will you let others know about the results?

Writing and Submitting the Proposal

Although the need for a project and its various activities may be vitally important, equally important is that the grant proposal be written in a way that is easy to read and understand. Simply put, grant-funding agencies will discard any proposals that are difficult to read. Therefore, in some cases it is best to hire a grant writer (Appalachian Regional Commission, 2020). A grant writer may be asked to submit the grant proposal online or in paper format. When preparing the proposal for an online format, the grant writer can prepare the work offline by using a word processor. The writer should pay particular attention to issues such as word count, composition of the proposal, spelling, and grammar (BarCharts, 2012). In addition, information in the proposal should be clear, concise, and easy to understand. Finally, the proposal must observe all guidelines, not exceed the word count, and not include anything specifically prohibited.

When submitting in paper format, keep the proposal clear and concise. The proposal should present a chronological history of the organization along with any connection with the funding agency. The grant writer must make a logical presentation for the community, client, or organizational need. They should highlight the board of directors and key staff along with the qualifications of any contractors and consultants. If figures, charts, tables, or photos are included in the proposal, they must be relevant. Regarding finances, the past five years should be reviewed, and an overall fundraising plan should be presented not only for the organization but also for the specific project (BarCharts, 2012). The following four issues are fundamentally important for grant writers to get right (Thompson, 2018):

1. *Tie the program to the funder's interests.* First, make sure that the program really does fit the interests specified in the guidelines by the funder. Second, never parrot the language used in the guide-

CHAPTER 8 • Grant Writing in Sport   189

Formatting Suggestions for the Proposal

Although the content of the proposal is important, so is the formatting. Licklider (2012) provides the following recommendations for formatting a proposal:

Fonts

- Times New Roman, Garamond, and Courier are the most readable fonts.
- Do not use more than two types of font.
- Typefaces like Arial and Helvetica are good for titles and headings.
- Boldface and all caps should not be used unless necessary.
- Underlining in the document slows down the reader.

General Formatting Tips

- Always check the funding guidelines for rules about font, headers, layout, type, size, and style.
- Be consistent and use similar highlighting devices.
- Anticipate that the reader will skim the proposal.

Graphics and Color

- Do not use complicated graphics.
- Color should be used carefully in graphics, type, and paper.

Lists

- Bulleted lists should be used for items of equal importance.
- Use a numbered list for items that need to be understood based on sequence or ranking.

Margins

- Left and right margins should be an inch (2.5 cm).
- Left justify the text with ragged right margins.

Proposal Design

- Use color as an organizer and as a way to portray emotion.
- The width of captions should fit the graphics.
- Use the whole page by using margins but do not fill the whole page.
- Direct the eye of the reader to important information by using graphics.
- Always double-check the appearance of color.

Sentence and Paragraph Length

- Paragraphs should be limited to 8 to 10 lines.
- Use no more than two commas in a sentence.
- Limit sentences to about 15 words.

Titles and Headers

- Use no more than three levels of headings.
- Limit titles to about 10 words.
- Do not use generic headers and subheaders; use headers specific to the proposal.
- Do not place headers in the lower third of the page.
- Left justify headings and captions.

lines. Instead, paraphrase the guidelines to show you understand what the funder wants to support.

2. *Ask for the right amount of money.* Look carefully at the list of grants that the funder has awarded and make sure that your request falls within the range of grants typically awarded.

3. *Make a logical, structured argument for support.* The easiest way to do so is to begin with a statement of the problem, follow that with your nonprofit's qualification to address that question, and end with specifics regarding what you will do with the funding requested.

4. *Write in a clear, concise style.* Writing in a clear and concise manner has never been more important because so many nonprofits are seeking funding. Funders are finding it difficult to review all the applications they receive, so they will immediately throw out proposals that are difficult to read or understand.

Letters of Support and Affiliation Agreements

A letter of support can make a big difference in convincing a funding organization to support your funding request. The letter provides some form of testimonial for the competence of the organization seeking the grant, and it is often submitted in conjunction with the grant proposal. The merits of the proposal should always be highlighted in the letter of support. Letters of support may come from various organizations, such as a local government entity, educational organization, or public official. Often, these letters pledge to help the project or program for which the funds are being requested. Some letters pledge in-kind support. In some cases, a donor may agree to fund a certain part of the project for a certain amount of money or loan volunteers who are willing to work pro bono on the project. In some cases, a letter from a member of Congress may be requested for federal funding. Proposals to a federal agency may ask for the exact areas of the proposal that are being sanctioned and whether any form of in-kind support is included.

Before approving or awarding a grant, many federal agencies require a submission in writing of any affiliation agreements. An affiliation agreement is a mutual agreement between agencies to share services (Congressional Research Service, 2019b). Often, the result of these types of agreements between two parties is the formatting of a **memorandum of agreement (MOA),** or memorandum of understanding (MOU), which in written form describes how two organizations will work together on a project. The document often includes the various details of the partnership along with the terms of the agreement and the various roles and responsibilities of everyone involved. The terms *MOA* and *MOU* are often used interchangeably, and although some may believe that the word *agreement* signifies greater commitment, there is no legal difference between them. You can find a sample MOU in HK*Propel*.

After Submitting the Proposal

After submitting the proposal, the nonprofit anxiously awaits word on whether the funding agency will fund the grant. When the nonprofit organization is awarded with the grant, the funding agency often sends a **notice of grant award (NGA).** The NGA typically specifies the amount and duration of the award and provides other pertinent information concerning the grant. In some cases, the funding agency requires some postaward training that covers topics vital to the successful implementation and administration of the grant. Typically, funding agencies also ask to be notified of any changes to the project as specified in the grant proposal. A timeline will report when the grantee needs to provide various reports to the funding agency.

After receiving notice that the proposal will be funded, the grantee organization's chief financial officer must be informed of the grant. The nonprofit board will also need to be notified. In some cases, grant agreement forms must be signed by the nonprofit board. If the funder does not want to remain anonymous, a press release should be prepared for approval by the board (Browning, 2014). Finally, of course, the grant writer should thank the PO with the funding agency after being awarded the grant.

When a grant writer receives notice that the proposal is going to be funded, celebrating success is wonderful. But like sales, grant writing can be heartbreaking. The result following grant submission is often bad news from the funding agency indicating that a program will not be funded. The success rate is only 30 to 40 percent for grant writers submitting to a new funder (Clinton, 2018). The 30 to 40 percent rate also applies when a grant writer is submitting an application for a new program. The good news is that success rates go up significantly when a grant writer is submitting an application to an already established funder with whom there is an existing relationship. In fact, acceptance rates go up to 80 percent when a grant writer is seeking to expand an existing program and up to 90 percent when submitting an already existing program. A grant writer should expect a success rate of between 50 and 60 percent when submitting applications to a combination of existing and new funders (Clinton, 2018).

What happens when a grant writer receives news that their program will not be funded? As with sales, a grant writer should never take rejection personally and must always embrace the rejection as a call to perseverance for getting the program or project funded. Being persistent, however, does not mean that the grant proposal cannot be improved. The grant writer should examine the proposal for flaws. Remember the tips provided previously. Reviewers of the grant are likely to reject proposals that are not clearly stated and fail to provide a concise and compelling argument for why the funding is needed. The easiest way to get rejected is failing to follow the guidelines provided by the funding organization, which are normally clearly stated. Another common reason for rejection is a poorly written proposal or one that has poorly stated methods and design for the program. Often, the grant writer will receive feedback from those reviewing the application. Analyzing weaknesses in the pro-

posal often leads to improvement and greater success in the future. Sometimes, however, the reason the proposal was denied has nothing to do with the proposal. The reviewers may have liked the ideas in the proposal but could not accommodate the funding request because of limited funds. In other instances, reviewers may have been looking for specific priorities in the proposal. In many cases, the competitiveness of the applicant pool was so great that other proposals were deemed more worthy.

After receiving a funding denial email, the grant writer may want to adhere to at least a 24- to 48-hour cool-down period. After working extremely hard and coordinating with many key stakeholders to develop the proposal, the grant writer may be highly emotional after receiving news that the funding was denied. Shooting back a quick email to the PO after receiving bad news is never a great idea. Take a day or two to digest the news and determine why the proposal was denied funding. Depending on the type of grant, feedback from reviewers will vary. In some instances, little will need fixing. In other cases, reviewers can be very harsh and deliver numerous criticisms of the proposal.

Next, the writer needs to determine if the problems outlined by reviewers are fixable. Poor writing and errors in grammar and spelling are easy fixes, and in some cases you can hire or bring in someone to help with writing. The more difficult issues to fix are cases in which another agency is already meeting the needs that you are seeking funds for or situations in which reviewers do not think that the program is important or judge that the methods for solving the problem are poor. Finally, after taking some time to digest the funding denial, contact the PO for feedback. Whether in sales, fundraising, or grant writing, you want to understand why someone or some entity chooses not to fund your request. Learning the reason behind the decision always helps the grant writer to improve and avoid making the same mistakes in the future. Thank the PO for taking the time to consider the proposal. Finally, remain confident and keep applying for new grants.

Summary

Grant writing is a form of fundraising that is fundamentally important to understand, especially for those working in development departments in intercollegiate athletics, non-profit sport organizations, and government organizations such as community recreation departments. These types of organizations apply for various types of grants from both public and private funding sources. A fundraising professional needs to understand the nuances of grant writing. Although it is a type of fundraising, it is not the same as sales and it involves an understanding of unique terminology. At the same time, grant writing requires many of the skills necessary in sales. A good grant writer needs to know how to network with the program officer. Excellent communication skills are vital, especially writing skills. Perseverance and competitiveness are also key characteristics for a grant writer because grants are often not funded.

The process of grant writing starts with an important idea that needs funding. Many hours of research are often needed to determine the best sources of funding. The grant writer must understand how to write an LOI, a letter proposal, and, most important, the full proposal. The proposal includes several key parts, such as an executive summary or abstract, needs statement, goals and objectives, methods and implementation, evaluation, timelines, budget, and sustainability. Each of these individual sections contains subtleties, and the grant writer must understand how to write in collaboration with other contributors. Style and content matter, so the grant writer must attend to details when writing. For a grant writer, the consequences of not paying attention to detail are significant and could lead to having a proposal discarded for simple grammatical or spelling errors.

Few sport management programs within the United States focus on the importance of grant writing. This type of fundraising is often ignored, and many students are not aware of the advantages to being skilled in grant writing. But jobs are available to students who possess these skills. For example, development professionals in collegiate athletics who can write grants have tremendous potential to climb the management ranks within the institution. The skills are also transferable to other departments within most colleges and universities, such as the advancement office. Students may also consider starting their own nonprofit sport organization. Many small nonprofits can fund important programs that rely on either public or private grants. Students interested in community recreation may find it helpful to create new programs by writing grants. Finally, a number of jobs in sport are available with less traditional nonprofit organizations, such as sport and athlete foundations or associations like the NCAA, National Baseball Coaches Association, or the NFL Player Care Foundation.

APPLIED LEARNING ACTIVITIES

1. Search the Internet for a grant related to sport, recreation, or fitness. You might try one of the youth sport grants at instrumentl.com. Think about some of the activities that might take place to implement the grant. Next, develop a brief budget to make these activities happen.

2. Go online to the Justin J. Watt Foundation (n.d.), which provides after-school athletics opportunities for middle-school-aged children and donates items such as game jerseys and safety equipment like helmets. Imagine you work for a local middle school and are contacting the foundation for a donation. If you were writing a letter to the foundation, what are some important topics you would mention? Write a one-page letter to the foundation that includes those topics.

CASE STUDY

OVERCOMING BARRIERS

Empowerment3 is a center at James Madison University that runs a program called Overcoming Barriers (OB), which is a mentoring program that serves children and adults with disabilities. This program is used as a vehicle for empowering people with disabilities, along with parents, educators, and community organizations. OB staff was awarded a grant by the National Institutes of Health (NIH) that helped to launch the program. The program does pre- and post-testing for participants' fitness level, social capabilities, and involvement in the community. The testing is used to determine the level of efficacy that the participants possess. The grant was awarded funding by the NIH for several reasons. The most important of these was that the grant proposal aligned with the NIH's focus of funding, the idea was innovative, the proposal discussed how OB would leverage partners within the local community, and the program outlined how it would be sustainable and have a lasting impact.

Courtesy of Empowerment3, James Madison University

Discussion Questions

1. What factors made the Overcoming Barriers grant successful? List in detail.

2. A needs statement should clearly and concisely define the need, be simple, contain no jargon, be easy to read, and be supported with evidence such as statistical facts and data. Using this information, what you can gather from the case, and what you learn at empowerment3.jmu.edu, write a needs statement for the Overcoming Barriers program.

Go to HK*Propel* to complete the activities for this chapter.

CHAPTER 9

Food and Beverage, Hospitality, Tourism, and Merchandising Revenues

CHAPTER OBJECTIVES

After completing the chapter, you should be able to do the following:

- Highlight the economics of sport, hospitality, tourism, and merchandising
- Identify key terms in the industry
- Understand the importance of the hospitality industry
- Explain the intersection between sport, hospitality, and retail sales
- Describe sport tourism and its impacts
- Demonstrate how the sport industry has changed
- Be aware of jobs in these industries for sport management students
- Apply the PRO method to food and beverage, hospitality, tourism, and retail merchandising

Working as a sport industry professional is impossible without having some understanding of the intersection between sport, hospitality, tourism, and retail sales. Perhaps you have witnessed how these industries operate in conjunction with one another while traveling for a sport event, eating at a restaurant, staying at a hotel, or buying merchandise. The US Travel Association (2019) reports that sport travelers spend on average almost four nights in a destination with an average party size of three people. Almost half bring children on the trip. Almost 40 percent of international travelers coming to the United States indicate interest in attending an NBA, NFL, or MLB game, amounting to almost 30 million visitors. The economic impact for youth sports was estimated to be $17 billion, including travel, equipment, and team membership.

The overlap of sport with the hospitality industry is also apparent in the business practices adopted by the various industries. For example, sport has adopted practices used within the hospitality industry, such as variable ticket pricing and in-stadium food and beverages (Mitchell et al., 2018). Like many restaurants, the right field pavilion at MLB's Los Angeles Dodgers Stadium offers an all-you-can-eat menu with the purchase of a game ticket. Most sport venues now offer upscale restaurants and merchandise stores, and in some places you can stay at the hotel next to the stadium or arena. For example, The Battery, an entertainment district built next to Truist Park, home of MLB's Atlanta Braves, is marketed as a place to dine, play, and shop. It offers numerous hotels, restaurants, and shops, including a lush nail spa, cigar lounge, boxing studio, escape room, and 9,100-square-foot virtual reality park (Gargis, 2019). These types of entertainment projects spur economic development in the area. In 2018 Thyssenkrupp Elevator Americas announced a new 420-foot skyscraper to serve as its Atlanta headquarters. The project spurred 650 new jobs and incentivized thousands of visitor clients to the area for three- to five-night stays (Lucie, 2018).

Many students in sport management aspire to work in professional sport. But the sport industry is broad and encompasses jobs that cross over into recreation, hospitality, tourism, and retail sales. One segment of the industry that students often do not consider is resorts, which encompass various places that involve vacations, tourism, and recreation. In 2016, there were 463 ski resorts alone. Among the many other types of resorts are beach, mountain, all-inclusive, golf, island, mountain, spa, tropical, and theme park (Lock, 2018). In 2018 there were 1,058 waterparks in the United States; the Midwest and South accounted for 407 and 362 respectively (Hotel & Leisure Advisors, 2018). The golf industry employs more than 300,000 people who are engaged in operating golf courses and country clubs that have dining and recreational facilities (IBIS World, 2021). Revenues in the industry totaled $24.4 billion in 2020, including services such as food and beverage, equipment rental, and golf instruction.

Food and Beverage Sales and Revenues

Over the years, we have witnessed considerable changes in consumer demand for food and beverage. The concession trends for food and beverage in the sport industry will include more innovative food offerings, lower prices, and local options along with a greater emphasis on serving fans quicker and more efficiently with technology (Evans, 2019). One example of lower prices can be found with Arthur Blank, owner of the Atlanta Falcons in the NFL and Atlanta United in MLS. Mr. Blank implemented a new value menu when the teams moved into Mercedes-Benz Stadium. Instead of the traditional high-price items, Blank's value menu included bottomless soft drinks, $2 hot dogs, $5 cheeseburgers, and other affordable items. The result of lowering prices by 50 percent was a 16 percent increase in food spending per fan (Belson, 2018).

Sport events are inextricably linked with food and beverage. Consumer behavior has changed from the old-time concession stands of hot dogs, hamburgers, and popcorn to upscale restaurants, specialty foods, and events that offer alcohol before the event. In all four professional leagues in North America, stadiums are providing upscale services by employing executive chefs, roaming mixologists, and pastry artisans and appealing to the fans by offering locally inspired cuisine more often associated with upscale restaurants than bleachers (Smith, 2018). Stadium food choices are likely to come from hometown celebrity chefs and local gourmet shops and to incorporate regional ingredients and twists (Tep, 2013). Fans attending games at the Barclays Center in Brooklyn, New York, can enjoy pulled-pork sandwiches from chef Pelaccio or tacos with beer-battered cod and mango salsa at Calexico. At FirstEnergy Stadium in Cleveland, Browns fans can enjoy chef Jonathon Sawyer's Carnegie Dip, made with beef brisket that has been smoked at the stadium for three weeks and topped with caramelized onions, aged cheddar, and jus. Finally, at Seattle's CenturyLink Field, fans attending a Seattle Sounders MLS or Seahawks NFL game can enjoy the famous Pike Place Market's Beecher's Handmade Cheese.

Another area where food and beverage play a big role is with luxury suites in sport stadiums and arenas. For example, if you are relaxing in a luxury suite at Staples Center in Los Angeles, Levy Restaurants will serve you crispy fried chickpeas in flavors like sea salt, smoked chipotle, and barbeque along with some Cakebread Cellars Chardonnay. When you attend an MLS game with the Portland Timbers and sit in the Key Bank Club, you can enjoy custom-made bowls of pho and pasties (hand-held meat pies) or Timber Bacon, a peppery center cut dipped in chocolate. Perhaps the best is Saratoga Race Track, where a waiter will hand carve pistachio-encrusted beef tenderloin along with dijonnaise lamb chops, red-wine-soaked prime rib eye, and bourbon-glazed pork loin (Tredwell, 2011). The least expensive suite for fans attending the February 2, 2020, Super Bowl game at Hard Rock Stadium in Miami between the Kansas City Chiefs and San Francisco 49ers cost $13,000 per ticket inclusive of food and beverages, alcohol, a dedicated suite staff, and parking (Slingland, 2020). Meanwhile, up to 26 guests could be accommodated in the sideline suite that cost $691,767, or more than $26,000 per person, and included food and beverage, alcohol, two parking passes, and a support staff. The mezzanine suites accommodated 18 guests, were fully catered, and included food and beverages that cost $518,670 for the entire suite, or $28,815 per person. Finally, a Red Zone Suite that could accommodate up to 19 people and included food and beverage, alcohol, and support staff cost $585,596, or $30,820 per person.

In-House Versus Outsourcing Food and Beverage Services

Whether traveling to participate in an event (e.g., marathon) or to spectate (e.g., NFL game), sport consumers expect to have access to food and beverage (F&B) services. With this said, sport properties must determine how they will serve the consumer. Sport properties deliver F&B services in two primary ways: (1) in-house or (2) by outsourcing F&B services to another company.

In-House

A sport property may operate concessions on their own for several reasons. The advantages of in-house concessions include having complete control over the following:

- Revenues and profits
- Item selection, purchasing, and pricing of the menu served to consumers
- Management, training, hiring, and firing of all F&B personnel
- Purchase and maintenance of all equipment, including point-of-sale systems
- Selection and purchase of all F&B personnel uniforms
- Marketing and promotion of all food items on various menus
- Cash management and security
- Health, safety, and insurance

Control over all those items provides the sport property with greater flexibility on many issues. Just a few examples of the flexibility of in-house concessions includes the ability to change the price of a menu item, hire or fire an employee, and choose the type of equipment purchased. Keeping F&B services in-house offers several other advantages, but many of the same advantages can also be counted as disadvantages. For example, human resource issues like hiring and firing can be expensive and time consuming. Many sport properties do not have the expertise in F&B services to manage large-scale production of food. For those reasons, the trend for many sport properties is to outsource their concessions.

Outsourcing F&B Services

Sport organizations outsource their concessions for a variety of reasons. First, by outsourcing to a company that specializes in food service, the sport property can focus their time on areas where they have more expertise. The property does not have to worry about issues related to capital resources, management expertise, hiring and firing personnel, providing a flexible menu, ordering food, equipment, and promotion. The property can transfer risk to the concessionaire while receiving a guaranteed amount of concessions revenue. The biggest issue by far when it comes to risk has to do with alcohol. For example, many colleges

and universities are concerned about issues of risk when it comes to alcohol sales. Many are moving toward selling alcohol at games because less binge drinking then occurs during tailgating parties before a game, reducing risk. Most sport venues also cut off alcohol sales at a certain point late in the contest such as the seventh-inning stretch or in the fourth quarter. For professional sport contests, especially at the minor league level, alcohol sales can be a significant source of revenues, in some cases contributing up to 50 or 60 percent of overall profits.

National concessionaire companies like Aramark, Centerplate, Levy Restaurants, and Sportservice operate in many of the professional facilities around the country. These companies work with a variety of local and national companies to provide mini food courts in stadiums and arenas. Only one concessionaire and no more than two traditionally hold a contract within a facility (Steinbach, 2008). Although a company like Levy Restaurants may be the primary lease holder for the concessions space within the entire stadium or arena, they often sublet to a third-party provider such as a local restaurant and receive a cut of their sales. Traditional food items such as hot dogs, sausages, popcorn, nachos, candy, and soft drinks constitute 70 percent of total sales, but 30 percent

Concessions area at Camelback Ranch, spring training home of the Los Angeles Dodgers and Chicago White Sox.

comes from offering fans a variety of branded items like Chick-Fil-A sandwiches, Domino's pizza, Starbucks coffee, or Dippin' Dots ice cream. As menus continue to become more sophisticated, consumers demand even more sophisticated fare. In professional venues, concessions agreements can vary in any number of ways. The sport property could have a deal for general concessions, a deal for vending, a deal for suites, a deal for clubs, and a deal for restaurants.

When considering prospective concessionaires, the sport property often sends out a request for proposal (RFP) (Steinbach, 2008). Colleges and universities seeking bids from prospective concession providers may send out an RFP asking the amount the provider is willing to invest up front and the percentage of concession sales to be returned to the property. Concessions agreements may have different deals for vending, corporate suites, club sections, restaurants, and general concessions. Some properties can make up to 90 percent profit on soft drinks and do not allow outside vendors to sell them. In some cases, the concession company may take 40 to 45 percent of gross sales of food or may have a 50-50 split with the sport property. Some schools establish contracts with concession companies that cover all aspects of the institution. Other schools separate their concessions contracts between athletics and the larger institution. Furthermore, concessions served to fans in general seating areas are different from those for ticket holders in suites or club sections. Finally, other schools (e.g., University of Pittsburgh in football, Georgetown University in basketball) schedule their home games at off-campus facilities owned by the community or a professional sport franchise, which affects how concessions are managed and how much profit is received.

Role of Technology in F&B Services

Technology also plays a big part in the sales of food and beverages within the sport industry. Sport stadiums and arenas will need to continue building out digital connectivity with innovations like biometric technology using digital fingerprints, making it easier for customers to get into the stadium and purchase concessions. Similarly, wayfinding tools can help attendees navigate throughout the venue, parking lots, and transportation options (Hamstra, 2020). New technologies also allow high-end suite owners to be recognized with geolocation devices as soon as they arrive at the venue, thus triggering the preparation of their food in their luxury boxes.

Some of the technologies driving concession sales include table and mobile phone ordering, self-serve beverages, wristbands, and ID cards (Arnett, 2015). The Charleston RiverDogs use an app that allows season ticket holders in bowl-level seating to receive restaurant-style service. The app immediately transmits orders to remote printers in the kitchen. The switch to a mobile application over traditional pen-and-paper ordering cut the wait time in half from the normal 35 to 40 minutes. In the private luxury suites, the RiverDogs added touch pads for food and beverage orders that were staffed by two servers. Self-service beverage stations, such as frozen drink machines, can be found at various venues. At the United Center in Chicago, pour-your-own beer is on tap when you attend a Blackhawks (NHL) or Bulls (NBA) game. At Churchill Downs in Louisville, Kentucky, you can find cocktail dispensers in the private suites for pouring mint juleps and other bourbon cocktails during the Kentucky Derby. Wristbands and ID cards are increasingly used across multiple venues. Amusement parks like Cedar Point in Ohio allow attendees to purchase all-day dining plans using wristbands to pay for meals, snacks, and beverages. At the University of Southern Florida Sun Dome, stadium concessions are synced with a student's residence hall meal plan using their ID card. In 2019 the Denver Broncos and Aramark added some technologies to Empower Field at Mile High. Included among the new technologies were artificial intelligence (AI) self-checkout scanners used for quick payment, self-ordering kiosks that allow fans to customize and pay for

B2C REVENUE GENERATION

Examples of Biometric and Wayfinder Technologies

Used at airports, stadiums, and other venues throughout the United States, Clear is a company that uses biometric identifiers such as eyes, face, and fingerprints to identify a person. Clear allows fans to use their fingerprints instead of paper or digital tickets to enter a sport stadium and purchase concessions, including alcohol. The convenience for the fan is not having to show identification or open their wallets. Citi Field, home of the New York Mets professional baseball team, uses Clear's technology in conjunction with a self-checkout kiosk where fans can self-scan items, including alcoholic beverages, and check out using Clear's fingerprint technology (Hamstra, 2020).

At U.S. Bank Stadium, home of the Minnesota Vikings, a fan can use their smartphone to do everything from learning about traffic conditions and parking to ordering tickets and chicken wings so that they are not waiting at the ticket or concessions window. Fans can even find out about crowd levels at the concession stand or the restrooms. After the fan taps the concession order and purchase button, they simply go to pick up their food. The technology also allows a fan to push a notification to receive a coupon for nachos and soft drinks (Olson, 2015).

orders using touch screen technology, point-of-sale systems with Apple Pay, and handheld credit card reader technology that allows fans to pay with credit card.

Upscale Dining

Although upscale dining is the trend, concession stands with various food choices still exist at sport venues. Most sport teams outsource concessions to sport food and hospitality companies like Levy Restaurants, Delaware North Sportservice, Aramark, and Centerplate. But these concessionaires are increasingly being replaced by subcontractors, such as Starbucks, Chick Fil-A, Dominoes, Dippin' Dots, Bojangles, and local restaurants. By outsourcing to these third-party vendors, teams not only transfer the risks that come with having to hire and fire personnel, manage food margins, and maintain sustainable environments but also gain the expertise of companies who specialize in concessions. As we noted earlier, the greatest risk that most organizations seek to transfer is alcohol sales. Although alcohol sales can generate substantial profits, many sport organizations are cognizant of the legal implications that stem from serving alcohol. This concern is

especially important for intercollegiate athletics departments who seek to mitigate risks.

Teams are famous for their crazy concessions. For example, the Texas Rangers' Triple-A affiliate, Round Rock Express, serves a dish called Lava Rock Fire and Ice platter, prepared on volcanic rock that can be heated up to 700 degrees. The dish is surf-n-turf comprising "Nolan Ryan beef tenderloin" and local Gulf Coast shrimp. Also appealing to fans are partnerships with breweries built within or next to stadiums and arenas. The first brewery inside an MLB ballpark was Sandlot Brewery, located inside Coors Field in Denver, Colorado. The brewery is in the basement of an old warehouse that was restored and incorporated into the architecture of the stadium when it was built in 1995. Inside Citi Field, home of the New York Mets, is Mikkeller Brewing NYC, a brewery based in Denmark. The location at the ball park has 60 beers on tap, plus burgers, hot dogs, and eclectic eats. Inside Camden Yards in Baltimore, Dempsey's Brew Pub and Restaurant is open for lunch and dinner year-round on both game days and nongame days. Named after former Orioles catcher Rick Dempsey, the pub and restaurant includes upscale American fare and is highlighted by specialty beers brewed on-site (Minard, 2020).

Sport Tourism Sales and Revenues

One area of significant growth and opportunities for jobs that new entrants into the sport industry should consider is sport tourism. Sport tourism can be defined as "leisure-based travel that takes individuals temporarily outside of their home communities to participate in physical activities, to watch physical activities, or to venerate attractions associated with physical activities" (Gibson, 2003, p. 207). The sport tourism marketplace in the United States was anticipated to be around $17 billion in 2020 (Middleton, 2020a). In 2019 almost 180 million people traveled to sporting events in the United States either as spectators or participants, and the sports tourism industry generated around 740,000 jobs (Reau, 2020).

Sport-Related Travel

In 2018, approximately 190 million travelers attended or participated in a sport event, spending $41 billion during their trip (US Travel Association, 2019). Most communities now recognize that visitor expenditures on room nights, restaurant meals, local attractions, and retailers are good for the local economy. Cities across the country compete vigorously to host sports events or attract various sport activities, and most of these events take place whether the economy is booming or in recession (Schumacher, 2015). Perhaps you are familiar with a new facility built in your hometown that expects to attract tourists who travel to participate in softball, baseball, soccer, volleyball, basketball, hockey, or some other sport.

The people who travel to these facilities are called sport tourists. Gibson (2003) refers to three primary types of sport tourism: (1) active sport tourism, (2) event sport tourism, and (3) nostalgia sport tourism. Using Gibson's framework, Shonk (2006) suggests that four primary motivations explain why people travel for sport: (1) to participate in an organized sport event (e.g., active sport tourism by traveling to New England to participate in the Boston

Marathon), (2) to participate at a specific location (e.g., active sport tourism by traveling to a specific location like Aspen, Colorado, or the Swiss Alps to ski at a resort), (3) to spectate at an organized event (e.g., event sport tourism by traveling to Tokyo to watch the Olympic Games), and (4) to visit a hall of fame or a specific place to see the stadium or visit facilities (e.g., nostalgia sport tourism by traveling to the Baseball Hall of Fame in Cooperstown, New York, or visiting Fenway Park in Boston, Massachusetts).

Tourists who travel to a place can be primarily motivated by sport-related or tourism-related purposes (Gammon & Robinson, 2003). For example, a tourist may visit Boston specifically to attend a Red Sox game, or the person may already be in Boston for other reasons (e.g., attending a conference) and decide to attend a Red Sox game. The phenomenon of business travelers combining their business trips with leisure outings, often extending their duration of travel, is sometimes called **bleisure**. For example, after a visit to Boston for business travel, a tourist may extend their stay for two days to visit Cape Cod. Globally, approximately one of every three business travelers add a leisure component to at least one of their business trips each year (BBC, n.d.). About 60 percent of business trips qualify as bleisure, 48 percent of people list entertainment and activities as a leading factor for extending a business trip, 64 percent of people travel solo when combining business and leisure, and 50 percent of travelers stay an average of two to three nights (see figure 9.1) (Wesfield, 2018).

Sport Tourism Sales

Within the sport tourism sector, numerous jobs are available with organizations such as sport-related facilities, sports commissions, convention and visitor centers, resorts, and even hotels in various areas related to sales of sport, hospitality and tourism, fitness, and recreation (Greenwell et al., 2019). U.S. sports travelers, event organizers, and venues spent a total of $45.1 billion in 2019 and generated

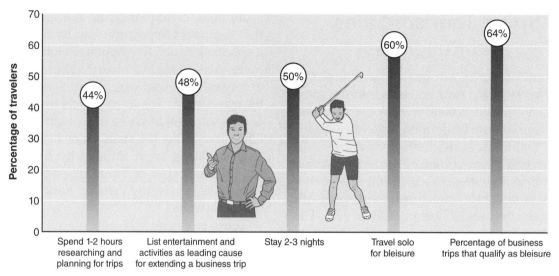

FIGURE 9.1   Sport tourism often occurs as part of bleisure: the blending of business and leisure travel.

Data from Wesfield (2018). www.guesty.com/blog/grow-your-business-using-bleisure-trend/

B2C REVENUE GENERATION

Impact of COVID-19 on Sport Tourism

Perhaps no two industries combined suffered more economically from the COVID-19 pandemic than the sport and tourism industries. The United Nations World Tourism Association (2021, January 28) reported 1 billion fewer international arrivals in 2020. Sport tourism was severely affected. Direct spending fell by $2.5 billion because 10 million fewer people traveled to watch or participate in sport events. Furthermore, $20 billion in direct spending was lost between March and December 2020 because 75 million fewer people traveled for those events (Reau, 2020).

$103.3 billion in direct, indirect, and induced business sales. Sport tourism generated $14.6 billion in tax revenues in 2019, and the number of people traveling to sport events in the United States increased by more than 10 million between 2015 and 2019 (Reau, 2020).

Jobs with free-standing sports commissions and convention and visitor bureaus focus on the sales and service of a place. An example is the Indiana Sports Corp (n.d.), based in Indianapolis, which seeks to promote tourism and economic development statewide. The organization has hosted more than 450 national and international sport events, resulting in over $4 billion in direct spending in the community. The marketers of towns and cities throughout the world seek to gain advantage for their particular place by attracting tourism and inward investment revenues. These inward

investment revenues are generated by the flow of new tourists into the city or region (Warnaby & Medway, 2013).

The people who work in these positions engage in place marketing and branding. Rainisto (2003) describes place marketing in the United States as "a multibillion-dollar industry where places have been 'commodities to be consumed,' and sold aggressively" (p. 12). A place marketer is branding a certain destination. The way that cities are branded in the mind of the consumer differs. The consumer has what Zenker and Braun (2017) refer to as a network of associations in their mind based on their visual, verbal, and behavioral expressions of the place. These associations create certain images of the place in the mind of a consumer. The image of a place is how it is perceived, and a place has a positive image when those associations are perceived as favorable (Boisen et al., 2018). "The sum of beliefs and impressions people hold about place" is defined as the **destination image** in the mind of the consumer (Kotler & Gertner, p. 251). Images are a representation of a larger number of associations connected to the place, and the mind tries to process a large amount of essential information and data about a place (Martin, 2015). Therefore, the role of someone working for a convention and visitors bureau (CVB) or sports commission as a salesperson is to shape the image of the destination they are selling.

Some fundamental terms are important to understand because of the intersection of the sport, hospitality, and tourism industries. For example, sales in sport tourism often works from what is commonly referred to as an RFP, which stands for **request for proposal**. An RFP is a formal request by a company or event to a potential vendor requesting a bid on satisfying a particular specification. Rights holders, such as the National Collegiate Athletics Association (NCAA), National Football League (NFL), and Amateur Athletic Union (AAU), often send out RFPs to communicate their event needs to a variety of venues, hotels, and **destination marketing organizations (DMOs)**. DMOs include organizations such as convention and visitors bureaus, tourism authorities, chambers of commerce, and sports commissions whose primary purpose is to market the geographic area as an attractive place to travel. Numerous organizations like this around the country hire employees to sell their destination as a place to bring sport events.

Youth Sport

CVB and sports commission representatives spend most of their time selling to sport properties in youth sport. Although professional sport, as we have discussed, is certainly a large component of the sport tourism industry, amateur sport such as youth travel sport, intercollegiate sport, and in some cases interscholastic sport are also important to the industry. Examples include youth traveling with their parents for AAU tournaments, volleyball tournaments, and baseball and softball tour-

naments. Spending in the youth travel market for sport events was approximately $17 billion in 2019 (SportsEvents Media Group, 2019). In 2019 the average spending per athlete was $980 per event (Middleton, 2020b). Intercollegiate teams travel regularly for sport events and stay in hotels. On occasion, interscholastic sport teams travel and stay in hotels. Increasingly, millennials are driving the sport travel market as they participate in wellness tourism related to adventure and outdoor experiences. To appeal to this demographic, sport events are increasingly also operating activities related to food, alcohol, and music to create experiences with social interactions (Middleton, 2020b).

Overnight sport travel included 96.4 million people in 2019, and travelers, event organizers, and venues spent $12.5 billion on transportation, $9.2 billion on lodging, and $8.6 billion on food and beverages. Estimated annual spending for sport-related travel in 2019 was $24.4 billion, which was spent on the following types of travel activities (Miller & Washington, 2019):

- Travel by sport spectators: $9.4 billion
- Travel related to youth sport: $7.0 billion
- Collegiate sport teams' travel: $2.0 billion
- Professional sport teams' travel: $1.0 billion
- Other sport-related travel: $5.0 billion

Youth sport events often require parents and athletes to travel to an athletic competition that will take place at a certain sport venture. In some cases, they travel a relatively long distance and stay overnight at a hotel or other form of accommodation. When they travel 50 miles (80 km) or more beyond their home and stay overnight, they are referred to as sport tourists. When parents and youth athletes travel over 50 miles for a sport event but return home the same day, we can refer to them as **daytrippers**.

Hospitality Sales and Revenues

Sport and tourism are now concomitant. In many facility projects around the country a fan can come early to the game to enjoy an event, eat at a restaurant, or stay at a hotel. An example of this type of facility project is a public-private partnership between Loews Hotels & Co., the Cordish Companies, the Texas Rangers, and the city of Arlington, Texas. Public-private partnerships are "a long-term contract between a private party and a government entity, for providing a public asset or service, in which the private party bears significant risk and management responsibility, and remuneration is linked to performance" (World Bank, 2018). According to the Texas Rangers (2017), the $150 million flagship Live! by Loews—Arlington, Texas, hotel and convention center is positioned between the Texas Rangers' Globe Life Field and the Dallas Cowboys' AT&T Stadium. Around $1.25 billion in construction occurred in the Arlington Entertainment District including the hotel, the Rangers' new ballpark, and Texas Live! Accordingly, the partnership was projected to exceed $100 million per year in economic output to the City of Arlington and Tarrant County and over $2 billion in direct and indirect salaries during its first 40 years, as well as create approximately 3,025 new jobs for local and regional residents. More than 50 million annual visitors were projected to dine in the entertainment district. The hotel property was promoted as a luxury resort-style upscale hotel within a sport and entertainment district that provides a location for meetings, events, and conventions and is a destination for sports fans, visitors, and families.

Lodging

Sales in sport and tourism is inextricably linked with the lodging industry. In the following section, we discuss hotel stays and the impact of COVID-19 on lodging.

Hotel Stays

Approximately 54 percent of people traveling for sport spend the night at the destination. The sport event organizer must be able to collaborate with the hotel industry. The American Hotel and Lodging Association (AHLA) reports that the hotel sector comprised more than 54,200 properties that hosted 5 million guests per day in 2018 (Miller & Washington, 2019). The average daily hotel rate for hotels in September 2020 was $99. The **average daily rate (ADR)** is the revenue generated by the income from hotel rooms sold divided by the total number of rooms sold.

$$\text{average daily rate} = \text{hotel room revenue} \div \text{total rooms sold}$$

Sport event planners work with DMO sales and marketing representatives to secure room blocks. A **room block** refers to the number of hotel rooms that are reserved for an event. A room block normally starts with 10 or more rooms and provides a discount of 15 to 40 percent to the occupant of the room. One of the challenges with room blocks for sporting events is that the intent of the attendee to travel to the destination and stay in the hotel ultimately depends on whether athletes qualify for the event. When athletes do not qualify for an event, numerous room nights may be cancelled at a late date, thus affecting event revenues (Judah, n.d.). The price for rooms in the room block is less than the standard asking price for any hotel room before any discounts, which is referred to as the **rack rate**. In some cases, however, sport properties book what are called contract rooms, which are stipulated by contracts. Examples include airline crews and permanent guests; within the sport industry, contract rooms are reserved for umpires and players.

Hotels may charge a penalty if the actual event uses fewer rooms than were originally booked in the hotel contract. Within the contract between a sport event rights holder and a hotel is an **attrition rate** that indicates the number or percentage of rooms the rights holder can release without penalty. Attrition occurs when a group (e.g., sport team, block of rooms for fans, parents, athletes, etc.) does not honor their commitment to the number of rooms blocked and a payment is required to make up for the rooms not rented, according to the terms of the clause in the contract (CVent, n.d.). Sport organizations can mitigate or avoid attrition penalties by negotiating with hotels in the following ways (Patel, 2010):

- Be conservative when estimating the number of rooms needed because asking for additional guest rooms is easier than having them released.

- Negotiate a clause in the hotel contract that allows a reduction in the room block on designated dates without penalty.

- Review the prearrival block periodically and plan a course of action to boost activity when reservations are coming in slower than historical data indicates.

- Negotiate up front to pay damages on profit, not gross revenue, in the event you do have to pay penalties.

Increasingly, more sport tourists are booking Airbnb than hotel rooms (Middleton, 2020b). An **Airbnb** is an online marketplace that helps to connect persons wanting to rent out their homes with others who are looking for accommodation in a certain location. In 2019 the hotel occupancy rate was down, as was the revenue per available room (RevPAR). This trend is a general concern for the sport tourism industry. **Occupancy rate** can be measured in the following way:

occupancy rate = total number of rooms occupied ÷ total number of rooms available × 100

Hotels often ask the rights holder to have some investment with their room block by asking them to sign a 50 or 60 percent **performance clause**. Rights holders often ask hotels for an accumulative performance clause; otherwise, hotels may claim that the performance clause is day by day. A day-by-day clause means that even if the sport event rights holder has filled 100 percent of their block, they can still be charged attrition penalties if 100 percent of the rooms are not filled every day. This can even apply to cases where the rights holder has filled more than the required number of rooms on other days (Judah, n.d.). A performance clause includes various criteria or standards, the most important of which is RevPAR. **RevPAR**, which stands for revenue per available room, can be calculated by multiplying a hotel's average daily room rate by its occupancy rate. It can also be calculated by dividing the hotel's total room revenue by the total number of rooms available. RevPAR represents the revenue generated per available room, whether or not the rooms are occupied, and it helps in measuring revenue-generating performance and pricing rooms accurately. RevPAR provides a metric for hotels to measure themselves against other properties or brands.

Effects of COVID-19

Although the COVID-19 pandemic that started in 2020 had a devastating economic effect on jobs and revenues within the sport industry, perhaps no industry suffered more than hospitality. The lodging sector was particularly hard hit because many people feared staying at a hotel. Industry research in 2020 predicted that recovery to pre-COVID 19 levels for the hotel industry would take until 2023 or later (Krishnan et al., 2020). With that said, consider how the sport and tourism industry worked in collaboration with sport rights holders to make events happen during the pandemic.

For example, the NBA suspended play because of the coronavirus in March 2020 and resumed play again in late July. Before play resumed, the NBA sent teams a detailed 113-page health and safety manual. The health and safety guidelines outlined six phases. In phase 4 the guidelines suggested that only "healthy, no-risk individuals of teams" were to travel to the Bubble in Orlando, Florida, and members of the travel party had to self-isolate in their rooms for over 24 hours (Kosel, 2020). During this time, players were allowed to mingle, eat, and play various games with players from other teams that were staying at the same hotel as long as physical distancing and other procedures were followed. Players were asked to limit interactions with players staying at different hotels. While in Orlando, the teams were split into three hotels based on seeding, the Gran Destino, the Grand Floridian, and the Yacht Club. The top teams stayed at the Grand Destino, which was the newest hotel in Disney World, having opened in July 2019. The players had access to amenities such as special culinary teams, players-only lounges with TVs and gaming options, swimming pools, trails for

Douglas P. DeFelice/Getty Images

The Los Angeles Lakers won the 2020 NBA title, which was contested in a Bubble with no spectators.

running and riding bikes, barbers, manicurists, pedicurists, daily entertainment like movie screenings, Ping-Pong, pool and lawn games, yoga, meditation, and mental health services (Elkins, 2020; Medworth, 2020).

Although Major League Baseball (MLB) did not compete in a Bubble as the NBA did during the regular season, beginning with the division series the postseason was played in Bubble environments at four neutral sites in Southern California (Los Angeles and San Diego) and Texas (Houston and Arlington). The American League Championship Series was played at San Diego's Petco Park, and the National League Championship Series at Globe Life Field in Arlington, Texas. The World Series was also played at Globe Life Field in Arlington, a retractable-roof stadium with artificial turf (Borelli, 2020; Fagan, 2020). As with the NBA, the hotel industry was used as a way to isolate players, mostly during the postseason in this case, and to provide a safe

environment for MLB players. Hotels are often located next to the ballpark and provide easy access for players along with entertainment and eating options. Family members of players who wanted to join them at Bubble hotels had to undergo a seven-day quarantine, and strict rules prohibited players and family members from congregating in indoor areas like bars and restaurants in the hotels (Nightengale, 2020).

Food and Beverage

When selling within the industry, sport managers must not only understand the sales of food and beverage, but also be able to negotiate with restaurants, hotels, and attractions. For example, the consumption of a sport event (e.g., professional baseball game) often includes a visit to a local sports pub or restaurant after the game. Youth who participate on travel sport teams often visit a restaurant as a group after games. Planning for a sport event may require astute sales and negotiating skills with hotels and venues where a team has a prefunction meeting or banquet.

Revenues from food and beverage within the hospitality industry derive from the sale of food and beverages, as well other sources like meeting-room rentals, audiovisual equipment rentals, and cover or service charges. Banquets often include plated or buffet service. The entrees for plated service usually include chicken or beef along with a veggie, dessert, and beverage. Plated meals are often used for dinner when a group has more time to relax and enjoy the meal and perhaps listen to a speaker. A buffet is more common during breakfast and lunch periods when a group has less time because of other commitments. Plated meals are more formal and have a set event timeline. In contrast, buffet style is more relaxed and casual. Guests can control their choices and have more options. Because people can eat as much as they want, the costs are often higher for buffets than they are for plated service. Receptions and break items are also popular. Before an event, chilled and hot hors-d'oeuvres are often served to athletes or event attendees who do not want to eat too much before the event. Break items during an event may include fruits, granola bars, water, and other items that do not cost much but provide a quick pick-me-up for event attendees. Regardless of the style chosen, one of the most important factors is the **guest count**, which is the number one factor in managing the budget for an event. Guest count is the number of people who will be fed during the function.

Merchandising and Licensing Sales and Revenue

Merchandising and licensing is big business in the sport industry. Revenues that derive from merchandising consist of the sale of products licensed with sports logos or trademarks (DeGaris, 2015). Merchandising in the North American sport market increased from $13.5 billion in 2014 to $14.6 billion in 2018 and is projected to rise to $15.4b by 2023 (PwC, 2019). PwC defines merchandising as the sale of licensed products with team and league logos, player likenesses, and other intellectual property. The first professional league to generate revenues from licensing was the NFL in 1963 with its licensing agreement with the Topps Company, a trading-card manufacturer, and a company called Sport Specialties that made NFL hats (Mullin et al., 2000). If you wear an officially licensed jersey of your favorite player or play a game like NBA 2K, you understand what we mean when we say merchandising and licensing is big business. In licensing deals with video game publishers like Electronic Arts and Sony and trading-card maker Panini America, the NFL and MLB Players Associations receive approximately $120 million in combined annual revenues (Maestas & Belze, n.d.). Video game publisher Take-Two Interactive pays the National Basketball Association and its players' union approximately $1.1 to make NBA 2K. In 2019,Manchester United sold more than 3.25 million soccer jerseys.

Licensing is defined as "the right to use proprietary and intellectual properties for designated marketing activities" (Fullerton, 2007, p. 256). Another way of describing licensing is to say that it is a process in which the firm that owns a brand (the licensor) enters into an agreement with another firm (the licensee) to manufacture, promote, distribute, or sell products using the brand name. A licensing contract defines the terms of use of the asset, such as compensation to the licensor and geographic restrictions (Jayachandran et al., 2013). Licensing is a value-added process that helps to generate revenues through the right to use another organization's intellectual properties for commercial purposes (Fullerton, 2007). It is an agreement through which a licensee leases the rights to a legally protected piece of intellectual property from a licensor for use in conjunction with a product or service (Licensing International, 2020a). Intellectual properties are intangible assets and may include the name, slogan, logo, symbol, image, or likeness for which an organization can claim ownership (Fullerton, 2007). These intangible assets are registered with the U.S. Patent and Trademark Office and are called trademarks. Under the Federal Trademark Act of 1946, called the Lanham Act, a trademark is any word, name, symbol, device, or combination thereof.

The licensee does not own the property, but rather is given permission to use it for specified marketing purposes. Licensees are often sport apparel and footwear companies like Nike, Under Armour, Adidas, Russell Athletic, and others who plan to sell the merchandise. Licensing allows teams and leagues to increase revenues with little risk because the licensees assume the risk by manufacturing the product. In return for licensing the brand, its owner receives a payment, often a royalty, determined as a percentage of the revenues generated through the licensed asset (Jayachandran, et al., 2013). Royalty fees vary depending on the product. For example, royalties for toys and games are 4 percent, for apparel 11 percent, for player-identified items 15 percent, and for trading cards and video 20 percent. (Mullin et al., 2007). The licensor is the owner of the properties that are designated in a contract and grants the right to use its intellectual properties to a second party (Fullerton, 2007). The licensor is the entity that owns or represents the sport property. Sports equipment and apparel companies such as Nike and Adidas leverage their brands to drive retail product sales (DeGaris, 2015). In contrast with merchandising, which is a strategy that teams and leagues use primarily to drive retail sales, licensing has more to do with growing the brand to increase other revenues such as ticket sales.

Collegiate Sport Licensing

For both sport properties and licensees, licensing is an important source of revenue. The licensee gains a new revenue stream, and the property receives a royalty for each licensed product sold. The NCAA's Collegiate Licensing Company generates revenue to support and enhance various programs and provide funds for scholarships and programs or services to athletes who are students at NCAA-affiliated colleges (Linton, n.d.). On April 28, 2020, the board of governors of the NCAA (2020a) approved what they called modernized rules

for name, image, and likeness. The new rules allow compensation for third-party endorsements without school or conference involvement and compensation to student-athletes for opportunities like social media, new businesses, and personal appearances without institutional involvement or the use of trademarks or logos. In addition, the board emphasized that schools should not pay student-athletes for name, image, and likeness (NIL) activities.

Publishers of games like EA Sports pay major league sports leagues an amount that ranges between 10 to 15 percent of the game's revenues (Maestas & Belzer, n.d.). The NCAA football game published by EA generates approximately $80 million per year. EA agreed to pay about $40 million to more than 29,000 current and former players. The payments averaged $1,200 per student-athlete, depending on the number of games in which they appeared. The maximum payment per student-athlete was $7,200.

As we move forward, it will be interesting to view the effect of the new NIL rules because customers will have more options than they used to. For example, does the sponsor invest their money directly with a student-athlete (e.g., Trevor Lawrence) or with the college or university (e.g., Clemson University)? Likewise, NIL opens opportunities for a lesser-known athlete (e.g., a tennis player) who may have a million followers on social media. Intercollegiate athletics has always tried to emphasize the affiliation with the team and coach, rather than the player. But with NIL, fans can rally around greater attachment to players.

Collegiate Licensing Company

The Collegiate Licensing Company (CLC) is the licensing representative for the NCAA that is responsible for administering the licensing program, processing applications, collecting royalties, enforcing trademarks, and pursuing new market opportunities (NCAA, 2020b). The company was founded in 1981 by Bill Battle after he made a licensing agreement with legendary Alabama football coach Paul "Bear" Bryant. CLC is headquartered in Atlanta, Georgia, has a staff of around 90 people, and represents more than 150 colleges and universities, bowl games, athletics conferences, the NCAA, the College Football Playoff, and the Heisman Trophy. As the largest and most influential agency in collegiate licensing, CLC represents a total of $4.6 billion in retail sales (CLC, 2020; Georgia Tech, 2020).

The idea behind CLC was to acquire licensing rights to as many colleges and universities as possible and sell the rights to national sponsors as a bundle. Bundling occurs when a company packages two or more of their products or services together as a single unit. For example, in 2013, IMG College and CLC sold a national sponsorship in a deal with Green Mountain Coffee Roasters Inc. in which the company's Keurig brewing system became the official coffee and tea system for over 24 schools across the country during the first 3 years of the deal. Both national and local licenses exist. For local licenses, a pizza shop in, say, Gainesville can approach the University of Florida and pay a local licensing fee. National licensing expands licensing potential because it offers a one-stop shop for national brands to offer several hundred licenses at one time. It also gives a national sponsor like Keurig the opportunity to reach regional markets (e.g., Storrs, Connecticut, and Fayetteville, Arkansas) that are not accessible through professional sport.

Professional Sport Licensing

Each professional league in North America has its own process for licensing various companies to sell their merchandise, such as hats, jerseys, apparel, and other items, with their name and logo. Prospective licensees must provide their business history and distribution information. Prospective licensees send applications to NFL Properties (NFLP), the organization that represents the merchandising and licensing interests of the NFL. As you can see from table 9.1, the NFL ranked second behind Major League Baseball in total licensing sales in 2019. In-house merchandising does not occur because NFL Shop.com runs all the licensing for the NFL. Therefore, regardless of the team you cheer for, you must buy from the same website, which then distributes revenue to teams. Teams can opt out of this agreement, but only the Dallas Cowboys have done so. Likewise, NBA Properties (NBAP) represents the NBA. NBAP requires the licensee to make payments on royalties, provide an annual minimum guarantee, and provide merchandise credit on licensed items. A prospective licensee must provide information about their business, including the number of years the business has operated, the number of salespersons employed, and the number of distributors in the company's network. In addition, the NBAP requires the prospective licensee to provide an overview of their business plan, bank references, and details on how their merchandise is distributed (e.g., through sporting goods stores, over the Internet, or through independent chains) (Luthor, 2019).

The global licensed sport merchandise market in 2018 was valued at approximately $26.47 billion and was forecast to reach a value of $33.99 billion dollars by 2023 (Statista,

TABLE 9.1 Top Sport Licensors in 2018

Sport property	Yearly retail sales
Major League Baseball	$5.5 billion
National Football League	$3.3 billion
National Basketball Association	$3.2 billion
Ferrari	$2.6 billion
US Polo Assn and USPA Global Licensing	$1.7 billion
NFL Players Association	$1.65 billion
National Hockey League	$1.3 billion
NASCAR	$1.0 billion
WWE	$1.0 billion
PGA Tour	$855 million

Source: Cronin (2019).

2020). The International Licensing Industry Merchandisers Association (LIMA) reported four straight years of growth in 2020 for sport licensing and $698 million in royalty revenue on retail sales of $12.8 billion. Total revenues from collegiate licensing were $209 million on $3.88 billion in retail sales (MyTVChain, 2020). Nike's licensing deal with the NBA amounts to $1 billion over eight years, which calculates to approximately $275,000 per player annually. For collegiate apparel, the average annual value amounts to about $8 million per school, or about $10,000 per student-athlete (Maestas & Belzer, n.d.).

Approximately 30.3 million people purchased NFL merchandise in 2019. Males made up 60 percent of customers and females 40 percent. The largest group of purchasers were between the ages of 35 and 49. More than 26.2 million people purchased MLB licensed merchandise in 2019, most of whom were male (57 percent male, 43 percent female), and the largest segment was between the ages of 35 and 49 (28 percent). The NBA had approximately 13.5 million buyers of licensed apparel; 58 percent were male, 42 percent were female, and 45 percent were within the range of 18 to 34 years of age. Finally, licensed merchandise of NHL apparel was bought by 8.3 million people; 67 percent were male, 33 percent were female, and 37 percent were within the range of 18 to 34 years of age (SBR Net, 2020).

Sporting Goods Retail Sales

The sales of products like athletics footwear, licensed sports merchandise, exercise equipment, and athletics apparel accounts for more than $40 billion annually at sporting goods stores in the United States (Statista, 2021). Bass Pro Shops and Dick's Sporting Goods account for more than 30 percent of the market share in the industry, and the top four companies account for 43.9 percent of the market. But more than half (50 percent) of the companies in the industry are owner-operated sporting goods stores with no additional employees. Larger chains like Dick's Sporting Goods can leverage their size to reduce costs (Hiner, 2020).

Lightspeed (2018) explains several important terms that anyone working in sporting goods retail should understand. Sporting goods stores like Play It Again Sports are an example of a franchise. Franchises are businesses that expand by distributing products with a licensing relationship. **Franchisors** issue a license for the sporting goods products to a **franchisee** to operate under the business name. At checkout, sporting goods retail stores use **point-of-sale (POS)** systems consisting of computers and cash registers that capture transaction data at the time and place of sale. Both sales and purchasing jobs are prevalent in the industry. The period between when a purchaser places an order with a sporting goods supplier and when the product arrives in the store is the order **lead time**. Discounts that sporting goods retailers make on merchandise are called **markdowns.** After accounting for expenses, the sporting goods store can calculate net profit. **Shrinkage** occurs when goods are lost because of employee theft, shoplifting, administrative errors, vendor fraud, cashier error, and damage in the store or in transit.

Other outlets where sporting goods sales are important in sport are golf courses and country clubs. Club managers must interact with golf, tennis, and fitness professionals while also understanding food and beverage and membership sales. Golf and tennis professionals are often paid a percentage of the golf income, which includes proceeds from the sale of soft goods and hard goods at the pro shop, cart fees, bag storage fees, and lesson fees (Tucci, 1997). **Soft goods** are apparel items in retail like golf slacks, shirts, shoes, and sweaters. **Hard goods** are traditional equipment like clubs, bags, and other items that are not apparel.

Applying the PRO Method to Food and Beverage, Hospitality, Tourism, and Merchandising

Throughout this book, we have used the same five-step method, which we refer to as the PRO method, to explain how to maximize revenue

B2B REVENUE GENERATION

NFLPA and Record-Breaking Sales

The NFL Players Association (NFLPA), through NFL Players, Inc., the licensing and marketing arm, surpassed $193 million in revenues in 2019. Player-licensed merchandise surpassed $1.65 billion in retail sales. Because of the affinity of fans for NFL players, licensees such as EA Sports, Panini America, and Fanatics experienced record-breaking sales. Multiyear licensing deals and various groundbreaking partnerships have made the NFLPA the most progressive, innovative, and athlete-driven business in modern professional sport (Licensing International, 2020b).

generation. We apply this method within the context of ticket sales, sponsorships, corporate and foundation sales, fundraising, social media, grant writing, broadcasting, and media. Sidebars have been used throughout the text to discuss both B2B and B2C sales. For example, when we talk about corporate and foundation sales, we are discussing a situation in which one business is selling to another. In some cases, ticket sales can be between two businesses, but more often individuals are buying single-game and season tickets. Within the context of food and beverage, hospitality, tourism, and merchandising, sales often occur as B2C transactions. But in some scenarios within sport, B2B sales occur when a sport property reserves a room block at a hotel, plans a meal function at a restaurant, or orders a bulk order of merchandise for their team. As we noted in chapter 2, consumers are often purchasing an intangible service. In the following sections, we have applied each step of the PRO method within the context of these multiple industries. Note that sales can be quite complex because interactions occur between multiple large industries like sport, hospitality, tourism, and retail merchandising. Therefore, rather than trying to suggest that there is a one-size-fits-all formula, we want to point out some key points to each step of the PRO method. First, we start by suggesting that several key differences between B2B and B2C selling come into play within these industries.

Sincavage (n.d.) with Tenfold highlights six important distinctions between selling to the B2B versus the B2C market. First, the pool of leads is much larger in the B2C market. Consider, for example, the number of leads for people who may stay at a hotel or eat at a restaurant. Second, greater product knowledge is required for selling B2B. Consider how much you need to know when selling a sponsorship in comparison with selling a shirt or a meal. The third difference has to do with the number of decision-makers. As we discussed in an earlier chapter, selling sponsorships may entail working with several decision-makers. In contrast, often only one decision maker is involved in B2C sales of a hotel room, meal, or piece of merchandise. The fourth distinction is the difference in responses between B2B and B2C sales. We have talked about the emotional nature of sport, and someone buying a ticket may be excited. The same may be true for staying at the hotel next to the stadium or purchasing the latest merchandise for your team. B2B purchases, on the other hand, often comprise more rational thought processes. A fifth distinction is the duration of the decision-making process. B2B decision-making may involve months of phone calls, but B2C sales often occur spontaneously, such as by picking up the phone and reserving a hotel room. Finally, the business relationship can be quite different between B2B and B2C sales. Often B2C sales are a one-off transaction, whereas sales of corporate partnerships require developing a long-term relationship with the customer.

Step 1: PROspect for Qualified Customers

As noted earlier, prospecting within the context of food and beverage, hospitality, tourism, and merchandising can entail a large number of leads when considering individual consumers.

But B2B sales also occur, such as when sport properties are planning events and use requests for proposals (RFPs) to receive bids from hotels, restaurants, sporting goods companies, and other companies within the hospitality industry, such as rental car companies and theme parks. Therefore, the manner of selling will vary depending on whether you are selling to another company or a single person who is attending a sport event over the weekend.

Step 2: PRObe for Information With Open-Ended Questions

A salesperson should always probe for information regardless of the situation. For example, a hotel reservations agent asks the consumer questions about the type of room required, need for amenities, dates for arrival and departure, accessibility needs, and others. Likewise, food and beverage sales requires probing for answers to questions like the customer's food preferences, cooking requirements, and manner of preparation. These open-ended questions can be particularly important when sport properties are working with various companies in the hospitality and tourism industries. For example, a representative of an organization like the Tampa Bay Sports Commission may be working with a property such as the National Football League to plan the Super Bowl. One of the first questions asked is how many hotel rooms are needed. If the destination cannot provide the required number of hotel rooms or the appropriate sport venues, then they will never be able to meet the needs of the sport property that is planning the event.

Step 3: PROvide Solutions by Matching Product Benefits With Customer Information

The planning of most sport events involves a collaborative effort between the sport property, hotels, transportation providers, airlines, restaurants, local accommodations, government officials, and destination marketers. Rarely does the event occur with a single B2C sale. In these cases, the various partner organi-

zations planning the event must be in constant communication to provide solutions for the needs for the event. For example, if representatives from Special Olympics are working with the Indiana Sports Corporation to plan an event in Indianapolis, communication would have to take place regarding lodging needs. Suppose that Special Olympics needs 500 accessible hotel rooms. In that case, the sports corporation must be networking and communicating with multiple hotels around the city to make this happen.

Step 4: PROpose an Offer That Best Fits the Customer's Needs

How the offer is proposed may vary depending on whether the sale is B2B or B2C. For example, a sale of a single hotel room to one person does not require any formal offer. In many cases, this transaction may be done online with little or no interaction between a consumer and salesperson. But a DMO working with a sport property to plan an event may offer a sophisticated proposal that talks about everything from sport venues, hotel rooms, and meal functions to transportation, airports, local businesses, and beyond. Bids, planning, proposals, and contracts for large sporting events are comprehensive and often happen many years in advance.

Step 5: PROtect the Relationship by Maintaining Contact and Customer Service

The final step in the PRO method entails customer service and staying in close contact with the consumer. As noted earlier, a B2C sale in hospitality can be a one-off transaction, such as the purchase of a hotel room for a specified period. But sport properties often deal with B2B sales in which they are interacting with multiple stakeholders such as the sports commission, equipment providers, stadium authorities, transportation providers, and others. Because of the complexity of planning sport events, maintaining contact and providing superior customer service is imperative. DMOs are often in contact with sport properties throughout the year, and providing a good customer experience can often lead to future sales.

Summary

We have outlined some of the statistics in this chapter that suggest the importance and intersectionality between sport, hospitality, tourism, and retail sales. Sport properties may provide food and beverage services in-house or outsource it, but either way it is an important component within the industry. Likewise, many sport venues now provide some form of upscale dining, which is expected by the average consumer. Sport-related travel is a multibillion-dollar business and continues to grow. Youth sport is an important contributor to the growth in sport tourism. The sport tourist, whether traveling to participate or to spectate, expects to have excellent service relative to hotels, meals, travel, and other amenities. More than 50 percent of attendees at sporting events will spend the night, and they often require discounted rates. The chapter also covers merchandising and licensing. As the college sport landscape continues to change with NIL, sport managers must be aware of its effect on merchandising and licensing. From prospecting for customers to protecting the relationship, the PRO method of sales can be applied effectively to both individual and business customers in the hospitality, tourism, and merchandising industries.

APPLIED LEARNING ACTIVITIES

1. Have you ever traveled 50 miles (80 km) or more to a sporting event? If so, you are considered a sports tourist. Complete a three- to four-minute video that explains where you traveled, why you traveled, and what you spent money on. For example, perhaps you stayed at a hotel, had dinner at a restaurant, and bought a souvenir.

2. The chapter is focused on the intersection between sport, hospitality, tourism, and merchandising retail sales. Each of these are large industries. Which one of the industries do you believe is most important to sport? Write a two-page paper explaining the importance of the industry you choose. The first page should provide background about the industry you deem most important: its operation, characteristics, and role in the sport industry. The second page should provide practical application by way of various examples you have seen related to hotels, restaurants, or merchandising.

CASE STUDY

A NEW $44 MILLION YOUTH SPORTS COMPLEX IN CLARK COUNTY, OHIO?

The Chamber of Greater Springfield released a study in 2017 that called for the development of a $44 million youth sports complex at a site that was occupied by the Upper Valley Mall. Springfield is in Clark County, Ohio, just northeast of Dayton. The proposal was to develop 83 acres of property to create sport venues that would attract tournaments year-round for sports such as basketball, baseball, and volleyball. Officials suggest that the development would lead to millions in new investment in the area and provide an economic boost to area businesses and hotels (Sanctis, 2017). To boost economic development, the chamber had considered trying to attract more conventions and business meetings to downtown Springfield but decided that other nearby communities already had those types of facilities in place. Before doing the study, the Greater Springfield Convention and Visitors Bureau had formed a sports tourism committee to consider how to draw more sport tournaments to Clark County. Officials are counting on the fact that the new youth sports complex in Clark County would have access to a regional population of over 37 million people, giving it a significant population size advantage over more isolated destinations. The project would take years to develop, but officials believe it would lead to new hotels, restaurants, and retail and would make Clark County a top destination for youth and amateur sport tournaments.

Discussion Questions

1. Suppose you work for the Greater Springfield Convention and Visitors Bureau and your job is to bring sport events to the area. What are some ways that you would attract tourists to the area? Talk about how you might market the area. In other words, what forms of media (social media, television, etc.) would you use? Also, provide a slogan for promoting Greater Springfield.

2. Go online and research the area around Greater Springfield, Clark County, within the state of Ohio, and regional areas. Where do you believe most travelers would be coming from if the new project were completed? How would you market to those areas?

Go to HKPropel to complete the activities for this chapter.

Stringer/Anadolu Agency via Getty Images

CHAPTER 10

Social Media for Revenue Generation

CHAPTER OBJECTIVES

After completing the chapter, you should be able to do the following:
- Understand the scope of social media in sport
- Identify motivations of people who use social media to consume or supplement sport
- Describe common social media platforms
- Differentiate between using social media to sell sport and using it to sell through sport
- Understand the inventory available for those using social media to sell through sport
- Use ratios and social media metrics to evaluate performance
- Apply the PRO method to revenue generation using social media
- Observe netiquette when interacting on social media

Social media can touch every segment of the sport industry, so an element of social media could appear in every chapter of every textbook on sport. In this chapter, we remain focused on how to use social media to generate revenue directly for a sport organization. That said, keep in mind that the impact of social media on sport likely reaches far beyond direct revenue. Social media platforms have been used for marketing, communication with fans, gameday operations, security, and even directly enhancing the fans' experience of the game. Social media platforms emerge and disappear every year, and even the common platforms frequently change their interfaces. Therefore, this chapter does not provide a how-to guide on usage of these platforms, but instead highlights the differences and emphasizes how salespeople can best use the various platforms.

Growth of Social Media in Sport

Most Americans understand the size and scope of social media. Likewise, most Americans understand the size of professional sport. But the degree of the influence of social media on sport is likely less obvious to most fans. The numbers regarding social media usage pertaining to sport are staggering: According to a Google report, searches for sport content on YouTube (mainly highlights) increased 80 percent between 2016 and 2017. The same report suggested that 80 percent of fans watching a live sporting event supplement their viewership with a phone or tablet, which often involves some form of social media interaction (Google, 2018). Furthermore, the NBA and NFL ranked third and sixth nationwide in a survey of overall user engagement by media companies; Walt Disney Company, AT&T, Comcast, and Fox were the other leaders (Shareable, 2021). Even single events have drawn massive social media numbers, such as the 44 million engagements during Super Bowl LIV (Nielson, 2020).

Although interactions occur before and after sporting events all over the world, an interesting phenomenon known as the second screen has caught the eyes of sport organizations and salespeople alike. **Second-screen viewing** is a term coined to describe fans' use of a second device (usually a phone or computer) simultaneously with their television. The effect carries over into live sporting events as fans use social media to supplement their experience while they are in the stadium or arena itself. Research has shown increased levels of enjoyment from fans who use a second screen for both televised broadcasts and live attendance (Rubenking & Lewis, 2016; Smith et al., 2019). This finding suggests that teams can use social media not simply as a preevent tactic but also as a way to supplement fan enjoyment and engagement during games.

These points all prove that social media is important in sport, whether it is being used to generate revenue directly or just as a marketing engine to increase interest in the product itself.

Social Media Platforms in Sport

What started as a few websites designed to allow friends to stay in touch with each other has developed into the world-changing phenomenon known as social media. **Social media** can be defined as technologically delivered engagement between a person and another person or organization using the Internet. One of the best and worst things about social media is that it is always changing. New **social media platforms**, or software designed to support social media engagements, are introduced every year, and existing platforms are always changing. This constant change leads to a never-ending cycle of change in how social media is used for revenue generation. In 2014 and 2015, a popular social media app called Vine boasted over 200 million users. By the end of 2016, the user base had plummeted and support for the app was discontinued. In this chapter we focus on the "big three": Facebook, Twitter, and Instagram, as well as pseudo-social platform YouTube, business-centric LinkedIn, and a few less-developed platforms. Although specific features are likely to change as these platforms evolve, understanding some of the larger fundamental differences between them is important in exploring how to use them for sales.

Facebook

Facebook is one of the earliest forms of social media. With over 2.7 billion users, it remains the biggest social media platform in the world. Facebook differs from its competitors in a few ways. First, it is much more substantive in its offerings. Facebook allows users to post social content to each other's personal **feed** (content area visible to other users), like other platforms, but it also offers users the ability to join groups, livestream content, pay friends, shop for items directly through the platform, and play games. Facebook allows users to "friend" each other, which gives them access to additional content on others' feeds and makes friends' content more visible. Facebook also collects considerable demographic information for targeted advertising, and users can choose whether to display those demographics publicly. Aside from just posting their name and birthday, users can post where they went to school; where they work; the names of their friends, spouses, and family members; and lists of hobbies. A lot of background information is available about people who choose to show those details to the public.

The Facebook groups feature, one of its most popular elements, separates Facebook from other forms of social media. Strangers who would otherwise be unlikely to encounter each other can join groups that create a separate feed of content for people with similar interests. For example, a fraternity or sorority can create a group to stay in touch with each other and share content. Likewise, a group could be made for an MLS fan club. Lastly, Facebook offers an internal messaging system that allows one-on-one communication between members.

Facebook for Revenue Generation in Sport

As one of the earliest forms of social media, Facebook also offered one of the earliest opportunities for sport organizations to provide content for their fans and attempt to generate revenue. Most sport organizations have a Facebook business page, which acts as a secondary website for the team, player, or league. Facebook's platform allows the display of robust content. The business page of a team can display highlight videos, photos, contact information, links to merchandise, upcoming events, and livestreaming of interviews or other content. Although other social media platforms offer many of the same features, having a home page on the platform organizes it all into a one-stop shop that a Twitter or Instagram bio cannot accommodate. In other words, Facebook offers more real estate for teams to use.

Sport organizations commonly attempt to generate revenue in multiple ways through their business page. First, the sheer amount of content space available allows teams to post links to their ticket pages, merchandise pages, and sponsors without running up against character or space limitations. Additionally, the Facebook feed of posted content is optimized for linking articles and outside webpages in a way that is superior to most other social media platforms. Teams can share ticketing promotions, sponsor promotions, merchandise sales, and other revenue-generating opportunities quickly and easily. Although other platforms offer similar opportunities, Facebook may truly be the best option for connecting outside content to a media platform.

Twitter and Instagram

Twitter and Instagram both have some distinct features, but most benefits of the two platforms are similar. Both are continuous feeds that, like Facebook, are driven by the accounts that the user "follows." Although the feed portions of Twitter and Instagram are similar to the Facebook feed, the biggest difference between these platforms and competitor Facebook is their simplicity. For Twitter and Instagram, usage patterns are straightforward. Both Twitter and Instagram users can post, "like," or comment on the content of other users. Both platforms allow users to search for people, companies, brands, and trends using a hashtag (#). Searching a specific hashtag displays all users posting content with (theoretically) similar motivations for consumption.

Twitter separates itself from Instagram by focusing more on text and information. Although tweets are limited to 280 characters so conversations must be concise, many users appreciate the brevity. Twitter adds the ability to "retweet," which allows a user to instantly link the post of any user to their own feed, and to "quote tweet," which is a retweet with a comment. This feature is important because a user can display content from other users on their own feed to be viewed by their followers, who may not follow the original source. For example, assume a user named Steve retweets a video or picture from his friend Evan. Also assume that Steve's mother, Janet, follows him on Twitter. Steve's retweet of Evan's original content will appear as an impression on Janet's feed, even though she may not know or have any association with Evan. This ability to push content to users who do not follow the original creator is what allows content to go **viral**, a term used to describe rapid expansion and impressions of content. The text-centric focus, ease of finding trending topics, and virality of the retweet and quote tweet feature help Twitter stand out as a platform for global conversation. The ability of Twitter content to go viral is a great feature, but it is not without its drawbacks. As a result of this feature, Twitter can sometimes be noisy because people are constantly exposed to content from unfamiliar creators and brands that they do not follow.

Instagram answers the call to the dilemma of noisy feeds and unwanted promotions. Instagram is far more focused on photos and videos and less on dialogue. Instagram does not allow users to retweet or quote tweet, meaning that Instagram feeds include only those whom the person follows, unless, of course, they choose to search for a particular trend or hashtag. As a result, Instagram content may feel more streamlined and intimate. The data seem to back up this claim, because interaction rates on Instagram are over 20 times higher than on Twitter (Leone, 2018). The increased interaction rate makes attracting followers on Instagram

much more valuable to a brand, but at the same time it is more difficult to be visible. Instagram loses some of the virality effect, and it restricts the ability of unknown brands to gain market share through exposure to nonfollowers. Note that Facebook owns Instagram, so the company may believe that Instagram's more restricted environment is complemented by Facebook's more commercial applications. Both Instagram and Twitter offer a private messaging system similar to Facebook's, although users can choose to block messages from nonfollowers.

Selling Sport Through Twitter and Instagram

Organizations can use both Twitter and Instagram effectively to sell their products in multiple ways. Although many sport organizations use both platforms for various purposes, the dialogue-focused tweets may be more attractive for content that requires a lengthy explanation. For example, a ticket sales representative who wants to highlight the features of partnering with an organization may write a short success story from one of their clients, followed by contact information. Additionally, not requiring users to follow one another means that Twitter is more commonly used for quick-response service issues. Customers who have problems or questions are typically quick to post on social media sites, and savvy salespeople may use keywords to identify those customers, resolve issues, and, they hope, build a future relationship with the customer. Lastly, sales content produced for Twitter may differ slightly because the ability for retweeting and quote tweeting the content vastly increases the reach of the salesperson. Clever, funny, or agreeable posts may put an organization, or even a salesperson, in touch with a large audience rapidly if their tweet goes viral.

Instagram is used in many of the same ways as Twitter. Instagram posts can highlight sponsors, tickets, merchandise, and other content areas as effectively as a tweet. Where Instagram really excels is in its ability to strengthen the relationship with existing fans or customers. Followers of a professional sport team's Instagram page have already volunteered their interest in the content, so they are likely to be invested in the team somehow. Instagram sales can leverage that connection to increase revenues. For instance, sport organizations may promote a sponsor who wishes to leverage the brand value of the team to sell their products. This post may appear as a picture of a prominent player or coach using the sponsor's products in a picture or video. Such an advertisement does not require much of a dialogue, and the content would relate to fans who are attached more intimately to the brand than to the worldwide view of Twitter.

LinkedIn

LinkedIn is like Facebook in that it includes a feed and the ability to follow, find users, and view content. The biggest distinction between LinkedIn and Facebook is that LinkedIn is designed specifically for creating business content. User profiles on LinkedIn, which calls itself the largest professional network in the world, are hyperfocused on the professional life of the user. They include work and education experience, as well as opportunities for users to endorse the professional abilities of other users in several ways. The profiles are so business-centric that there is even a feature that allows the user to attach a resume at the front of their profile, along with an indicator as to whether they are actively looking for jobs. LinkedIn profiles also allow users to view the network, or "connections," of other users, including how they are connected professionally. One unique feature of LinkedIn is the ability to see which other users have viewed your profile, an interesting piece of information rarely disclosed to users on other platforms.

Where LinkedIn shines for salespeople lies in the way that it displays information on an individual's network and the ease by which it finds similarities between users. Searching any user on LinkedIn automatically generates a web of "second-degree connections" that includes various ways that two strangers may have something in common. Results show shared coworkers, places of employment, alma maters, and even "third-degree connections," which mean that although you have no direct connections to the user, they have a link with one of your second-degree connections. LinkedIn does not pretend to be a purely social platform, and it does not allow users to search for themes or hashtags quite as easily as some of the other platforms, limiting its viral ability. But the extensive database of business information on users and the web of connections displayed allows salespeople to find a common point of connection between themselves and millions of people.

Selling Sport Through LinkedIn

As we previously mentioned, LinkedIn is a goldmine of professional networking. Thus, the biggest benefit for sport salespeople lies in LinkedIn's ability to prospect. Ticket salespeople can drill down into a specific group of people who are more likely to buy. For example, the salesperson of a college athletics department may use the site to browse for alumni of the university who still live close by. Combined with the messenger feature, this tool can be a powerful way to get in touch with prospects whose contact information is not in the department's database. Likewise, the professional nature of LinkedIn makes it a natural fit for B2B prospecting. For B2B sales, one of the most challenging steps of the PRO method can be probing for information about the business. LinkedIn provides the prospect's job title as well as information about the company, including its location and number of employees!

YouTube

Sometimes considered a form of social media and sometimes considered a form of broadcast media, YouTube has one of the largest networks of users of any of the platforms mentioned. YouTube is primarily a hosting service for recorded or live videos. Users upload content that can be searched for by other users. When a user watches a video they like, they can "follow" that channel to received updates on new videos as they are posted. Users also have the option to "like," "dislike," and comment on videos. Additionally, YouTube includes an algorithm that recommends videos to users based on previous views. YouTube hosts a massive amount of sport content videos that are viewed and shared millions of times each day. But the recorded YouTube videos tend to lack the ability for live interaction that other platforms offer.

Selling Sport Through YouTube

YouTube livestreaming seems to be a more promising option for salespeople because it gives them the ability to join a live chat with other users enjoying the same live content. The challenge of using YouTube livestreams for sales is that engaging in sales behavior in chats is generally frowned upon and often results in action from moderators, who aim to keep the channel strictly social. The broadcast potential of YouTube was previously discussed in chapter 4, but the potential for direct sales or sales activities through the platform is limited. Salespeople can most effectively use YouTube to host and share content videos that provide information to customers (information, high-lights, success stories, etc.). Note that YouTube monetizes videos and offers a share of the revenue to the creators, although a user needs hundreds of thousands of views to generate significant revenue. Although this opportu-nity is typically not the priority for most sport organizations, it is worth tracking as YouTube's popularity grows.

Other Social Media Platforms

Social media is constantly evolving, and there will always be a new platform gaining pop-ularity while another fades into uselessness. The big three mentioned earlier—Facebook, Instagram, and Twitter—have withstood the test of time and are likely to remain as assets to a salesperson looking to use them for direct revenue generation. Additionally, LinkedIn provides a valuable resource that may be more useful to salespeople than socially focused media, and YouTube can be used to deliver video content easily to customers. That said, some niche forms of social media can provide sales value, and other emerging forms of media that have not yet been used extensively for sales have potential.

Blogging

Blogging, once thought of as more of an online journal, has reemerged as a form of social media consumption alongside some of the newer, flashier platforms. A blog is usually a series of written posts on a particular topic. Posts can go into far more depth than a traditional social media post that would only include a few sentences. Blogs are often focused on a particular topic, and the writer of the blog (the blogger) is often viewed as an expert in their area by consumers (Wright, 2017). Although blogs contain far fewer active engagement opportunities than traditional social media, they, like YouTube videos, are useful as a way to deliver information. A salesperson may decide to start a blog on common questions they have gotten from customers and the way that they were resolved. Likewise, a series on how to use tickets for B2B purposes may attract new customers who had never realized how a ticket purchase may help their business.

Snapchat

Snapchat is a relatively new social media platform that operates similarly to Instagram with followers, feeds, and special filters that can add effects to pictures or video. Snapchat's primary difference is that pictures and videos are only temporary, meaning that they show up on the user's feed for only a few seconds before they are lost. Sustaining interaction is thus somewhat difficult, but direct messaging on Snapchat does allow for text communica-tion. The lack of trend-based interaction and the temporary nature of the content means diminishing value for salespeople, although some sport organizations have successfully marketed large Snapchat audiences. Generally, Instagram tends to offer most of the same ben-efits with fewer drawbacks.

TikTok

TikTok, the newest platform on the list, has already accumulated 80 million users, thanks to its innovative integration of music and video without the need for complicated software. The basis of TikTok content is a video loop, usually recording the user performing some activity or

B2C REVENUE GENERATION

Atlanta Hawks and Tinder Creatively Use Platform to Drive Ticket Sales

In one of the more creative and viral social media promotions in recent memory, the Atlanta Hawks partnered with Tinder in 2015 and again in 2016 using the dating application to drive fans to Phillips Arena. The app has been programmed to match fans in the arena with others who have bought tickets. If both parties "swipe right," Tinder opens communication for them to chat during the game. Matched fans who wish to meet during the game can be directed to one of several meeting areas, which contain complimentary roses and breath mints to help the pair get to know each other. Furthermore, fans were encouraged to use other forms of social media to post pictures with their newfound acquaintances, and Hawks' security wore T-shirts proclaiming them "Swipe left patrol." The promotion was a major success; 1,500 tickets were reportedly sold in the first five days and countless more afterward (Bieler, 2015). The viral promotion ended up trending on Twitter in Atlanta and caught the attention of the entire country the following year when the Hawks paid for the wedding of one lucky couple who met during the previous year's game. Most sport organizations would not have thought a dating app could be cross-promoted with an NBA team to add value to a game and sell tickets, but by being creative and fully utilizing multiple forms of social media, the Hawks were able to develop their bottom line as well as a few relationships!

sharing a video. The short video repeats in an endless loop until a user swipes up or down to view the next video. Follows, likes, and comments continue as features form other social media platforms, but TikTok's most distinct value comes from the nature of its viral challenges and dances, combined with a "For you" page that uses algorithms to suggest videos that users may like. Although sport organizations are already racing to engage in TikTok content, the simplistic nature of the app limits its value to salespeople. But the sheer popularity and rapid growth of the app make it worth monitoring, and savvy sellers may soon find a way to tap into the audience.

Selling Sport Versus Selling Through Sport Using Social Media

Sport-marketing texts often discuss the idea of marketing sport versus marketing through sport and highlight the distinctions between the two: One involves getting butts in seats and eyeballs on screens, whereas the other involves using the sport product to market the products of outside companies (Mullin et al., 2014). We believe a similar concept applies to sales as it relates to social media; selling sport through social media is completely different from selling through sport using social media. Selling sport through social media refers to the sales agent using social media platforms to engage customers, build interest in their products, and ultimately influence them to buy a product offered by the sport organization (tickets, merchandise, concessions). Meanwhile, selling through sport is what the sponsor does when they buy sponsorship inventory; their goal is not to influence a buyer to buy products of the team, but to buy products of the sponsor. When selling sport, the product being sold is the game itself and the direct revenues that come with it. When selling through sport, the product is access to the audience watching the game and influencing them to buy the products of the sponsor. The easiest way to differentiate between the two is to ask yourself who the fan's money goes to. If the fan's money is going directly to the team, the sport organization is likely selling sport. If the goal is to build the brand or get a customer to spend money with an outside company, and the outside company is the one who pays the team, the sport organization is selling (and marketing) through sport.

Both are significant ways that sport organizations can earn revenue, but the approaches and structure to each are fundamentally different. Therefore, later in the chapter we separately discuss the PRO method for the different forms.

Selling Sport Through Social Media: Seeing Yourself as the Brand

When selling sport, you are using your own social media channels to promote the brand. You are using your individual accounts as the platform for selling. The inventory that you are selling remains the same as that used in other forms of sales (ticketing, merchandise, concessions), but the delivery method of communicating with customers changes. The seller themselves are creating the content to attract buyers to buy from them, and the seller is the actual brand being promoted. Sales representatives using social media to sell sport are creating their own individual content, which may be endorsed by or affiliated with a team, but the name of the salesperson is on the account, not the team. When taking this approach, salespeople should think of themselves as an individual brand; they are trying to promote to their audience (future customers) that they are the best route for buying sport products. To sell sport effectively using social media, the seller should think of how the PRO method will be slightly different when the medium of communication is a social media account and adjust accordingly. This process will be discussed more thoroughly later in the chapter.

Selling sport using social media is certainly not easy, and it is time consuming. A salesperson interacting on Twitter is unlikely to close sales immediately and generate leads on their first attempt. As with other methods of sales communication, time and practice are required. Similarly, a blog or YouTube channel highlighting success stories and promoting to future buyers may be effective content, but it will take time to develop. Salespeople should continue to self-evaluate what is working and adjust their strategies constantly to maximize effectiveness. As social media becomes more integrated into everyday life, the salespeople who succeed in traditional sport sales may be the ones willing to use untraditional mediums of communication. In fact, some research shows that customers feel more comfortable communicating about sales through email and social media, even though the depth of communication available to the salesperson is limited (Vanheems et al., 2013; Norris, 2007).

Selling Through Sport Using Social Media

Whereas selling sport products using social media involves the same inventory and a different method of communication, selling through sport using social media involves entirely separate inventory. Additionally, selling through sport differs in that it involves the social media accounts of the team rather than the accounts of the individual salesperson. As a seller you are not using your personal platforms to sell products, but instead pitching the actual platforms of the team as the product itself. Most professional sport teams have active accounts on the big three social media platforms, and those who do not should, because the opportunities for sponsorship are endless.

Each social media platform has multiple unique ways to use their content to promote sponsors, and the available content on social media channels is always changing, so specific inventory that is available today may be obsolete tomorrow. What usually remains unchanged, however, are the general categories that these inventory items fall into: affiliate marketing, direct endorsement or advertisement, and indirect endorsement or advertisement. By studying the effectiveness of each of these three categories and the way in which they work, you can apply these same principles to future social media platforms and inventory as they evolve.

First, teams can use affiliate marketing, which focuses on a direct sale of an outside product to the customer. The sales to a consumer who was led to the product by an affiliate marketer are typically tracked using a specific web link and paid to the affiliate by way of a royalty. This mode is less common in professional sport and more likely to occur in minor league sport, teams with a smaller audience, or individual athletes. When affiliate links are provided, they are usually also part of a direct or indirect advertisement by the team.

Direct advertisements are clear advertisements or content created by the sponsor and posted on the official social media accounts of the sport organization. For example, Kingsford Charcoal created video ads featuring grilling with their charcoal, and they were tweeted out on the Washington Nationals' feed. This example is a direct advertisement because most of the content is directed toward the sponsor, not the team. On the other hand, a tweet from Kaiser Permanente on the Nationals' feed promoted an "inning of excellence"—an inning with six hits, a walk, a sac fly, a sac bunt, and seven runs! Their graphic included photos of these plays, focusing mainly on the team itself, with a small Kaiser logo. This tweet served as **indirect advertisement** because the purpose of the post was not solely to promote Kaiser Permanente but to promote their "inning of excellence."

Direct advertisements leave little room for attention to something else, so they are more effective in promoting a company that wants to deliver a longer, more detailed message about their brand. A company might post short tweets, as in the Kingsford example, but they can use other platforms for longer messages. Meanwhile, indirect advertisements often leave little room to deliver a lengthy brand message and tend to be more effective for sponsors who just want the exposure of being associated with the team's social media accounts. Direct advertisement tends to be more expensive because it requires most of the content from the post to be directed toward the brand and because it clearly leaves the impression on the viewer that the post is an advertisement. Teams hesitate to offer too many direct advertisements in a short period because they do not want to appear "spammy." To offer transparency, many organizations use the hashtag #ad to disclose to their customers that the content is a direct advertisement and not an effort to trick them. Likewise, indirect advertisements are more

subtle and typically less expensive because they use less of the social media content and can be posted more often.

Using the PRO Method for Social Media Revenue Generation

As we mentioned, selling sport and selling through sport are two completely different processes, with different inventory. Selling sport through social media relies on the social media platforms as the method of communication. Thus, going through the full five-step PRO method using social media to communicate is extremely unlikely. For selling through sport, this is not a problem because only the inventory has changed; most of the PRO method is still done on the phone or through email as you seek to gain sponsors who want to sell their products in this way. For selling sport through social media, it is common to get only to step 1 before the communication method changes and the sale become more traditional. Therefore, when we apply the PRO method to this chapter, we cover step 1 twice: once for selling sport and once for selling through sport. After that, we focus on the areas of the PRO method that are unique to social media inventory, rather than repeat things already discussed in chapter 4.

Step 1 (Selling Sport): PROspect for Qualified Customers

Prospecting through social media is one of the most effective ways to use the platforms. Social media can reach hundreds of millions of people, and most platforms include a way to reach out directly to the individuals, so prospects are certainly plentiful. What makes this step challenging is qualifying the prospect. Qualified customers have the means, ability, and interest to purchase your product. For instance, some fans may be interacting about a particular sport team but live nowhere near the team's stadium or arena. In these cases, trying to sell this person tickets or concessions would make no sense, although they might be interested in merchandise sales. Additionally, because of the sheer volume of customers following, interacting with, and commenting about sport teams, you often have to qualify the degree to which the customer is a fan. Normally, nonfans or low-identification fans can still be decent leads, but when using social media as a method of communication, they may be less valuable. Passionate, involved fans would be the best leads to start with.

Prospecting Through Facebook

One of Facebook's most useful features is that it gives the user the ability to join groups and interact with those groups. Nearly every professional sport team has a fan group on Facebook, which would be a fantastic place to start prospecting for leads. After you become a member of the group, avoid the urge to post a generic message asking people to contact you about tickets (or other inventory). Social media communities tend to be sensitive to "fishing" or generic posts asking large groups of people vague questions. Instead, do some research within the group. Read comments and learn about the members. Who mentioned that they go to games? Who mentioned that they have not been to a game in a long time? Which members live in the area where the team plays? Which members seem to be the most passionate? You can find the answer to many of these questions before you ever reach the probing stage of the process.

After you have identified a potential prospect, you must make the initial contact carefully on all forms of social media, especially Facebook. People tend to be less accustomed to strangers sending messages on Facebook, so you should be friendly and passive. The good news is that most of the time you will be able to message someone on Facebook even if they are not a "friend." In making the first contact, you should be transparent and identify yourself as an employee but also suggest that you can help them. Ultimately, these should be "soft" asks that give the customer a comfortable way to say no. This approach is not always recommended in sales, but we believe it is warranted when reaching out to people on social media. Here

are some examples of introductions through Facebook:

> Example 1: *Turner, I am a member of the Panthers Facebook group as well. I saw what a passionate fan you are and didn't know how many games you have been to in person. I sell tickets for the Panthers and would love to help if you want to see a game live.*

> Example 2: *Penny, I belong to the central Virginia business networking group you are a part of and have been helping some of the members entertain their VIPs at our soccer games this year. If you need information on hospitality and club services, we have some unique experiences to offer.*

Prospecting Through Twitter and Instagram

Prospecting through Twitter and Instagram is different from prospecting through Facebook because you cannot use a Facebook group as an introductory point and the public profiles on Twitter and Instagram are far more limited. You will not know as much about the person you are messaging, and you will not have common ground to start with. But what Twitter and Instagram lose in information they make up for with volume. Twitter tends to have more informational and conversational posts, which makes it perfect for tapping into a global conversation on a topic surrounding a sport team. Searching a hashtag for a sporting event or team can give you hundreds of people who may be interested. Quickly looking at someone's Twitter profile page may reveal their location or even fandom because it is common content for a Twitter bio. If you can send a message to the prospect, you structure the conversation as you would a Facebook message. But as we said, the volume of prospects you can get from Twitter comes with a few costs. People on Twitter commonly do not allow messages from strangers. It is even more common on Instagram for private messaging to be blocked. Unfortunately, in these cases you are left only with the option of leaving a public comment. Again, people on social media are often suspicious of individuals reaching out to them through the app to sell something, so you must be transparent and honest. You typically want to offer only a one-sentence explanation of what you can do for them and your contact information. This approach sounds like the bulldogging sales method mentioned in chapter 3, which involves pitching sales before you do step 2 or 3 of the PRO method. The difference is in the intent and the platform. The goal of reaching out to a prospect on social media is not to complete an entire sale through the site's messaging system. The goal is to get them to call you or email you so that you can start the PRO method normally. Social media just requires that you give a little more information when you approach the customer compared with a regular phone call. If you must reach out to someone by commenting on their post, make sure that your response is related to the team or product you are selling, and make it straight to the point. A few examples follow:

> Example 1: *That's a great photo of you two! If you want to come to another game, shoot me a message; I work in ticket sales for the team.*
>
> Example 2: *Glad to hear you care so much about our student-athletes! I am working on development for our scholarship endowment and would love to talk more if you are interested in supporting these young men and women even more. Go Wildcats!*
>
> Example 3: *What a cool watch party! If your company wants to do the next one at the actual game, let me know; I can help set it up.*

Notice that in the examples, you do not introduce yourself in the typical sense. The interaction does not include a traditional salutation or "Hi, I'm . . ." moment. With social media, you normally do not need to introduce yourself because your name is clearly displayed on your account. Additionally, these comments are a one-time soft ask designed to provide information to the buyer and then allow them to make their own decision without feeling pushed. Considering how skeptical people tend to be when they are approached

on social media platforms, we believe that this is the best method. Lastly, remember that the goal of using social media to sell traditional sport inventory is almost entirely in the prospecting portion of the PRO method. Ideally, the customer responds that they are interested, the salesperson sets up a call, and the sale moves forward in a more traditional sense. Probing for information, resolving objections, and pitching a sale through the messenger feature of a social media platform is certainly possible, but it is not generally recommended.

Prospecting Through LinkedIn

LinkedIn may have the most B2B potential for prospecting compared with other forms of social media. The business focus of LinkedIn makes it extremely easy to approach a B2B customer because users who frequent the platform tend to consume the content for business purposes anyway. Offering a way to improve sales, hospitality, or morale would be considered far more normal on LinkedIn than it would on one of the other platforms. Aside from the sheer nature of its content, LinkedIn has a few other advantages you can take advantage of. If you have built a large network yourself, you can go through your contacts and see how many of them are qualified in terms of location or interest. You may even be able to get information about their company, including how many employees they have and what those employees have said about their company. Additionally, the search features on LinkedIn allow you to sort your network for similarities, such as schools or employers that you have in common with others on the site. These touchpoints are a good way to start a conversation. Lastly, LinkedIn allows you to work in reverse on B2B prospecting. That is to say, if you have already targeted a company but need to find the person who oversees events, you can use LinkedIn to help you. By finding the company information page and searching for a job title such as "human resources" or "events," you may be able to identify exactly the person you need to contact. The following are some ways that you can create the introduction for a B2B sales lead:

Example 1: *Emilia, congrats on the new promotion! Since you are the new director of marketing let me know if you want to promote your business at any Saints games this year. I have been working with a lot of similar businesses who have found it beneficial. Just tell me what time works best for you and we can set something up.*

Example 2: *Hello, Jalen, I noticed that your job description mentions handling corporate events for your company. That is right up my alley because I coordinate corporate events for the Bulls. I'd love to chat about what we can do for you if you are interested.*

Example 3: *Good morning, Jeremy, I was looking at your company's website and noticed that you seem to have a huge emphasis on providing a premium experience for your clients. I wanted to reach out to you regarding some of our premium seating options. I'm sure your clientele would love it.*

LinkedIn introductions can be a little longer and provide more information than an introduction on Facebook, Twitter, or Instagram because users on LinkedIn are used to being solicited. Because the idea of being "sold to" is not as foreign on LinkedIn, you can treat the message more like a traditional phone or email introduction, although shorter is always better. The goal remains the same as it is on other forms of social media; ideally, you do not want to have too much of the conversation through the message system. Instead, try to secure a phone call so that you can properly go through the steps of the sales process.

Step 1 Again (Selling Through Sport): PROspecting for Qualified Customers

When selling through sport, we want to focus on customers who are interested in the social media platforms of the sport organization. This form of selling merges the process from chapter 4 with the content from this chapter. When prospecting for businesses that would be interested in partnering to use your social media platforms, you want to focus on your audience more than anything else. What are the demographics of your followers on social media? Note that these demographics may be different from those of the typical fan. Also, look at how your fans are interacting. What are they posting? What themes emerge in their content? Social media advertising is all about audience, and you need to have a strong idea of your audience before you try to sell it to a business.

After you analyze your audience, prospecting consists of trying to find businesses that would find value in advertising on your social media channels. One way to do this is to look at your competitors and see if you can find sponsors who already invest in this space. Although this method of prospecting is certainly easy and effective, your organization probably has only a limited number of competitors, and the leads are likely to dry up quickly. Other ways you could prospect would be to note what brands and products your fans mention in their posts. If you notice one company being mentioned several times, you have a great lead to approach them and try to build on an audience that already has an interest. One tip to prospecting and making initial contact on these sales is to offer a little bit of information regarding your audience or why you believe that you are a good fit. This approach helps especially with businesses that are not as familiar with social media marketing. Here are some ideas about how you might approach these businesses:

Example 1: *Hi, I work with local businesses to promote their brands on our social media pages. We have over half a million followers between the ages of 18 and 25, so it seems like a really good fit for your business. I'd like to set up a time to chat more if you think we can help you.*

Example 2: *Luigi, I work with the Tampa Bay Rowdies and have been creating promotional programs for local businesses using our social media platforms. I'd love to chat more about our programs if you have a free moment sometime this week.*

These approaches sound a lot like traditional sponsorship prospecting, but the social media inventory and marketing process is so different from traditional sponsorship that the salesperson may need to educate the business partnering with the sport organization. Note that social media is often a supplement to traditional sponsorship inventory, but this chapter focuses on the social media inventory by itself.

Step 2: PRObe for Information With Open-Ended Questions

Probing for information to make a social-media-based sale involves a lot of the same sorts of questions that a regular sponsorship sale would include: Who is your audience? What are you looking to do with your marketing budget? These sorts of questions will help in the next step when you are creating the content that will be used for the business. Some probing questions that are more specific to social media selling include these: How do you measure success on your social media campaigns? What current trends are you trying to associate with your company? How many of your customers use social media? All these questions give you specific insight into how to design social media content for the business.

Finding the trigger statement can be a bit tricky when talking about social media, because the obvious end goal of the customer is usually to increase sales. But you want to find out what the customer believes is the engine that will drive those sales. Is it brand building? Awareness? The ability to demonstrate a new feature of their product? Getting past the "make more money" trigger statement is similar to getting past the generic "having fun" trigger statement from ticket sales customers.

Step 3: PROvide Solutions by Matching Features and Benefits With the Customer's Needs

Step 3 requires that you match the features and benefits of the product with the wants and needs of the customer. A good seller should have identified the goals of the sponsor or corporate partner in the previous step. Features of the social media inventory include the audience and the ability to gain exposure and reach that audience. Matching these features with benefits involves two main factors in a social media campaign: choosing which social media platform will deliver the content and explaining what that platform offers to help deliver the message from the content. This step can vary widely because of the numerous possibilities. The following are some examples of suggesting platforms and methods of delivery:

> Example 1: *Carole, your extra-messy buffalo wings sound delicious. How about we create a Twitter campaign that asks our fans to respond to a tweet with pictures of themselves covered in barbeque sauce and to show us their "game face"? We will link your restaurant and provide your logo on the original tweet.*

> Example 2: *Phil, you mentioned that your car-detailing company needs to show folks how good your work is. In this case, it sounds like Instagram is the way to go because it is all centered on pictures. Perhaps we can take some pictures of our players' cars detailed and shiny in the parking lot and give you a shoutout for doing such great work.*

> Example 3: *Samir, your tutoring business is probably best promoted by our Facebook account. The audience is a bit older and more likely to have kids. Since you have to explain what a mobile tutor is, it is probably best for us to just post a direct advertisement so that you can use all the space to explain your product to our fans.*

> Example 4: *Warren, if your goal is to reach millions of impressions, we need to make this go viral and Twitter is probably the best bet. We can come up with a witty 10-second video, but it will have to be hilarious to get the viral response you're looking for. Let's start thinking of ideas.*

B2B REVENUE GENERATION

Secret Deodorant Wins on Multiple Levels With USWNT Social Media Campaign

Secret Deodorant has found an audience who is listening with their social media campaign, which celebrates the success of the U.S. Women's National Soccer Team, targets a perfectly matched demographic, and supports a cause close to the hearts of their audience. The All Strength, No Sweat campaign is part of a collaboration with the USWNT that highlights barrier-breaking women who are successful without "sweating" the obstacles they face. Their social media campaign has included numerous posts, which started by congratulating the UWSNT on their 2019 World Cup victory and quickly shifted the discussion to the pay disparity between the players and the players on the Men's National Team. This conversation created a strong attachment to their female demographic for two reasons: First, the idea of unequal pay is a cause that women related to. Second, it rallied UWSNT supporters in support of brokering a new compensation agreement. Lastly, Secret donated $529,000 to the players themselves to help close the gap ($23,000 for all 23 players). The social media campaign received tens of thousands of retweets and quote tweets, adding to the exposure, and the hashtag #dontsweatfairpay was trending across the United States because of the campaign. Although Secret's partnership with the USWNT does not end with social media inventory, the campaign showed the value that a single retweet from an official sport account at the right time can have on the exposure that a brand gets. In fact, the #dontsweatfairpay and #equalsweatequalpay hashtags have remained a staple of Secret's marketing campaign, which includes the sponsorship of several other women's sporting events and causes.

Step 4: PROpose an Offer

Truthfully, proposing the offer using social media as the inventory does not differ much from traditional sponsorship. What may change is how often the sponsorship is paid out. Larger sponsorship agreements typically include fixed amounts of money and more inventory than a simple social media campaign. But some agreements have bonuses that can be reached if social media content reaches certain milestones on likes, retweets, comments, and impressions. Additionally, smaller sport organizations may be more willing to be creative on compensation, perhaps agreeing to an affiliate marketing agreement or a variation of a royalty on sold products through the campaign. As always, the most important part of the offer is asking for the sale at the end. Here are a few ways you can summarize and ask for the sale:

> Example 1: *Tristan, you mentioned that impressions were more important to you than anything. We can have your auto repair shop featured as the presenter of our "Clutch plays of the game" video. We tweet it out at the end of every game, so you would get 82 instances of the promotion. I'd love to get you signed up so that we can start the promotion for tomorrow's game. What do you think?*

> Example 2: *Luigi, I can completely understand how you are afraid of wasting your marketing dollars and want to ensure that every penny you spend gets a return. How about this: If you can provide us with a promotional code that gives our fans 10 percent off, we will promote it on all our social media channels. You pay us the same 10 percent on sales using the promo code. That way you are spending money only when you know it led to an actual sale. How does that sound?*

> Example 3: *Luna, we can release your new commercial on our Facebook, Twitter, and Instagram pages for the amount we discussed. You mentioned that you really want this video to go viral, but that is impossible to guarantee. How about we discuss a bonus that applies only if the video gets a combined 100,000 engagements?*

Step 5: PROtect the Sale With Continuing Customer Service

As with all forms of sales, after you complete a sale the job is not over. With social media inventory, the results are so quantifiable that you always have information to provide to your customer. Good salespeople constantly communicate about what is and what is not working within a social media campaign. The nature of social media allows the customer to change their message if it is not working, so do not be afraid to report lower than expected numbers. Instead, use the numbers as an opportunity to improve the message or switch platforms to see if something else works better. Additionally, do not be afraid to interact with the fans who comment on the customer's content that you retweeted. Doing so adds legitimacy to the partnership because it shows that the sport organization is invested in the product, not simply posting an ad.

Upselling and cross-selling to other inventory items is a great way to increase revenue from a corporate partner who typically invests only in the digital side of the team. Do not forget that there is more than one way to accomplish the goals of the customer; even if a social media campaign is already working, you can supplement it with inventory from another form of sponsorship. Similarly, you can cross-sell completely different inventory such as tickets or hospitality events to businesses who would normally use only social media content. A few brief examples follow:

> Example 1: *Sony, I was thinking about how well the Facebook campaign is going, and I was thinking it may be beneficial to also set you up with a table during the games so that you can reach the older demographic you might be missing with the social media side.*

> Example 2: *Chelsea, I'm sure that your sales team is getting bombarded with calls after how much interaction this Twitter campaign is getting. Once things die down, let me know if you would like to treat them to a game at the ballpark. I'm happy to help.*

CUSTOMER SERVICE

Chiefs Kingdom Reigns Through Social Media

The 2019 Kansas City Chiefs knew from the beginning that they had a championship-caliber team and wanted to build their fanbase throughout the season. Season ticketholders (called season ticket members) received a surprise gift from the Chiefs: a box full of gifts along with their season membership card. Designed to look like playing cards, the cards featured star players, along with the member's name. Additionally, fans were treated to a throwback towel featuring a vintage Chiefs logo.

Scott Winters/Icon Sportswire via Getty Images

Where the Chiefs really capitalized off this promotion was in how they used social media to make season ticketholders feel special. First, they encouraged fans to post pictures of themselves holding their membership card or flag with the hashtags #chiefsstmflag and #chiefskingdom and interact with each other over their excitement about the upcoming season. Additionally, the Chiefs' official accounts began to reply, retweet, and comment on fans' pages who used the hashtag. The promotion gained considerable traction as thousands of excited fans publicly shared the benefits of membership.

Summary of the PRO Method for Social Media Revenue Generation

If you are selling traditional sport inventory, the most effective use of social media is as a prospecting tool and as a way to make contact with millions of fans. The prospecting capabilities of social media platforms are endless, but after a customer is interested, the recommended approach is to move the sale to a more traditional form of communication such as phone or email. If you are not selling traditional inventory but want to use social media as a niche form of sponsorship or as a supplemental add-on to an existing sponsor, the PRO method can be used more thoroughly. Sponsorship has already been discussed in detail in chapter 5, but this section shows you some of the differences between social media inventory and traditional sponsorship inventory.

Measuring Success: Impressions, Engagements, and Ratios

One of the reasons that businesses love social media is that tracking success is relatively easy. Over the years, strategies have been developed to tell which social media campaigns are effective and which are not. Social media tends to be delivered completely through the Internet and is easily quantifiable, so measuring and reporting performance metrics have become standard practice. Salespeople looking to sell sport through social media or sell through sport using social media should be familiar with these measurements.

Affiliate Marketing and Impressions

You may remember that **affiliate marketing** involves someone promoting a product and receiving a share of sales from viewers who purchase the product because of the affiliation. Affiliate marketers track their success in a couple of ways. The first is a trackable link. Certain web links save a cookie, which digitally tracks a website viewer and reports when the viewer purchases an item. The purchase can then be traced back to the individual link provided to the affiliate marketer to receive their commission. Alternatively, some businesses use a specific promo code or discount opportunity that identifies the customer as someone who visited the site because of the social media content of the affiliate. Businesses may also track affiliates by looking at increased traffic immediately following a social media campaign or during a certain time of day, but these methods are less precise and less common.

Aside from affiliate marketing, regular social media content is often measured by the sheer number of impressions that they create. In social media, an **impression** is every person who viewed the content for any reason. Whether they view it from following the original creator, stumble on it because of a hashtag, or see it retweeted by a friend, it is considered an impression. An important point is that impressions are counted regardless of whether the viewer interacts with the post.

Social Media Ratios

Counting impressions is one way to measure the effectiveness of a social media campaign, but the quantity of impressions or interactions may not give you as much information as you would like. For instance, getting 10,000 likes on a tweet would be considered a strong performance most of the time, but if the creator of the tweet had several million followers, it would mean that most of that person's audience was not interested in the content. Ratios are useful here, and several are used for social media evaluation. They can be broken down into three general categories: awareness ratios, engagement ratios, and conversion ratios.

Awareness Ratios

Awareness ratios measure the audience who is viewing the post, as well as the general growth of the account who created the content. The first ratio to look at is the **audience growth rate**, which is more a measure to gauge performance of an entire social media account rather than an individual post. Audience growth rate is calculated by dividing the number of new followers in any given timeframe (month, year, day) by the total number of followers of the account. This number shows you not only how many new followers you gained but also how fast you gained them or how much momentum you are building on that social media platform.

When looking at a specific post, many people want to consider the **virality rate** of the content. This ratio is calculated by the number of people who shared or retweeted a post divided by the number of impressions on that post. This ratio gives an idea of the general quality or interest in the content of the post. A post that is retweeted 500 times may seem to be performing poorly, but if those 500 retweets came from only 2,000 views, then the content of the tweet may be very good and it only needs to get in front of more viewers to make rapid gains in exposure.

Social share of voice is a ratio that measures how much an account is mentioned compared with their competitors. It is calculated by compiling the number of mentions that an official account receives on social media as well as the number of mentions that the competitors receive. The proportion of mentions that belongs to the account of interest versus the competitors shows the social share of voice. This ratio gives information relating to how visible a particular account or brand is within their space or among their competition.

Engagement Ratios

Engagement ratios measure the degree to which content is relating to the audience who is viewing it. Although engagement ratios are a category of ratio, the **engagement rate** is a specific ratio that falls into this category. This ratio can be used for both accounts and particular content. It is calculated by the number of engagements (likes, retweets, comments, shares, etc.) divided by the total number of followers of the account. To calculate the engagement rate for an individual over a certain length of time, accumulate the total number of engagements over that time, divide

by the number of posts during that time, and then divide again by the number of followers of the account. This number gives you an idea, in general, of how much engagement the account offers. If someone wants to look specifically at a particular post, you can simply divide the number of engagements on the post by the number of follows belonging to the person who created the content. Generally, an engagement rate above 1 percent is considered good, and 5 percent is considered exceptional. Note that Instagram has a high average engagement rate; some creators routinely boast engagement rates of 6 percent or more.

The **applause rate** is similar to the engagement rate, but it includes only engagements of agreement, such as likes, favorites, thumbs-up icons, and similar responses. This ratio measures the degree to which the followers of an account value the content of the posts. The reason that this ratio is different from the engagement rate is that the engagement rate includes retweets and comments. Oftentimes, interesting or controversial content can result in a lot of retweets, quote tweets, and comments because of the nature of the tweet, not necessarily because the viewer found it valuable. In fact, posts are often shared or retweeted with a caption from the re-poster making fun of the original author or disagreeing with them. These sorts of hostile or negative engagements would be included in the engagement rate but not in the applause rate.

Conversion Ratios

Although awareness ratios and engagement ratios are useful for branding, judging the quality of content, and getting an idea of how followers of an account behave toward that account, **conversion ratios** are focused on bottom-line objectives. These ratios measure how effectively an account can persuade their followers to do something. These ratios are often also used for digital sponsorship marketing, so you will probably recognize clickthrough rate (CTR) and bounce rate as two of the most common ratios in this category. As a reminder, CTR measures the percentage of viewers who actually click on the link or advertisement. It is calculated by dividing the total number of clicks by the total number of impressions. Likewise, bounce rate is the percentage of viewers who left the site shortly after clicking the link.

Conversion ratios are often used in social media "calls to action" when an influencer or social media account calls on followers to perform some action, such as follow a friend of theirs. Conversion ratios measure the increase in followers that the person gets in the next day. Conversion ratios could also be used when an account asks followers to perform an action such as posting a picture of themselves that supports an advertiser. For example, a social media account who partnered with a cleaning product may ask their followers to post pictures of the dirtiest bedroom using a hashtag that is tied to their sponsor. The last form of calls to action would be affiliate marketing, which has already been discussed in this chapter. Affiliate marketers closely track the ability of their social media accounts to convert into full sales.

Social Media Netiquette

Social media interactions can be quite different from interactions with customers in a traditional sense. The following guidelines can help salespeople maximize their effectiveness:

- *Be yourself*—trying to pretend to be something that you are not is often obvious.
- *Be honest*—be truthful with customers as much as you can. If you deceive them once, they will never be customers again.
- *Be transparent*—do not pretend that the product has no disadvantages or that the customer risks nothing. Customers are more likely to respond positively if you address the negative aspects and let them decide for themselves.
- *Be professional*—although you obviously want to be yourself, you should also make a point to use complete sentences and speak professionally. Slang or "text talk" is generally not recommended

- *Avoid sensitive or controversial topics, profanity, and other inappropriate interactions*—these things are bound to surface in some of the conversations you encounter on the Internet. As a salesperson, you should remain professional and either ignore the comment or politely address it if you must.

Summary

The purpose of this chapter is to examine social media and the multiple ways it is used to generate revenue in sport. We discussed the growth of social media, the way it is used to enhance viewership, and the various social media platforms available. Keep in mind that generating revenue through social media can be done in two different ways: Selling sport means using social media platforms to engage in traditional sport sales, and selling through sport using social media means that the actual product being sold is content from an official sport organization's platform. The social media platforms that have remained entrenched in the sporting world are Facebook, Twitter, Instagram, and LinkedIn. Specialty or niche platforms such as YouTube, TikTok, and blogs have more recently become popular as well, although they have not become staples for all professional sport organizations. Selling sport through social media really involves only step 1 of the PRO method, because when the prospecting is completed, the goal is to convert the prospect into a traditional sales medium. Actually selling social media content is completely different, so each step of the PRO method can be used, although the steps will be applied in slightly different ways for social media sales than for traditional sponsorship. Lastly, businesses and customers evaluate the effectiveness of social media campaigns using ratios, and salespeople need to take care to observe etiquette when selling on social media.

APPLIED LEARNING ACTIVITIES

1. *Comparing social media platforms.* Assign a random sport organization to each student and require them to compare how the team promotes their products on various social media platforms. Students should find the team's official Twitter page, Instagram page, Facebook home page, Snapchat accounts, YouTube channels, and any official blogs, podcasts, and other forms. Students then discuss the different forms of media, tone, atmosphere, and sales strategies attempted on the various platforms.

2. *LinkedIn prospecting.* Have students log into their own LinkedIn accounts and go through the prospecting process. Students should select (or be assigned) a sport organization to represent and use the LinkedIn search feature to come up with a list of 10 prospects that may be qualified to purchase something from the team (most commonly, sponsorship or tickets). Have the students probe for information on the prospect's LinkedIn pages and explain how and why they may be qualified. An extra step would be to require students to craft an opening line to introduce themselves to the prospect.

CASE STUDY

WHEN SOCIAL MEDIA BACKFIRES

Coming up with the perfect social media sales campaign is exceedingly difficult. For some teams, especially controversial or unsuccessful ones, trying to connect with fans can be as dangerous as it is helpful. When sport organizations, or salespeople, attempt to use social media to promote customer service, they should always be aware of how it can go wrong.

For example, in 2014 the New York Jets and (then) wide receiver Eric Decker ran a promotion for free merchandise asking Jets fans to show why they love the Jets on social media. Fans, frustrated by the team's lack of success, quickly latched onto the promotion and posted sarcastic responses. The promotion turned even uglier when Decker's wife lashed out with a tweet: "You think he really cares what y'all think haters?" The tweet was later deleted, likely at the request of the Jets' PR team, but the damage had been done. This example shows that although social media can be a fantastic way to connect and build relationships for future sales, it must be done carefully and with as much foresight as possible.

Discussion Questions:

1. What topics or areas of social media are best avoided when communicating with fans? Why do you believe they should be avoided?

2. What are the risks of using players to help promote or sell merchandise and tickets?

Go to *HKPropel* to complete the activities for this chapter.

Fizkes iStock / Getty Images

CHAPTER 11

Sales Force Management

CHAPTER OBJECTIVES

After completing the chapter, you should be able to do the following:

- Explain external and internal factors in sales
- Describe the human resource process
- Discuss sales training and provide an example of sales role-play
- Describe customer relationship management and its use by sales managers
- Explain bonuses and commissions as a way to incent sales staff
- Understand the importance of motivating the sales force
- Provide guidance on types of leadership that sales managers can use
- Apply the PRO method to sales training

As you have learned by now, one of the easiest ways to enter and stay in the sport industry is to be willing and able to sell. Sport organizations hire many recent college graduates to sell season tickets, memberships, group tickets and outings, various ticket packages, and birthday parties. Those who succeed in sales will have many opportunities to move into new sales positions and progress into management positions. Although an excellent salesperson could transition into becoming an excellent sales manager, it is not guaranteed. Often the greatest athletes do not become the greatest coaches, and the same can be said for sales managers. Although an outstanding salesperson should work within a team setting, a good salesperson does not always have to depend on others. A sales manager, however, is fully dependent on the success of everyone on the sales staff working together. And a sales manager can have a significant effect on the production of the sales staff.

Must a sales manager understand the fundamental steps unique to sales? The answer to this question is yes, absolutely. More important, the sales manager must be a good teacher or trainer, motivator, and leader, besides having other skills and abilities. Motivation, leadership, and teaching or training are all skills that can be learned. In this chapter, we outline some of these key skills and describe motivational factors that help in understanding the needs of the sales staff. In addition, sales managers need to be proficient in using customer relationship management (CRM) systems. This chapter focuses on the most important parts of the job for any sales manager. First, the manager must understand basic concepts in human resources management having to do with hiring and training good people and motivating the sales force. Leadership is crucial to retaining the sales force. Finally, the sales manager should understand the fundamentals of management and the use of technology.

Sport managers must coordinate both human and material resources along with relevant technologies and situational contingencies to support the efficient exchange of sport services (Chelladurai, 2017). All these elements come into play for a sales manager in sport who must coordinate with sales staff, understand customers, interact with new technologies, introduce new products or services, handle legal and ethical challenges, resolve complaints, and devise strategies to beat the competition, all within a constantly changing environment. Within sport, the core product is the game itself, and salespeople have little or no control over the outcome. The manager is responsible for interacting with both internal and external forces in sport. External environmental changes affect the sales force in relation to four categories: (1) customers, (2) competitors, (3) technology, and (4) the ethical and regulatory environment (Jones et al., 2005). To adapt to these changes, organizations seek to modify and change internal structures and processes that affect sales force management. These internal structures and external changes are depicted in figure 11.1, along with the core product in sport (the contest itself) and in fitness (change in body or health and wellness). Although the sales manager has control over the internal structure and process, they have little or no control over the core product and external environmental changes that affect the organization.

Beyond the core product and external changes, sales managers must manage the internal structure and processes within the organization. These elements may include the introduction of new products, purchase of new technology, implementation of new sales strategies, use of CRM systems, allocation of new sales positions, and the hiring of new salespersons. All these internal processes and structural issues may result from changes in the external environment. Changes in the external environment may include new ticket holders, changing expectations of customers, and changing demographics of the customer base. Sales managers must be cognizant of how the customer is changing and interacting with the core product. Changing demographics in the United States has a big effect on the core product, the game itself. For example, the slow

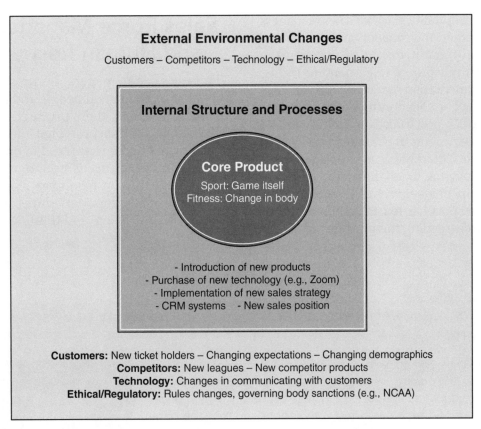

External Environmental Changes

Customers – Competitors – Technology – Ethical/Regulatory

Internal Structure and Processes

Core Product

Sport: Game itself
Fitness: Change in body

- Introduction of new products
- Purchase of new technology (e.g., Zoom)
- Implementation of new sales strategy
- CRM systems   - New sales position

Customers: New ticket holders – Changing expectations – Changing demographics
Competitors: New leagues – New competitor products
Technology: Changes in communicating with customers
Ethical/Regulatory: Rules changes, governing body sanctions (e.g., NCAA)

FIGURE 11.1   Core product, internal structure, and external environmental changes.
Adapted from Jones et al. (2005).

nature of the game of baseball is not as appealing to a changing fan base, and over the years football has become the most popular sport in the United States. Monitoring competition is also important. The commercialization of intercollegiate sport over the years has changed how the NCAA operates. Factors like cost of attendance; conference realignment; rules regarding name, likeness, and image (NLI); and the emergence of new competition are rapidly changing college sport. New leagues and new products are factors for sales managers to monitor when considering the competition. Technologies are also playing a big part in the changes within the external environment. COVID guidelines made communication in person next to impossible, so organizations moved to online platforms such as Zoom to communicate with both customers and employees. Ethical and regulatory changes are also of concern. Rules changes, new government guidelines, tax laws, gov-

erning-body sanctions, and many other factors are important for a sales manager to consider when making structural and process decisions.

In the end, the point remains that sales is not easy. Three key issues face all salespeople and sales managers: complexity, collaboration, and accountability (Ingram et al., 2005). These three issues are highly important in the sport industry. As the industry continues to expand, the inventory becomes more complex. Consider the complex inventory now being sold in ticketing. In the old days, tickets consisted of box and reserved seats along with general admission. Now, salespeople sell all sorts of inventory, including club seats, various levels of premium suites, and many types of season ticket packages, using dynamic ticket pricing and various types of technology to sell. And ticketing is only one category of sales. Consider as well the increasing complexity of selling sponsorships, merchandise, concessions, events, and hospitality. Further, sales managers must understand the concept of collaboration as teams sell these items. In cases when the organization outsources (e.g., naming rights, concessions, media and marketing rights), sales managers may be collaborating with salespeople who do not report directly to them. Multiple teams or departments in ticketing, luxury club and suite sales, marketing, events, and others must work together to sell the product. Finally, the complexity of inventory, collaboration, and the focus on sport has led to greater accountability for those selling the product.

Sales Force Management and Human Resources

The best sales managers are those who can recruit and retain good people and are accomplished at selling their product or service. Salespeople are often promoted into sales management positions. To succeed in this position, the sales manager needs to understand basic concepts in human resources management. Some of the most important duties of the manager are hiring, firing, and training.

INDUSTRY PROFILE

Dan Jankoski, Legends General Manager, University of Wisconsin property

Legends is a company that specializes in delivering solutions for sales, hospitality, merchandise, and technology to sports and entertainment venues. In 2019 the University of Wisconsin athletic department partnered with Legends to manage general ticketing, premium seating, annual fundraising, marketing, and business intelligence capabilities. As part of his work with collegiate partnerships with Legends, Dan Jankoski also served as the general manager for this effort at the University of Wisconsin.

© Daniel Jankoski

Question: What are your primary responsibilities related to managing the sales force?

Answer: We have four managers who focus on key areas of our partnership with the Wisconsin property. We have a ticket sales manager, manager of data analytics, premium seat manager, and a manager of strategic development. Legends at Wisconsin has 21 team members who, either directly or through their manager, report to me. My primary responsibility is to manage this partnership between the Wisconsin property and our team. Part of this is making sure our goals between the two organizations align and that our team members at Legends have the resources needed to be successful. We at Legends want to deliver solutions to the Wisconsin property to ensure they are moving forward with what they are trying to accomplish. Also, I want to ensure that our Legends team on the ground is put into position to execute the strategy. Generally speaking, for me this consists of implementing a one-to-one management style where I need to get to know each person on our team both professionally and personally. I try to understand what motivates them, their strengths, and how the team dynamic needs to work together cohesively. I want to ensure that there is cross-collaboration between the individual departments as there is a lot of opportunity for us to make our teammates successful. Team objectives should be clear for everybody. We generate revenue in a lot of different areas, so it is important that we are able to collaborate with each other. Furthermore, our team needs should be aligned with all of the core objectives of our partnership with the

Wisconsin property.

Question: What is your approach to training salespeople? What has worked well, and what has not worked at all?

Answer: Training for us starts with administering a survey and then observation. First, I need to understand what people want to learn and what they are doing well or what needs improvement. Surveying our salespeople helps me to understand their interests. I speak about it as continual training and empowered training. Once you have someone on your team who has mastered something, you can have them teach their teammates, and in turn this also helps them to become empowered. Second, observation is a technique that allows me to witness what a team member is doing well along with any struggles. Observation helps us to focus on the training areas that need to be considered and continually worked on. I challenge our managers to observe their team members as they are going through a campaign. Using these observations helps us to create training specific to each individual team member. In the observation stage, data and analytics are also vitally important. Especially with young salespeople, it is very helpful to have data and analytical insights to identify what parts of the sales process they need to improve upon. It also helps us to identify why they are losing sales. We can then help them to overcome objections and to identify what they are not saying that may be helpful. In the end, it helps to identify what parts of the sales process can be improved upon for each individual team member.

Question: What are some effective methods you have used to motivate salespeople?

Answer: Each person needs to be managed individually so you understand what motivates them. Friendly competition seems to resonate with a lot of our sales professionals. We will create teams and then track metrics. In addition to their individual goals, each team member is part of a larger team, the Legends team. Utilizing unique incentives is another motivator. For example, some salespeople enjoy receiving a unique sport experience (e.g., tickets to other games or lunch with the athletics director). What makes it effective is that not everyone has access to these types of rewards. We also provide each individual team member with their overall individual and team goals, but I also challenge them to create their own goals and incentives. This works because most team members want to hold themselves accountable. At Wisconsin especially, we try to celebrate successes over the entirety of the team. For example, if the premium seats team has a goal that has been reached, then everyone celebrates. This reminds all of us that while we have our own smaller teams, we are all part of one larger team.

Question: Describe your idea of leadership within the context of sales.

Answer: Leadership for me entails putting my team members in a position to be challenged and empowered to make decisions. I would rather team members be positive and solutions oriented, and try something that doesn't work out, rather than just say they have a problem. I want to hire great people whom I can challenge and then empower them to make decisions with a solutions mindset. Ultimately, this level of empowerment will help them if they go into management positions down the road. I heard a quote from Jay Wright when I was at the Villanova property that I have always liked. He said, "Everyone's job is different, but everyone's status is the same." This quote reminds me that if one of the wheels falls off, then the whole partnership at Wisconsin is not going forward as it should. We as a team at Legends need to execute across all parts of our partnership.

Question: What is the most valuable piece of advice you have been given in regard to sport sales?

Answer: To be solutions oriented is first and foremost. The reason it is so important in sales is because great sales reps find opportunities that good sales professionals do not. The only way to find these opportunities is to be solutions oriented. If a prospective customer says they are not interested, then the salesperson needs to find out why. If you bring a solutions-oriented mindset you can tackle this objection. A great salesperson should always say, "Yes if . . ." as opposed to saying, "No because . . ." The question the salesperson must answer is "What does it take for this to be a win?" as opposed to "Why this is a loss?"

Hiring and Firing

Hiring salespeople who are productive and a good fit for an organization can be one of the most fulfilling experiences for the sales manager. The fundamental components of the human resource process are writing a job description, determining compensation, recruiting, interviewing, and extending an offer. Hiring the wrong person can lead to a lot of heartache and costly mistakes. Hiring and training any employee costs money, and you do not want to hire someone who will come in and disrupt the culture of the organization. An organization must advertise the position and pay for candidates to travel, eat, and stay in a hotel during the recruitment period. Organizations pay not only the cost of recruitment but also the cost of losing customers, credibility, and contact information (Martini & James, 2012). Often, organizations interview multiple candidates, thus increasing the cost. After the applicant is hired, the organization must pay for training, benefits, salary, commissions, bonuses, and other forms of compensation. If the candidate is not the right fit and lasts less than a year, then the organization is back to hiring again. Therefore, hiring the right person is important, and sales managers must know what to look for in a sales candidate. In addition, the personality and leadership style of the manager and the organization need to be a good fit for the sales applicant.

What do we mean by a good fit? Understanding the mission and vision of the organization is crucial here. The mission of any organization is the purpose of the organization, and the vision communicates where the organization aspires to be in the future. Who is responsible for communicating this mission and vision to the sales staff? If you said the sales manager, you would be correct. A sales manager must commit to starting everything with a specific vision before hiring and then must hire to fulfill that vision (Klymshyn, 2006). During the hiring process, the sales manager must ask what they want people to think of or speak about when describing the sales environment. As the sales manager, are you interested in fostering healthy competition between salespeople, creating a fast-paced environment, or ensuring that everyone offers mutual respect within the sales arena? Klymshyn highlights three Ps that are fundamental for both the manager and the operation of the sales team:

- Professionalism
- Preparation
- Productivity

These three Ps can be arranged in any order. For example, sales teams who are professional and prepared will be productive. Likewise, we could say that productive and professional sales teams are prepared, or we could say that prepared and productive teams are professional.

Feigon (2013) claims that most sales organizations are not well equipped to compete for top sales talent. Meanwhile, the competition continues to increase while the talent pool shrinks. Furthermore, Feigon suggests that more skills are now needed to hire salespeople and that traditional recruitment, screening, and hiring practices do not work as well as they did in the past. Managers must evaluate experienced salespeople who may be set in their ways and less willing to prospect or cold call. On the other hand, managers must deal with recent college graduates who are familiar with technology and networking but have little knowledge of basic sales skills and require a lot of training. Therefore, Feigon provides the following advice about hiring. Sales managers need to be able to recognize the talent that makes for strong salespeople, place salespeople in the right roles, learn where to find good talent, create the right messaging, build a fun culture, and screen applicants effectively. The ego of some sales managers can create problems within the workplace, although that same ego may have made them a good and competitive salesperson in the first place. Feigon says that what he calls sales superheroes have the following characteristics:

- Are curious about people and businesses and are motivated to provide a solution to customer needs
- Are good written and oral communicators who give clear messages to customers during presentations
- Can be persuasive using logic and knowledge
- Can collaborate, especially when using technology or engaging customers with entertaining content and relatable conversation
- Understand financial value and can explain ROI to the customer
- Are tenacious, focused in the face of distractions, and can rebound from constant rejection

Many sport organizations conduct two or three interviews before they make an offer to a job candidate. Often, sales managers use behavioral interviewing techniques. Even so, sales managers estimate that only 40 to 60 percent of their sales staff at any one time can execute basic sales strategies (Martini & James, 2012). Asking a candidate how they would react in certain situations can give the sales manager a better idea about how a potential salesperson will perform in the job. To tease out responses from the job candidate, some sales managers use role-play scenarios. They may ask for an **elevator pitch**, a persuasive pitch to sell yourself to an employer that is short enough that you could pitch it while riding in an elevator. The presentation must be brief, persuasive, and emphasize your skills. Here are some examples of behavioral role-play scenarios:

- Demonstrate or provide an example of how you have closed a sale in the past.
- Give me an elevator pitch suggesting why you are the best applicant for the job.
- In the next five minutes, sell me a season ticket or membership for our organization.

- How would you respond to the following objections?
  - Not interested.
  - I cannot afford it.
  - I don't have time to speak to you.
  - Email or mail me something.
  - No thank you.

Sales Training

The goal of sales training is to improve the individual competency of sales team members (Siegfried, 2009). Training activities facilitate learning and help to develop new and existing skills that will improve the performance of specific sales-related tasks. Among these activities are classroom-based courses, videos, role-play, on-the-job training, and business or simulation games. But for those who are being trained, nothing is worse than attending a day or days of training from someone who has not done what is being discussed, reads from a book, or lacks experience in facilitating the training (Seidman, 2012). Siegfried (2009) suggests that the two highest priorities when conducting sales training are (1) teaching sellers how to sell and (2) teaching them what it is they are selling.

Over the course of a year, teaching selling skills normally consumes 34.5 percent of total training time. In descending order, the remainder of training time is spent on product training (28.3 percent), sales management training (13.9 percent), company-specific training (12.8 percent), and industry training (10.5 percent). Siegfried suggests that trainers should ensure that the following core skills or competencies are evident in each sales training:

- Salespeople understand how to ask customers effective questions and become better at listening.
- Salespeople can sell while keeping the best interests of the customer in mind.
- Salespeople make ethical decisions.
- Salespeople can leverage sales approaches that are transferable

- from one situation to another.

The sales trainer should have a deep understanding of several key concepts, including the sales process, pipeline, cycle, and forecast (Lambert, 2009). The trainer must understand the **sales process**, the steps like prospecting and qualifying that salespeople complete to create value for both the customer and the sales organization. According to Robinson (n.d.), when an organization puts together their sales training, they need to consider issues like the value proposition. For example, the training should address how to explain why their product is better than the competitor's product. Also, the trainer must ask if the sales process is clear and easily explained.

Sales managers often role-play with the sales staff. Every manager uses a different approach to role-playing and teaching sales. The sales manager is ultimately responsible for keeping their sales staff knowledgeable about the current sales environment. A good sales manager teaches fundamental concepts about sales and ensures that the sales staff are prepared to walk into any sales situation. Teaching and role-playing can be done in many ways that can be equally effective. Some sales managers like to make it competitive, others focus more on sales techniques, and still others make it fun.

Incorporating the PRO Method in Sales Training

Sales trainers can incorporate the PRO method into their programs, which may be virtual or in-person. PRO method training may include information about prospecting, probing for information with open-ended questions, providing solutions by matching product benefits with customer information, proposing an offer, and protecting the relationship by maintaining contact and providing customer service.

Step 1: PROspect for Qualified Customers

Prospecting for qualified customers can be a challenge. According to Schultz (n.d.), sales-people fail to prospect correctly for several reasons. First, many salespeople are not motivated and do not dedicate the time and energy needed to prospect for new customers. Another reason for poor prospecting is poor targeting, which results from not knowing how to work with gatekeepers or not targeting the right people. Still other salespeople give up too early and do not reach out by phone to potential customers. Finally, salespeople often do not research prospects or customize their messages to each customer. Training for prospecting should explain how to tackle these challenges. Several training tips may be helpful here, such as being friendly and familiarizing yourself with prospective customers through personalized emails, building relationships with the customer, being a knowledgeable resource, and prospecting on a daily basis (Kakar, 2019).

Step 2: PRObe for Information With Open-Ended Questions

Closed-ended questions generate responses that shut down conversation and may elicit yes or no responses. In contrast, open-ended questions give the prospect the opportunity to talk and to open up about their experiences, passions, and more generally about things of interest. Good salespeople ask good questions and are good listeners. Trainers can help salespeople develop open-ended questions. In the same way, salespeople can learn how to be good listeners. Probing questions help to gather more information about a topic and help the salesperson gain a better understanding about how their solution will improve the customer's situation (Mayer, 2021). Trainers can create an activity in which salespeople develop open-ended questions. Mayer suggests that these open-ended questions should be specific to keep the prospect from drifting away from the topic. The following are some examples of open-ended questions that are specific:

- What does your organization do on a daily basis?
- What makes your organization unique?
- Can you tell me about yourself?

Novice salespeople can learn a great deal by listening to and learning from experienced sales managers.

Oonal/E+/Getty Images

- How did you get into this occupation?
- Why is this initiative important for your organization?
- What are your goals?

Step 3: PROvide Solutions by Matching Product Benefits With Customer Information

Trainers can make a couple of important points in this step, during which the salesperson is providing solutions. First, product knowledge is vitally important in being able to provide the best benefit to the customer. Therefore, the trainer can spend time talking to salespeople about product benefits and helping them understand how various products add value to a consumer. An activity for trainers to do here is to have salespeople complete an elevator pitch that sells the benefits of an individual product or service. Salespeople can do this in

front of the whole class, or the trainer can break salespeople into groups of two. Second, this is a good time to talk about the concept of listening to the consumer. Hearing and listening are different. Hearing is an involuntary, continuous process that is passive. Listening is a voluntary, temporary process that is active and requires engagement (Lewkovich, 2018). The following are some activities to help develop stronger listening skills.

- *Listening activity I*: Have the speaker talk about their background—where they are from, siblings, schooling, interests, and experiences. This talk should last for about two minutes. Then have the responder in the group repeat back what they heard.
- *Listening activity II*: To help salespeople better understand what was said, you can have the groups add an activity by

having another speaker provide their background. Next, have the responder ask clarifying questions by restating what they heard and then summarizing. Restating does not mean repeating back what you heard, but rather paraphrasing what you heard, or saying it in your own words. Summarizing entails having the responder put the facts together and then respond to the speaker by saying, "It sounds to me like . . ."

Steps 4 and 5: PROposing an Offer and PROtecting the Relationship

In chapter 2 we discussed step 4 and talked about summarizing the offer. During the training you should have the salesperson practice emphasizing the trigger statement. The trigger statement is the single most important reason that the customer would be interested in the product. As noted in chapter 2 the salesperson emphasizes the trigger statement using some of the following words:

> "I know you mentioned . . ."
>
> "You told me that . . ."
>
> "It seems like . . ."
>
> "It looks to me like . . ."

Next, have the salesperson summarize the offer and, finally, ask for the sale. Asking for the sale is crucial, and the sales trainer should spend considerable time focusing on this step. As noted in chapter 2 the first part of asking for the sale involves telling the customer that they can have everything you offered if they are willing to commit to buying it. Then follow this statement by asking for their thoughts. We provided three examples of how to ask for the sale in chapter 2. The following is some wording taken from chapter 2 while asking for the sale:

> *The entire season package is only $2,000 and I can get it taken care of for you right now. What do you think?*
>
> *I can have a contract sent over immediately and we can go ahead and get started on helping your business. How does that sound?*

> *A gift of $50,000 would keep us on track to break ground by the end of the year. What are your thoughts on helping us today?*

Finally, you want to emphasize to the salesperson the importance of customer service. A good salesperson stays in constant contact with their customers. A good exercise here is to ask the group to brainstorm some ways to stay in contact with the customer. Some ways to do this include sending birthday or holiday cards, calling to check in with the customer, inviting the customer to events or activities, asking the customer to provide feedback, and staying in contact on social media.

Customer Relationship Management

Customer relationship management (CRM) systems are critical for both the sales team and the sales manager to save time and money and can be a helpful tool for closing deals (Stockdill, 2019). With a CRM system, customers respond to campaigns, or salespeople enter customer data to capture purchase history, demographics, and website interaction. Sales staff can use the system to identify and segment customers for campaigns that will appeal to them, thereby increasing sales success. CRM helps the sales manager analyze salesperson performance, coach the sales team, appropriate resources, and optimize sales moving forward (Insight Squared, n.d.). According to Tanner et al. (2005), CRM is a "strategy resulting in developing the most appropriate relationship with a customer, a process that is supported by technology and that may not necessarily yield deep or strategic partnerships with all customers" (p. 169). Scott (2018) notes that almost all sport teams and leagues use CRM for a variety of reasons, including all of the following:

- To build a detailed profile of their fan base
- To send messages or promotions targeted to certain fans
- To increase their ticket sales

B2C REVENUE GENERATION

Sales Role-Play

One of the best ways to become an effective salesperson is to role-play. Use the task and process below to role-play with a group of peers in your class.

Task

Drawing on what you have learned about sales, set up and make a sales call using a mock scenario. The primary task is to sell the customer your product or service.

Process

The sales trainer provides students with sales collateral to be used in the 10- to 20-minute sales presentation. This face-to-face sales presentation is conducted individually between the student and customer. Although sales collateral will be provided for each salesperson, students are expected to conduct outside research to understand the sport industry, the sport organization they represent, and any competitors. Although there is no single way to conduct a sales call, the following criteria can be used to evaluate the sales student:

- The student is knowledgeable about the product or service they are selling.
- The student asks open-ended questions
- Evidence shows that the student has researched the product or service and is informed about their organization and its competitors.
- The student demonstrates strong interpersonal skills and is able to develop a bond with the customer.
- The student is perceived by the customer as a consultant, not just another salesperson.
- The student demonstrates effective listening skills.
- The student demonstrates the ability to overcome objections raised by the customer.
- The student asks for the order by proposing an offer that best fits the customer's needs.
- The student appears relaxed, confident, and enthusiastic during the presentation.
- The student dresses in professional business attire.

- To gain support from sponsors
- To engage fans

CRM is useful for salespeople because it provides a safe storage space, allows more time with customers, provides activity reports, helps segment data, keeps the salesperson up to date on what is happening, tells when customers should be contacted, streamlines the sales cycle, analyzes customer needs, cuts down on administrative tasks, and saves money (Plaksij, 2020). But the sales manager should expect some sales personnel to resist using CRM because of the lack of control they feel, especially when it is forced on them (Kinnett, 2017).

Sales and Motivation

Companies spend a lot of time and money trying to determine how to motivate the sales force. Sales force compensation is the single largest marketing investment for most B2B companies, and U.S. companies spend more than $800 billion incentivizing employees (Steenburgh & Ahearne, 2012). Sales managers may sometimes have difficulty relating to how to motivate the sales force because many of them are former high performers. Salespeople who are stars often accomplish any goals in their path but stop working if an incentive ceiling is put in place. Steenburgh and Ahearne suggest that pay should not be capped for these types of salespeople and that companies should offer overachievement compensation rates. Core performers, the largest percentage of salespeople, can be incented with multitier targets that include sales contests with prizes that vary in nature and value. Finally, laggards, those salespeople at the bottom, can be incentivized with quarterly bonuses and some social pressure from peers.

Bonuses and Commissions

Bonuses and commissions can be a motivational factor for many salespeople. One of the biggest reasons that many people pursue a career in sales is the dynamic nature of earning an ever-increasing salary. As we have mentioned, you have control of your salary, and the more you sell, the more money you typically make. Bonus and commission structures, however, can be tricky to implement and should be done strategically. Done well, bonuses and commissions motivate employees to perform at extremely high levels. Done poorly, bonuses and commissions can derail the morale of a department and lead to dysfunction and communication issues within the organization.

Most sales organizations offer bonuses or commissions to incentivize their salespeople. Both are considered forms of variable pay, which is money that results from sales in addition to a salesperson's fixed (base) pay. For example, if a salesperson's salary is $25,000 per year, both bonuses and commissions would add to this base salary. The sales manager must understand the key differences between these two types of incentives. A commission is a payment made to an employee based on a percentage of sales they bring to the company. In contrast, a bonus is often a payment based not on individual sales but usually on departmental sales or when certain revenue targets are met (Smith, 2019). Made at the discretion of management, a bonus is usually a payment made for achieving or surpassing a set level of performance, and it is useful in directing salespeople's efforts toward specific strategic objectives (Churchill et al.,

1993). Bonuses, therefore, are based not only on sales volume but also on meeting other various goals important to a sales organization and for superior rather than customary performance (Joseph & Kalwani, 1998).

Commission

Commissions are paid per sale. Most commonly these are represented as a percentage, though sometimes you may see a fixed amount per sale. Commissions can contribute a large portion of a salesperson's income in certain industries. They most commonly range between 1 percent and 10 percent. Higher salesperson commissions are certainly possible, though less common. Traditional commissions are paid regardless of a salesperson's goal performance, although creative commission structures have become popular as well.

Various commission structures are used in sport. Patel (2019) highlights some of these structures, including commission-only, or **straight commission plan**. Some sport organizations use this system by employing what they call a street team who sell tickets. Sport executives tell stories of starting their careers in this way by being told they had a job only if they came back at the end of the day with a signed contract. Patel suggests that this type of structure is motivational because the salesperson has control of their income and can work more hours if desired to make more money. For the sales organization, this structure is easier because a salesperson is considered an independent contractor, saving the company money on hiring, benefits, and taxes. Although this type of structure can be a motivating scenario for some salespeople, it does not consider external factors like the economy and situational factors like the COVID-19 pandemic, when sales simply were not happening because sporting events were cancelled. These types of structures do not promote stability and traditionally result in large-scale turnover among the sales staff, most of whom are young and need significant training.

The most common structure for sport organizations is what is called a **base salary**

plus commission structure. The salesperson's salary in this structure is not enough to live on comfortably, but the commission allows them to make a viable income (Patel, 2019). More important, the company typically pays for benefits for the salesperson and provides some stability should the market fluctuate, causing sales to become more difficult. Another common way that sport organizations motivate their sales force is by using a **tiered commission structure**. In this structure, a salesperson's commission rate increases as they hit certain revenue benchmarks. For example, the commission rate may be set at 5 percent for all sales up to $25,000, increase to 10 percent for sales between $25,001 and $50,000, to 15 percent for sales between $50,001 and $75,000, and then to 20 percent for sales of $75,001 and above. As Patel suggests, this type of structure motivates high performers. Some companies may also implement systems whereby underperformers have their commission reduced if they meet only a certain percentage of their quota. For example, if the sales goal is $30,000 and the salesperson sells only $15,000, the company may pay the salesperson only 50 percent of their commission.

Although commission only, base salary plus commission, and tiered commissions are the most common structures found in sport, a few other types are sometimes used, including a revenue commission model, gross margin commission model, and commission draw structure (Patel, 2019). A **revenue commission** model pays a salesperson based on the revenues they generate. This structure is common for organizations who are entering new markets or want to increase market share and for companies that sell products with set price points. With a slight twist, the **gross margin commission** model considers the revenues generated but then deducts the expenses; therefore, a sales rep earns a percentage of the profit. The **commission draw structure** includes elements of the commission only and base pay plus commission structure whereby the salesperson earns some amount of pay each month regardless of sales. Normally used for new hires, this structure helps the salesperson adjust when they first come aboard without affecting their commissions. The salesperson is essentially guaranteed the draw amount in commission. For example, if the draw is $3,000 in commission, but the salesperson earns only $2,000 in commission, they would still receive the full draw of $3,000.

Chung (2015) states that the research clearly shows that companies sell more when they eliminate thresholds. Therefore, he advises that companies not place a cap on commissions that limits the amount of compensation a salesperson can earn. Chung suggests that a pay system should have multiple components, such as quarterly performance bonuses for high performers and overachievement bonuses for lower performers. In addition, Chung notes that although companies should experiment with their pay systems, they should keep it fairly simple. Too much complexity may allow salespeople to game the system.

State laws may vary regarding payment of commissions and bonuses. Parsons (2018) notes that companies may require continued employment on the date that a bonus is paid out, although in some states an employer is limited as to what conditions it can impose on payment after the employee has taken all the steps to make a sale. The sales manager must understand these laws along with benchmarks for commissions as they relate to commission activators and multipliers.

Commission Activators and Multipliers

Occasionally, sport organizations require sales representatives to achieve a certain benchmark before they begin to earn commission. For instance, a sponsorship department may require a sales representative to reach 80 percent of their annual sales goal before they receive commission on anything. These sorts of commissions come with higher risk for the salesperson and usually result in a high-reward commission being paid out after they are activated. Similarly, a **multiplier** can exist in either a traditional or activated commission.

A multiplier includes a commission percentage that increases as the salesperson achieves certain benchmarks. An organization who uses a commission multiplier must clarify whether the multiplier applies retroactively to all sales or only to sales following attainment of the benchmark. An example of a commission multiplier is shown in table 11.1.

Bonuses

Bonuses differ from commissions because they are not accumulated on a per-sale basis. Instead, they are rewards for achieving a particular goal or benchmark. Bonuses may be more appropriate for the manager of a sales department who is not actively selling or for a group goal such as renewals that could be difficult to calculate as a commission. Alternatively, bonuses may be a way to incentivize smaller, easier sales that may not warrant a commission. Although many people think of bonuses as large, annual payments, a sales manager may want to offer smaller bonuses throughout the year. Even a "free lunch bonus," an inexpensive and simple incentive, can motivate the sales department to reach a goal. Bonus structures can be simple or quite complicated, and methods for applying them vary. A simple bonus may be listed as $1,000 for a manager whose salespeople reached a particular quarterly goal. A more complicated, progressive annual goal is illustrated in table 11.2.

Common Metrics and Ratios for Evaluation

When setting goals related to salesperson performance, numerous metrics can be used to evaluate salespeople, some of which go far past a simple revenue goal. Having sufficient data is crucial in evaluating the effectiveness of a salesperson. **Measurable metrics** are activities that can be quantified and recorded from the CRM software of the organization or from the salesperson's own tracking and recording. Several of the measurable activities for evaluation are discussed here.

Revenue Generation

The goal for all sales positions is to increase revenue. Therefore, one of the most commonly measured and evaluated elements for sales managers is the revenue generated by their employees. This metric can be represented as gross revenue or as a percentage of the goal for the salesperson.

Call Volume or Touchpoints

Aside from revenue and sales, call volume or touchpoints are the most common metrics tracked for salespeople. Typically, higher call volume increases the chances of sales, and high call volume is often associated with hardworking or passionate salespeople. But overemphasis on call volume can lead to "bulldogging" calls or rushing customers off the phone. A more modern metric is **touchpoints**, which include phone calls as well as any other form of correspondence between the sales representative and the customer. Because customers are becoming increasingly comfortable with email, text messaging, social media interactions, online video conferencing, and other face-to-face conversations, touchpoints have been used to encompass these interactions.

Attrition Rate

The **attrition rate** of the salesperson is calculated by dividing the number of renewed accounts by the number of accounts that

TABLE 11.1   Example of a Commission Multiplier

Sponsorship dollars sold	Commission
$0 to $100,000	1.0%
$100,001 to $150,000	3.5%
$151,000 and over	5.0%

TABLE 11.2 Example of an Annual Goal

(ANNUAL TARGET BONUS = 20% OF MANAGER'S ANNUAL SALARY)	
Percentage of annual property goal	Percentage of target bonus awarded
Less than 80% of goal	0% target bonus awarded
81% to 90% of goal	50% target bonus awarded
91% to 99% of goal	75% target bonus awarded
100% of goal	100% target bonus awarded
115% of goal	105% target bonus awarded
125% of goal	115% target bonus awarded

the salesperson started with in their book of business. Comparing the attrition rate of each salesperson to the sales team or organization is helpful to ensure that outside elements (coach leaving, price increase, etc.) are not the cause for a high attrition rate. If the sales representative has a high attrition rate compared with coworkers or with the organization as a whole, the salesperson may benefit from spending additional time calling and developing their existing business.

Conversion Rate

The **conversion rate** is calculated by dividing the number of sales by the number of active touchpoints generated by the salesperson. This measurement gives the manager an idea of how likely the salesperson is to complete a sale after they get a customer on the phone. Conversion rates typically do not include voicemails. A low conversion rate may suggest that the salesperson needs to focus more on steps 2 and 3 of the PRO method (PRObe for information with open-ended questions and PROvide solutions by matching product benefits with customer information).

Callback Rate

The **callback rate** is calculated by dividing the number of inbound calls by the number of voicemails left by the salesperson. Inbound calls that were not prompted by the salesperson are typically disregarded. A high callback rate suggests that the salesperson is using a particularly effective voicemail script or is showing strong energy on their voicemails, which is encouraging customers to call back. This ratio can also be used to gauge the effectiveness of a renewal campaign.

Upsell Rate

The **upsell rate** is calculated by the amount of new revenue generated by existing customers. Upselling is often overlooked, so this metric is important to evaluate. A low upsell rate may suggest that the sales representative could benefit from reaching back out to customers who have renewed to discuss additional inventory. Salespeople should continually review their current list of accounts to look for customers who may be in a position to move up to purchasing new or additional inventory.

Goals, Commissions, and Evaluation

Because sales and revenue generation is such a quantifiable segment of the sport industry, it is no surprise that employees in this area are often highly goal oriented. Thus, the organization and the sales manager must be able to set effective goals for their employees. Properly developed goals can motivate salespeople and communicate success. Note, however, that nothing can demotivate an employee faster than unrealistic or improperly developed goals, especially when salaries are often largely tied to commissions. Thus, managers and organizations can use multiple types of goals for different purposes.

Individual Goals

For many salespeople, especially in ticket sales, individual goals are the most prominent. Individual goals motivate the employee regardless of the performance of the rest of the sales department or the organization. Typically, commissions work best being paid for attaining individual goals. Individual goals should be weighted more heavily in positions in which the salesperson can operate largely independently of coworkers. For instance, ticket salespeople do not often require significant assistance from their coworkers to complete a sale. Reaching revenue goals related to concessions, however, may be more of a team effort, so individual goals may be weighted less.

Although emphasizing individual goals offers advantages, negative consequences can occur as well. First, managers who heavily emphasize individual goals and commissions should keep a keen eye on the morale of the office and the attitudes of sales representatives toward one another. When individual performance is most highly prized, the environment can become more competitive. Competition is good, but too much competition can be harmful. The sales manager needs to monitor attitudes in this environment. Lastly, some things will always be beyond the control of a sales representative. Emphasizing individual goals can be frustrating to someone who thinks that they performed better than what their metrics show. For instance, a big win or big announcement by the team may cause the inbound phone line to be flooded with calls, resulting in easy sales for whichever sales representative is answering the phone. Coworkers who were not present are likely to become frustrated in this scenario, because they were unable to reap the benefits. Although individual goal setting has pros and cons, many organizations use a combination of various goals.

Group Goals

Group goals consist of larger goals that reward an entire group of people. For instance, a sponsorship department may have a goal to sell $1 million in new business in a given year.

Likewise, a ticket sales department may have a goal to retain 90 percent of season ticket holders. The benefit of a group goal is that it promotes teamwork and morale in the office. Many sales departments have these goals listed in large letters somewhere in the office so that everyone can see where the team currently stands. Because all the salespeople are working together, they have no reason to be ultracompetitive with one another or frustrated about the things outside their control. Group goals are most effective when there are multiple factors that the sales team cannot control or when multiple people are required to complete a sale. Lastly, group goals tend to place less stress on individual salespeople, because no one person feels responsible.

Although teamwork, cooperation, and less stress all seem like good things, group-focused goals have some shortfalls. Most notably, the lack of individual responsibility for goals makes it more difficult for good salespeople to stand out. Additionally, tension can develop when one person contributes significantly more than the others yet the success (and oftentimes bonuses) is shared evenly by all. College students engaged in team-based classes can relate to this problem. You may have done most of the work on a group project, but your teammates all got the same grade as you did. As mentioned earlier, a little competition can sometimes be a good motivator.

Property and Organizational Goals

Property and organizational goals are like group goals but on a larger scale. Typically, a goal is shared by two entire departments. Departments with the same goals may gain some advantages by sharing expenses and developing collaborative and synergistic relationships. For instance, an entire athletics department may have an overall revenue goal. Likewise, goals for gate revenue may be combined to include ticket sales, merchandise, and concessions. Placing large amounts of individual bonuses on such goals is difficult, so reaching these goals commonly involves smaller bonuses or even no tangible incentive. Additionally, these sorts of goals may be more commonly used to evaluate upper-level management people who oversee several departments.

Applying Motivational Theories to Sales

We have discussed some of the ways that commissions, bonuses, and goals tie into motivating salespeople. Sales managers can also consider both content-based and process-based motivational theories that can be applied to common situations in the workplace. Content-based theories focus on identifying and understanding the needs of employees that direct their behavior. Process-based theories focus on how employees choose behaviors to fulfill those various needs (Lussier & Kimball, 2020). Sales managers need to understand both employee needs and their fulfillment. Using the framework of several popular content-based and process-based motivational theories, we highlight in the following sections some important ways that sales managers can motivate their sales staff.

Meeting the Salesperson's Most Basic Needs

Understanding employee needs is important for the sales manager, but actually meeting their needs, especially their most basic needs, can be critical. Maslow's (1947) theory suggests that salespeople will be demotivated when their most basic needs are not being met. A salesperson who is not receiving a paycheck, is hungry, or feels threatened in the workplace will not be able to reach higher-level needs. Maslow's hierarchy consists of five needs (i.e., physiological, safety–security, belongingness, esteem, and self-actualization). He suggests that people must have their lower-level needs satisfied before they can move up. Salespeople are no different from any employee in the workplace. Their lower-level physiological needs (e.g., access to restrooms, food, water fountains) and safety needs (e.g., security, safe workplace)

must be met by the employer. Belongingness is important for the sales force as they develop relationships. As noted earlier, group goals can be beneficial in fostering a team atmosphere, and sales managers can facilitate social activities so that salespeople can talk and learn from each other. The last two needs, self-esteem and self-actualization, are important as well. Esteem needs can be met by sales managers through various recognition and appreciation programs. Most organizations have some type of recognition program that incentivizes salespeople to make the most sales with the allure of winning a trip, dinner certificate, or some other type of reward. By meeting these needs, the sales staff moves toward **self-actualization**, in which the salesperson reaches their full potential, feels personally fulfilled, and creatively solves problems.

Developing Important Relationships and Salesperson Growth

Some sales managers focus more on protecting their position than developing their employees. But the sales manager must remember that they are only as strong as the lowest seller on the sales staff. The manager should recognize that promoting important relationships and salesperson growth is important not only for building individual and team morale but also for maintaining their own job security. When the weakest salesperson is elevated, the team is also elevated, as is the sales manager's position in the eyes of the sales staff. Alderfer (1967, 1969) sought to extend Maslow's work concerning basic needs necessary for existence to the areas of interpersonal relationships and growth. Alderfer's relatedness needs, similar to belongingness and esteem needs, refer to a person's desire to maintain important interpersonal relationships. Relational selling, the constant focus on developing a relationship with customers rather than just selling a product, is important. Alderfer also focuses on growth needs that move toward Maslow's idea of self-actualization, referring to a person's desire

Great sales teams get along relationally and motivate each other professionally.

for personal development. Setting challenging but realistic goals can help salespeople strive toward some sense of self-actualization.

Understanding How to Recognize and Develop Employees

A sales manager must understand what motivates their employees in the same sense that a coach needs to know their players and their motivators. The sales manager must not be in it only for themselves, but rather seek to understand how employees can be recognized and developed so that they feel a sense of accomplishment or achievement. In 1959 Frederick Herzberg reclassified Maslow's needs into what he referred to as maintenance or hygiene factors and motivators. The lower-level needs were classified as the maintenance or hygiene

factors, and the higher-level needs were called motivators. Herzberg claimed that employees were motivated not by the hygiene factors, but by the motivators. The hygiene factors included supervision, interpersonal relations, physical working conditions, salary, company policy and its administration, benefits, and job security. The motivators included recognition, sense of achievement, growth, responsibility, advancement, and the work itself (Sanjeev & Surya, 2016). The traditional view of motivation was that satisfaction and dissatisfaction were at opposite ends of a continuum. Herzberg challenged this view by proposing two continuums; the maintenance factors comprise satisfaction or dissatisfaction with the work environment, and the motivators are satisfaction or dissatisfaction with the job itself. Employees are motivated when they are satisfied with maintenance factors (Lussier & Kimball, 2020). Sales managers should focus on motivators such as recognition, achievement, growth, and advancement. In fact, when you see organizations rewarding the top salesperson with a vacation, this is what they are doing.

Understanding Personality and the Need for Achievement, Power, and Affiliation

A good sales manager gets to know the personality of each member of the sales staff. Doing this takes time and is all about developing trust. But spending this time can be well worth it when the manager is better able to understand what motivates each person, including their need for achievement, power, and affiliation when considering how relationships are developed. According to McClelland (1971, 1975, 1985), all people are driven by and have a need for these three needs, but to varying degrees. These needs are based on personality and are developed as people interact with the environment. McClelland claims that those highest in the need for achievement often seek to perform at a higher level than their peers, which differentiates them. These salespeople may ask for feedback as they seek to attain the goals set for them, and they are effective leaders (Royle & Hall, 2012) whom sales managers may consider putting into team lead positions. High achievers are effective within sales departments and should be sought out in the recruitment process. A way to motivate salespeople high in the need for achievement is to provide them with nonroutine and challenging tasks that have attainable objectives.

The influence of power within a sales organization can be a great motivator, or it can cause a lot of political division within the workplace. Power can motivate a salesperson, and many of the best performers seek it in various ways. Sales jobs are a good fit for people seeking power because often they can plan and control their jobs. McClelland (1961, 1975, 1985) believed that people with a high need for power want influence or control over others. Power is a tremendous weapon when the salesperson can be influential and motivational in pre-senting a product or service to a prospective client. But power can create a severe headache to everyone within reach when it spills over and creates political or interpersonal tension between salespeople or between the sales manager and individual staff members.

Affiliation is one of the strongest motivational forces in sport. Consider the example of tens of thousands of fans attending a sporting event, most wearing the colors and logo of the home team. Much of the research in consumer behavior in sport discusses the idea of attachment and identification with a team. Alumni want to be affiliated with their school and love to immerse themselves in the nostalgia of yesterday. They can reunite with friends and cheer for their team while sharing a common bond. Rival alumni and students enjoy poking fun at each other leading up to the big game. Fans of a team may even poke fun at a rival fan wearing the wrong gear in the grocery store, or they may share stories with those wearing the correct hat or shirt. McClelland suggests that those seeking affiliation often seek relationships with others, engage in social activities, and are liked by others. This form of engagement and affiliation is important in sales. The sales leader should ensure that salespeople who have a high need for affiliation are a vital part of the team. Sales managers may build affiliation by offering incentives with rewards like pizza parties, happy hours, sport or music outings, or even activities like game nights or other types of theme nights.

Equity Within the Sales Organization

Some salespeople are inevitably going to be higher performers than others. Not everyone will be equal in what they bring to the sales organization in terms of skills, abilities, and ultimately performance. As we have discussed, higher performers must be motivated differently from low performers. Circumstances, however, also play a role in performance and must be taken into consideration. Measuring and rewarding effort is often much more difficult than measuring and rewarding performance. Take, for example, a salesperson who is making a lot of calls but simply is not making the same quantity of sales as another employee. What may not be accounted for is the fact that this salesperson is calling on new leads, whereas the other person is calling on renewals. Ultimately, in sales, performance in the form of revenue generation is the bottom line and is the most highly rewarded.

Sales managers need to be aware of equity issues within the workplace. Behavioral psychologist John Stacy Adams (1963) proposed an equity theory by positing that an employee is motivated when their inputs are perceived to be equal to their outputs. But the employee is demotivated when they perceive that their inputs in the workplace are more significant than the outputs obtained for their work endeavors (Lăzăroiu, 2015). In contrast, they are motivated when they perceive they are being equitably rewarded relative to others. The inputs may include factors like experience, seniority, status, effort, and intelligence, whereas the outputs may include factors like recognition, praise, pay, benefits, promotions, increased status, and a supervisor's approval (Lussier & Kimball, 2020). An example in sales is a salesperson who is working hard and making a lot of sales calls but is not rewarded appropriately. Another issue in sales has to do with seniority. A senior salesperson may be demotivated if they see a new salesperson coming into the organization with a potential list of clients that was not offered to them.

Setting Specific and Challenging Goals

Earlier in the chapter we discussed the importance of goals in relation to commissions and bonuses. We suggested that properly developed goals can motivate salespeople and communicate success. At the same time, poorly developed goals can be a demotivating force for salespeople. The most effective performance happens when goals are specific and challenging, are used to evaluate performance,

are linked to feedback about results, and create commitment and acceptance (Lunenburg, 2011). Goals affect performance because they direct attention and effort toward goal-related activities. Higher goals lead to greater effort, prolonged effort, or persistence, and they affect action (Locke & Latham, 2002). Sales managers should work alongside the salesperson to determine goals. All too often, the sales manager or someone from the top of the organizational hierarchy sets individual goals without any input from the person seeking to achieve it. The takeaway for sales managers when it comes to setting goals is that they should be difficult but achievable (Lussier & Kimball, 2020) and set in collaboration with the salesperson.

Reinforcing the Actions of a Salesperson

What happens in sport when a player comes off the field after making a great play or demonstrating passion, hustle, and effort? Often, the coach reinforces this behavior by giving the player a high five or a tap on the shoulder. What is the coach saying here? The coach is applauding the player and reinforcing this type of play or effort. In the same way, sales managers need to reinforce the behaviors of their sales staff. In his study of operant conditioning (i.e., the changing of behavior through reinforcement), Skinner (1948) suggested that reinforced behavior tends to be repeated, whereas behavior that is not reinforced tends to die out. Sales managers may use several types of reinforcement, including positive, negative, punishment, and extinction.

- *Positive reinforcement*—Sales managers may use positive rewards, the best motivator for increasing productivity, for employees who exhibit a positive or desired performance. For example, a manager may put an incentive into the contract for a salesperson to receive a certain monetary reward for attaining a certain (desired) level of sales.

- *Negative reinforcement*—Also called avoidance reinforcement, this type involves the removal of certain negative obstructions to reinforce the desired behavior. For example, daily meetings with a sales manager to talk about performance may be discontinued after a salesperson meets certain sales benchmarks.

- *Punishment*—This reinforcement occurs when a sales manager imposes a negative consequence or removes a positive consequence to prevent a salesperson from repeating an undesired behavior. Punishment can be negative when a sales manager takes away certain accounts and funds when the salesperson does not make the required sales. Punishment can also be in the form of removing a positive consequence (e.g., a bonus) when the salesperson does not meet the required behavior.

- *Extinction*—The sales manager uses extinction as a type of reinforcement when they try to reduce or eliminate a form of undesirable behavior by withholding reinforcement when the behavior occurs. The difference between punishment and extinction is that negative punishment means something may be taken away, whereas extinction does not add or take away. An example of extinction occurs when a manager simply does not send bonus information for a salesperson to the human resources department.

Leading the Sales Force

Numerous books on the topic of leadership can be found at almost every bookstore. Leading a group of highly driven people who are constantly competing is as difficult and challenging as leading a group of professional athletes. The manager is responsible for interacting with multiple personalities, most of whom are highly competitive. At the same time, the manager must navigate team dynamics, politics, and power plays. All this must be done while directing the sales staff toward predetermined goals in a similar manner to a coach leading players toward winning a championship, increasing player grade point averages, or having a 100 percent graduation rate.

Leadership is key, and the best leaders can influence their sales staff to achieve both individual and organizational goals. Great leaders have many characteristics, including the ability to motivate, influence, listen, and transform others. There is room for sales managers to use multiple types of leadership styles when influencing their sales staff to achieve certain performance objectives. Martin (2015) interviewed over 1,000 sales managers and found that the highest performing leaders had the following attributes.

- Were target and deadline driven, blocked out distractions, and compartmentalized negative news that sidetracked the team.

- Held their team to a high level of accountability by exercising the power of their title and position.

- Had the ability to hire quality talent that helped the sales organization achieve success. The highest performing sales managers were able to hire quality talent because they focused on hiring people who were skillful builders of relationships and were persuasive and experienced.

- Were able to dispense advice and add value during customer meetings.

- Controlled their sales teams by closely monitoring and strictly enforcing a particular sales process.

- Could adapt their style to each employee.

- Were able to derive strategies for the best course of action to maximize revenue.

Kruse (2019) suggests that the most successful sales leaders provide their salespeople with regular feedback, have weekly one-on-one meetings, are good coaches, leverage the strength of their team, and care for them. Leadership styles used by successful sales managers vary, and the best managers use more than one type, including transactional, transformational, and laissez-faire.

Transactional Sales Leadership

Transactional leadership can be defined as "leaders who lead primarily by using social exchanges for transactions" (Robbins, 2007, p.475). Through these exchanges, leaders accomplish their performance objectives, complete required tasks, and maintain the current organizational structure. Followers can fulfill their own self-interest, experience minimal workplace anxiety, and concentrate on meeting clear organizational objectives, such as increased quality, customer service, reduced costs, and increased production (McCleskey, 2014). Transactional leaders have been found to be effective in sales, often because of social and economic exchanges that occur through rewards. Transactional leadership describes a relationship between leaders and followers as one with a series of exchanges of gratification that are designed to maximize organizational and individual gains (Burns, 1978). A transactional leader can better monitor, evaluate, and direct salespeople and thus provide them with greater direction on how to improve their performance (Domingues et al., 2017. Transactional leadership is common in companies with sales teams (Sandilands, n.d.). When the salesperson agrees to meet a certain sales target, the exchange is the payment of a predetermined commission. If the salesperson fails to meet the targeted amount, the punishment is loss of the commission.

MacKenzie et al. (2001) suggest that sales managers who monitor employee sales performance and praise and recognize their contributions will experience higher levels of employee performance. Likewise, MacKenzie et al. claim that sales managers who discipline sales representatives who are not living up to performance expectations will increase sales performance. These types of leaders thrive on enforcing routine and depend on an established system of rewards and punishments to get salespeople to perform at high levels (Abbott, n.d.). Transactional leadership works best in situations where salespeople are driven by intrinsic desires, but it can also result in their doing just enough to earn a bonus or keep their jobs.

Transformational Sales Leadership

Transformational leaders are often able to come into a sales organization and enact widespread change. A transformational leader is "one who raises the followers' level of consciousness about the importance and value of desired outcomes and the methods of reaching those outcomes" (Burns, 1978, p. 141). Organizations that are experiencing declining sales or low morale are likely to hire someone to come in and transform the organization. According to MacKenzie et al. (2001), a change in values, goals, and the aspirations of followers occurs with transformational leadership. This is made possible when followers adopt the leader's end values and raise each other's motivation and sense of purpose. Research by MacKenzie et al. suggests that sales leaders need to do a better job of articulating a vision, fostering the acceptance of group goals, and providing individualized support. The transformational leader in sales will set high expectations, expect their team to reach for the improbable, and encourage them to look beyond their own self-interests, which pushes them to do more when it comes to sales (Abbott, n.d.).

Autocratic Sales Leadership

Many coaches in sport are autocratic in their style of leadership. An autocratic style suggests that group members contribute few to no ideas and only the leader makes decisions. The advantages of this style of leadership occurs when decisions need to be made quickly. In addition, teams under pressure may benefit from this style. But autocratic leadership can be frustrating to group members when they are not heard because input is not encouraged

(LeMarco, 2019). Nevertheless, autocratic leaders may be able to benefit team performance under certain conditions by providing direction and clarity (De Hoogh et al., 2015). In addition, autocratic leaders may offer team members ease and peace of mind.

This style of leadership can be appropriate when a sales manager is leading and training a young and inexperienced sales staff. We often see this in sport with minor league sport teams where the low pay leads to frequent turnover and new, inexperienced sales staff. The autocratic leader who teaches and explains to sales employees why certain decisions are made can provide an excellent learning experience to the sales members. For example, a sales manager who does not allow the sales team to discount or trade certain inventory (e.g., signage) may have a good reason for having this policy. When young sales employees understand the reasoning, they are likely not only to buy in but also to sell more.

Democratic Sales Leadership

Sales managers who have an experienced sales force are more likely to be democratic in style by asking for feedback and input from employees. Democratic leadership is an excellent style because it is more inclusive and brings diverse and multiple opinions into the decision-making process (Abbott, n.d.). Sales leaders who use this style are still likely to make the final decision, but not without input. A democratic approach is effective when trying to solve complex problems. It encourages creativity and strengthens the relationships of a team (Gaille, 2018). Operating in this way, however, can be time consuming. Sales leaders who use the democratic style may develop highly motivated but smaller teams (Dyczkowska & Dyczkowski, 2018).

Laissez-Faire Leadership

Although less common, a laissez-faire approach may at times be a sales mangers best option.

The concept of laissez-faire means "to leave alone" or to use a hands-off approach (Abbott, n.d.). Here, leaders allow employees to make decisions, confident that they possess the skills, knowledge, and follow-through necessary to complete a project (Cherry, 2020). The advantages of employing a laissez-faire style are that it encourages personal growth, innovation, and faster decision making. The downside is that it can also lead to poorly defined roles for group members, poor involvement, low accountability, and passivity of group members. Laissez-faire can be a good style of leadership with an experienced sales force. It may work well for some sales departments but result in lower productivity and performance for other departments (Abbott, n.d.).

Authentic and Servant Leadership

Most people, regardless of the industry, will follow someone who seems confident and trustworthy. Authentic leaders are described as people who are confident, optimistic, hopeful, resilient, and of high moral character (Avolio et al., 2004). Aydın and Kaya (2016) suggest that authentic leaders are needed in sales organizations because they have high moral and ethical standards, respect their followers, and appreciate the importance of well-being. Findings from their study suggest that authentic leadership positively affects the individual task-related outcomes of a salesperson. Servant leadership is a style in which the primary focus of the leader is on the welfare of others with a sincere, selfless underlying motivation (Greenleaf, 2002).

Servant leaders are better able to help less-experienced salespeople because they need more guidance, organizational socialization, and mentoring early in their professional careers (Jaramillo et al., 2009). Servant leadership is not always the answer, but it will often help garner the attention and respect of employees when implemented by a sales manager.

Summary

As the salesperson gains experience and wants more responsibility, they need to develop managerial experience, demonstrate success, and learn from managerial failures. Although sales managers have control over the internal structure and sales process, they have no control over the core product and external environmental changes that affect the organization. In this challenging environment, sales training is extremely important. Role-playing is an effective method for training sales staff. CRM systems are used to target the right customers with the promotional campaigns that would interest them the most. Bonuses and commissions, when designed correctly, can motivate staff. The sales manager must be able to motivate the sales staff by applying various motivational theories to the sales environment. Sales managers can use multiple styles of leadership, but many argue that the most effective styles for the long term are those that incorporate altruistic aspects.

APPLIED LEARNING ACTIVITIES

1. After reading the section of the chapter that involves hiring and firing and sales force tactics, you should be familiar with behavioral role-play scenarios, such as these: "Demonstrate or provide an example of how you have closed a sale in the past" and "In the next five minutes, sell me a season ticket or membership for our organization." One of the most common requests by an interviewer to a sales candidate is to give an elevator pitch, defined as a persuasive pitch to sell yourself to an employer that is short enough that you could pitch it while riding in an elevator. Type your elevator pitch and share it with a small group within your class.

2. In the section Goals, Commissions, and Evaluations, you became familiar with several types of goals related to sales. Which type of goal would best align with a sale that would benefit two entire departments? Explain why.

3. By now you should be familiar with transactional sales leadership. Transactional leadership involves leaders using social exchanges for various transactions to accomplish their performance objectives, complete required tasks, and maintain the current organizational structure. In a similar manner, followers can fulfill their own self-interest, experience minimal workplace anxiety, and concentrate on meeting clear organizational objectives such as increased quality, customer service, reduced costs, and increased production. In short, when staff perform well, they get something in return. Do some research to find a real-world example of transactional sales leadership and record your findings.

CASE STUDY

YOU ARE THE SENIOR SALES MANAGER

Imagine that you are the senior sales manager for an MLB team. In this position you make the big decisions that affect the inside sales team, including hiring, firing, and promotion. In this case you are deciding whether to hire candidate X or candidate Y. Both have adequate resumes for the job, but they show different traits while interviewing. You sit down with a few members of your sales team to assess the interviews to decide whom you will hire.

Candidate X: This candidate showed great technical understanding of how sales works. He referenced his knowledge of how to navigate a sales funnel, as well as his experience with cold calling and persuasion. But upon checking with his professional references, you found some flaws. Candidate X was a toxic team member and was not comfortable with collaboration. He tended to do things on his own without notifying team members, he rarely asked questions and seemed unmotivated, and he showed no signs of the three Ps (professionalism, preparation, productivity). Additionally, candidate X gave a lackluster elevator pitch about why he was right for the job.

Candidate Y: This candidate did not have a great understanding of the technical aspects of how sales works. She was unfamiliar with cold calling, sales funnels, and persuasion. But her references raved about her teamwork and collaboration abilities. She was described as driven, motivated, a communicator, and a leader. She was proficient with the CRM system and showed skills that encompassed the three Ps. On top of this she said she is driven by learning new things and that her lack of knowledge of sales could be easily corrected if she was in the right training program.

Discussion Questions

1. Based on this information and what you have read in the chapter, which candidate would you hire and why?
2. For each candidate, what is an area they could improve upon?

Go to HK*Propel* to complete the activities for this chapter.

Eva-Katalin/E+/Getty Images

CHAPTER 12

Future Trends in Revenue Generation

CHAPTER OBJECTIVES

After completing the chapter, you should be able to do the following:

- Discuss the impact of sport betting
- Highlight the effect of new tax laws on revenue generation
- Understand future technologies to be used in generating revenue in sport
- Identify new events that help to generate revenue
- Describe new markets for sport
- Be familiar with future trends in revenue generation
- Be prepared to manage revenue generation during times of uncertainty

In this chapter we attempt to forecast the future of sales and revenue generation in sport. The changing nature and uncertainties of technology, business environment, cultural and societal norms, and external and internal factors affecting the sport industry make it difficult to predict the future. COVID-19 had and will continue to have an impact on sport and the way in which it is sold. Virtual meetings will likely become more sophisticated and normalized as a sales method for meeting with prospective customers. This chapter summarizes and highlights the importance of the PRO method within sales and fundraising. The unique nature of emotion within sport is discussed as it applies to sales and fundraising. New revenue trends are presented, such as legal sport betting, effect of tax laws, future technologies, new sport events, expanding markets, youth sport participation and specialization, international sport, sporting goods, and fitness.

Do You Want to Work in the Sport Industry?

Throughout the textbook, we noted the fundamental differences between fundraising and sales and the way that various segments (e.g., collegiate and nonprofit sport versus professional sport) of the industry can use the steps of the PRO method. This process is critical to success for anyone wanting to generate revenues. Just as a coach uses a system or game plan to help athletes succeed, so the salesperson can use the basic process outlined in the PRO method for success in revenue generation. Although the coach can draw up an excellent game plan, the athlete is ultimately responsible for studying it, training for physical strength and endurance, developing emotional intelligence, having a competitive spirit, applying a strong work ethic during practice and games, and working with teammates, coaches, and others in a collaborative manner. In the same way, the PRO method means nothing to a salesperson who does not study the process,

practice through role-play, apply a strong work ethic, collaborate with others in learning, and seek to compete for sales. Sales and the generation of revenues is not for the faint of heart. Some people may naturally gravitate toward sales and fundraising. But the relevant skills can be taught, and success does not come only to those with one type of personality. Are you willing to put in the hard work? If so, sales and fundraising can offer one of the most effective paths to the top of any sport organization.

Sport is unique because of the emotion that it generates within the consumer, whether participating or spectating. This truth cannot be understated when it comes to the function of sales. Great passion is generated by affiliations in sport, especially when it comes to certain teams. Salespeople who understand how to appeal to these emotions will be successful within the industry. Equally important, those who can generate this type of emotion and demonstrate enthusiasm and passion for their product (team, program, service, etc.) can be successful influencers or persuaders of prospective consumers. Although most sales jobs in sport ask you to take off your fan hat, they simultaneously require you to generate a level of enthusiasm equal to or higher than that of the fan when selling the product.

Regardless of their industry, salespeople must understand new forms of technology, best practices and shifts in how companies are selling, and basic principles that apply to any form of sales. But we would like to focus on some important points that we hope you take away from reading this book. Sales and revenue generation are fundamentally important to every organization, and they are vital to every sport organization. Others have called sales the lifeblood of sport. We will go a step further by suggesting that any sport organization who does not have first responders ready to inject and pump blood into the system (sport organization) will simply die. We make this statement with all due respect to the true heroes in the medical field who save the lives of so many people.

The PRO Method Moving Forward

First, salespeople must understand and master the process. Just as an athlete trains for excellence in their sport, so a salesperson must practice the sales process. We reiterate the five-step sales process called the PRO method that was laid out in chapter 2 (see figure 12.1).

- Step 1: PROspect for qualified customers
- Step 2: PRObe for information with open-ended questions
- Step 3: PROvide solutions by matching product benefits with customer information
- Step 4: PROpose an offer that best fits the customer's needs
- Step 5: PROtect the relationship by maintaining contact and customer service

Prospecting is the process of trying to figure out who you should be contacting, including both inbound and outbound customers. Fundraising also calls this process prospecting or identification. Identifying potential new customers in the future may use artificial intelligence (AI), and AI may be used to manage CRM data in this stage of the process. Some predict that AI, machine learning, and automation will enhance the sales force. For example, software will provide personalized call confirmation reminders to clients, and sales representatives and AI will manage CRM data to help qualify prospects (Signorelli, 2020). Although we currently use a device such as a laptop or smartphone as our sales assistant, within 10 years the device may be something we can talk to like Amazon Echo. Within 20 years sales interactions may be more fully engaged with virtual reality. Many salespeople are concerned about being replaced by these types of AI. The principal takeaway for students and industry practitioners is to continue to learn about AI. You are more likely to be replaced by another salesperson who understands AI technology than by the machine itself (Schwartz, n.d.).

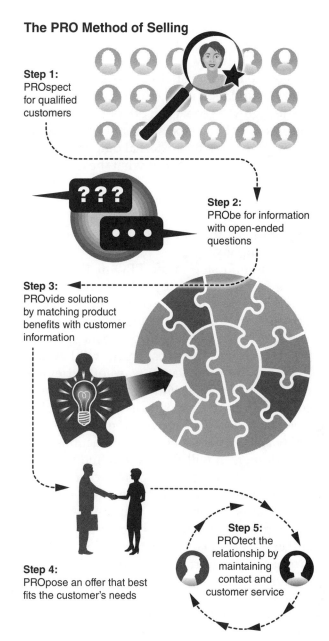

The PRO Method of Selling

Step 1: PROspect for qualified customers

Step 2: PRObe for information with open-ended questions

Step 3: PROvide solutions by matching product benefits with customer information

Step 4: PROpose an offer that best fits the customer's needs

Step 5: PROtect the relationship by maintaining contact and customer service

FIGURE 12.1 The PRO method of sales guides a salesperson through the sales process, from finding qualified customers to maintaining the relationship after the sale.

Sport industry professionals will require the ability to adapt as new technologies for identifying prospective consumers come online. As biometric, ID, and chip technologies become more prevalent in the industry, they will likely provide valuable identifying information. Video content and virtual reality will also lead to greater interactions with prospective fans or participants. Although adopting more augmented and creative ways of working within the sales industry is important, still others suggest that we must always seek to gain an intimate understanding of our customers and create highly personalized offers and purchasing options. The salesperson should continue to leverage internal and external data that helps to answer questions about what the customer wants to buy and how the purchase fits with previous purchases (KPMG, 2020). Data also help to provide context for understanding the consumer's mindset and current perceptions of the company.

The second step in the PRO method is to probe for information by asking open-ended questions. Often, this type of probing is done in person. As technology and automation become more prevalent, fewer face-to-face interactions will take place. The salesperson will have to learn new and innovative ways of retrieving personal information without as much personal contact. Virtual technologies like Zoom, WebEx, Google Meet, and others will become more critical ways to achieve personal interactions. But the salesperson will also need to find ways to gain access to in-person, face-to-face meetings that are more personal in nature than interactions that occur on online platforms. Despite the heightened use of technology, many people still crave personal connections. This concern is especially important to donors as the dollar amount of their investment goes up.

Step 3 of the PRO method recommends that the salesperson match product benefits with customer information. Before engaging with the salesperson, the consumer arrives with preconceived assumptions about the product or service. As discussed in chapter 4, the sale of any product or service requires that the prospective buyer perceives its value. With this said, visual content is becoming more important. Salespeople need to become proficient with developing sophisticated content, such as videos, presentations, and other various types of visuals that explain value and benefits to the consumer.

Finally, steps 4 and 5 are to propose an offer that best fits the customer's needs and to protect the relationship by maintaining contact and customer service. Creating more personalized offers in the future will require offering more flexible purchasing and service consumption options (KPMG, 2020). Some consumers will require bundling with the best price and terms for both parties, whereas others will need more personalized service offers whereby the solution is consumed over time on a subscription or usage basis. Salespeople will need to understand how to engage with consumers personally and how to meet their pricing needs using the most convenient methods.

New Revenue Trends

Current trends can point to the future of revenue generation in sport. Online technologies will surely continue to pave the way in which we communicate. Although the process of selling does not change, new vehicles and forms of communicating with the customer will arise. This chapter considers various trends moving forward, including legal sport betting, effect of tax laws, future technologies, new sport events, expanding markets, youth sport participation and specialization, international sport, and sporting goods and fitness.

Legal Sport Betting

In 2018 the Supreme Court of the United States (SCOTUS) struck down a federal law that banned commercial sport betting in most states, thereby legalizing the estimated $150 billion in illegal wagers that Americans make every year on professional and amateur sport (Liptak & Draper, 2018). Each U.S. state and sovereign tribal nation can now set their own policy and legalize and regulate sport betting. Although sport betting had been legal in Nevada for years, Delaware was the first U.S. state to launch single-game betting. New Jersey followed. By May 2020, two years after the Supreme Court decision, the number of

People lined up to place their wagers on June 14, 2018, in Monmouth Park in Oceanport, New Jersey, on the first day of legal sport betting in the state.

states with live single-game sport betting was 18, including Washington, DC (American Gaming Association, 2020). Research by the American Gaming Association suggests that nearly 80 percent of Americans claim to support legalized sport betting in their state and more than 70 percent say it is important to place bets through legal, regulated providers (Ponseti, 2019).

By June of 2020, the **sport-betting revenues** from the 18 states totaled $1.5 billion. The amount wagered between June 2018 and June 2020, also called the **handle**, was $21.8 billion. The term *handle* refers to an amount wagered over a period, whereas the term *sport-betting revenues* refers to the amount of money kept by sportsbooks out of the amount wagered. States also make some money, in the sum of

$206 million. Referred to as **taxes or state revenues**, these tax monies are collected by state and local jurisdictions; they are the state share of proceeds in revenue-sharing markets (Legal Sports Report, 2020).

Not all states that allow legal sport betting use online or mobile wagering platforms. Some allow online and mobile wagering anywhere within state lines, whereas others require all bets to be placed inside a casino (Legal Sports Report, 2020). Daily fantasy sports (DFS) are a significant contributor to legal sport betting. DFS mirrors season-long fantasy sports but condenses it into a shorter period. Two of the largest providers of DFS are DraftKings and FanDuel. DraftKings is a DFS contest and sport-betting provider that operates a lot like a bank within their Boston-based headquarters.

FanDuel Group is a New York City–based bookmaker and daily fantasy sports provider.

Although legalized sport betting was still in its infancy at the time of publication of this book, it is and will continue to be a large revenue producer. In particular, the four major sport leagues in the United States have a lot to gain from sport betting. The American Gaming Association commissioned a Nielsen sports study that examined annual revenues by league. Their findings suggest that the four major sports leagues will earn a collective $4.2 billion from widely available legal sport betting. The report also analyzed revenue streams that legal sport betting could generate for Major League Baseball (MLB) and the National Basketball Association (NBA). Their findings suggest that greater fan engagement and viewership could boost the total annual revenue from media rights, sponsorships, merchandise, and ticket sales in the amount of $952 million for MLB and $425 million for the NBA from increased consumption of products (Ponseti, 2018).

Effect of Tax Laws

Tax laws can have a big effect on both organizational and individual revenues in sport. The Tax Reform Act, signed into law by President Trump in December 2017, doubled the standard deduction for individuals and put a $10,000 cap on the amount that individuals could deduct for state and local taxes paid (Delaney & Thompson, 2019). According to projections by the congressional Joint Committee on Taxation, 28.5 million fewer Americans will itemize their deductions, thus significantly reducing tax incentives for Americans to donate to charitable sport organizations. Within intercollegiate sport, the Tax Reform Act does not allow a charitable deduction for any payment made to an institution of higher education in exchange for the right to purchase tickets or seating for athletic events (Nussbaum et al., 2018). The law repealed the existing rule that allowed the purchaser to claim a charitable deduction equal to 80 percent of the amount paid for the right to purchase tickets. In addition, the law also repealed the exception to the deduction disallowance for entertainment, amusement, or recreation directly related to or associated with the active conduct of the taxpayer's trade or business. Therefore, a taxpayer can no longer take a deduction for the cost of tickets to sporting events purchased to entertain clients or other business prospects. The law also has an effect on professional athletes because they are no longer able to exempt business expenses (e.g., agent fees, union dues, travel, gym) from their taxes (Prete, 2019).

Long-standing state and local taxes have been an issue for many years. Professional athletes pay taxes on income not only in their team's home state but also in some of the states that they travel to for away games. This tax, often referred to as the jock tax, taxes the incomes of visiting players. The tax can be levied on a **duty-duty basis**, whereby the athlete is taxed based on the percentage of their contract's time that they were present in the jurisdiction and earning an income. It can also occur on a **per-game basis**, whereby the player is taxed on the percentage of the game schedule played in that jurisdiction (Northeastern University, 2020). The duty-duty tax is based on the amount of time a player contributes to income-related work in a particular state. The calculation for the tax is made by taking the amount of time a player spends in another state and dividing this number by the total amount of income-related work days, which starts at the beginning of training camp (Prete, 2019). Some states, such as Florida, Washington, Nevada, Tennessee, and Texas, do not collect a jock tax. During the COVID-19 pandemic, the National Basketball Association held its season in a bubble in Florida, a state with no state income tax. Major League Baseball held the National League Championship Series and World Series in Texas, another state with no income tax. Likewise, the National Hockey League played its games in Canada. Do you notice a trend? None of these locations is subject to the jock tax (Zeitz, 2020). Although the absence of a jock tax may not have been the primary reason for choosing these locations, in the future, leagues may consider the effect of the jock tax when choosing site locations for events.

Future Technologies in Sport

Sometimes it is difficult to imagine that many sales representatives within sport operated without a computer, or shared one, as recently as the 1990s. Hard tickets were common back in the 1980s and early 1990s. The perforated tickets came in the mail and had to be separated. Social media platforms such as Facebook, Twitter, Instagram, and Snapchat that many organizations and consumers use today were still many years in the future. The dynamic world of sport continues to evolve, so whatever is written now may be obsolete in the days ahead. Still, we need to consider how sport will evolve in terms of technology and the continued focus on sales and generating revenues. Another unknown as we write this book is how COVID-19 will affect sales and revenue generation within the sport industry.

From devices like wearable monitors to clothing and equipment with embedded sensors, sport organizations and manufacturers can collect large amounts of data, such as an athlete's heart rate, glucose level, breathing, gait, strain, and fatigue (Lazzarotti et al., 2019). Opperman (2020) provides several examples. The Adidas MiCoach system is used by Major League Soccer (MLS) during both practice and games to track athletes' heart rates, speed, jump height, running distance, and other data. The technology uses miniaturized GPS, gyroscopes, and accelerometers that are embedded into a small system that is lodged in athletes' jerseys and cleats. Wearable technologies are likely to continue to increase in popularity. In the future, products similar to Google Glass, a wearable computer that allows users to use augmented reality glasses to talk to friends and send messages, may create a pay-per-gaze business model that will allow companies to monetize advertisements.

Because we live in a world that is driven by technology, we may forget that technology is not the end, but rather the tool for reaching the audience. For technology investors, capital ventures will be focused on areas such as media and content-related platforms, esports and measurement platforms for data, and analytics and biometrics (Proman, 2019). Other ventures in the future will be related to athlete tech and performance optimization, in-venue technology, gambling and gaming, and recovery health and home fitness.

B2C REVENUE GENERATION

Whoop and the PGA Tour

A great example of how new forms of technology are being implemented by sport leagues is the partnership between Whoop and the PGA Tour. Whoop is the official fitness wearable of the PGA tour, and when the tour resumed in Summer 2020 after a break due to COVID-19, approximately 1,000 of these devices were distributed to players, caddies, and other personnel. The wearable device not only helps with training, but also provides metrics like heart rate and respiratory rate, which could help detect infections. PGA players like Justin Thomas have commented on social media how much they enjoy learning more about key metrics like heart rate. To build excitement and show the emotion in golf, the PGA implemented "Whoop Live," which provides player heart rates and other biometrics in real time (Van Deusen, 2021). As the partnership between Whoop and the PGA continues to evolve, additional data points like sleep and strain scores may be included. These metrics are often broadcast alongside emotional displays by PGA players and posted on various social media sites (LeMire, 2021).

Although some smaller sport venues still use hard tickets, almost every sport team now uses a ticketing system (e.g., TicketMaster, Tickets.com, Paciolan). Post COVID-19, paperless ticketing will be the norm. Teams continue to look for ways to integrate systems that allow their technologies to interact. For example, using a digital device, fans will have a "loaded ticket" that allows them to scan their ticket at the gate and use their phone to scan at the concession. GiveX is one example of a company that offers a type of gift card, loyalty, and stored-value ticketing solution. NCR is another example of a company that provides a digital banking platform. Ticketing platforms like Groupmatics help sport organizations manage group sales and collect event attendee data. The platform allows group leaders to promote their outing at a sporting event by email or social media while tracking their sales.

Although the fundraising professional has traditionally relied on the importance of human contact or human touchpoints, a fundamental shift occurred during the COVID-19 crisis. According to John Meck (personal communication, July 2020), the director of corporate relations at James Madison University in Virginia, fundraisers navigated a learning curve as they engaged with potential donors through virtual meetings and completed contactless transactions. Many donors will donate without much human contact, but Meck believes that there is a threshold point. Although virtual meetings and contactless transactions were prevalent during the pandemic, a shift back to personal contact will occur. Meck suggested that those who can swing back to this role sooner with fundraisers will probably be the most successful.

New Sport Events

Undoubtedly, esports will continue to grow, and new revenue streams in sport will be generated from this niche segment of the industry. Market revenues for global esports amounted to a little over US$1 billion in 2020 and were expected to reach almost $1.6 billion by 2023 (Gough, 2020). Most of these revenues will be generated from sponsorships and advertising along with media rights, publisher fees, merchandise and tickets, digital, and streaming. Asia and North America are the largest esports markets. The number of esports fans increased from 335 million in 2017 to 454 million in 2019. Because of the rise in technology, many teenagers are identifying more strongly with pro gamers than with traditional athletes. The League of Legends World Championship recently had more viewers than the Super Bowl. With the rise of virtual reality, the esports sector will continue to grow, and augmented reality may one day bring esports and traditional sports together to form a new category (LWO Sports, 2020).

New sports continue to develop. The question becomes how to monetize them and create customer value. Consider pickleball, which was virtually unknown two decades ago and is now a multimillion-dollar business. Dimengo (2014) highlights some of the newer sports, such as bandy, footgolf, and sepak takraw, that perhaps you have never heard of. Played primarily outside the United States, bandy is a game with 8 to 11 players that combines ice hockey and soccer. Footgolf, a game that uses soccer balls and the players' own feet instead of golf balls and clubs, is more well known. The American Footgolf Federation (footgolf.us) and the American Footgolf League (AFGL) are good sources for learning more about the sport. Using elements of volleyball, soccer, and gymnastics, players in sepak takraw use several body parts, except their hands or arms, to volley balls back and forth, scoring when a ball hits the ground. Although sports like footgolf are organized and have a governing body, others will continue to evolve and seek new ways to be monetized.

Expanding Markets

Where will new opportunities for sales and revenue growth be generated? If you are a student in sport management, you should look at areas for growth if you want to find a job within the industry. Revenues within the sport industry

Sepak takraw is gaining in popularity around the world.

were strong in late 2019 and early 2020 but came to a screeching halt in March 2020 because of the COVID-19 pandemic. The global sports market had a value of nearly $488.5 billion in 2018, growing at a compound annual growth rate (CAGR) of 4.3 percent since 2014 (Business Wire, 2019). The largest markets for the sport industry are in North America (30.5 percent of the global market), followed by Western Europe, Asia-Pacific, and other regions. The fastest growing regions moving forward will be Asia-Pacific and the Middle East, followed by North America and South America.

New sales jobs will morph out of the growth of rising areas like esports, new sports, and new trends in virtual and augmented reality. Many students do not consider the wealth of opportunities in sport tourism, resorts, nonprofits, and recreation. Jobs in minor league baseball will decrease as Major League Baseball (MLB) reduces the number of affiliates from 160 to 120. This process of elimination began in September 2020 when MLB converted the Appalachian League to a college summer circuit for rising freshmen and sophomores. The good news is that new revenue opportunities will require

Rebeca Figueiredo Amorim/Getty Images

New sales jobs are emerging in exciting sectors, including esports.

salespeople, as noted in this statement by Morgan Sword, MLB's executive vice president of baseball economics and operations:

> *Fans are going to get to see top prospects right in their hometowns, communities are going to see an influx of new revenue opportunities and players are going to receive state-of-the-art training, visibility to our scouts and educational programming that's designed to prepare them for careers as professional athletes. (Dykstra, 2020)*

Youth Sport Participation and Specialization

An issue that has a substantial effect on sport is the participation of youth. Unfortunately, participation in youth sport in the United States is declining. This trend is partly responsible for childhood obesity, poor nutrition habits, lack of physical and social development along with self-confidence, and a decline in leadership skills, among other negative outcomes. By fall 2020, in the midst of the COVID-19 pandemic, almost 40 percent of parents said that their children were no longer interested in participating in organized sport. Unfortunately, youth from lower-income homes face increasing barriers to participation, and those from the lowest income homes are more than three times as likely to be physically inactive. Each year the Aspen Institute (2019) publishes their *State of Play* report. Among the interesting findings from the 2019 report are the following:

- For kids between the ages of 6 and 12, only 38 percent played team or individual sports on a regular basis in 2018, down from 45 percent in 2008.
- For kids between the ages of 6 and 17, only 24 percent engaged in at least 60

minutes of physical activity per day, down from 30 percent a decade earlier.

- Up to 22 percent of youth ages 6 to 12 in households with incomes under $25,000 played sports in 2018 on a regular basis, compared with 43 percent of youth from homes earning $100,000 or more.

Sport specialization is another issue facing youth sport. Approximately 70 percent of youth within the United States drop out of sport by the age of 13. Several factors contribute, including burnout, injury, poor coaching, new social relationships, pressure to win and not having fun, and pressure by parents and coaches for kids to specialize at increasingly younger ages. Many parents put an extraordinary amount of pressure on their kids to participate. Too often, the pressure stems from improper motives by parents who are seeking college scholarships and living vicariously through their children. Athletes are being recruited at younger ages, and travel leagues put more pressure on children to perform instead of simply have fun. Numerous examples could be cited regarding the sport recruitment of youth athletes. The youngest female athlete to be recruited in lacrosse was an eighth grader from Florida who made a verbal commitment to play for Syracuse University (Wallace, 2016).

The increase of sport specialization and the privatization of sport has led to mixed outcomes. "Sports specialization is defined as intense, year-round training in a single sport with the exclusion of other sports" (Jayanthi et al., 2013, p. 252). Numerous jobs have been created with recruiting services such as Next College Student Athlete (NCSA), Field Level, and many others. Collegiate showcase camps (e.g., Rivals, Headfirst, and Showball) are rampant. Athlete development organizations (e.g., Baseball Factory) have sprung up. Athletic training facilities have evolved where prospective athletes can train specifically for one or more sports. The services offered by these facilities include specific developmental instruction and lessons, strength training, access to various training facilities, travel teams, contact and access to college coaches, video analysis, software and analytics, showcase tournaments, and uniforms. The travel teams often provide intense competition for the youth athletes, but as the number of teams grows the level of competition narrows.

As the professional model of sport continues to dive deeper into youth sport, these types of organizations and programs that appeal to youth athletes and parents have created jobs. In many cases these jobs are sales related. Salespeople in these various organizations identify and contact parents and athletes to ask them to register or purchase a membership. Many of the camps and programs can be quite expensive, but parents are often willing to pay the fee with the hope that their child will be better prepared for high school sports or receive a scholarship to college. Critics of this form of specialization and privatization note the tremendous pressures leveled on athletes at a young age. Many argue that children are still developing and should be encouraged to try numerous sports rather than be forced to choose one over another. Collegiate coaches are increasingly seeking players who have been exposed to multiple sports and are more athletic.

Moving forward, what can we do to help solve some of the issues facing youth sport? One of the biggest challenges is lack of the opportunities for those in lower socioeconomic categories. The *State of Play* report from the Aspen Institute (2019) suggested that children residing in families who are making under $25,000 are severely disadvantaged when it comes to playing organized sport on a regular basis. In addition, the report highlighted the trend toward declining participation by youth in general. Public entities are increasingly unable to solve these types of problems because of state and federal budget shortfalls. The private sector can and should continue to address these issues.

Social justice is an increasingly important topic within the United States. Private organizations can be formed to solve these types of problems, but, of course, funds will be needed. New nonprofit organizations are founded every day, and many of them are focused on social issues like poverty, community enrichment, and youth development. In an earlier chapter, we discussed several corporate social responsibility (CSR) initiatives and cause-related activities that are funded by corporations and foundations. People who understand sales and fundraising will be well positioned to develop these types of organizations and programs. Sustainable programs will need to be deeply rooted in the fundamentals of sales and fundraising that you learned in this textbook. You must be able to identify and prospect for potential funders, solicit funds, and cultivate and steward partners. Fundraising events can provide opportunities to showcase to donors both the incredible potential of youth athletes and the great need resulting from socioeconomic inequalities. Grant writing is another important skill that students can develop in college. As with role-playing in sales, students can practice their writing skills by registering for classes that focus on grant writing.

International Sport

As North American markets for sport leagues become more saturated, the emphasis on international sport is increasing. Leagues like the NBA, NFL, and MLB are playing both preseason exhibitions and regular season games overseas. The NBA has played games in Brazil, China, Germany, Philippines, Spain, and the United Kingdom. The NFL International Series are regular season games that take place in the United Kingdom and Mexico. MLB has played exhibitions or games in Australia, Japan, Mexico, Puerto Rico, and the United Kingdom. As leagues continue to expand to overseas markets, students who can speak multiple languages will have an advantage. For example, the NBA has 12 international offices in NBA Asia (Hong Kong, Manila), NBA Canada (Toronto), NBA China (Shanghai, Beijing, Taipei), NBA Europe (London, Madrid), NBA India (Mumbai), NBA Latin America (Mexico City, Rio de Janeiro), and NBA South Africa (Johannesburg).

Selling sport in international markets requires more than just understanding and speaking multiple languages. Students who wish to work in these markets must also have a keen understanding of the cultural differences at play in each market. Selling a sport product in the United States is different from selling in China or Latin America. Vargas (2019) offers the following advice when selling across cultures:

1. Be culturally aware and learn about other countries. In the United States, for example, launching right into the sales presentation is not unusual. In other countries, such as Brazil, launching directly into the sales presentation would be a mistake.

2. Consider the language along with how you will communicate when making the presentation. Do you need an interpreter? If so, the interpreter should have strong technical knowledge and should meet with the clients before the sales meeting.

3. Pay attention to both your own body language as well as the body language of others. For example, in the United States and certain parts of Europe, eye contact is important. In China and Japan, hierarchy is important, so you should present your speech in a way that acknowledges the most senior person at the table. Watching the body language of others is also important. For example, a nod or affirmative gesture in an Asian country may mean I hear you rather than I agree.

4. Maintain formality and be careful with the use of titles. How you address someone can be very specific to the culture. For example, in many cultures jumping straight to first-name terms is highly offensive. In Germany you may be very formal and use Mr. for men and Mrs. for all women. In the Middle East, status is important and an individual should be addressed as "Sheikh" or "Sayed."

Several cultural issues need to be considered when understanding how sport is consumed around the world. As just discussed, these issues may include determinants like religion and social, economic, geopolitical, and cultural norms. Many ball and stick sports have their origins in European countries like the United Kingdom and made their way to the United States. Soccer and badminton are the two sports with the highest participation numbers throughout the world. Although many are aware of the popularity of soccer, perhaps you were surprised to hear about badminton. Over 6 million people participated in badminton in 2019 (Sports & Fitness Industry Association, 2020). More than 1.1 billion people watched the debut of badminton in the Olympic Games in 1996 (Clement, 2004). Soccer and badminton are popular sports throughout the world because they are relatively inexpensive to play.

The governance of sport in the United States is different from that in many parts of the world. North American models of sport are based on local governments. For example, a person growing up in the United States may start at a very young age by participating in a local recreation program, advance to a travel team, and then play on a middle and high school sport team. The highly skilled may play a sport in college, and the exceptionally skilled may play professionally. Except for bidding on sport megaevents like the Olympic and Paralympic Games, the U.S. federal government is not highly involved. In contrast, in many countries, such as Brazil, the Dominican Republic, Australia, and China, there is a minister of sport at the federal level. In addition, the North American model of sport is based on league structures, whereas other models (European, Latin American) are based on clubs. For example, a youth in Europe may begin playing on their local team or on official youth teams for professional football clubs. They may continue to play for better teams until they are eventually contracted to play professionally.

Cultural norms, geography, and fan avidity are also important sales factors that differ between countries. For example, the large number of lakes and cold weather in Canada are key reasons why the country produces many professional hockey players. The Board of Control for Cricket in India (BCCI) is one of the richest sport organizations in the world. Cricket in India is wildly popular, and cricketers can make a lot of money by playing or betting on the sport. Almost everyone in India knows Sachin Tendulkar, the "God of Cricket" in the country. In the Dominican Republic not everyone is good at baseball, but almost everyone has played the sport. More than 10 percent of all MLB players are Dominicans. Most people know of the popularity of soccer in Brazil, but if you go to any beach in the country you will see people playing a sport called footvolley. A mix of soccer and volleyball, the sport permits players to use both their feet and their head to get the ball over the net.

Sporting Goods and Fitness

Retail sales of sporting goods make up a sizable chunk of the sport industry and offer numerous sales opportunities. Sporting goods stores traditionally sell new items such as bicycles, camping equipment, exercise and fitness equipment, apparel, footwear, and other goods and accessories. Although declining youth sport participation has had a negative effect on industry revenues, new and alternative forms of exercise like CrossFit and yoga have generated increased demand for products. Revenues in the sporting goods store industry in 2020 amounted to $44.5 billion (IBIS World, 2020).

Revenues for the online sporting goods industry are expected to increase at an annualized rate of 2.8 percent from 2020 to 2025 (Roth, 2020). During this time, participation in sport is expected to rise at an annualized rate of 1.5 percent. Roth suggests that the COVID-19 pandemic has permanently changed consumer behavior, so at-home workouts and activities will continue to be in high demand in the future. Increasingly, consumers are buying everything from weights for strength training to cardiovascular machines like elliptical and treadmill machines. What this says for the sporting goods industry is the need to continue to meet the needs of online consumers. Online consumption can be challenging when ordering sporting goods equipment. Sporting goods companies will continue to use new technologies to deliver their products and services to consumers. If you are selling sporting goods, you will need to understand these technologies to reach consumers. As noted in chapter 9, half of the companies in the sporting goods industry are owner operated and have no additional employees. These smaller organizations will be at a disadvantage in terms of technology in comparison with larger companies like Dick's Sporting Goods.

Crisis Management

The date March 11, 2020 (3/11), is the day that sport officially shut down because of the coronavirus pandemic (COVID-19) in the United States. COVID-19 is an illness caused by a virus that can spread from person to person. Starting in China, the virus spread worldwide and caused unprecedented shutdowns in most countries and severely impacted the United States. The economy in the United States was largely shut down for a time. Intercollegiate athletics programs at many institutions across North America cut sports programs. On March 11, 2020, the National Basketball Association (NBA) announced that it was suspending its season after a player, Rudy Gobert, tested positive for the virus. One day earlier, on March 10, the Ivy League announced they would cancel their men's and women's basketball tournaments. After 3/11, the dominoes began to fall. Major League Baseball suspended the remainder of spring training and pushed back the start of the regular season by two weeks. The Masters golf tournament was suspended, and the National Hockey League (NHL) and Major League Soccer (MLS) suspended play. The NCAA basketball tournament was canceled, and events like the Kentucky Derby were either moved to a later date or canceled. Leagues in Europe and Asia were shut down. And the largest event of all, the 2020 Summer Olympic Games to be held in Tokyo, was pushed back to 2021. No sport, recreational activity, or physical activity was spared. In the United States, as many as 40 million jobs were lost. Unemployment rose to almost 15 percent, a level not seen since the Great Depression of the 1930s.

In the midst of the COVID-19 pandemic, on May 25, 2020, George Floyd, an African American man, was killed in Minneapolis, Minnesota, by a white police officer. This event significantly changed the landscape in the United States, and it will have an enduring effect on sport moving forward. George Floyd's death led to a call against racism and injustice in the United States that had not been seen since the Civil Rights Movement of the 1960s. Protests and riots ensued on the streets of many cities in the United States and across the globe. Meanwhile, athletes, coaches, and representatives from sport organizations across the country spoke out against racial inequalities. Some coaches came under scrutiny for racist remarks. Some companies walked away from sponsorships or put pressure on sport organizations or brands with alleged racist logos or names. On July 2, the title sponsor for the Washington Redskins, FedEx, asked the organization to change their name.

This book was written during the COVID-19 pandemic, and one of the lessons learned from this time was how quickly decisions can change during a crisis. Therefore, predicting the outcomes for sport moving forward is difficult. Many jobs within the industry were lost, and organizations lost millions of dollars because of the pandemic. Sales and fundraising came to a standstill. Sport marketers worked from their homes, and fundraisers could meet with potential donors only through teleconferencing. By July 2020 MLB resumed spring training. Marketers had to reconsider how to sell with no fans in the stadium. The traditional method of selling season tickets was suspended, and many teams considered how they could sell variable groups of tickets to fans similar to what is called a flexible ticket package.

The COVID-19 pandemic is only one example of a crisis situation that a person working in sport sales may face. By the summer of 2021, many North American professional leagues were gearing up for increased fan attendance. For example, in May 2021 the Washington Nationals announced that Nationals Park would be back to full capacity by June 10, 2021. However, there are a lot of lessons that can be learned from these types of crisis situations for anyone working in sport sales, including the following:

1. *Safety is key.* The first priority for every sport organization is the safety of their patrons. While customer service is vitally important to every sport organization, it is imperative that sport organizations protect their customers, whether it be a fitness center, recreational facility, or professional sport venue.

2. *Practice flexibility and adaptability.* Sales professionals must not be set in their ways: If you are going to generate revenues, you need to be willing and able to adapt. This type of flexibility means that you may have to learn new forms of technology, use new and different processes, be flexible concerning the needs and wants of your consumer, and have an open mindset that accepts change. For example, like many other sales professionals, during the pandemic Deron Marchant in business development with the Baltimore Orioles had to be flexible as his computer was moved to a home office where he was selling.

3. *Use creativity.* During the COVID-19 pandemic professional teams had to think of new and creative ways to appeal to fans. For example, fans who received a COVID vaccine at Yankee Stadium or Citi Field received a free ticket to a future Mets or Yankees game (Traub, 2021). Seats were sold at limited capacities at various ballparks. Fans attending a game at Nationals Park in May 2021 sat in groups of socially distanced pods of 1 to 6 people. Seats around these pods were zip tied so that others could not sit in them.

4. *Brainstorm new ways to service your consumer.* While safety is a first priority, salespeople should never forget that serving the customer is still vital. In some cases, this may mean brainstorming new ways to communicate with,

relate to, and serve the customer. The sales team may have to be flexible and creative in coming up with new and novel ways to influence the consumer. Selling can still take place during most crises, but the sales staff may need to brainstorm the best ways to proceed.

Summary

We have discussed in this chapter the changing nature of sales, especially within the sport industry. Technology continues to change the way that salespeople identify and converse with prospective and returning donors. Salespeople who understand how to use new forms of technology will have a competitive advantage. At the same time, however, the sales process still includes a very personal component. Many donors demand personal communications and interactions that do not involve technological solutions. As face-to-face in-person interactions become less prevalent, salespeople will do well to continue to reach out to donors and prospective donors in person and make personal touches.

The unique component to selling sport is the emotion that results from attending, viewing, or participating in a sport event. In addition, the salesperson is selling an uncertain outcome that derives from the sporting event. Consumers of other goods and services simply do not experience the same emotion. For example, automobiles, furniture, electronics, housing, and groceries do not elicit the same level of emotion as sport. Regardless of the product or industry, there is a process for selling that helps to engage prospective consumers or donors. We have outlined a five-step process called the PRO method. Salespeople who are aware of this process and can actively apply it will be the most successful.

If you are a student and are just now learning about the sales process, you have learned the importance of sales to the sport industry. In addition, you have broadened your perspectives about the many ways to get involved in selling a sport product or service. Perhaps you were not aware of the intersection between sales, hospitality, tourism, and retail sales. Sales skills are transferable, and a person can move from a hospitality sales job to one in sport or vice versa. In this chapter, we have speculated about trends for the future. Legalized sport betting will likely have an increasing impact on sport. We discussed future technologies like virtual reality, artificial intelligence, and wearable technologies. New sport events will create new opportunities for selling sport, and expanding markets in Asia and the Middle East may provide opportunities for sales jobs. The trends in youth sport are declining par- ticipation in organized sports and increased specialization. Sales of sporting goods will continue to increase, and more consumer spending will take place online. Finally, the COVID-19 pandemic has had a tremendous effect on sport, although the long-term impact of the pandemic may take years to understand. We have outlined some useful ways to handle crisis management, which include putting safety first, being flexible and adaptable, using creativity, and brainstorming new ways to serve the customer. The most effective salespeo- ple will be able to use these skills to navigate turbulent situations.

APPLIED LEARNING ACTIVITIES

1. In this chapter we discuss several trends regarding sport sales for the future. Choose one of these trends (e.g., youth sport and specialization, new technologies) and think of some examples of these trends you have experienced. Discuss these trends in a paragraph.

2. One of the trends we have discussed is new technologies. Brainstorm a new type of social media platform that you would create. What would be the primary purpose of the social media platform? Who would be the primary audience for the social media platform? Finally, and most important, how would you monetize the platform?

CASE STUDY

ZEBRA AND RFID CHIPS IN THE NFL

In 2014 the National Football League partnered with a company called Zebra Technologies that manufactures a radio-frequency identification (RFID) system called MotionWorks. In retail stores, the RFID is the sticker on boxes of electronics that set off alarms when a cus- tomer walks out of the store. In the NFL, the primary motive for using RFID is to improve the television experience by helping viewers track athletes and their performance, but teams like the 49ers, Lions, and Saints are using it to track the distances and speeds that their athletes run in practice (Taylor, 2015). The NFL is not the only league using RFID tags. The Tampa Bay Lightning of the National Hockey League has implanted RFID tags in the jerseys of their season ticket holders to allow them to purchase discounted food and merchandise. Developers are working to improve RFID, most importantly by decreasing the size of tags, increasing effectiveness, improving antennas, and making more versatile chips (RFID, 2014).

Discussion Questions

1. The case references ways that professional teams in the NFL and NHL have used RFID technology. Can you think of some other ways that RFID technology could be used in sport? Talk about them in a one- to two-minute video that you create on YouTube.

2. The case talks about the Tampa Bay Lighting using RFID technology with season ticket holders. How can this technology be used to monetize other inventories for the team?

Go to HK*Propel* to complete the activities for this chapter.

above the fold—The area immediately visible at the top of a website page that does not require one to scroll down.

ad-based video on demand (AVOD)—Similar to the model used by satellite and cable providers where programs were interrupted by commercials, a type of video monetization in which advertisers pay a fee for every ad rendered on a video.

affiliate marketing—A form of sales in which a marketer refers a product to the customer and receives a commission on the completed sale.

agent disclosure—Refers to how much information the customer receives (and remembers) about the salesperson.

Airbnb—An online marketplace that helps to connect people wanting to rent out their homes with others who are looking for accommodation in a certain location.

annual fund—A type of fundraising that is an organized effort to solicit regular donations from donors that support the daily operation of a nonprofit organization and its ongoing programs.

applause rate—An engagement ratio that measures only the positive engagements on any piece of content. It is calculated by dividing the number of likes or thumbs-up interactions by the number of followers of the account.

arbitrary allocation—A top-down approach whereby the budget is set solely based on what decision-makers believe is necessary.

artificial intelligence (AI)—A branch of computer science that is concerned with building smart machines capable of performing tasks that typically require some form of human intelligence.

athlete endorsement—An agreement between an individual who enjoys public recognition (an athlete) and an entity (e.g., a brand) to use the celebrity for the purpose of promoting the entity.

attrition rate—A metric for measuring performance of a salesperson, calculated by dividing the number of renewed accounts by the number of accounts that the salesperson started with in their book of business. *In the hospitality industry*, the number or percentage of rooms that the rights holder can release without penalty in a contract between a sport event rights holder and hotel.

audience growth rate—A measurement to gauge overall social media account growth.

average daily rate (ADR)—An indicator of a hotel's income, calculated by the revenue generated from hotel rooms sold divided by the total number of rooms sold.

base salary plus commission structure—A commission structure in which the salesperson makes a set salary plus a commission.

benefits (of products) —The result of how the features affect the customer.

bleisure—Refers to the phenomenon of business travelers combining their business trips with leisure outings, often extending their duration of travel.

blockchain technology—Used for transactions made for cryptocurrencies, a blockchain is a digital record of transactions whereby individual records, called blocks, are linked together in a single list, called a chain.

boilerplate proposals—Generic template proposals that include general information about the property.

bonus—A payment based not on individual sales, but usually on departmental sales or when certain revenue targets are met.

bounce rate—Measures when a user lands on a website and views only one page.

B2B sales (business-to-business sales)—An activity in which a business is selling its products or services to another business.

B2C sales (business-to-consumer sales)—Refers to sales to individuals rather than businesses.

bulldog—A quantity-based sales technique in which sales representatives try to qualify a customer quickly and immediately pitch a sale before moving on to the next prospect.

callback rate—A metric that is calculated by dividing the number of inbound calls by the number of voicemails left by the salesperson.

capital award—Funds that help to build or remodel a facility or equipment.

capital campaign—An organized effort to raise funds for a relatively large project within an existing organization that has a fixed budget and timeline.

challenge grant—Funds that are matched by either the applicant or another source.

charitable gift annuity—A legal contract between a donor and a nonprofit organization that involves the irrevocable transfer of property (cash, real property, or securities) in exchange for paying the donor or donor's designee an annuity for life.

charitable remainder annuity trust—An annuity in which the amount paid to the donor each year is a fixed percentage of the value of the trust at the time it is established.

charitable remainder unitrust—A type of planned giving that allows the donor and other designated beneficiaries to receive income over either the donor's life, donors' joint lives, or for life plus a stated term of years.

charts—Graphic representations of data that may include project management tools (e.g., Gantt charts), timelines, representations that describe similarities and differences between concepts (e.g., Venn diagrams), maps, process diagrams, and other graphic displays of information. Sites like Vizzlo and Infogram can be used to create various types of charts.

cinemagraph—A GIF that contains subtle motion that plays in a short, never-ending loop, while the rest of the image remains still.

click-through rate—Measures how many times an ad was clicked on by users.

commission—A payment made to an employee based on a percentage of sales that they bring to the company.

commission draw structure—A commission structure that includes elements of the commission only and base pay plus commission structures whereby the salesperson earns some amount of pay each month regardless of sales.

community foundation—Foundation that maintains and administers funds on behalf of multiple donors primarily to meet the needs of the geographic community or region where it is based.

competitive parity—A top-down strategy whereby a company sets a budget of marketing activities at par with their competitors or the industry average.

conscientiousness—Having a strong sense of duty and being responsible and reliable.

conversion rate—A metric that is calculated by dividing the number of sales by the number of active touchpoints generated by the salesperson. *In fundraising,* the percentage of people who visit the webpage for a fundraising event and sign up to attend.

conversion ratios—Measurements that gauge the degree to which followers of a social media account complete a desirable task. Common conversion ratios include clickthrough rate and bounce rate.

cooperative intentions—Refers to the degree to which the customer believes the salesperson has their best interests in mind.

cord-cutting—A term used to refer to when a consumer cancels a cable or satellite subscription in place of getting content by other means.

core product (sport)—The actual game being played on the court or field.

corporate foundations (or company-sponsored foundations)—A type of private foundation that is a separate legal entity and is created and financially supported by a corporation.

cost per acquisition (CPA)—Measures the cumulative expense of acquiring one paying customer on a specific marketing campaign or channel.

cost per click (CPC)—A method of billing advertising based on the number of times a visitor clicks on an advertisement.

cost per thousand (CPM)—An advertising term that stands for cost per thousand (the *m* in CPM stands for *mille*, which is French for "thousand").

cultivation—A step in the fundraising process in which the fundraiser starts to build a relationship with the prospective donor.

customer disclosure—Refers to how much information the customer has willingly offered to the salesperson about themselves.

customer needs—Requirements that must be met for the customer to get reasonable value from the purchase.

customer wants—Factors of the purchase that are preferable, although not necessarily required.

data mining—The process of selecting, exploring, and modeling raw data to uncover trends and patterns.

daytripper—A person who travels over 50 miles (80 km) but returns home the same day.

decision maker—The person who has the ultimate authority to decide on a sponsorship purchase.

deflecting—Highlighting a different positive benefit to outweigh a negative objection.

designated market areas (DMAs)—Geographic areas that represent specific television markets that can receive the same programming.

destination image—The sum of beliefs and impressions that people hold about place.

destination marketing organizations (DMOs)—Organizations whose primary purpose is to market the geographic area as an attractive travel destination.

direct advertisements (social media)—Content created by a sport organization solely for the purpose of advertising or promoting the sponsor.

direct sponsorship objectives—Objectives that focus on increasing sales for the sponsors and have a short-term effect on the behavior of the consumer.

donor-advised fund (DAF)—An account administered by a third-party sponsor, such as a community foundation, who handles all the business and legal matters, thus freeing the donor from those responsibilities.

donor prospecting—A step in the fundraising process in which the fundraiser identifies individuals who are capable of making a gift to their organization.

donor's bill of rights—Highlights various ethical issues germane to philanthropy to foster respect and trust in the public and build donors' confidence in the organizations they support.

duty-duty basis—A tax based on the percentage of the time in an athlete's contract when they were present in the jurisdiction and earning an income.

dynamic pricing—A pricing strategy that allows the price of an item to change in real time with availability.

dynamic ticketing—Refers to the concept whereby the price of single-game tickets fluctuates based on a range of supply and demand market factors such as the opposing team and the night of the week.

ego drive—The drive of a salesperson such that they want and need to make the sale in a personal, or ego, way, not merely for the money to be gained.

80–20 rule—States that a salesperson should spend 80 percent of their time listening and no more than 20 percent of their time talking to the customer.

elevator pitch—A persuasive pitch to sell yourself to an employer that is short enough that you could pitch it while riding in an elevator.

empathy—The ability to feel as another person does to be able to sell them a product or service.

endowment grant—An investment whereby some of the annual income is used for a specific purpose.

engagement rate—An engagement ratio that determines the percentage of an audience that relates positively or negatively to a piece of content. It is calculated by dividing the total number of engagements by the total number of followers on the account. *Informally*, measures how much users are interacting with a brand by considering factors like the number of comments on a post or shares received.

engagement ratios—A series of measurements that can be used to determine the degree to which the audience relates to the content being posted.

facilities and administrative costs (F&A)—The label often used by federal agencies to describe expenses that are difficult to assign to a particular project but are at the same time required by the project.

family foundation—A type of private foundation that is typically funded through an endowment from a family whose members have substantial roles in governance.

features (of products)—Facts about the product. Features are indisputable.

feed—In social media, continuous content areas on a social media platform visible to others.

fixed pricing—A pricing strategy that maintains the price of an item regardless of availability.

formative evaluation—An evaluative technique that provides immediate feedback by monitoring any group to determine where problems may be emerging.

franchisee—The company or person who is issued a license to sell merchandise and operate under a franchisor's business name.

franchisor—A company or person who issues a license to a franchisee.

fundraising—The creation and ongoing development of relationships between a not-for-profit organization and its various donors for the purpose of increasing gift revenue to the organization.

Gantt charts—Timelines used by project managers that display the progress on a project by showing activities vertically and time horizontally. They help managers break down a project into manageable pieces of work, stay organized, and visualize dependencies between tasks.

gatekeeper—Any person who restricts access to the actual prospect. Often, the person who answers the phone, directs phone calls, and usually protects decision-makers from the constant barrage of phone calls from salespeople.

GIF—Stands for graphical interchange format, a series of images or soundless video that loops continuously without anyone needing to press play.

goods—Tangible items produced for sale.

grant—A specific quantity of money that is awarded by a government agency, foundation, organization, or person to an organization or individual for a specific activity or purpose.

grantee—The individual or organization designated to receive the funds from the grantor.

grantor—The organization or agency that receives the funding request and consequently decides whether to fund or reject the request.

grants research—The systematic collection and analysis of information that will lead to the submission of a proposal.

gross margin commission—A commission structure that considers the revenues generated but then deducts the expenses; therefore, a sales rep earns a percentage of the profit.

gross ratings points—A measure of the size of an audience reached by a specific media vehicle or schedule.

group ticket sales—Discounted tickets bought in bulk.

guest count—The number of people who will be fed during a function and the primary factor in managing the budget for an event.

handle—The amount wagered over a period.

hard goods—In retail sales, includes equipment like sporting goods that are not apparel.

hard money—A regular appropriation of money.

hot lead—A prospect who has high interest in purchasing a product and simply needs to be contacted.

impression—Any instance in which a person viewed social media content.

inbound sales—Customers who have actively reached out to the sport organization and expressed interest in their product.

independent foundation—A type of private foundation that is funded by endowments from a single source (e.g., individual or group of individuals) but is not governed by the benefactor, the benefactor's family, or a corporation.

indirect advertisement (social media)—Content created by a sport organization that allows sponsor advertisement but has as its main purpose the promotion of something other than the sponsor.

indirect sponsorship objectives—Objectives that lead to the goal of enhancing sales and include aims such as generating awareness, reaching new target markets, improving image, and building relationships.

influencer marketing—A recent trend in sport sponsorship that uses not only celebrity endorsements but also influencers, people who would never be considered famous in an offline setting. Brands create collaborations with influencers because they have the power to affect purchasing decisions of others because of their authority, knowledge, position, or size of their social media following.

infographics—A collection of imagery, charts, and minimal text that covers a complex topic, but provides an easy-to-understand overview of the topic.

interaction intensity—Refers to how often and under what circumstances the salesperson contacts the customer.

international foundation—A type of private foundation that typically makes grants to their own country and overseas and is based outside the United States. It can also refer to any foundation in any country that primarily engages in giving across borders.

key performance indicators (KPIs)—Metrics (e.g., click-through rate, engagement rate, bounce rate) used to track the performance of social media campaigns.

lead—An unqualified contact. A contact who is unqualified does not fit one or more of the following three criteria: (1) fits the target market, (2) has the money to buy, and (3) is authorized to make a buying decision.

lead time—The period between when a purchaser places an order with a sporting goods supplier and when the product arrives in the store

letter of inquiry (LOI)—A one- to three-page letter that many funding agencies ask for and is a non-legally binding document that includes an introduction to your project, contact information at your agency, a description of your organization, a statement of need, your methodology or an achievable solution to the need, a brief discussion of other funding sources, and a final summary.

leveraging—The investment in communicating about and through the sponsorship that is in excess of the sponsorship deal.

live read—Advertisement in which a presenter or announcer talks about the product or service live and on air, used primarily in radio.

making the ask—Refers to asking a person to donate a certain amount of money to the organization.

markdowns—Discounts that sporting goods retailers make on merchandise.

marketing—All activities designed to meet the needs and wants of sport consumers through exchange processes.

measurable metrics—Activities that can be quantified and recorded from the CRM software of the organization or from the salesperson's own tracking and recording.

meme—An image, video, or piece of text that is copied, slightly altered, and spread rapidly by Internet users.

memorandum of agreement (MOA)—A document that describes how two organizations will work together on a project. It often includes various details of the partnership along with the terms of the agreement and the roles and responsibilities of everyone involved.

multiplier—Exists in either a traditional or activated commission and includes a commission percentage that increases as the salesperson achieves certain benchmarks.

new sales—A sale to a customer who was not a customer (or not a season ticketholder) in the previous year. These sales typically have higher commissions.

notice of grant award (NGA)—A letter that specifies the amount and duration of a grant award and provides other pertinent information concerning the grant.

objective and task method—A bottom-up approach to budgeting whereby funds are allocated based on sponsorship objectives.

occupancy rate—A metric used by hotels that is calculated by dividing the number of rooms occupied by the number of rooms available and multiplying the result by 100.

open-ended questions—Questions that cannot be answered with a simple yes or no.

operating foundation—A special form of private foundation that uses the bulk of its income to run its own charitable programs or services.

operating or general-purpose grant—Funds that are donated to an organization with no expectation that the funds will be used for any specific purpose or activity.

outbound sales—When sales representatives reach out directly to customers.

outsourcing—Turning over all or part of an organizational activity to an outside vendor.

over-the-top (OTT)—The productized (i.e., making or developing into a product) practice of streaming content to customers directly over the web.

panel—A group of people chosen by companies that measure ratings (e.g., Nielsen) that is representative of a larger universe of people.

partner—A term that is used interchangeably at times with the term *sponsor*. Although a partnership includes payment, it also implies working toward a common goal or having common interests at heart.

percentage of sales—A top-down approach whereby decision-makers determine advertising and promotion budgets based on product sales.

performance clause—Criteria or standards in a contract between a hotel and a sport event rights holder.

per-game basis—A tax based on the percentage of a player's game schedule that occurred in a particular jurisdiction.

PERT diagram—A timeline used by project managers to illustrate who is responsible for what and when specific events are scheduled. The diagram highlights the interdependence of activities by diagramming their network. The key components include activities, events, time, the critical path, and cost.

planned giving—Charitable donations made with some level of professional guidance that normally involve a process of making a significant charitable gift during a donor's life or at death that is part of their financial or estate plan.

point-of-sale (POS)—Systems consisting of computers and cash registers that capture transaction data at the time and place of sale.

presenting sponsor—Often the key partner for an event with benefits such as the use of the event's name or image, prominent positioning of the sponsor's logo, appearance on the event's website or social media channels, and involvement with hospitality packages.

price lining—A pricing strategy in which a product is advertised with several different price points based on different benefits.

primary ticket market—Tickets sold directly by the team.

private foundation—A 501(c)(3) organization that is established to fund charitable activities through grants and other gifts.

private operating foundation—A type of private foundation that operates its own charitable programs (although some also make grants) and is required to spend a certain portion of its assets each year on charitable activities.

private sector grants—Grants that are funded by foundations or corporate grant makers that use funds from private sources (e.g., investments, contributions, grants, or donations) to fund eligible grantees.

probing—Asking targeted questions to gather information.

products—Any items that are offered for sale.

program announcements—A method used by a funding source to provide information about grants that have flexibility in terms of their procedures, methods, timeline, and targets to be served in the grant.

program officer (PO)—The point of contact for understanding the funding agencies' response to the grant submission.

program-related investments—Loans or equity investments made by a private foundation or public charity, primarily for charitable purposes.

project or program grant—Funds that are awarded to achieve specific outcomes within a specified period. Activities that are fairly limited in scope are often referred to as projects, whereas programs are wider in scope.

promotional efforts—The various means through which sport organizations persuade consumers to make a purchase decision.

prospecting—The act of searching for and finding qualified leads and turning them into prospects for a sale.

public sector grants—Grants that are funded by government agencies at the federal, state, county, or local level with money that is subject to congressional approval, federal pass-through programs that may or may not be funded by federal money, and taxpayer dollars.

qualified leads—Cases in which the prospect has shown some interest or had contact with the sport property.

qualifying distribution—A distribution made by a private nonoperating foundation that may consist of a grant, gift, or what are called program-related investments along with rea-

sonable administrative expenses incurred by the private foundation in carrying out its charitable purposes, and amounts paid to acquire assets used in carrying out the foundation's exempt purposes.

rack rate—The standard asking price for a hotel room before any discounts.

rate card—a document or brochure with the various advertising inventory for sale in newspapers, television, and radio along with the pricing.

ratings—The percentage of households tuned into the medium (e.g., television or radio) at any given moment.

reach—Measures the number of viewers that have the opportunity to view an ad during a given period time.

reciprocation—A principle that suggests we should repay, in kind, what another person has provided us.

referrals—When a current customer provides a lead on another customer who may be interested.

regional broadcast networks—Cable broadcasting channels that provide sport programming in local geographic markets.

relationship marketing (also relationship selling)—A method that prioritizes the long-term relationship with the customer over the short-term sale.

renewals (ticketing)—A season ticket sale to a customer who had tickets in the previous season.

request for proposal (RFP)—*In the context of grants,* correspondence by a funding source that outlines information such as the type of program, geographical or targeted groups to be served, range of acceptable costs, timeline, criteria for selecting recipients, and acceptable procedures or methods. *In the hospitality industry,* a formal request by a company or event to a potential vendor requesting a bid on satisfying those specifications.

restricted funds—Funds that are set aside for a particular purpose normally because the donor has requested that the funds be used for that purpose.

return on investment—An educated approximation of how much additional profit a company has earned based solely on the sponsorship.

return on objectives—A metric that uses company objectives (e.g., factors like sales or website visits because of the sponsorship) to measure the value of a sponsorship.

revenue commission—A commission structure that pays a salesperson based on the revenues they generate.

revenue per available room (RevPAR)—Revenue generated per available room, whether or not the rooms are occupied. Hotels use this metric to measure themselves against other properties or brands.

role-playing—A method that encourages thinking and creativity, lets students develop and practice new language and behavioral skills in a relatively nonthreatening setting, and can create the motivation and involvement necessary for learning to occur.

room block—The number of hotel rooms that are reserved for an event. A block normally includes 10 or more rooms and provides a discount of 15 to 40 percent to the occupant of the room.

sales process—The tasks or steps like prospecting and qualifying that salespeople complete to create value for both the customer and the sales organization.

satellite radio—Radio broadcasting that uses satellites to transmit content, covers an entire content instead of a local geographic region, and requires a compatible head unit or a portable satellite tuner as well as a monthly subscription.

scarcity—A principle that suggests that opportunities seem more valuable to us when their availability is limited.

screenshot—An image of data displayed on the screen of a computer or mobile device that can help to communicate complex ideas.

season membership—See season ticket package. A season ticketholder who receives year-round contact and benefits.

season ticket package—A single purchase for the entire home season of a team.

secondary benefit (tickets)—A B2B concept that suggests that a business may give tickets to a person with a motivation of gaining a benefit as part of the customer's enjoyment.

secondary ticket market—Tickets that were purchased from a team and then resold.

second-screen viewing—A term coined to describe fans' use of a second device (usually a phone or computer) simultaneously with their television.

self-actualization—The last stage in Maslow's hierarchy of needs, in which the salesperson reaches their full potential, feels personally fulfilled, and creatively solves problems.

services—Actions or work done for a person or organization.

share—The percentage of televisions tuned to a program among those in use.

shotgunning—A sales technique in which the sales representative bombards the customer with several pitches for various inventory without qualifying them first, in an attempt to stumble on a good fit.

shrinkage—Occurs in retail when goods are lost because of employee theft, shoplifting, administrative errors, vendor fraud, cashier error, and damage in the store or in transit.

social media—Technologically delivered engagement between a person and another person or organization using the Internet.

social media platforms—Software designed to support social media engagement.

social proof—A principle that suggests that we try to find out what other people think is correct to determine what is correct.

social share of voice—A ratio that measures how much an account is mentioned compared with their competitors. It is calculated by compiling the number of mentions that an official account receives on social media as well as the number of mentions that the competitors receive.

soft goods—Apparel items in retail like golf slacks, shirts, shoes, and sweaters.

soft money—Money obtained by grants or contracts that has a deadline date.

solicited designation—Donation by an individual or corporation for a particular cause directly solicited by a nonprofit organization.

sponsee—The property providing value in a sponsorship.

sponsor—The party that pays or provides compensation to be officially associated with a specific property.

sponsorship—The acquisition of rights to affiliate or directly associate with a product, person, organization, team, league, or event for the purpose of deriving benefits related to that affiliation or association.

sponsorship activation—Communications that promote the engagement, involvement, or participation of the sponsorship audience with the sponsor.

sponsorship assets—The benefits and rights that the sponsor negotiates with the sport property.

sponsorship objectives—Part of the promotional process that should be linked to the broader promotional planning process and objectives.

sport-betting revenues—The amount of money kept by sportsbooks out of the amount wagered.

sport property—Refers to a league, team, event, venue, governing body, or association that sells sponsorship rights.

stadium naming rights—A transaction in which money or consideration changes hands to secure the right to name a sports facility.

start-up or seed money—Funds given to an individual or organization to help begin the process for an initiative.

sticky—A website is considered sticky when a user visits the site repeatedly and spends more time browsing than the average user.

straight commission plan—Commission structure whereby the salesperson is paid only the commission they make on each sale.

subscription video on demand (SVOD)—A subscription-based (e.g., weekly, monthly, or quarterly) method of video monetization that allows viewers to have unlimited access to a video library for as long as their subscription lasts.

summative evaluation—A type of evaluation technique that is the final or concluding task or the final formative evaluation of a project.

support statement—Confirmation that the customer is correct and that the salesperson agrees with them.

taxes or state revenues—Tax monies collected by state and local jurisdictions; in this context, the share of sport-betting revenues collected by government units.

terrestrial radio—Radio broadcast by a land-based station that is limited to geographic regions, thus the content is broadcast and received locally.

tessera—Shards of pottery that formed the earliest tickets during the Roman Empire.

3-to-1 ratio—A customer service guideline that suggests contacting customers three times without asking for money before contacting them to sell something.

tiered commission structure—A commission structure whereby a salesperson's commission rate increases as they hit certain revenue benchmarks that are set.

title sponsor—An organization that contracts to provides money, goods, or services in exchange for the exclusive right to have their name appear prominently before the title of the event.

touchpoint—A metric for measuring call volume that includes phone calls as well as any other form of correspondence between the sales representative and the customer.

transaction video on demand (TVOD)—Better known as pay-per-view, a type of video monetization whereby viewers pay a certain amount of money for what they want to watch.

transition statement—Positive statement that connects a feature to a benefit for the customer.

trigger statement—Single most important reason that the customer wants to buy the product.

unrestricted funds—Funds used by a nonprofit organization for any purpose they deem necessary and that often go toward normal operating costs.

unsolicited designation—Donation by an individual or organization without having been directly solicited by the charity.

upsell rate—A metric that is calculated by the amount of new revenue generated by existing customers.

viral—A term used to describe rapid expansion and impressions of content.

virality rate—A measurement taken to gauge the general quality of social media content on Twitter. It is found by dividing the number of retweets by the number of views.

web scraping—A set of techniques used to automatically get information from a website instead of manually copying it.

website takeover—This occurs when the publisher of the website allows an advertiser to place creative content in each available ad spot in the layout or into the site background, or provide interactive content.

win–win scenario (ticket sales)—Situation in which the customer is paying for the services and is happy with the product they received for their money.

REFERENCES

Chapter 1

Baker, T. (2015). *The new influencing toolkit: Capabilities for communicating with influence.* Palgrave Macmillan.

Barthelemy, J. (2003). *The seven deadly sins of outsourcing. Academy of Management Executive, 17*(2), 87-99.

Barrick, M.R., Mount, M.K., & Judge, T.A. (2001). Personality and performance at the beginning of the new millennium: What do we know and where do we go next? *International Journal of Selection and Assessment, 9*(1-2), 9-30.

Blustein, A. (2019, January 18). *Advertisers spent over \$3bn on TV ads during playoff across major US sports.* The Drum. www.thedrum.com/news/2019/01/18/advertisers-spent-over-3bn-tv-ads-during-playoff-across-major-us-sports

Burden, W., & Li, M. (2009). Minor League Baseball: Exploring the growing interest in outsourced sport marketing. *Sport Marketing Quarterly, 18*(3), 139.

Busi, M. (2008). Editorial. *Strategic Outsourcing: An International Journal, 1,* 5-11.

Bynum. M. (2007, August). *Outsourcing sports programs allows a department to do more with less.* Athletic Business. www.athleticbusiness.com/staffing/outsourcing-sports-programs-allows-a-department-to-do-more-with-less.html

Chelladurai, P. (2014). *Managing organizations for sport and physical activity: A systems perspective.* Routledge.

Click, E. (2014). One development project, two economic tales: The St. Louis Cardinals' Busch Stadium and Ballpark Village. *Missouri Policy Journal, 2,* 21-34.

Cialdini, R. (2007). *Influence: The psychology of persuasion* (rev. ed.; 1st Collins business essentials ed.). Collins.

Ciconte, B.L., & Jacob, J. (2011). *Fundraising basics: A complete guide* (3rd ed.). Jones & Bartlett.

Cohn, C. (2015, June 16). Differences in selling B2B vs. B2C. *Forbes.* www.forbes.com/sites/chuckcohn/2015/06/16/differences-in-selling-b2b-vs-b2c/#397a3f834fb2

Connolly, E. (2019, January 17). *"We sit and we think, what are we missing?" Inside Snapchat's sports content strategy.* Sports Pro. www.sportspromedia.com/quick_fire_questions/snapchat-sport-content-strategy-copa-90-interview

Content Marketing Institute. (2019). *What is content marketing? Useful content should be at the core of your marketing.* https://contentmarketinginstitute.com/what-is-content-marketing/

Craig, R., & Amernic, J. (1994). Roleplaying in a conflict resolution setting: Description and some implications for accounting. *Issues in Accounting Education, 9*(1), 28.

Crockett, Z. (2019, January 5). *Are gym memberships worth the money? More than half of all gym members never actually go to the gym—yet year after year, they continue to pay for a service they don't use. Why?* The Hustle. https://thehustle.co/gym-membership-cost

Cvetkoska, V., & Iliev, F. (2017). How to choose your next top salesperson: Multiple-criteria approach. *Business Systems Research Journal, 8*(1), 92-112.

DeSena, J. (2003). *The 10 immutable laws of power selling: The key to winning sales, wowing customers, and driving profits through the roof.* McGraw-Hill Professional.

Dinu, A.M. (2015). The risks and benefits of outsourcing. *Knowledge Horizons—Economics, 7*(2), 103.

Driver, S. (2020, December 22). *Instagram for business: Everything you need to know.* Business News Daily. www.businessnewsdaily.com/7662-instagram-business-guide.html

Duermyer, R. (2019, June 25). *What is blogging and how can it help my home business?* The Balance Small Business. www.thebalancesmb.com/blogging-what-is-it-1794405

Facebook Business. (2019). *Columbus Blue Jackets: Selling tickets in a multi-phase campaign built on Facebook lead ads.* www.facebook.com/business/success/columbus-blue-jackets

Farris, P.W., Bendle, N.T., Pfeifer, P.E., & Reibstein, D.J. (2010). *Marketing metrics: The definitive guide to measuring marketing performance.* Pearson Education.

Florida, R. (2015, September 10). *The never-ending stadium boondoggle.* Bloomberg. www.bloomberg.com/news/articles/2015-09-10/u-s-sports-stadiums-continue-to-be-funded-with-taxpayer-money

Fulks, D.L. (2017, September). *Revenues and expenses 2004-2016.* NCAA. www.ncaa.org/sites/default/files/2017RES_D1-evExp_Entire_2017_Final_20180123.pdf

Gallagher, D., Gilmore, A., & Stolz, A. (2012). The strategic marketing of small sports clubs: From fundraising to social entrepreneurship. *Journal of Strategic Marketing, 20*(3), 231-247.

Greenwell, T.C., Danzey-Bussell, L.A., & Shonk, D. (2019). *Managing sport events.* Human Kinetics.

Herring, S., Scheidt, L., Bonus, S., & Wright, E. (2004). Bridging the gap: A genre analysis of weblogs. In *Proceedings of the 37th Hawaii International Conference on System Sciences. Los Alamitos.*

Hsu, T. (2020, August 12). Postponed college football games could disrupt $1 billion in TV ads. *New York Times.* www.nytimes.com/2020/08/12/business/media/college-football-ads-coronavirus.html

IBIS World. (2017, December). *Online event ticket sales in the US: Market research report.* www.gao.gov/assets/700/691247.pdf

Irwin, R.L., Sutton, W.A., & McCarthy, L.M. (2008). *Sport promotion and sales management.* Human Kinetics.

Kang, S.J., Ha, J.P., & Hambrick, M.E. (2015). A mixed-method approach to exploring the motives of sport-related mobile applications among college students. *Journal of Sport Management, 29*(3), 272-290.

Kelly, W. (2012. April 1). Town ponders privatization for Recreation Department services. *Palm Beach Daily News.* www.palmbeachdailynews.com/article/20120401/SPORTS/304018513

Kurlan, D. (2009). *The modern science of salesperson selection.* Westborough, A White Paper, Objective Management Group.

Leeds, E.M., Leeds, M.A., & Pistolet, I. (2007). A stadium by any other name: The value of naming rights. *Journal of Sports Economics, 8*(6), 581-595.

Lieberman, L. (2019, August 19). UG tells T-Bones to get off my field. *Kansas City Business Journal.* www.bizjournals.com/kansascity/news/2019/08/19/unified-government-tbones-baseball-eviction-notice.html

Lindahl, W. (2010). *Principles of fundraising: Theory and practice.* Jones & Bartlett Learning.

Martin, S.W. (2011, June 27). Seven personality traits of top salespeople. *Harvard Business Review.* https://hbr.org/2011/06/the-seven-personality-traits-o

Maxwell, H., & Lough, N. (2009). Signage vs. no signage: An analysis of sponsorship recognition in women's college basketball. *Sport Marketing Quarterly, 18*(4).

Mayer, D., & Greenberg, H.M. (1964). What makes a good salesman? *Harvard Business Review, 42*(4), 119-125.

Miller, R.K., & Washington, K. (2018). *Sports marketing 2018-2019.* Richard K. Miller & Associates.

Misener, K. (2011). Community relations. In L.E. Swayne and G.J. Golson (Eds.), *Encyclopedia of sports management and marketing.* Sage.

National Recreation and Parks Association (2021). *2021 NRPA performance agency review.* www.nrpa.org/siteassets/2021-agency-performance-review_final.pdf

Nations, D. (2019, March 29). *What is Facebook? Learn why so many people can't stay away from Facebook*. Lifewire. www.lifewire.com/what-is-facebook-3486391?print

NASSM. (2020). *Academic programs*. www.nassm.com/Programs/AcademicPrograms

NCAA. (2020). *Finances of intercollegiate athletics*. www.ncaa.org/about/resources/research/finances-intercollegiate-athletics

Pink, D.H. (2012). *To sell is human: The surprising truth about moving others*. Penguin.

Plunkett Research. (2018). *Sports & recreation business statistics analysis, business and industry statistics*. www.plunkett research.com/statistics/sports-industry

Popp, N., Simmons, J., & McEvoy, C.D. (2017). Sport ticket sales training: Perceived effectiveness and impact on ticket sales results. *Sport Marketing Quarterly, 26*(2), 99.

Popp, N., Simmons, J., & McEvoy, C. (2019). Effects of employee training on job satisfaction outcomes among sport ticket sellers. *International Journal of Sport Management and Marketing, 19*(3-4), 147-160.

Ramsey, S. (2016, October 20). *Twelve craziest minor league promotions*. Fox Sports. www.foxsports.com/southwest/gallery/top-12-craziest-minor-league-promotions-081014

Reese, J.T., & Thomas, D. (2013). Ticket operations history and background. In J.T. Reese (Ed.), *Ticket operations and sales management in sport*. Fitness Information Technology.

Reilly, K.F. (2019). *Clubs in town & country* (North American ed.). A report prepared by PBMares, LLP in conjunction with Club Services Group.

Schmitt, B., Rogers, D., & Vrotsos, K. (2003). *There's no business that's not show business: Marketing in an experience culture*. FT Press.

Shonk, D.J. (2011). Promotion. In L.E. Swayne & G.J. Golson (Eds.), *Encyclopedia of sports management and marketing*. Sage.

Simmons, S. (2018, August 21). Digital marketing changing the sports industry. *Management Tips in Business*. https://sens-international.org/digital-marketing-changing-the-sports-industry/

Smith, D.P. (2018, May). How sports stadiums are upping their foodservice game. *QSR*. www.qsrmagazine.com/menu-innovations/how-sports-stadiums-are-upping-their-food-service-game

Sport England. (2019). *How does sport bring communities together? Understanding the context*. www.sportengland.org/our-work/partnering-local-government/scenarios/how-does-sport-bring-communities-together/

Statista. (September 23, 2016). *Largest sports league TV contracts worldwide as of September 2016 (in billion U.S. dollars per year)* [Graph]. www.statista.com/statistics/316617/largest-tv-sports-league-contracts-usa/

Stevens, H. (2018, July 16). 5-year-old Glenview baseball fan wrote every team asking for a pocket schedule. The results have been delightful. *Chicago Tribune*. www.chicagotribune.com/columns/heidi-stevens/ct-life-stevens-sunday-baseball-schedule-collection-0716-story.html

Sutton. (2017, August 7). A new look at outsourcing your marketing rights. *Sports Business Journal*. www.sportsbusinessdaily.com/Journal/Issues/2017/08/07/Opinion/Sutton-Impact.aspx

Tompkins, P.K. (1998). Role playing/simulation. *Internet TESL Journal, 4*(8), 143-150.

Vinchur, A.J., Schippmann, J.S., Switzer III, F.S., & Roth, P.L. (1998). A meta-analytic review of predictors of job performance for salespeople. *Journal of Applied Psychology, 83*(4), 586.

Warr, P., Bartram, D., & Martin, T. (2005). Personality and sales performance: Situational variation and interactions between traits. *International Journal of Selection and Assessment, 13*(1), 87-91.

Williams, J., Chinn, S. J., & Suleiman, J. (2014). The value of Twitter for sports fans. *Journal of Direct, Data and Digital Marketing Practice, 16*(1), 36-50.

Yakasai, A.M., & Jan, M.T. (2015). The impact of big five personality traits on salespeople's performance: Exploring the moderating role of culture. *Kuwait Chapter of the Arabian Journal of Business and Management Review, 4*(5), 11.

Chapter 2

Arli, D., Bauer, C., & Palmatier, R.W. (2018). Relational selling: Past, present and future. *Industrial Marketing Management, 69*, 169-184.

Crosby, L.A., Evans, K.R., & Cowles, D. (1990). Relationship quality in services selling: An interpersonal influence perspective. *Journal of Marketing, 54*(3), 68-81.

Duke Sports Information. (2016). Duke sellout streak keeps building. https://goduke.com/news/2016/6/8/211005197.aspx

Hoffman, K.D., Howe, V., & Hardigree, D.W. (1991). Ethical dilemmas faced in the selling of complex services: Significant others and competitive pressures. *Journal of Personal Selling & Sales Management, 11*(4), 13-25.

Johnson, D.S., & Grayson, K. (2000). Sources and dimensions of trust in service relationships. *Handbook of Service Relationship, 357*-370.

Johnson, E.M. (1969). *Are goods and services different? An exercise in marketing theory.* Ph.D. dissertation, Washington University.

Sharma, A., Levy, M., & Kumar, A. (2000). Knowledge structures and retail sales performance: An empirical examination. *Journal of Retailing, 76*(1), 53-69.

Chapter 3

Carroll, B. (1991). The American Football League attendance, 1960-67. *The Coffin Corner, 13*(4), 6-7. www.profootballresearchers.org/archives/Website_Files/Coffin_Corner/13-04-430.pdf

Cavanaugh, J. (2006). *Tunney: Boxing's brainiest champ and his upset of the great Jack Dempsey.* Ballantine Books.

Colosseumrometickets.com. (2018). *Seating at the Colosseum.* https://colosseumrometickets.com/seating-colosseum/

Dowd, K. (2019, April 15). *The priciest seats at the Warriors' new Chase Center? $2 million per year.* SFGate. www.sfgate.com/warriors/article/sf-chase-center-ticket-prices-warriors-13768493.php

Forbes. (February 27, 2020). *Gate receipts as percentage of total revenue in the National Basketball Association from 2010/11 to 2019/20.* In Statista. www.statista.com/statistics/193410/percentage-of-ticketing-revenue-in-the-nba-since-2006/

Gast, J. (2014). *The Astrodome: Building an American spectacle.* Aspinwall Press.

Haupert, M., & Winter, K. (2003). Pay ball: Estimating the profitability of the New York Yankees 1915-1937. *Essays in Economic & Business History, 21*(1), 89-101.

Hopkins, K., & Beard, M. (2011). *The Colosseum.* Harvard University Press.

McGinn, B. (2012). *The ultimate Super Bowl book: A complete reference to the stats, stars, and stories behind football's biggest game.* MVP Books.

NCAA. (2019). *2019 football attendance.* http://fs.ncaa.org/Docs/stats/football_records/Attendance/2019.pdf

Pierce, D., Petersen, J., Clavio, G., & Meadows, B. (2012). Content analysis of sport ticket sales job announcements. *Sport, Business and Management, 2*(2). 137-155.

Platner, S.B. (2015). *A topographical dictionary of ancient Rome.* Cambridge University Press.

PwC. (2019). *Total sports gate revenues in North America from 2006 to 2023.* In Statista. www-statista-com.esearch.ut.edu/statistics/194224/sports-gate-revenue-in-north-america/

Ramirez, F. (2020). *SoFi Stadium preview with it set to open on Sunday.* SI.com. www.si.com/nfl/chargers/news/sofi-stadium-preview-with-it-set-to-debut-on-sunday

Reese, J.T. (2012). *Ticket operations and sales management.* Fitness Information.

Shoemaker, C. (2011). *History of premium seating and future trends.* Ballparkratings.com. www.

ballparkratings.com/article/history-of-premium-seating-and-future-trends/

Spanberg, E. (2012). Employee benefits: Companies use sports sponsorships to motivate employees and recognize their accomplishments. *Sports Business Daily*, March 26. www.sportsbusinessdaily.com/Journal/Issues/2012/03/26/In-Depth/Employees.aspx

TicketIQ. (2020, July 22). Potential ticket revenue loss in selected sports leagues due to the coronavirus (COVID-19) pandemic in the United States in 2020 (in billion U.S. dollars). Statista. https://www-statista-com.esearch.ut.edu/statistics/1130000/ticket-revenue-loss-sports-leagues-corona/

Uhrich, S., & Benkenstein, M. Sport stadium atmosphere: Formative and reflective indicators for operationalizing the construct. *Journal of Sport Management*, 24(2), 211-237.

Chapter 4

Baltimore Orioles. (2020). *Broadcast affiliates*. www.mlb.com/orioles/schedule/broadcast-affiliates

Baseball Reference. (2020). *Revenue sharing*. www.baseball-reference.com/bullpen/Revenue_sharing

Bengel, C. (2020, February 19). *Athletics become first MLB team to switch to streaming-only platform from traditional radio*. CBS Sports. www.cbssports.com/mlb/news/athletics-become-first-mlb-team-to-switch-to-streaming-only-platform-from-traditional-radio/

Blattberg, E. (2015, April 23). *What are the upfronts?* Digiday. https://digiday.com/marketing/upfrontses-wtf-upfronts/

Bollapragada, S., & Mallik, S. (2008). Managing on-air ad inventory in broadcast television. *IIE Transactions*, 40(12), 1107-123.

Brandi. (2020, October 16). The top digital marketing terms you need to know. *Lyfe Marketing*. www.lyfemarketing.com/blog/marketing-terms/

Brebion. (2018, February 4). Above the fold vs. below the fold: Does it still matter today? *AB Tasty*. www.abtasty.com/blog/above-the-fold/

Carp, S. (2020, December 8). *Georgia Tech brings revenue streams under one umbrella in Legends deal*. SportsPro. www.sportspromedia.com/news/georgia-tech-yellow-jackets-legends-multimedia-rights-ticketing-ecommerce

Center for Research in Intercollegiate Athletics. (2018). *Intercollegiate multimedia rights agreement report*. https://ec951b37-ca10-47f8-94e6-1f6d4139c58a.filesusr.com/ugd/1ee3b7_bfe5d0a43d8e4db685fe9bbc39c02943.pdf

Congressional Research Service. (2013). *Selected laws governing the broadcast of professional sporting events*. www.everycrsreport.com/reports/R43096.html

Daniels, T. (2018, November 15). *MLB, Fox announce new TV rights contract worth reported $5.1 billion*. Bleacher Report. https://bleacherreport.com/articles/2806206-mlb-fox-announce-new-tv-rights-contract-through-2028-season

Danjou, A. (2018, April 2). *Why a proper GIF strategy is so important for sport on social media*. Digital Sport. https://digitalsport.co/gifs-sport-clubs-leagues

Deloitte. (2020). *Perspectives: A whole new ball game: Navigating digital transformation in the sports industry: Why technological changes are important in sports*. https://www2.deloitte.com/us/en/pages/technology-media-and-telecommunications/articles/digital-transformation-and-future-changes-in-sports-industry.html

Dixon, E. (2020, April 7). *IMG in discussions over withheld FA Cup rights payments*. SportsPro. www.sportspromedia.com/news/img-fa-cup-tv-rights-payments-coronavirus

Egan, S. (2020). *Television broadcasting in the U.S.* Ibis World. https://my.ibisworld.com/us/en/industry/51512/industry-performance#current-performance.es/digital-transformation-and-future-changes-in-sports-industry.html

FSGA. (n.d.). *Industry demographics*. https://thefsga.org/industry-demographics/

Faris, S. (2019, April 15). *What is a typical CPM?* Chron. https://smallbusiness.chron.com/typical-cpm-74763.html

Federal Communications Commission (FCC). (2020). *Digital radio.* www.fcc.gov/consumers/guides/digital-radio

Gallegos, M. (2020, February 18). *A's games to be streamed exclusively on TuneIn.* www.mlb.com/news/a-s-games-to-be-streamed-exclusively-on-tunein

Ganekar, B. (2018, February 2). Impact of digital media on sports. *Webbutterjam.* www.webbutterjam.com/blog/impact-of-digital-media-on-sports/

Gough, C. (2020, June 2). *Total broadcasting rights in sports industry by league 2019/20.*

Statista. www.statista.com/statistics/1120170/broadcasting-rights-sports-by-league/

Grand View Research. (2020, June). *Video streaming market worth $184.2 billion by 2027, CAGR 20.4%.* www.grandviewresearch.com/press-release/global-video-streaming-market

Green, A. (2020). *All you need to know about streaming in 4K HDR.* Moshi. https://support.moshi.com/hc/en-us/articles/360040344212-All-you-need-to-know-about-streaming-in-4K-HDR

Guttman, A. (2019, May 13). *Social media marketing penetration in the U.S. 2013-2019.* Statista. www.statista.com/statistics/203513/usage-trands-of-social-media-platforms-in-marketing

Harris, N. (2020). *The impact of social and digital media on sport.* La Trobe University. www.latrobe.edu.au/nest/the-impact-of-social-and-digital-media-on-sport/

Harvey, S. (n.d.). *The history of sports talk radio stations: An entertainment home run.* Radio Fidelity. https://radiofidelity.com/history-of-sports-broadcasting/

Hendricks, M., & Vockrodt, S. (2019, February 6). Kansas City Chiefs' tax returns provide rare look inside the business of pro football. *Kansas City Star.* www.kansascity.com/sports/nfl/kansas-city-chiefs/article225279155.html

Hurwitz, D. (1984). Broadcast ratings: The missing dimension. *Critical Studies in Mass Communication, 1*(2), 205-15.

IAB. (2018, June 13). *Live video streaming: A global perspective.* www.iab.com/insights/live-video-streaming-2018/

IMG. (2020). *Rights and distribution.* http://img.com/expertise/media/

Johnson, D. (2019, June 30). *NBA TV will be integrating VR and AR for new content.* Trend Hunter. www.trendhunter.com/trends/mixed-reality-broadcasts

Kariyawasam, K., & Tsai, M. (2017). Copyright and live streaming of sports broadcasting. *International Review of Law, Computers & Technology, 31*(3), 265-288.

Kerr-Dineen, L. (2017, April 5). Why Augusta National turns down hundreds of millions of dollars every year. *USA Today.* https://ftw.usatoday.com/2017/04/augusta-national-the-masters-2017-television-rights-cbs-tournament

Kidd, R. (2020, March 10). How an AI-automated sports broadcaster is shaking up soccer streaming. *Forbes.* www.forbes.com/sites/robertkidd/2020/03/10/how-an-ai-automated-sports-broadcaster-is-shaking-up-soccer-streaming/#6d003a2222a6

Krings, E. (2020, June 9). AVOD: The definitive guide to ad-based video on demand. *Dacast.* https://www.dacast.com/blog/avod/

Lane, T. (n.d.). *How to measure the reach of TV advertising.* Chron. https://smallbusiness.chron.com/measure-reach-tv-advertising-66414.html

Lange, D. (2020, November 26). *Live sport viewership in the United States 2020.* Statista. www.statista.com/statistics/1127341/live-sport-viewership/

Laukonnen, J. (2020, February 5). *HD radio vs. satellite radio: Which is better?* Lifewire. www.lifewire.com/hd-radio-vs-satellite-radio-534594

Leblebici, H., Salancik, G.R., Copay, A., & King, T. (1991). Institutional change and the transformation of interorganizational fields: An organizational history of the US radio broadcasting industry. *Administrative Science Quarterly*, 333-363.

Leboff, G. (2017). *Digital selling: How to use social media and the web to generate leads and sell more.* Kogan Press.

Lee, S., Seo, W.J., & Green, B.C. (2013). Understanding why people play fantasy sport: Development of the Fantasy Sport Motivation Inventory (FanSMI). *European Sport Management Quarterly, 13*(2), 166-199.

Lippmann, S. (2007). The institutional context of industry consolidation: Radio broadcasting in the United States, 1920–1934. *Social Forces, 86*(2), 467-495.

Maestas, A.J. (n.d.). *Negotiating college sports multimedia rights deals.* AthleticDirectorU. https://athleticdirectoru.com/articles/negotiating-college-sports-multimedia-rights-deals/

McAdams, M. (2019, April 18). *What is OTT?— understanding the modern media streaming landscape.* Tapjoy. www.tapjoy.com/resources/what-is-ott/

MediaRadar. (2020, March 16). Are traditional TV ads really getting shorter? *MediaRadar Blog.* https://mediaradar.com/blog/are-traditional-tv-ads-really-getting-shorter-2019-numbers/

Miles, S. (2019, March 25). *Metered, hard, or dynamic? Choosing the best paywall strategy.* WebPublisher Pro. webpublisherpro.com/metered-hard-or-dynamic-choosing-the-best-paywall-strategy/

Mullin, B., Hardy, S., & Sutton., W. (2007). (2014). *Sport marketing* (3rd ed.) Human Kinetics.

Nielsen (2020). TV ratings. www.nielsen.com/us/en/solutions/measurement/television/

Octoparse. (n.d.). *Easy web scraping for anyone.* www.octoparse.com

Ourand, J. (2019, November 27). *Octagon hired to sell multimedia rights for minor league baseball.* New York Business Journal. www.bizjournals. com/newyork/news/2019/11/27/octagon-sells-minor-league-baseball-media-rights. html

Ozanian, M. (2019, March 8). New York Yankees buy back YES Network for $3.47 billion. *Forbes.* www.forbes.com/sites/mike-ozanian/2019/03/08/new-york-yankees-buy-back-yes-network-for-3-47-billion/#4de7018483c

Pallota, F. (2014, December 3). *As new viewing options gain ground, live television viewership is slipping.* CNN. https://money.cnn. com/2014/12/03/media/nielsen-trends-total-audience-measurement/index.html?-section=money_media

Pavlova, I. (2017). How to boost your business by using cartoon characters in marketing. *Graphic Mama.* https://graphicmama.com/blog/cartoon-characters-in-marketing/

Peters, J. (2017, March 4). Media Buying 101— reach & frequency. *Media Buying and Inbound Marketing Blog.* www.mediamanagement servicesinc.com/blog-media-buying-social-media-consultant/bid/108082/media-buying-101-reach-frequency

Petersen, L. (2019, March 5). *Advantages & disadvantages of radio advertising.* Chron. https://smallbusiness.chron.com/advantages-amp-disadvantages-radio-advertising-40629.html

Phala, N. (2019, September 26). *Three reasons why you should use live reads for radio advertising.* www.mediaupdate.co.za/marketing/147174/three-reasons-why-you-should-use-live-reads-for-radio-advertising

PwC. (2019). *At the gate and beyond: Outlook for the sports market in North America through 2023.* www.pwc.com/us/en/industries/tmt/library/sports-outlook-north-america.html

Quicksprout. (2018, March 14). *How to optimize your mobile websites for google searches.* www.quicksprout.com/mobile-seo

Quinn, A. (2019, February 14). *How live streams became the mainstream for sports fan.* MarketScale. marketscale.com/industries/sports-and-entertainment/live-streaming-sports

Radio Advertising Bureau. (2020). *Radio facts.* www.rab.com/whyradio.cfm#facts

Santana, D. (2019, December 3). *Augmented reality has its limits, but is here to stay in sports.* Front Office Sports. https://frontofficesports.com/augmented-reality-growth-in-sports/

Sarokin, D. (2017, April 19). *Difference between ratings & shares.* Pocket Sense. https://pocketsense.com/difference-between-ratings-shares-1518.html

Sehl, K. (2019, April 10). All the different ways to calculate engagement rate. *Hootsuite.* https://blog.hootsuite.com/calculate-engagement-rate/

Shultz, R. (2021, February 8). *"Sports Illustrated" seeks new revenue stream through metered paywall.* Media Post. www.mediapost.com/publications/article/360363/sports-illustrated-seeks-new-revenue-stream-thro.html

Sherman. (2019, August 19). 12 social media KPIs you should not ignore. *Lyfe Marketing.* www.lyfemarketing.com/blog/social-media-kpis/

Shilina, S. (2019, November 1). *Video streaming and blockchain: A tale of two paradigm shifts.* Medium. https://medium.com/paradigm-fund/video-streaming-and-blockchain-a-tale-of-two-paradigm-shifts-867664c899a0

Small, N. (2020, October 12). How to create a live streaming pay per view sports broadcast. *Dacast.* www.dacast.com/blog/how-to-create-live-stream-pay-per-view-sports/

Social SEO. (2018, October 4). *Understanding cost per acquisition.* www.socialseo.com/understanding-cost-per-acquisition

Sports Business Media. (2019, February 7). *United States market report, 2019.* https://media.sportbusiness.com/2019/02/the-us-market-report-2019/

Staples, A. (2016, March 28). The future of college sports media rights: How will deals evolve with the landscape? Punt, pass & pork: How will college sports media rights deals evolve with the changing landscape? *Sports Illustrated.* www.si.com/college/2016/03/28/how-are-college-sports-media-rights-deal-evolving

Steinberg, B. (2020, September 9). "Thursday Night Football," "Monday Night Football" could change networks in TV's NFL rights scramble. *Variety.* https://variety.com/2020/tv/news/thursday-night-football-monday-night-football-tv-networks-nfl-rights-1234763560/

Sterne, J. (2010). *Social media metrics: How to measure and optimize your marketing investment.* Wiley.

Stoll, J. (2021, February 1). *Most watched primetime telecasts in the U.S. 2020.* Statista. www.statista.com/statistics/320934/prime-time-programming-viewers-usa/

Swayne, L.E., & Dodds, M. (Eds.). (2011). *Encyclopedia of sports management and marketing.* Sage.

Tainsky, S. (2010). Television broadcast demand for National Football League contests. *Journal of Sports Economics, 11*(6), 629-640.

Tainsky, S., Xu, J., & Zhou, Y. (2014). Qualifying the game uncertainty effect: A game-level analysis of NFL postseason broadcast ratings. *Journal of Sports Economics, 15*(3), 219-236.

Tokareva. (2018, February 2). The difference between virtual reality, augmented reality and mixed reality. *Forbes.* www.forbes.com/sites/quora/2018/02/02/the-difference-between-virtual-reality-augmented-reality-and-mixed-reality/#4c554702d07c

Tsiotsou, R.H. (2011). Broadcast rights. In L.E. Swayne & G.J. Golson (Eds.), *Encyclopedia of Sports Management and Marketing.* Sage.

TV by the numbers. (2009, March 21). *Top 100 rated TV shows of all time.* Archived from the original on March 19, 2020. https://web.archive.org/web/20200319070342/https://tvbythenumbers.zap2it.com/reference/top-100-rated-tv-shows-of-all-time/

USC Annenberg Center for the Digital Future. (2016, May 19). *USC Annenberg/ThePostGame: GenZ and younger Millennial sports fans are driving fundamental changes in programming, platforms and purchasing.* www.prnewswire.com/news-releases/usc-annenbergthepostgame-genz-and-younger-millennial-sports-fans-are-driving-fundamental-changes-in-programming-platforms-and-purchasing-300271545.html

Vargiu, E., & Urru, M. (2013). Exploiting web scraping in a collaborative filtering-based approach to web advertising. *Artificial Intelligence Research, 2*(1), 44-54.

Wilbert (2020, August 14). OTT video monetization: The ultimate guide for professional broadcasters. *Dacast.* www.dacast.com/blog/over-the-top-video/

World Intellectual Property Organization (WIPO). (2020). *Broadcasting & media rights in sport.* www.wipo.int/ip-sport/en/broadcasting.html

Wulf, S. (1989, November 15). Puppies, poison ivy and a dashing duke: The first *SI* was a far cry—in both form and substance—from the one we now publish, but we have always been guided by Henry Luce's promise to cover sport with heart and humor. *Sports Illustrated.* https://vault.si.com/vault/1989/11/15/puppies-poison-ivy-and-a-dashing-duke

Chapter 5

Activate Annual 2018/19: Sports marketing, sponsorship, activation & partnership leverage. 2018 overview. https://strivesponsorship.com/wp-content/uploads/2018/12/Activative-Annual-2018-2019.pdf

Allen, S. (2014, March 20). *A brief history of jersey sponsorship.* Mental Floss. www.mentalfloss.com/article/27776/brief-history-jersey-sponsorship

Arthur, D., Scott, D., & Woods, T. (1997). A conceptual model of the corporate decision-making process of sport sponsorship acquisition. *Journal of Sport Management, 11*(3), 223-233.

Association of National Advertisers. (2017). *Use of social media and advanced technologies for sponsorship.* www.talkingnewmedia.com/wp-content/uploads/2017/09/Social.Media_.Sponsoships.Final_.pdf

Bergkvist, L., & Zhou, K. (2016). Celebrity endorsements: A literature review and research agenda. *International Journal of Advertising, 35*(4), 642-663.

Bower (2019, March 27). *How to write a corporate sponsorship proposal.* Nonprofit Information. Retrieved from https://nonprofitinformation.com/how-to-write-a-corporate-sponsorship-proposal/.

Brown, M. (2017, August 25). *Exclusive infographics show NFL, MLB, NBA and NHL sponsorship growth over last decade.* Forbes. www.forbes.com/sites/maurybrown/2017/08/25/exclusive-inforgraphics-show-nfl-mlb-nba-and-nhl-sponsorship-growth-over-last-decade/#5041df63d907

Brown, M. (2018, August 14). *NASCAR sponsorships show that while a few have left, blue-chips are still drawn to racing.* Forbes. www.forbes.com/sites/maurybrown/2018/08/14/nascar-sponsorships-show-that-while-few-have-left-blue-chips-still-drawn-to-racing/#5edaae5c5bc9

Brown, N. (2020, February 1). *13 minutes, $13 million: The logistics of pulling off a Super Bowl halftime show.* Reuters. www.reuters.com/article/us-football-nfl-superbowl-halftime/13-minutes-13-million-the-logistics-of-pulling-off-a-super-bowl-halftime-show-idUSKBN1ZV3TC.

Burton, T. (2008). *Naming rights: Legacy gifts and corporate money.* Wiley.

Chanavat, N., Desbordes, M., & Chadwick, S. (n.d.). *Routledge handbook of sports marketing.* Routledge.

Charge (n.d.) *Evaluating your sponsorships: The basics.* https://chargesponsorship.com/evaluating-your-sponsorships-the-basics/

Cornwell, T.B. (2017). Soliciting sport sponsorship. In T. Bradbury and I. O'Boyle (Eds.). *Understanding sport management: International perspectives* (pp. 172-183).

Cornwell, T.B. (2021, January 2). *Sponsorship expectations for 2021.* www.linkedin.com/pulse/sponsorship-expectations-2021-t-bettina-cornwell?trk=read_related_article-card_title

Cornwell, B.T., Pruitt, S.W., & Clark, J.M. (2004). *The official paper on official sponsorships: The impact of major league sports official sponsorship announcements on the stock prices of sponsoring firms.* Working paper.

Cutler, M. (2020, May 18). *Sponsorship spend to fall $17.2bn; financial services by $5.7bn.* Two Circles. https://twocircles.com/gb-en/articles/projections-sponsorship-spend-to-fall-17-2bn

Dees, W., Walsh, P., McEvoy, C.D., McKelvey, S., Mullin, B.J., Hardy, S., & Sutton, W.A. (2021). *Sport marketing* (5th ed.). Human Kinetics.

DeGaris, L. (n.d.). *Sports marketing: A practical Approach.* Routledge.

DeGaris, L., Dodds, M., & Reese, J.T. (2015). A data-driven approach to sponsorship planning: Multiple sponsorship selection. In *Routledge handbook of sports marketing* (pp. 96-107). Routledge.

DeGaris, L., West, C., & Dodds, M. (2009). Leveraging and activating NASCAR sponsorships with NASCAR-linked sales promotions. *Journal of Sponsorship, 3*(1), 88-97.

Demir, R., & Söderman, S. (2015). Strategic sponsoring in professional sport: A review and conceptualization, *European Sport Management Quarterly, 15*(3), 271-300.

Drape, J., Chen, D.W., & Hsu, T. (n.d.). 2020: The year in sport when everybody lost. *New York Times.* www.nytimes.com/interactive/2020/12/13/sports/coronavirus-sports-economy-wisconsin.html

Duke Sports Information. (2008, August 22). *Duke & Nike enter into 10-year sponsorship for all varsity athletics teams.* https://goduke.com/news/2008/8/22/1566867.aspx

Eddy, T., & Cork, B.C. (2016). Sponsor- and team-related intentions of salient market segments in a naming-rights sponsorship scenario. *Journal of Issues in Intercollegiate Athletics, 9*, 142-162.

Elmira Enforcers. (n.d.). *Official site of the Elmira Enforcers pro hockey team.* www.elmiraenforcers.com/home

emarketer. (2020, June). *Total media ad spending, US, 2020-2024.* https://forecasts-na1.emarketer.com/584b26021403070290f93a2f/59652cd00da12c0424803964

Enoch, B.J. (2020, February 13). Opendorse. *Social media in sports marketing.* https://opendorse.com/blog/social-media-in-sports-marketing/

Forbes. (2020). *The business of baseball.* www.forbes.com/mlb-valuations/list/

Fullerton, S. (2007). *Sports marketing.* McGraw-Hill Irwin.

Funk, D.C., & James, J. (2001). The psychological continuum model: A conceptual framework for understanding an individual's psychological connection to sport. *Sport Management Review, 4*(2), 119-150.

George Mason University. (2020). *In-game promotions—basketball.* George Mason Athletics. https://gomason.com/news/2012/1/13/205360471.aspx

Greenberg, K. (2010, February 9). *Return on objective key in sports partnerships.* Media Post. www.mediapost.com/publications/article/122132/return-on-objective-key-in-sports-partnerships.html

Hoehn, T. (2006). 21 Governance and governing bodies in sport. In W. Andreff and S. Syzmanski (Eds.), *Handbook on the economics of sport* (pp.227-240). Elgar.

Hookit. (2018, December 6). *How technology companies are leveraging sports sponsorships to grow their brand.* www.hookit.com/insights/how-technology-companies-are-leveraging-sports-sponsorships-to-grow-their-brand/

Hoye, R., & Cuskelly, G. (2007). *Sport governance.* Routledge.

Hsu, C.L., & Liao, Y.C. (2014). Exploring the linkages between perceived information accessibility and microblog stickiness: The moderating role of a sense of community. *Information & Management, 51*(7), 833-844.

Hu, L., Min, Q., Han, S., & Liu, Z. (2020). Understanding followers' stickiness to digital influencers: The effect of psychological responses. *International Journal of Information Management, 54*, 102169.

IEG. (January 16, 2018). *Global sponsorship spending from 2007 to 2018 (in billion U.S. dollars)*

[Graph]. Statista. www.statista.com/statistics/196864/global-sponsorship-spending-since-2007/

IEG. (March 19, 2018). *Sponsorship spending on college athletics to total $1.24 billion in 2017/18 season.* www.sponsorship.com/Report/2018/03/19/Sponsorship-Spending-On-College-Athletics-To-Total.aspx

IEG. (December 18, 2017). *Year-end recap: Sponsorship spending on the four major U.S. pro sports leagues.* www.sponsorship.com/Report/2017/12/18/Year-End-Recap--Sponsorship-Spending-On-The-Four-M.aspx

IEG. (2017). *IEG's guide to sponsorship: Everything you need to know about sports, arts, event, entertainment, and cause marketing.* www.sponsorship.com/ieg/files/59/59ada496-cd2c-4ac2-9382-060d86fcbdc4.pdf

International Olympic Committee. (2020). The Olympic Partner Programme. www.olympic.org/partners

Irwin, R., Sutton, W., & McCarthy, L. (2008). *Sport promotion & sales management.* Human Kinetics.

Jensen, J.A. (2017). Assessing corporate demand for sponsorship: marketing costs in the financial services industry. *Marketing Letters, 28*(2), 281-291.

Jensen, J.A., & Cornwell, T.B. (2018). Assessing the dissolution of horizontal marketing relationships: The case of corporate sponsorship of sport. *Journal of Business Research, 124*(2).

King, B. (2020, July 20). *2020 betting: MLB doubling down.* Sports Business Journal. www.sportsbusinessdaily.com/Journal/Issues/2020/07/20/Gambling/MLB.aspx?hl=sponsorship+&sc=0

Koerber, C. (2019, April 18). *The fast-changing world of sports sponsorship.* Medium. https://medium.com/@14ideas/the-fast-changing-world-of-sports-sponsorships-7bffdd9bd7ff

Koronios, K., Dimitropoulos, P., Travlos, A., Douvis, I., & Ratten, V. (2020). Online technologies and sports: A new era for sponsorship. *Journal of High Technology Management Research*, 100373.

Kte'pi, B. (2011). Pass-through rights. In L.E. Swayne & M. Dodds (Eds.), *Encyclopedia of sports management and marketing* (Vol. 1, pp. 1087-1088). Sage. https://doi.org/10.4135/9781412994156.n542

Lynde, T. (2007). *Sponsorships 101.* Lynde & Associates.

Maestas, A.J. (2009). Guide to sponsorship return on investment. *Journal of Sponsorship, 3*(1).

Mickle. (2013). *7-Eleven joins action sports tour thanks to Mountain Dew pass-through rights. Sports Business Journal.* www.sportsbusinessdaily.com/Journal/Issues/2013/06/03/Marketing-and-Sponsorship/Mountain-Dew.aspx

Miller, R.K. (2020). Part II: Sports market segments: Chapter 7: Advertising & sponsorships: 7.1 Market assessment. (2020). In *Sports Marketing* (pp. 61-62).

Miller, R.K., & Washington, K. (2018). Advertising & sponsorships. In *Sports marketing 2018-2019* (18th ed.). Richard K. Miller & Associates.

Miller, R.K., & Washington, K. (2020). *Sports Marketing 2019-2020.* Richard K. Miller & Associates.

Mullin, B.J., Hardy, S., & Sutton, W.A. (2014). *Sport marketing* (4th ed.). Human Kinetics.

National Federation of State High School Associations. (2020). *Marketing opportunities.* www.nfhs.org/marketing.aspx

Olejniczak, M., & Aicher, T., (2012). Leveraging sponsorships to meet organizational marketing objectives: A case study of a consumer packaged good product with the Super Bowl. *Case Studies in Sport Management, 1*(10), 1-9.

O'Reilly, N., & Huybers, T. (2015). Servicing in sponsorship: A best-worst scaling empirical analysis. *Journal of Sport Management, 29*(2), 155-169.

Quester, P.G., & Thompson, B. (2001). Advertising and promotion leverage on arts sponsorship effectiveness (1998 Adelaide Festival of the Arts). *Journal of Advertising Research, 4,* 33–47.

Rose-Redwood, R., Vuolteenaho, J., Young, C., & Light, D. (2019). Naming rights, place branding, and the tumultuous cultural landscapes of neoliberal urbanism. *Urban Geography*, 40(6), 747–761.

Shin, H., Lee, H., & Perdue, R.R. (2018). The congruity effects of commercial brand sponsorship in a regional event. *Tourism Management*, 67, 168-179.

Skildum-Reid, K., & Grey, A. (2014). *The sponsorship seeker's toolkit* (4th ed.). McGraw-Hill.

Sports Business Journal. (2018, April 30). *Top naming-rights deals*. www.sportsbusinessdaily.com/Journal/Issues/2018/04/30/Marketing-and-Sponsorship/Naming-rights-deals.aspx

Steinbach, P. (2005, April). Signs of the times. *Athletic Business*. www.athleticbusiness.com/marketing/signs-of-the-times.html

Tafà, R. (2017, September 21). *What is a title sponsor?* RTR Sports Marketing. https://rtrsports.co.uk/blog/what-is-a-title-sponsor

Texas State University. (2020). *Contests & in-game promotions*. https://txstatebobcats.com/sports/2010/7/29/GEN_0729103931.aspx

Thieringer, J. (2018, October 15). *Sports sponsorship: These are the marketing trends 2019*. ISPO. www.ispo.com/en/trends/sports-sponsorship-marketing-trends-2019

Thornburg, R.H. (2002). Stadium naming rights: An assessment of the contract and trademark issues inherent to both professional and collegiate stadiums. *Virginia Sports and Entertainment Law Journal*, 2, 328.

Trex, E. (2008, November 27). *A brief history of stadium naming rights*. Mental Floss. www.mentalfloss.com/article/20239/brief-history-stadium-naming-rights

Waterhouse, D. (2017, June 21). 4 stats that prove the power of emotions in sports advertising. https://unruly.co/blog/article/2017/06/21/stats-emotions-sports-advertising

Weeks, C.S., Cornwell, T.B. , & Drennan, J.C. (2008). Leveraging sponsorships on the Inet: Activation, congruence and articulation. *Psychology & Marketing*, 25(7), 637-654.

Wolfe, T. (2018, June 14). Monongalia County Ballpark announces new features for Black Bears season. *Times West Virginian*. www.timeswv.com/sports/monongalia-county-ballpark-announces-new-features-for-black-bears-season/article_e4fa3eb4-6f88-11e8-b90a-cbf6b43da60a.html

Chapter 6

Alexanderson, P. (2017, October 26). *How to qualify for and retain your status as a private operating foundation*. www.mossadams.com/articles/2017/october/how-to-become-a-private-operating-foundation

American Heart Association. (2020). *NFL Play 60*. www.heart.org/en/professional/educator/nfl-play-60

Babiak, K., & Wolfe, R. (2006). More than just a game? Corporate social responsibility and Super Bowl XL. *Sport Marketing Quarterly*, 15(4).

Benjamin, A. (2017, March 10). *NHL Green focuses on environmental sustainability: League believes clean water, cold temperatures vital to growth of hockey*. NHL. www.nhl.com/news/nhl-celebrating-green-week/c-287597386

Bethmann, S., von Schnurbein, G., & Studer, S. (2014). Governance systems of grant-making foundations. *Voluntary Sector Review*, 5(1), 75-95.

Carlson, M., & O'Neal-McElrath, T. (2008). *Winning grants: Step by step* (3rd ed.). Jossey-Bass.

Ciconte, B.L., & Jacob, J. (2001). *Fundraising basics: A complete guide* (2nd ed.). Aspen.

Coffman, S. (2001, August 1). Just what are public charities and private foundations, anyway? *GuideStar Blog*. https://trust.guidestar.org/just-what-are-public-charities-and-private-foundations-anyway

Community Foundation of Harrisonburg and Rockingham County. (2020). *Summary report on 2019 Great Community Give*. www.tcfhr.org/nonprofit-organizations/nonprofit-organizations-services/greatcommunity give/great-community-give-2020-summary-report/

Corporate Grants Guide. (2020). *Corporate funding: Rolling deadlines.* https://corporategrantsguide.com/grants-by-deadline/corporate-funding-rolling-deadlines/

Council on Foundations. (n.d.). *Independent foundations.* www.cof.org/foundation-type/independent-foundations

Dean, D.H. (2002). Associating the corporation with a charitable event through sponsorship: Measuring the effects on corporate community relations. *Journal of Advertising, 31*(4), 77-87.

Dick's Sporting Goods. (n.d.) *Donations & sponsorships.* www.dickssportinggoods.com/s/community-programs

Di Mento, M. (2021, February 9, 2021). The philanthropy 50. *Chronicle of Philanthropy.* www.philanthropy.com/article/the-philanthropy-50/#id=browse_2019

Di Mento, M., & Lindsay, D. (2018, February 6). America's superrich made near-record contributions to charity in 2017. *Chronicle of Philanthropy.* www.philanthropy.com/article/America-s-Superrich-Made/242446

Djaballah, M. (2016). Corporate social responsibility in sport. In Wagner, R., Storm, R.K., & Nielsen, K. (Eds.). *When sport meets business: Capabilities, challenges, critiques.* Sage.

Donate a dollar at the register? Checkout charity is big business for nonprofits. (2013, September 1). *Tampa Bay Times.* www.tampabay.com/news/business/retail/donate-a-dollar-at-the-register-checkout-charity-is-big-business-for/2139533/

Double the Donation. (2020). *Corporate matching gift programs: Understanding the basics.* https://doublethedonation.com/tips/corporate-matching-gift-programs/

Engelhardt-Cronk, K. (n.d.). *What US nonprofits need to know about in-kind contributions.* Mission Box. www.missionbox.com/article/56/what-us-nonprofits-need-to-know-about-in-kind-contributions

English, B. (2012, August 7). Sox 1st in standings—in charity: Over 10 years, team raised $52m, tops in baseball. *Boston Globe.* http://archive.boston.com/news/local/massachusetts/articles/2012/08/07/red_sox_charity_exceeds_50_million_in_10_years/

Foundation Center. (n.d.a). *What is a community foundation? Where can I learn more about them?* https://learning.candid.org/resources/knowledge-base/community-foundations/

Foundation Center. (n.d.b). *What should be included in a letter of inquiry?* https://learning.candid.org/resources/knowledge-base/letters-of-inquiry/

Fidelity Charitable. (n.d.). *What is a private family foundation?* www.fidelitycharitable.org/guidance/philanthropy/private-family-foundation.html

Foundation Group. (n.d.) *What is a private foundation?* https://www.501c3.org/what-is-a-private-foundation/

Foundation Source. (2020). *Starting a foundation.* https://foundationsource.com/start-a-foundation/

Foundation Source. (2019). *Adding a corporate foundation to your company's philanthropy.* www.foundationsource.com/corporate-philanthropy/

Fritz, J. (2019, May 23). *Checkout charity campaigns succeed because most consumers say yes.* The Balance Small Business. www.thebalancesmb.com/checkout-charity-capaign-best-practices-2501825

Fundraiser Help. (2020). *Corporate grants for nonprofit list.* www.fundraiserhelp.com/corporate-grants-source-list.htm

Gannon, J. (2020, May 14). COVID-19 pandemic spurs companies to donate and boost their brands. *Pittsburgh Post-Gazette.* www.post-gazette.com/business/career-workplace/2020/05/14/COVID-19-companiesdonations-brand-reputation-Pittsburgh/stories/202005060064

Gates, B., & Gates, M. (2020, February 10). Why we swing for the fences. *Gates Notes.* www.gatesnotes.com/2020-Annual-Letter

Giving USA. (2019, June 18). *Giving USA 2019: Americans gave $427.71 billion to charity in 2018 amid complex year for charitable giving.* https://givingusa.org/giving-usa-2019-americans-gave-427-71-billion-to-charity-in-2018-amid-complex-year-for-charitable-giving/

Goldman, T. (2020, August 26). *"Tired of the killings": Pro athletes refuse to play to protest racial injustice.* National Public Radio. www.npr.org/sections/live-updates-protests-for-racial-justice/2020/08/26/906496470/a-dramatic-day-in-pro-sports-where-the-action-was-no-action

Good Sports. (2017). *Annual report.* www.goodsports.org/assets/GSP-137_2018_Annual Report_r5-2.pdf

Hessekiel, D. (2019, July 17). Charity checkout remains strong, even in a changing retail landscape. *Forbes.* www.forbes.com/sites/davidhessekiel/2019/07/17/charity-checkout-remains-strong-even-in-a-changing-retail-landscape

Hikind, L. (2020, September 22). *How to write a LOI=letter of intent, letter of interest, letter of inquiry.* Grant Watch. www.grantwatch.com/blog/ask-libby/how-to-write-a-loiletter-of-intent-letter-of-interest-letter-of-inquiry-2/

Horoszowski, M. (2015, May 5). 7 research-backed reasons your business needs to be socially responsible. *Moving Worlds.* https://blog.movingworlds.org/7-research-backed-reasons-your-business-needs-to-be-socially-responsible/

Internal Revenue Service. (n.d.). *Private operating foundation.* www.irs.gov/charities-non-profits/private-foundations/private-operating-foundations

Kain, R. (2019, November 25). *Corporate philanthropy: A comprehensive guide for nonprofits.* Re: Charity. https://recharity.ca/corporate-philanthropy/

King, B. (2019, September 9). Feeling the impact: Social responsibility in sports. *Sports Business Journal.* www.sportsbusinessdaily.com/Journal/Issues/2019/09/09/In-Depth/Social-responsibility.aspx

Koenig, M. (2019, January 16). *7 tips on asking for donations—it's intimidating, we get it.* Nonprofit Hub. https://nonprofithub.org/fundraising/7-tips-on-asking-for-donations-its-intimidating-we-get-it/

Leat, D. (2016). Private and family foundations. In Jung, T., Phillips, S.D., & Harrow, J. (Eds.). *The Routledge companion to philanthropy.* ProQuest Ebook Central. https://ebookcentral.proquest.com

Lee, M.C. (2019). *An examination of the organizational structure and practices of grant-making foundations and their impact on grassroots organizations* (Order No. 28091060). ProQuest Dissertations & Theses Global. (2439597765). https://search.proquest.com/docview/2439597765?accountid=11667

Manos. (2020, April 17). How 2020 is ushering in a new era for corporate social responsibility. *Forbes.* www.forbes.com/sites/theyec/2020/04/17/how-2020-is-ushering-in-a-new-era-for-corporate-social-responsibility/#34fdc88b76f8

Mazany, T., & Perry, D.C. (2014). *Here for good. Community foundations and the challenges of the 21st century.* ProQuest Ebook Central. https://ebookcentral.proquest.com

Milwaukee Bucks. (2020). *Our mission.* www.nba.com/bucks/community

National Center for Family Philanthropy. (n.d.). *What is a private operating foundation, and should we consider using this option?* www.ncfp.org/knowledge/what-is-a-private-operating-foundation/

National Council of Nonprofits. (n.d.). *State associations collaborating with community foundations.* www.councilofnonprofits.org/state-associations-collaborating-community-foundations

Morand, T. (2020, January 20). Everything your organization needs to know about in-kind donations. *Wild Apricot.* www.wildapricot.com/blog/in-kind-donations

NFL. (n.d.). *Crucial Catch.* www.nfl.com/causes/crucial-catch/

North Carolina State University. (2020). *Zero waste Wolfpack*. https://gopack.com/sports/2016/4/27/sustainability-update.aspx

Northwestern University Foundation Relations. (2020). *Letter of inquiry*. www.northwestern.edu/foundationrelations/grant-writing-guide/proposal-resources/letter-of-inquiry/

Norton, L. (2013). *How to be a global nonprofit: Legal and practical guidance for international activities* (1st ed.). Wiley.

O'Leary, B., Olsen-Phillips, P., & Daniels, A. (2018). Drug, tech, and financial-services companies top list of corporate donors. *Chronicle of Philanthropy*. www.philanthropy.com/interactives/corporate-giving#id=table_2017

Parent, B. (2018). Social responsibility in sports: Current landscape. *Journal of Legal Aspects of Sport, 28*, 126.

Preston, C. (2016, June 22). The 20 most generous companies of the Fortune 500. *Fortune*. https://fortune.com/2016/06/22/fortune-500-most-charitable-companies/

Rader, D. (2020, April 8). *Mark Cuban will continue paying his employees amid coronavirus-induced economic downturn*. https://www.forbes.com/sites/doylerader/2020/04/08/mark-cuban-continue-paying-employees-coronavirus-economic-downturn/?sh=497878e84ea0

Scanlan, E.A. (1997). *Corporate and foundation fundraising: A complete guide from the inside*. Aspen.

Schiavo, A. (2019, December 27). *Why employers should consider adding volunteer time off benefits*. ebn. www.benefitnews.com/news/why-employers-should-consider-adding-volunteer-time-off-benefits

Schleifer, T. (2020, March 31). *Tech giants should give away their money instead of their products*. Vox. www.vox.com/recode/2020/3/31/21197652/coronavirus-philanthrophy-donations-google-cisc

Sheth, H., & Babiak, K.M. (2010). Beyond the game: Perceptions and practices of corporate social responsibility in the professional sport industry. *Journal of Business Ethics, 91*(3), 433-450.

Smith, S.R. (2016). Hybridity and philanthropy: Implications for policy and practice. In Jung, T., Phillips, S.D., & Harrow, J. (Eds.). *The Routledge companion to philanthropy*. ProQuest Ebook Central. https://ebookcentral.proquest.com

Starbucks. (2020). *The Starbucks Foundation*. Retrieved from www.starbucks.com/responsibility/community/starbucks-foundation

Starbucks Foundation. (2020, May 28). The Starbucks Foundation: Supporting community response and resilience during COVID-19. https://stories.starbucks.com/press/2020/the-starbucks-foundation-supporting-community-response-and-resilience-during-covid-19/

Stetson University College of Law. (n.d.). *Pro bono service*. www.stetson.edu/law/pro-bono/

Tampa Bay Lightning. (n.d.). *In-kind donations*. www.nhl.com/lightning/community/in-kind-donations

Tiny Pulse. (2020). *10 foolproof ideas for your company volunteer day*. www.tinypulse.com/blog/10-foolproof-ideas-for-your-company-volunteer-day

Valor. (2017, September 20). *What is a corporate foundation?* www.valorcsr.com/blog/what-is-a-corporate-foundation

Weinger, A. (2012, June 14). Five types of corporate giving. *101 Fundraising*. https://101fundraising.org/2012/06/five-types-of-corporate-giving

Weinger, A. (2015, June 5). *It's never too late for donors to submit matching gift requests*. Double the Donation. https://doublethedonation.com/tips/tag/matching-gift-deadlines/

Weinger, A. (2016, November 3). *7 outstanding corporate matching gift programs*. America's Charities. www.charities.org/news/blog/7-outstanding-corporate-matching-gift-programs

Weinger, (2017, November 10). 10 Corporate philanthropy programs nonprofits should know. *GuideStar Blog.* https://trust.guidestar.org/10-corporate-philanthropy-programs-nonprofits-should-know

Weinger, A. (2019, November 20). *Corporate charitable giving programs for nonprofits.* The Balance Small Business. www.thebalancesmb.com/corporate-programs-help-nonprofits-2502073

Wex. (2020). *Corporate grants.* www.wexinc.com/about/community/grants

Wimbish, J. (2020, March 28). *Coronavirus: How sports teams, players are helping arena, stadium workers affected by COVID-19 outbreak.* CBS Sports. www.cbssports.com/nba/news/coronavirus-how-sports-teams-players-are-helping-arena-stadium-workers-affected-by-covid-19-outbreak/

Wisconsin Philanthropy Network. (2020). *Independent foundations.* https://wiphilanthropy.org/learn/for-grantmakers/independent-foundations/

Chapter 7

AGN. (2017). *Understanding the difference between annual fund and annual giving.* https://agnresources.com/2017/11/26/difference-annual-fund-annual-giving/

Alborough, L. (2017). Lost in translation: A sociological study of the role of fundraisers in mediating gift giving in non-profit organisations. *International Journal of Nonprofit and Voluntary Sector Marketing, 22*(4), e1602.

American Cancer Society (n.d.). *Relay for life.* www.cancer.org/involved/fundraise/relay-for-life.html

Aspen Institute. (2019). *State of play: Trends and developments in youth sport.* https://assets.aspeninstitute.org/content/uploads/2019/10/2019_SOP_National_Final.pdf

Beem, M.J., & Sargeant, A. (2017). Planned giving. In A. Sargeant & Y. Sargeant (Eds.), *Fundraising principles and practice* (2nd ed.). Wiley.

Brown University. (n.d.). *Sports foundation donor recognition.* https://alumni-friends.brown.edu/giving/donor-recognition/sports-foundation-donor-recognition

Bucy, M. (2013). The costs of the pay-to-play model in high school athletics. *University of Maryland Law Journal of Race, Religion, Gender and Class, 13*(2),278-302 (2013). https://digitalcommons.law.umaryland.edu/cgi/viewcontent.cgi?article=1227&context=rrgc

Buff Club. (2020). *Why annual giving?* https://cubuffclub.com/sports/2018/8/1/annual-giving.aspx

Charlotte-Mecklenburg Schools. (n.d.). *Athletic participation fee.* www.cmsathleticzone.com/page/show/539973-athletic-participation-fee

Cherico, C. (2014, March 25). Challenges and benefits of nonprofit event fundraising. *GuideStar.* https://trust.guidestar.org/blog/2014/03/25/challenges-and-benefits-of-nonprofit-event-fundraising/

Chung, E. (2020). How to create a strategic fundraising plan that you'll actually stick to. *Classy.* www.classy.org/blog/create-strategic-fundraising-plan-youll-actually-stick/

Ciconte, B.L., & Jacob, J.G. (2001). *Fundraising basics: A complete guide* (2nd ed.). Aspen.

DeWitt, B. (2011). *The nonprofit development companion: A workbook for fundraising success.* Wiley.

Dollhopf-Brown, E. (2013). *Prospect research fundamentals: Proven methods to help charities realize more major gifts* (4th ed.). Stevenson.

Donor Search. (2020). *Timeline for a capital campaign.* www.donorsearch.net/capital-campaign-timeline/

Double the Donation. (2020). *Nonprofit fundraising statistics* [updated for 2020]. https://doublethedonation.com/tips/matching-grant-resources/nonprofit-fundraising-statistics/

Dunlop, D.R. (2000, May). *Fundraising for the largest gift of a lifetime: From inspiring the commitment to receiving the gift.* Presented at the Council for Advancement and Support of Education (CASE) Conference, Charleston, SC.

Eisenstein, A. (2020). *How big is a major gift?* www.amyeisenstein.com/how-big-is-a-major-gift/

Eisenstein, A. (n.d.). *27 ways to cultivate donors and build deep, lasting relationships.* www.amyeisenstein.com/27-ways-cultivate-donors/

Elchlepp, K. (2019a). *GEICO ESPN High School Football Showcase returns, highlighting top talent and teams in the country* [Press release]. ESPN. https://espnpressroom.com/us/press-releases/2019/08/geico-espn-high-school-football-showcase-returns-highlighting-top-talent-teams-in-the-country/

Elchlepp, K. (2019b). *ESPN continues focus on top high school basketball teams and recruits, expands schedule to offer more games than ever* [Press release]. ESPN. https://espnpressroom.com/us/press-releases/2019/11/espn-continues-focus-on-top-high-school-basketball-teams-and-recruits-expands-schedule-to-offer-more-games-than-ever/

Elliot, N. (2010, November 17). *Best practices for fundraising in Division II.* NAADD. https://nacda.com/news/2010/11/17/best_practices_for_fundraising_in_division_ii.aspx

FastModel Sports. (2019, November 6). *Notre Dame Athletics partners with FastModel Sports to enhance engagement and fundraising via personalized messaging.* https://fastmodelsports.com/pages/notre-dame-athletics-partners-with-fastmodel-sports-to-enhance-engagement-and-fundraising-via-personalized-messaging

Fogal, R.E. (2005). Designing and managing the fundraising program. In *The Jossey-Bass handbook of nonprofit leadership and management* (pp. 419-435).

Frakes, J. (2018, September 27). St. Xavier-Trinity rivalry has had attendance dip in the past decade. *Courier Journal.* www.courier-journal.com/story/sports/preps/kentucky/2018/09/27/st-xavier-trinity-football-rival-game-attendance-drop/1446896002/

Fredricks, L. (2001). *Developing major gifts.* Aspen.

FreeWill. (2020). *2019 FreeWill planned giving report.* www.freewill.com/planned-giving-report-2019

Fritz, J. (2020, June 28). *What are the nonprofit fund types? Definition & examples of nonprofit fund types.* www.thebalancesmb.com/restricted-unrestricted-nonprofit-funds-2502167

Gattle, K. (2011). Personal solicitation. In Tempel, E., Seiler, T., Aldrich, E., Rosso, H., & Maehara, P. (Eds), *Achieving excellence in fundraising* (3rd ed.). Jossey-Bass.

Georgia Tech Athletics. (2020, September 25). *Ken and Trish Byers endow tennis head coach positions.* https://ramblinwreck.com/ken-and-trish-byers-endow-tennis-head-coach-positions/

Giving USA. (2019). *The annual report on philanthropy for the year 2018.*

GoFan. (2020). *Your complete high school ticketing solution.* www.huddletickets.com/gofan

Golden, J. (2015, July 29). *Youth sports: Kids' athletics are in danger.* CNBC. www.cnbc.com/2015/07/29/youth-sports-kids-athletics-are-in-danger.html

Greenwell, T.C., Danzey-Bussell, L.A., & Shonk, D.J. (2020). *Managing sport events* (2nd ed.). Human Kinetics.

Hansen, L. (2017, January 12). *Fundraising myths busted.* The Prowler. www.theprowler.org/1794/features/fundraising-myths-busted/?print=true

Hanson, A.R. (2019). *Examining the fundraising challenges faced and strategies utilized in the NCAA Division II athletics environment.* Master's thesis. University of Illinois at Urbana-Champaign.

Heyman, D.R., & Brenner, L. (2016). *Fundraising 101: A practical guide to easy to implement ideas & tips from industry experts.* Wiley.

Hobson, W., & Rich, S. (2015, December 23). Colleges spend fortunes on lavish athletics facilities. *Chicago Tribune.* www.chicagotribune.com/sports/college/ct-athletic-facilities-expenses-20151222-story.html

Jarvis, A. (2018, June 18). Six ways to punch up your fundraising appeals. *GuideStar Blog.*

https://trust.guidestar.org/six-ways-to-punch-up-your-fundraising-appeals

Jeff Brooks Fundraising. (2020). *About Jeff Brooks*. www.jeff-brooks.com/about

Karkaria, U. (2017, February 9). *Ticketing startup Huddle scores $11 million*. Atlanta Business Chronicle. www.bizjournals.com/atlanta/news/2017/02/09/ticketing-startup-huddle-scores-11-million.html

Kelley, D. (2012). *Sports fundraising dynamic methods for schools, universities and youth sport organizations*. Routledge.

Kirkpatrick, N. (2018). Collegiate = Corporate? The business and financial backgrounds of athletic directors at the "Power 5" conference level. *Journal of Issues in Intercollegiate Athletics*, *11*, 98-114. www.csri-jiia.org/wp-content/uploads/2018/05/RA_2018_05.pdf

Kolenich, E. (2018, October). *HS athletics depends on money made at football games*. Athletic Business. www.athleticbusiness.com/high school/span-class-c1-hs-athletics-depends-on-money-made-at-football-games-span.html

Lamb, D. (2011, January 19). Quest for the perfect proposal rating formula. *sgEngage*. https://npengage.com/nonprofit-fundraising/quest-for-the-perfect-prospect-rating-formula/

Lee, M. (2018, February 5). *Pay-to-play sports both help and harm athletics programs*. Scot Scoop. https://scotscoop.com/pay-to-play-sports-both-help-and-harm-athletics-programs/

Marcus, P. (2013). Using donations as intended. In Pettey, J. (Ed.), *Nonprofit fundraising strategy: A guide to ethical decision making and regulation for nonprofit organizations* (2nd ed.). Wiley.

McRay, G. (2017, March 23). *Are you misappropriating your nonprofit's funds?* www.501c3.org/misappropriating-nonprofit-funds/

Metrick, L.A. (2005). Successful strategies for effective stewardship. *New Directions for Philanthropic Fundraising*, *2005*(49), 29-41.

Myran-Schutte, L. (2020, February 12). *Booster clubs for high school athletics. One vs. multiple*. NFHS. www.nfhs.org/articles/booster-clubs-for-high-school-athletics-one-vs-multiple/

National Association of Collegiate Directors of Athletics. (2020, June 9). *Q&A with NAADD fundraiser of the year, Tim Folan*. https://nacda.com/news/2020/6/9/q-a-with-naadd-fundraiser-of-the-year-tim-folan.aspx

Nichols, J.E. (2004). Repositioning fundraising in the 21st century. *International Journal of Nonprofit and Voluntary Sector Marketing, 9*(2), 163-170.

North Carolina High School Athletic Association. (2020). *Planned giving opportunities*. www.nchsaa.org/planned-giving-opportunities

O'Connor, T. (2019). Our 14th annual state of the industry report. *SportEvents Magazine*, March, 18-30.

Pierce, D., & Petersen, J. (2011). Corporate sponsorship activation analysis in interscholastic athletics. *Journal of Sponsorship, 4*(3).

Polivy, D. (2014). *Donor cultivation and the donor lifecycle map: A new framework for fundraising*. Wiley.

Prince, R.A. (2016, July 5). What is planned giving? *Forbes*. www.forbes.com/sites/russalanprince/2016/07/05/what-is-planned-giving/#666b3f3d48a9

Ridpath, D. Pay-play panel sheds even more light on problems with American sport for development. *Forbes*. www.forbes.com/sites/bdavidridpath/2016/03/16/pay-to-play-panel-sheds-even-more-light-on-problems-with-american-sport-development/#5f0779dc2151

Rohrbach, J. (2013). Ethical considerations of making the ask. In J. Pettey (Ed.), *Nonprofit fundraising strategy: A guide to ethical decision making and regulation for nonprofit organizations* (2nd ed.). Wiley.

Rosen, R. (2012). *Money for the cause: A complete guide to event fundraising* (1st ed.). Texas A&M University Press.

Sargeant, A. (2013). Donor retention: What do we know & what can we do about it? *Nonprofit Quarterly*, Summer, 12-23.

Sargeant, A. (2017). The development of a profession. In A. Sargeant & Y. Sargeant (Eds.), *Fundraising principles and practice* (2nd ed.). Wiley.

Sargeant, A., & Shang, J. (2017). *Fundraising principles and practice* (2nd ed.). Wiley.

Schmidt, A. (2020, March 14). *Girl Scout Cookies and what to know about the $800M business.* Fox Business. www.foxbusiness.com/lifestyle/girl-scout-cookies-what-to-know

Sherman, M. (2012). *Corporate sponsorship in high school athletics* [Undergraduate honors thesis, University of Arkansas]. http://scholarworks.uark.edu/mktguht/15

Special Olympics. (2020). *Gifts that cost you nothing now.* https://solegacygiving.org/make-an-impact/gifts-that-cost-you-nothing-now/

Stevenson, S. (2009). *Fundraising for beginners: Essential procedures for getting a fundraising program up and running.* Stevenson.

Tedesco, B. (2020). *Identifying major gift prospects: 7 traits to investigate.* https://benefactorgroup.com/major-gifts-7-traits/

Tempel, E., Seiler, T., Aldrich, E., Rosso, H., & Maehara, P. (2011). *Achieving excellence in fundraising* (3rd ed.). Jossey-Bass.

UCATS. (2019, February 1). *Athletics annual thank-a-thon reaches more than 5,000 UCATS donors.* https://gobearcats.com/news/2019/2/1/athletics-annual-thank-a-thon-reaches-more-than-5-000-ucats-donors

United States Olympic and Paralympic Committee. (2018, November 1). *USOPF gift acceptance policy* [PDF document].

University of Arizona Wildcat Club. (2020). *Capital campaign.* https://arizonawildcats.com/sports/2017/10/26/capital-campaign.aspx

Virginia Tech Athletics. (2017, December 18). *Virginia Tech receives $15.2M gift to construct Student-Athlete Performance Center.* https://vtnews.vt.edu/articles/2017/12/athlete-performance-center.html

Walled Lake Consolidated Schools. (n.d.). *Pay-to-participate.* https://wlcsd.org/athletics/pay-to-participate

Waltasi, J. (2020, October 14). *Baseball alum Schmidt donates to practice field project.* San Jose State Spartans. https://sjsuspartans.com/news/2020/10/14/baseball-alum-schmidt-donates-to-practice-field-project.aspx

Weinstein, S. (2004). *Capital campaigns from the ground up: How nonprofits can have the buildings of their dreams.* Wiley.

Weinstein, S. (2009). *The complete guide to fundraising management* (3rd ed). Wiley.

Weinstein, S., & Barden, P. (2017). *The complete guide to fundraising management.* Wiley.

Women's Sports Foundation. (2020). *Planned giving.* www.womenssportsfoundation.org/support-us/planned-giving/

Young, R. (2020, April 25). *NFL raised more than $100 million during draft for coronavirus relief.* Yahoo Sports. https://sports.yahoo.com/nfl-draft-raised-100-million-for-coronavirus-covid-19-pandemic-relief-roger-goodell-235016606.html

Chapter 8

Appalachian Regional Commission. (2020). *How to write a grant proposal.* www.arc.gov/funding/HowtoWriteaGrantProposal.asp

BarCharts. (2012). *Grant writing.* ProQuest Ebook Central. https://ebookcentral.proquest.com/lib/jmu/detail.action?docID=4877136

Browning, B.A. (2014). *Grant writing for dummies.* https://ebookcentral.proquest.com

Bryant, M. (2019, January 28). *Difference between Gantt charts & PERT charts.* https://smallbusiness.chron.com/difference-between-gantt-charts-pert-charts-43848.html

Clinton, A. (2018, August 16). *About grant writer success rates.* Funding for Good. https://fundingforgood.org/about-grant-writer-sucess-rates/

Congressional Research Service. (2019a, May). *Federal grants to state and local governments: A historical perspective on contemporary issues.* https://fas.org/sgp/crs/misc/R40638.pdf

Congressional Research Service. (2019b, August 28). *How to develop and write a grant proposal.* https://fas.org/sgp/crs/misc/RL32159.pdf

Dartmouth College's Office of Sponsored Projects. (2020). *Budget.* www.dartmouth.edu/osp/resources/manual/pre-award/budget.html

Ford, R.D. (2019, September 26). *Why professional athletes are ditching charitable foundations*. Rosecrete Wealth Management. www.rosecrete.com/blog/why-professional-athletes-are-ditching-charitable-foundations

Foundation Center. (n.d.). *Foundation directory online*. https://fconline.foundationcenter.org/

Fritz, J. (2019, May 30). *How to write the evaluation section of your grant proposal*. The Balance Small Business. www.thebalancesmb.com/grant-proposal-evaluation-section-2501961

Gebicz, M. (n.d.). *What is a Gantt chart?* Atlassian. www.atlassian.com/agile/project-management/gantt-chart

Gitlin, L.N., & Lyons, K.J. (2014). *Successful grant writing: Strategies for health and human service professionals* (4th ed.). Springer.

Gottschalk, B. (2019). *Get money for your classroom: Easy grant writing ideas that work*. Routledge.

Hall, M.S. (1988). *Getting funded: A complete guide to proposal writing*. Continuing Education Publications, Portland State University.

Hall, M.S., & Howlett, S. (2003). *Getting funded: The complete guide to writing grant proposals*. Continuing Education Press.

Harvest Foundation. (2020). *Needs statement toolkit*. www.theharvestfoundation.org/library/documents/Needs%20Statement%20Toolkit.pdf

Iron Dukes. (2019, June 26). *Our mission*. www.irondukes.net/ViewArticle.dbml?ATCLID=211387391&DB_OEM_ID=5100&DB_OEM_ID=5100

Johnson, K. (n.d.). *How to present a solid sustainability plan for your grant proposal*. Nonprofit Academy. https://thenonprofitacademy.com/how-to-present-a-solid-sustainability-plan-for-your-grant-proposal/

Justin J. Watt Foundation. (n.d.). *Request funds*. http://jjwfoundation.org/request-funds/

Kachinske, T., & Kachinske, K. (2010). *90 days to success in grant writing*. Cengage Learning.

Larsen, B.A., Pekmezi, D., Marquez, B., Benitez, T.J., & Marcus, B.H. (2013). Physical activity in Latinas: Social and environmental influences. *Women's Health (London, England), 9*(2), 201-210. https://doi.org/10.2217/whe.13.9

LeBron James Family Foundation. (n.d.). *We are family*. www.lebronjamesfamilyfoundation.org/

Licklider, M.M. (2012). *Grant seeking in higher education: Strategies and tools for college faculty*. Wiley.

Lussier, R.N., & Kimball, D.C. (2014). *Applied sport management skills* (2nd ed.). Human Kinetics.

National Philanthropic Trust. (2020). *Charitable giving statistics*. www.nptrust.org/philanthropic-resources/charitable-giving-statistics/

Neilson, K.R. (2018, February 8). How to write the sustainability section of a grant. *Elevate*. www.elevatedeffect.com/writing-editing/sustainability-tips/

New, C.C., & Quick, J.A. (2003). *How to write a grant proposal*. Wiley.

Newman, C. (2017, March 20). 9 things to look for when evaluating a grant proposal. *sgEngage*. https://npengage.com/foundations/9-things-to-look-for-when-evaluating-a-grant-proposal/

Ohio Literacy Resource Center. (2018, August 6). *Advice and information on grant-seeking and proposal writing*. http://literacy.kent.edu/Oasis/grants/publicVSprivate.html

O'Neal-McElrath, T., & Carlson, M. (2013). *Winning grants step by step: The complete workbook for planning, developing, and writing successful proposals* (4th ed.). Jossey-Bass.

Orlich, D.C., & Shrope, N.R. (2013). *Developing a winning grant proposal*. Routledge.

Pain, E. (2020, April 6). A day in the life of a grant writer. *Science*. www.sciencemag.org/careers/2020/04/day-life-grant-writer

Porter, R. (2009). Can we talk? Contacting grant program officers. *Research Management Review, 17*(1), 10-17.

Price, S. (2018, December 18). *Is your organization eligible to receive grant funding?* Smart Grant Writing. https://medium.com/smartgrantwriting/is-your-organization-eligible-to-receive-grant-funding-2ce8bcf4da72

Redbooth Team. (2018, March 13). A super-quick guide to PERT, critical path, and all the other ways to manage a project: Finding the best way to manage your next project. *Redbooth*. https://redbooth.com/blog/quick-guide-pert-critical-path-project-management

Romeo-Velilla, M., Benyon, C., McGee, C., Murphy, R., Parnell, D., Hilland, T., Stratton, G., & Foweather, L. (2014). Formative evaluation of a UK community-based sports intervention to prevent smoking among children and young people: SmokeFree Sports. *Journal of Sport for Development*, 2(3).

Stanford Medicine. (2020). *The science and art of grant writing*. https://med.stanford.edu/researchofficebulletin/topics/The-science-and-art-of-grant-writing.html

Stephen & Ayesha Curry's Eat. Learn. Play Foundation. (n.d.). *Our mission*. https://eatlearnplay.org/

Stombaugh, H. (2013, December 4). *Making sense of summative evaluation: Three tips for making those "strings" work in your favor*. Charity Channel. https://charitychannel.com/summative-evaluation/

Thompson, W. (2018, March 28). The 4 most important things for grant writers to get right. *GuideStar*. https://trust.guidestar.org/the-4-most-important-things-for-grant-writers-to-get-right

Tufts Office of Research Development. (2018). *Guide for investigators: Contacting the program officer*. https://viceprovost.tufts.edu/RAD/proposal/contacting-the-program-officer/

Chapter 9

Arnett, L. (2015, August 15). Technology drives concessions. *FoodService Director*. www.foodservicedirector.com/operations/technology-drives-concessions

BBC. (n.d.). *The rise of the bleisure traveler*. www.bbc.com/storyworks/capital/bleisure-bound/bleisure-travel-trend

Belson, K. (2018, January 25). In Atlanta, concessions prices go down and revenue goes up. *New York Times*. www.nytimes.com/2018/01/25/sports/football/nfl-concessions.html

Boisen, M., Terlouw, K., Groote, P., & Couwenberg, O. (2018). Reframing place promotion, place marketing, and place branding-moving beyond conceptual confusion. *Cities*, 80, 4-11.

Borelli, M. (2020, September 6). *MLB rumors: Playoff teams may quarantine in hotels during final week of regular season*. Dodger Blue. https://dodgerblue.com/mlb-rumors-playoff-teams-quarantine-hotels-final-week-regular-season/2020/09/06/

CLC. (2020). *About us*. https://clc.com/home/about/

Cronin, B. (2019, August 8). *Major League Baseball tops list of sports licensors with $5.5bn in sales*. Sport Business. www.sportbusiness.com/news/major-league-baseball-tops-list-of-sports-licensors-with-5-5bn-in-sales/

CVent (n.d.). *Planner sourcing guide: Chapter 6: Negotiating with hotels*. www.cvent.com/en/resource/planner-sourcing-guide-chapter-6

DeGaris, L. (2015). *Sports marketing*. Routledge.

Elkins, K. (2020, July 8). *The NBA is set to resume its season at Disney World this month—here's what life for players will look like on campus*. CNBC. www.cnbc.com/2020/07/08/what-life-for-nba-players-will-look-like-at-disney-world.html

Evans, P. (2019, January 4). *Executives outline predictions for arena and stadium concessions in 2019*. Front Office Sports. https://frontofficesports.com/2019-concessions-predictions/

Fagan, R. (2020, September 28). *MLB playoff bubbles, explained: A complete guide to the rules, locations, schedule & more for 2020 postseason*. Sporting News. www.sportingnews.com/us/mlb/news/mlb-playoff-bubble-rules-locations-schedule/ekz3xsh112t6143x-muq2bd92v

Fullerton, S. (2007). *Sports marketing*. McGraw-Hill Irwin.

Gammon, S., & Robinson, T. 2003. Sport and tourism: A conceptual framework. *Journal of Sport Tourism*, 8, 21-26.

Gibson, H. (2003). Sport tourism: An introduction to the special issue. *Journal of Sport Management*, 17, 205-213.

Gargis, J. (2019, February 11). Braves official: More attractions to power the Battery in coming months, years. *Marietta Daily Journal*. www.mdjonline.com/news/braves-official-more-attractions-to-power-the-battery-in-coming-months-years/article_55463ca4-2e42-11e9-a6ac-db828192398d.html

Georgia Tech. (2020). *The Collegiate Licensing Company (CLC)*. https://licensing.gatech.edu/licensing/clc

Greenwell, T.C., Danzey-Bussell, L.A., & Shonk, D.J. (2019). *Managing sport events*. Human Kinetics.

Hamstra, M. (2020, January 2). *Sports stadiums tap tech to enhance fans' experience and fight lure of in-home media*. U.S. Chamber of Commerce. www.uschamber.com/co/good-company/launch-pad/sports-stadiums-attract-fans-with-new-tech

Hiner, J. (2020, June). *Sporting goods stores in the U.S.* IBIS World. https://my.ibisworld.com/us/en/industry/45111/about#additional-resources

Hotel & Leisure Advisors. (2018, April). *Waterparks: What's on deck in 2018?* https://hladvisors.com/waterparks-whats-on-deck-in-2018

IBIS World. (2021, February). *Golf courses & country clubs in the U.S.* www.ibisworld.com/industry-statistics/employment/golf-courses-country-clubs-united-states/

Indiana Sports Corp. (n.d.) *History*. www.indianasportscorp.org/about/history

Jayachandran, S., Kaufman, P., Kumar, V., & Hewett, K. (2013). Brand licensing: What drives royalty rates? *Journal of Marketing*, 77(5), 108-122.

Judah, A. (n.d.). *Innovative approaches for managing sports room blocks*. National Travel Systems. https://usagym.org/pages/memclub/biztips/articles/2017_0509.pdf

Kosel, O. (2020, June 17). *Breaking down the NBA health and safety manual and how it potentially affects the New Orleans Pelicans: A look at what awaits Zion and the rest of the gang*. SB Nation. www.thebirdwrites.com/2020/6/17/21294608/nba-health-safety-coronavirus-orlando-bubble-new-orleans-pelicans-zion-williamson-lonzo-ingram-jj

Kotler, P., & Gertner, D. (2002). Country as brand, product, and beyond: A place marketing and brand management perspective. *Journal of Brand Management*, 9(4-5), 249-261.

Krishnan, K., Mann, R., Seitzman, N., & Wittkam, N. (2020, June 10). *Hospitality and COVID-19: How long until 'no vacancy' for US hotels?* McKinsey & Company. www.mckinsey.com/industries/travel-logistics-and-transport-infrastructure/our-insights/hospitality-and-covid-19-how-long-until-no-vacancy-for-us-hotels#

Licensing International. (2020a). *What is licensing?* https://licensinginternational.org/what-is-licensing/

Licensing International. (2020b, June 24). *Nominees for best licensed brand—sports and collegiate*. https://licensinginternational.org/news/nominees-for-best-licensed-brand-sports-and-collegiate/

Lightspeed. (2018, September 3). *Your retail dictionary: 72 industry terms every small retailer should know*. www.shopkeep.com/blog/retail-dictionary#step-1

Linton, I. (n.d.). *Main goals & objectives in sports licensing*. Chron. https://smallbusiness.chron.com/main-goals-objectives-sports-licensing-37071.html

Lock, S. (2018, July 31). *Resorts in the U.S.—statistics & facts*. Statista. www.statista.com/topics/2109/resorts-in-the-us/

Lucie, C. (2018, July 26). *Braves unveil details for tallest building in Cobb County*. WSB-TV. www.wsbtv.com/news/local/cobb-county/atlanta-braves-to-unveil-details-for-tallest-building-in-cobb-county/798913118/

Luthor, J. (2019, June 17). *How to get permission to sell licensed team apparel*. Chron. https://smallbusiness.chron.com/permission-sell-licensed-team-apparel-25790.html

Maestas, A.J., & Belzer, J. (n.d.). *How much is NIL worth to student athletes?* AthleticDirectorU. https://athleticdirectoru.com/articles/how-much-is-nil-really-worth-to-student-athletes/

Martins, M. (2015). The tourist imagery, the destination image and the brand image. *Journal of Tourism and Hospitality Management, 3*(2), 1-14.

Medworth, W. (2020, June 16). *Every Disney hotel NBA teams are staying in, explained. The players will be staying in the best of the best Disney has to offer.* SB Nation. www.sbnation.com/nba/2020/6/16/21293622/disney-hotels-nba-players-florida

Middleton, S. (2020a, January 24). *New sports facilities opening to host a variety of events.* SportsEvents Media Group. https://sportseventsmagazine.com/2020/01/24/business-is-booming/

Middleton, S. (2020b, March). Our 15th annual state of the industry report: The tip of the iceberg: Undercurrents exist but the tourism market continues on a positive note. *SportsEvent Magazine.* https://lsc-pagepro.mydigitalpublication.com/publication/frame.php?i=652839&p=1&pn=&ver=html5

Miller, R.K., & Washington, K. (2019). *Travel & tourism market research handbook 2019-2020* (16th ed.). Miller Associates.

Minard, M. (2020, July 18). *Breweries in sports arenas.* Stadium Journey. https://stadium-journey.com/news/sports-arena-breweries

Mitchell, M., Clark, N., & Damonte, T. (2018, December 20). The migration of business strategies from the hospitality industry to athletics marketing. *Sport Journal.* https://thesportjournal.org/article/the-migration-of-business-strategies-from-the-hospitality-industry-to-athletics-marketing/#post/0

Mullin, B., Hardy, S., & Sutton, W. (2000). *Sport marketing (2nd ed.). Human Kinetics.*

Mullin, B., Hardy, S., & Sutton, W. (2007). *Sport marketing* (3rd ed.). Human Kinetics.

MyTVChain. (2020, January 11). *Sports licensing revenue is on the rise.* https://medium.com/@MyTVchain/sports-licensing-revenue-is-on-the-rise-e1661ff6237a

NCAA. (2020a). *Questions and answers on name, image and likeness.* www.ncaa.org/questions-and-answers-name-image-and-likeness

NCAA (2020b). *NCAA licensing program FAQs.* www.ncaa.org/championships/marketing/ncaa-licensing-program-faqs#four

Nightengale, B. (2020, September 15). MLB postseason will feature neutral-site "bubbles" and World Series in Texas—along with strict protocols. *USA Today.* www.usatoday.com/story/sports/mlb/columnist/bob-nightengale/2020/09/15/mlb-union-reach-postseason-deal-features-neutral-site-bubbles/5803119002/

Olson, R. (2015, May 21). Minnesota Vikings creating technology infrastructure to match scope of big stadium: New smartphone apps aim to engage fans from tailgate to touchdown. *Star Tribune.* www.startribune.com/minnesota-vikings-creating-technology-infrastructure-to-match-the-scope-of-big-stadium/304012281/

Patel, A. *How to manage attrition: Smart strategies for filling your room block and mitigating the damages if you fall short.* Meetings & Conventions. www.meetings-conventions.com/Resources/Meeting-Planning/How-to-Manage-Attrition

PwC. (2019) *At the gate and beyond: Outlook for the sports market in North America through 2023.* www.pwc.com/us/en/industries/tmt/library/sports-outlook-north-america.html

Rainisto, S.K. (2003). *Success factors of place marketing: A study of place marketing practices in Northern Europe and the United States.* Helsinki University of Technology.

Reau, J. (2020, September 1). Landmark study by Sports ETA on U.S. sports-related travel shows $45.1 billion impact, provides benchmark for post-Covid-19 impact measurement. *Sports ETA.* www.sportseta.org/blog/2020/09/01/landmark-study-by-sports-eta-on-us-sports-related-travel-shows-451-billion-impact-provides-benchmark-for-post-covid-19-impact-measurement

Sanctis, M. (2017, August 25). $44M youth sports complex might go in at Upper Valley Mall site. *Springfield News-Sun.* www.springfieldnewssun.com/business/economy/44m-youth-sports-complex-might-upper-valley-mall-site/wGeedw6YwrorGJmUp57ATL/

SBR Net. (2020). *Apparel.* www.sportsmarketanalytics.com/Subjects/Products/Apparel.aspx

Schumacher, D.G. (2015, October). *Report on the sport tourism industry.* National Association of Sports Commissions. www.sportseta.org/Portals/sportscommissions/Documents/About/NASC%20Sport%20Tourism%20Industry%20Report.pdf/

Shonk, D.J. (2006). *Perceptions of service quality, satisfaction and the intent to return among tourists attending a sporting event* [Unpublished doctoral dissertation]. Ohio State University.

Sincavage, D. (n.d.). *6 major differences between B2C vs B2B sales strategies.* Tenfold. www.tenfold.com/6-major-differences-between-b2c-vs-b2b-sales-strategies

Slingland, J. How much is a suite at the Super Bowl: Luxury suite pricing over the years. *TickPick Blog.* www.tickpick.com/blog/how-much-is-a-suite-at-the-super-bowl/

Smith, D.P. (2018, May). How sports stadiums are upping their foodservice game. *QSR.* www.qsrmagazine.com/menu-innovations/how-sports-stadiums-are-upping-their-foodservice-game

SportsEvents Media Group. (2019, August 5). *Youth sports boom continues; SFA says millions in facilities yet to be developed.* https://sportseventsmediagroup.com/youth-sports-boom-continues-sfa-says-millions-in-facilities-yet-to-be-developed/

Statista. (2020, September 22). *Global licensed sports merchandise market size from 2018 to 2023.* www.statista.com/statistics/940849/licensed-sports-merchandise-market-value-worldwide/

Statista. (2021, February 19). *Sporting goods industry—statistics & facts.* www.statista.com/topics/961/sporting-goods

Steinbach, P. (2008, July). *Concessions contracts capitalizing on brand loyalty.* Athletic Business. www.athleticbusiness.com/Marketing/concessions-contracts-capitalizing-on-consumers-brand-loyalty.html

Tep, R. (2013, May 15). America's best stadium food. *Travel+Leisure.* www.travelandleisure.com/trip-ideas/americas-best-stadium-food?

Texas Rangers. (2017). *Loews Hotels & Co, the Cordish Companies and Texas Rangers break ground on new $150 million flagship 'Live! by Loews' Hotel in Arlington, TX.* MLB. www.mlb.com/rangers/ballpark/globe-life-field/news/loews-cordish-and-texas-rangers-break-ground-on-live-by-loews

Tredwell, J. (2011, May 18). *Best stadium luxury box food spreads slideshow.* www.thedailymeal.com/best-stadium-luxury-box-food-spreads-slideshow

Tucci, L. (1997, April 13). *Golf pros at larger clubs make up to $500,000 a year.*

St. Louis Business Journal. www.bizjournals.com/stlouis/stories/1997/04/14/focus2.html

UNWTO. (2021, January 28). *2020: Worst year in tourism history with 1 billion fewer international arrivals.* www.unwto.org/taxonomy/term/347

US Travel Association. (2019, Jul 11). *The impact of sports on the travel industry.* www.ustravel.org/system/files/media_root/document/2019_Sports-Travel_07.11.19.pdf

Warnaby, G., & Medway, D. (2013). What about the 'place' in place marketing? *Marketing theory, 13*(3), 345-363.

Wesfield, Z. (2018, November 19). How short-term property managers can take advantage of the growing "bleisure" trend. *Guesty.* www.guesty.com/blog/grow-your-business-using-bleisure-trend/

World Bank. (2018). *What are public-private partnerships?* https://ppp.worldbank.org/public-private-partnership/overview/what-are-public-private-partnerships

Zenker, S., & Braun, E. (2017, August 17). Questioning a "one size fits all" city brand. *Journal of Place Management and Development, 10*(3).

Chapter 10

Bieler, D. (2015, January 7). Hawks hook up fans with Tinder "Swipe Right Night." *Washington Post*. www.washingtonpost.com/news/early-lead/wp/2015/01/07/hawks-hook-up-fans-with-tinder-swipe-right-night/

Google, (2018). *3 ways online video is changing what it means to be a sports fan.* www.thinkwithgoogle.com/marketing-strategies/video/sports-fans-video-insights/

Leone, C. (2018). *Which social media sites get the most engagement?* WebStrategiesinc.com. www.webstrategiesinc.com/blog/which-social-media-sites-get-the-most-engagement

Mullin, B.J., Hardy, S., & Sutton, W. (2014). *Sport marketing* (4th ed.). Human Kinetics.

Nielsen. (2020, February 3). *Super Bowl LIV draws nearly 100 million TV viewers, 44 million social media interactions* [Press release]. www.nielsen.com/us/en/press-releases/2020/super-bowl-liv-draws-nearly-100-million-tv-viewers-44-million-social-media-interactions

Norris, D.T. (2007). Sales communications in a mobile world: Using the latest technology and retaining the personal touch. *Business Communication Quarterly, 70*(4), 492-498.

Rubenking, B., & Lewis, N. (2016). The sweet spot: An examination of second-screen sports viewing. *International Journal of Sport Communication, 9*(4), 424-439.

Shareablee. (2021, March 9). *U.S. media 100 index February 2021.* www.shareablee.com/product/powerrankings/u-s-media-100-index-february-2021

Smith, L.R., Pegoraro, A., & Cruikshank, S.A. (2019). Tweet, retweet, favorite: The impact of Twitter use on enjoyment and sports viewing. *Journal of Broadcasting & Electronic Media, 63*(1), 94-110.

Vanheems, R., Kelly, J.S., & Stevenson, K. (2013). The Internet, the modern death of a salesman: Multichannel retailing's impact on the salesperson's role. *International Journal of Integrated Marketing Communications, 5*(2). 91-100.

Wright, C. (2017). Are beauty bloggers more influential than traditional industry experts? *Journal of Promotional Communications, 5*(3), 303-322.

Chapter 11

Abbott, T. (n.d.). *8 popular types of leadership styles.* www.socoselling.com/8-popular-types-of-leadership-styles/

Adams, J.S. (1963). Towards an understanding of inequity. *Journal of Abnormal and Social Psychology, 67*(5), 422-436.

Alderfer, C.P. (1967). Convergent and discriminant validation of satisfaction and desire measures by interviews and questionnaires. *Journal of Applied Psychology, 51*(6), 509-520.

Alderfer, C.P. (1969) An empirical test of a new theory of human needs. *Organizational Behaviour and Human Performance, 4,* 142-175.

Avolio, B.J., Luthans, F., & Walumba, F.O. (2004). *Authentic leadership: Theory building for veritable sustained performance.* Working paper. Gallup Leadership Institute, University of Nebraska-Lincoln.

Aydın, S., & Kaya, N. (2016). Authentic leadership in sales management: The effects on salespeople's task related outcomes. *Business and Economic Research, 6*(2), 133-155.

Burns, J.M. (1978). *Leadership.* HarperCollins.

Chelladurai, P. (2017). *Managing organizations for sport and physical activity: A systems perspective.* Routledge.

Cherry, K. (2020, July 2). *Pros and cons of laissez-faire leadership.* www.verywellmind.com/what-is-laissez-faire-leadership-2795316.

Chung, D.J. (2015). How to really motivate salespeople: New research challenges conventional wisdom about the best ways to pay your team. *Harvard Business Review.* https://hbr.org/2015/04/how-to-really-motivate-salespeople.

Churchill, G.A., Ford, N.M., & Walker, O.C. (1993). *Sales force management.* Irwin.

De Hoogh, A.H., Greer, L.L., & Den Hartog, D.N. (2015). Diabolical dictators or capable commanders? An investigation of the differential effects of autocratic leadership on team performance. *Leadership Quarterly, 26*(5), 687-701.

Domingues, J., Vieira, V.A., & Agnihotri, R. (2017). The interactive effects of goal orientation and leadership style on sales performance. *Marketing Letters, 28*(4), 637-649.

Dyczkowska, J., & Dyczkowski, T. (2018). Democratic or autocratic leadership style? Participative management and its links to rewarding strategies and job satisfaction in SMEs. *Athens Journal of Business and Economics, 4*(2), 193-218.

Feigon, J. (2013). *Smart sales manager* (1st ed.). AMACOM.

Gaille, B. (2018, March 15). *10 advantages and disadvantages of democratic leadership style.* https://brandongaille.com/19-advantages-and-disadvantages-of-democratic-leadership-style/

Greenleaf, R.K. (2002). *Servant leadership: A journey into the nature of legitimate power and greatness* (25th anniversary ed.). Paulist Press.

Ingram, T.N., LaForge, R.W., Locander, W.B., MacKenzie, S.B., & Podsakoff, P.M. (2005). New directions in sales leadership research. *Journal of Personal Selling & Sales Management, 25*(2), 137-154.

Insight Squared. (n.d.). Why sales managers need CRM. *Insight Squared Blog.* www.insightsquared.com/blog/why-sales-managers-need-and-love-crm/

Jaramillo, F., Grisaffe, D.B., Chonko, L.B., & Roberts, J.A. (2009). Examining the impact of servant leadership on sales force performance. *Journal of Personal Selling & Sales Management, 29*(3), 257-275.

Jones, E., Brown, S.P., Zoltners, A.A., & Weitz, B.A. (2005). The changing environment of selling and sales management. *Journal of Personal Selling & Sales Management, 25*(2), 105-111.

Joseph, K., & Kalwani, M.U. (1998). The role of bonus pay in salesforce compensation plans. *Industrial Marketing Management, 27*(2), 147-159.

Kakar, S. (2019, January 8). *5 sales prospecting techniques that aren't spammy.* Copper Chronicles. www.copper.com/resources/sales-prospecting-techniques

Kinnett, S. (2018). *How to win at CRM: Strategy, implementation, management* (1st ed.). CRC Press.

Klymshyn, J. (2006). *The ultimate sales managers' guide.* Wiley.

Kruse, K. (2019, September 10). The 5 habits of successful sales leaders. *Forbes.* www.forbes.com/sites/kevinkruse/2019/09/10/5-sales-manager-competencies/?sh=79abdf51d1d9

Lăzăroiu, G. (2015). Employee motivation and job performance. *Linguistic and Philosophical Investigations, 14,* 97-102.

LeMarco, N. (2019, January 24). *The effect of autocratic leadership.* Chron. https://smallbusiness.chron.com/effect-autocratic-leadership-2974.html

Lewkovich, A. (2018, August 16). Hearing vs. listening: What's the difference? *Footprints—Training and eTracking Solutions Blog.* www.yourtrainingprovider.com/hearing-vs-listening-whats-the-difference/

Locke, E.A., & Latham, G.P. (2002). Building a practically useful theory of goal setting and task motivation: A 35-year odyssey. *American Psychologist, 57*(9), 705.

Lunenburg, F.C. (2011). Goal-setting theory of motivation. *International Journal of Management, Business, and Administration, 15*(1), 1-6.

Lussier, R.N., & Kimball, D.C. (2020). *Applied sport management skills* (3rd ed.). Human Kinetics.

MacKenzie, S.B., Podsakoff, P.M., & Rich, G.A. (2001). Transformational and transactional leadership and salesperson performance. *Journal of the Academy of Marketing Science, 29*(2), 115.

Martin, S.W. (2015, September 11). The 7 attributes of the most effective sales leaders. *Harvard Business Review.* https://hbr.org/2015/09/the-7-attributes-of-the-most-effective-sales-leaders.

Martini, N., & James, G. (2012). *Scientific selling creates high-performance sales teams through applied psychology and testing.* Wiley.

Maslow, A.H. (1943). A theory of human motivation. *Psychological Review, 50*, 370-396.

Mayer, E. (2021, January 4). *30 best probing questions for sales to use in your next call*. Saleshacker. www.saleshacker.com/probing-questions-in-sales/

McClelland, D.C. (1961). *The achieving society*. Van Nostrand.

McClelland, D.C. (1975). *Power: The inner experience*. Irvington.

McClelland, D.C. (1985). *Human motivation*. Scott, Foresman.

McCleskey, J.A. (2014). Situational, transformational, and transactional leadership and leadership development. *Journal of Business Studies Quarterly, 5*(4), 117.

Parsons. (2018, July 2). When is a "bonus" really a "commission"? A helpful reminder to ensure your pay plans comply with state laws. *Labor & Employment Law Perspectives Blog*. www.foley.com/en/insights/publications/2018/07/when-is-a-bonus-really-a-commission-a-helpful-remi

Patel, S. (2019, July 17). *7 sales commission structures (& how to decide what's best for your team)*. Mailshake Blog. https://mailshake.com/blog/sales-commission-structures

Plasksij, Z. (2020, November 4). *10 Reasons why salespeople need CRM*. Super Office Blog. www.superoffice.com/blog/why-sales-people-need-crm/

Robbins, S.P., Judge, T.A., & Sanghi, S. (2007). *Organizational behavior* (12th ed.). Pearson Prentice Hall.

Robinson, R. (n.d.). *12 sales training techniques to build an unstoppable sales team*. https://blog.close.com/unstoppable-sales-team

Royle, M.T., & Hall, A.T. (2012). The relationship between McClelland's theory of needs, feeling individually accountable, and informal accountability for others. *International Journal of Management and Marketing Research, 5*(1), 21-42.

Sandilands, T. (n.d.). *What type of organizations employ transactional leadership?* Chron. https://smallbusiness.chron.com/type-organizations-employ-transactional-leadership-38770.html

Sanjeev, M.A., & Surya, A.V. (2016). Two factor theory of motivation and satisfaction: An empirical verification. *Annals of Data Science, 3*(2), 155-173.

Schultz, M. (n.d.) Top sales prospecting challenges. *Rain Group*. www.rainsalestraining.com/blog/top-sales-prospecting-challenges

Scott, G. (2018, November 2). *5 ways sports teams use CRM systems*. Biz Tech. https://biztechmagazine.com/article/2018/11/5-ways-sports-teams-use-crm-systems

Seidman, D. (2012). *The ultimate guide to sales training: Potent tactics to accelerate sales performance* (1st ed.). Pfeiffer.

Siegfried, A. (2009). *Sales training basics* (1st ed.). Association for Talent Development.

Skinner, B.F. (1948). Superstition in the pigeon. *Journal of Experimental Psychology, 38*(2), 168.

Smith, A. (2019, January 31). *The difference between commission & bonus*. Chron. https://smallbusiness.chron.com/difference-between-commission-bonus-25510.html

Steenburgh, T., & Ahearne, M. (2012, July-August). Motivating salespeople: What really works. *Harvard Business Review*. https://hbr.org/2012/07/motivating-salespeople-what-really-works

Stockdill, D. (2019, July 1). *4 things sales managers need from a CRM system*. Destination CRM. www.destinationcrm.com/Articles/Web-Exclusives/Viewpoints/4-Things-Sales-Managers-Need-From-a-CRM-System--132791.aspx

Tanner Jr., J.F., Ahearne, M., Leigh, T.W., Mason, C.H., & Moncrief, W.C. (2005). CRM in sales-intensive organizations: A review and future directions. *Journal of Personal Selling & Sales Management, 25*(2), 169-180.

Chapter 12

American Gaming Association. (2020). *Legal sports betting in the US*. www.americangaming.

org/wp-content/uploads/2020/01/AGA-Sports-Betting-Map-2020.pdf

Aspen Institute. (2019). *State of play: Trends and developments in youth sports*. https://assets.aspeninstitute.org/content/uploads/2019/10/2019_SOP_National_Final.pdf

Business Wire. (2019, May 14). *Sports—$614 billion global market opportunities & strategies to 2022*. www.businesswire.com/news/home/20190514005472/en/Sports---614-Billion-Global-Market-Opportunities

Clement, B. (2004, July 23). *Badminton second to soccer in participation worldwide*. ESPN. www.espn.com/olympics/summer04/badminton/news/story?id=1845228.

Delaney, T., & Thompson, D.L. (2019, January 14). The effects of 2019 tax-policy decisions will linger for decades. It's time to weigh in. *Chronicle of Philanthropy*. www.philanthropy.com/article/The-Effects-of-2019-Tax-Policy/245464

Dimengo, N. (2014, August 12). *Ridiculous new sports you've never heard of*. Bleacher Report. https://bleacherreport.com/artcles/2157441-ridiculous-new-sports-youve-never-heard-of

Dykstra, S. (2020, September 29). *Appy League becoming collegiate wood-bat circuit: Former Rookie Advanced loop introducing changes for 2021 season*. MLB. www.milb.com/app-first-pitch/tulsa/news/appalachian-league-becoming-collegiate-wood-bat-circuit

Gough, C. (2018, June 16). *Revenue of the global esports market 2018-2023*. Statista. www.statista.com/statistics/490522/global-esports-market-revenue/#statisticContainer

IBIS World. (2020). *Sporting goods stores in the US market size 2004–2026*. www.ibisworld.com/industry-statistics/market-size/sporting-goods-stores-united-states

Jayanthi, N., Pinkham, C., Dugas, L., Patrick, B., & Labella, C. (2013). Sports specialization in young athletes: Evidence-based recommendations. *Sports Health, 5*(3), 251–257.

KPMG. (2020, March). *Redefining sales to thrive in the connected economy. The future of sales*. https://advisory.kpmg.us/content/dam/advisory/en/pdfs/2020/future-sales-redefine-connected-economy.pdf

Lazzarotti, J.L., Costigan, M.T., & Solowan, A. (2019, April 5). *As wearable technology booms, sports and athletic organizations at all levels face privacy concerns*. Jackson Lewis. www.workplaceprivacyreport.com/2019/04/articles/health-information-technology/as-wearable-technology-booms-sports-and-athletic-organizations-at-all-levels-face-privacy-concerns

Legal Sports Report. (2020). *US sports betting revenue and handle*. www.legalsportsreport.com/sports-betting/revenue/

LeMire, J. (2021, January 6). *In a landmark deal, Whoop and the PGA Tour will show fans the heartbeat of golf*. www.sporttechie.com/whoop-pga-tour-partnership-fan-experience-golf-biometric-data

Liptak, A., & Draper, K. (2018, May 14). Supreme Court ruling favors sports betting. *New York Times*. www.nytimes.com/2018/05/14/us/politics/supreme-court-sports-betting-new-jersey.html

LWO Sports. (2020, July 3). *The rise in esports amidst live sports uncertainties KO*. https://lwosports.com/2020/07/03/rise-in-esports/

Northeastern University. (2020). Taxes in sport make game day complication. *D'Amore-McKim School of Business Blog*. https://onlinebusiness.northeastern.edu/blog/taxes-in-sports-make-game-day-complicated/

Nussbaum, A., Oram, J., Parnes, A., & Zeker, A. (2018, January 3). Tax reform's effect on the sports industry. *Proskauer Tax Blog*. www.proskauertaxtalks.com/2018/01/tax-reforms-effect-on-the-sports-industry/

Opperman, P. (2020). *How technology is changing contact sports*. The Innovation Enterprise. https://channels.theinnovationenterprise.com/articles/how-technology-is-chaning-contact-sports

Ponseti, C. (2018, October 18). *NBA & MLB could see combined $1.7 billion from legalized sports betting* [Press release]. American Gaming Association. www.americangaming.org/new/nba-mlb-could-see-combined-1-7-billion-from-legalized-sports-betting/

Ponseti, C. (2019, March 27). *Secure, convenient sports betting options crucial to eliminating illegal market: New report highlights overwhelming consumer support for legalized sports betting, low awareness of existing legal options* [Press release]. American Gaming Association. www.americangaming.org/new/secure- -sports-betting-options-crucial-to-eliminating-illegal-market/

Prete, R. (2019, September 10). *'Jock tax' poses financial burden for NFL non-players.* Bloomberg Tax. https://news.bloombergtax.com/daily-tax-report-state/jock-tax-poses-financial-burden-for-nfl-non-players

Proman, M. (2019, October 1). *The future of sports tech: Here's where investors are placing their bets.* Tech Crunch. https://techcrunch.com/2019/10/01/the-future-of-sports-tech-heres-where-investors-are-placing-their-bets/

RFID. (2014, November 19). *Benefits to fans.* Retrieved from https://rfidinsports.wordpress.com/

Roth, R. (2020, September). *Online sporting goods sales.* IBIS World. https://my.ibisworld.com/us/en/industry-specialized/od5105/about

Schwartz, P. (n.d.). *The future of sales is artificial intelligence.* Sales Force. www.salesforce.com/quotable/articles/future-of-sales/

Signorelli, B. (2020, July 3). How sales jobs could change in the next decade. *HubSpot.* https://blog.hubspot.com/sales/future-of-sales-predictions

Sports & Fitness Industry Association. (2020). *Badminton participation report 2020.* https://www.sfia.org/reports/856_Badminton-Participation-Report-2020

Taylor, T. (2015, March 5). NFL using Zebra RFID chips to track player movements, gather data. *SI.* www.si.com/edge/2015/03/05/nfl-player-tracking-technology-new-orleans-saints

Traub, M. (2021, May 10). *Sports and COVID-19: The impact on the sports-event industry.* www.sportstravelmagazine.com/sports-and-covid-19-what-happened-earlier-this-summer/.

Van Deusen, M. (2021, January 6). *PGA Tour partnership: Why WHOOP is golf's wearable of choice.* www.whoop.com/thelocker/pga-tour-partnership-golf-wearable/

Vargas, J. (2019, October 29). *15 Tips to boost your cross cultural sales skills.* www.rw-3.com/blog/fifteen-tips-for-cross-cultural-selling-with-a-global-mindset.

Wallace, K. (2016, January 21). *How to make your kid hate sports without really trying.* CNN Health. www.cnn.com/2016/01/21/health/kids-youth-sports-parents/index.html

Zeitz, R. (2020, November 23). Post pandemic tax policy and 'jock tax': AIRINC's Pat Jurgens on 'The View From The Top.' *Airshare.* https://airshare.air-inc.com/post-pandemic-tax-policy-and-jock-tax-airincs-pat-jurgens-on-the-view-from-the-top

INDEX

© David Shonk

David Shonk, PhD, is a professor in sport and recreation management at James Madison University, where he has taught courses on sales and marketing. In these courses, he has implemented a calling program for students and sales role-playing.

Shonk served as a marketing director for a Pittsburgh Pirates and Colorado Rockies professional baseball affiliate, where he was vitally involved in direct sales, marketing and promotion, telemarketing, ticketing, and concessions management. He has prior experience as a development director in the nonprofit sector, where he was involved in sales, fundraising and event planning.

Shonk is the editor of *Sport Management Education Journal* and a coauthor of *Managing Sport Events*.

© James Weiner

James Weiner, PhD, is an assistant professor in sport management at the University of Tampa, where he teaches classes in sport finance, sport marketing, and several contemporary issues, including sport sponsorship and multimedia sales. Weiner actively researches the sales process itself, including publications centered around sport sales classes in higher education, and his dissertation targeted several elements of service quality among box office sales representatives in college athletics.

Prior to entering academia, Weiner served as the general manager of sales and service for Duke University as an employee of IMG Learfield Ticket Solutions, an organization that offers ticket revenue generation solutions for college athletics departments. He also has prior experience as a senior account executive and has been responsible for selling single, group, season, and corporate tickets in the college athletics landscape.

Weiner has been published in several journals, including *Sport Management Education Journal*.